Surburg's Works

Vol V
Doctrine

Edited by
Herman J. Otten

LUTHERAN NEWS, INC., New Haven, Missouri

Surburg's Works

Library of Congress Card
Lutheran News, Inc.
684 Luther Lane
New Haven, MO 63068
Published 2017
Printed in the United States of America
IngramSpark, TN
ISBN #978-0-9864232-3-9

Table of Contents

History of Justification 1649

The Biblical Doctrine of Prayer 1649

The Salutary Relation Between Christian Doctrine and Christian Life... 1662

Divergent Approaches to the Nature of the Holy Scriptures Determine
Interpretation, Doctrine and Ethics 1679

Lent's Central Doctrine: The Biblical Teaching of the Atonement 1684

The Proper Use As Well As Misuse of The Law/Gospel Dichotomy In
20th Century Protestantism With Special Reference To American
Lutheranism 1695

The Domino Effect of the Rejection of One Doctrine Upon Other Doctrines
of the Bible 1716

The Removal of Satan or the Devil from the Old Testament by Modern Lutheran Theologians 1728

The Biblical Doctrine of the Angels (An Essay to Commemorate St.
Michael and All Angels, Sept. 29) 1733

The Descent Into Hell - What Happened Between Christ's Burial and His
Physical and Bodily Resurrection Appearances on Eastern Morn? 1751

Jesus Is God - The Variegated Witnesses and Testimonies to the
Deity of Christ as Set Forth in John's Gospel 1759

ELCA and the Jesus Seminar - The Resurrection of Christ 1769

Justification "By Faith" or Justification "Because of Faith" or
Justification as "The Result of Faith?" 1777

Lent's Central Doctrine: The Biblical Teaching of the Atonement 1786

The Holy Spirit -The Person and Activities of the Holy Spirit As Set
Forth in the Scriptures of the Old and New Testaments 1797

The Lord's Supper - Past and Current Teachings About the Lord's
Supper in Three Divergent Religious Traditions 1807

An Evaluation of Millennialism and Dispensationalism of Proponents
Using the Gulf War to Interpret the End Times Millennialism and
Israel Today 1823

The Teachings About The Holy Spirit in The Book of Acts 1842

Biblical Teachings Rejected and Contradicted by the Practitioners of
Human Abortion 1858

Dr. Raymond F. Surburg (1909-2001)

Dr. Raymond F. Surburg (1909-2001) - Teacher and Friend Ascended
Home to Heaven - A Tribute, By Dr. Phillip B. Giessler 1856

Dr. Raymond F. Surburg At Rest In Heaven, by Dr. Phil Giessler 1860

The Rev. Dr. Raymond F. Surburg- Called to the Church Triumphant 1862

Dr. Raymond Surburg " Brave Warrior" - Called by Name, Belonging to
God - Is. 43:1c, by Dr. Walter Maier III 1864

Index...1868

History of Justification

January 19, 1981
Dear Pastor Otten:
As you no doubt are aware I am scheduled to deliver an article at the International Center of Confessional Studies next week Friday. As a result of my reading on justification, I hit often the idea of writing a history of the doctrine of justification between 1531 and 1981.

If you are interested in printing such a piece you can let me know. I am sending you enough material for a number of installments to begin with. At least the opening part of my essay deals with the apology of the A.C. So far I have done considerable research and would continue to pursue the history of justification in Lutheranism and in recent times, if you would find it useful.

It might be worthwhile in view of the interest around by Preus' charge of erroneous teachings by Beck and Maier. I don't side with Dr. J.A.O. Preus.

May God bless you, your work, and your family in 1981!
Yours in Christ,
Raymond Surburg

The Biblical Doctrine of Prayer

Christian News, July 18, 1994

In the post-Reformation period of church history, the number of theological disciplines was increased and their boundaries and scope were more clearly defined. Subjects that were once considered to be part and parcel of Christian doctrine were separated and a distinction made between Christian doctrine and Christian ethics. Prayer was one of these topics transferred from Christian doctrine and assigned to Christian ethics. An examination of nineteen and twentieth century books on dogmatics will reveal that some did not discuss prayer, while others did. For example, the Lutheran doctrine books of Reu,[3] Stump,[4] Lindberg,[5] Schmid,[6] Hove,[7] do not treat the subject of prayer, while H.E. Jacobs,[8] Pieper,[9] J.T. Mueller,[10] Luther,[11] Hoenecke,[12] do include prayer in their dogmatics discussions. Among non-Lutheran theologians Buswell,[13] Berkhof,[14] Shedd,[15] Heppe,[15a] do not deal with prayer in their dogmatic works. Calvin in his *Institutes* has but one isolated reference,[16] while Reu-Buehring,[17] and Stump[18] have given an extensive discussion to prayer in their books on *Christian Ethics*.

The fifth Sunday after Easter or the sixth Sunday in Easter (as now called) is known as Sunday Rogate, calling attention to Biblical prayer, the epistle lesson for that Sunday is John 15:23-30, where Christ speaks about prayer.[19] *The Lutheran Hymnal* has a section where all hymns on prayer are grouped together.[20] The Lutheran Church-Missouri Synod in connection with the celebration of its centennial in 1947, one of the essays was by A. Behnke on "Prayer," and when appearing in print was placed among doctrines the Synod had taught for at least a century.[21] William Arndt in 1937 published a monograph *on Christian Prayer*.

The Frequency of Prayer in the Holy Scriptures

Both the Old and the New Testaments have considerable material and instruction pertaining to true prayer. From Genesis to Revelation the pages of the Bible are replete with all manner of information about God-pleasing prayer.

The observant reader will find that God commands prayer, the conditions under which prayers are acceptable, when prayer may take place, under what conditions they will be answered, see a classification of different prayers. He will find a delineation of Christ's exemplary prayer-life, set forth as a model, and also become aware of samples of God-pleasing prayer, the Bible gives examples of answered prayer, who and what to pray for, different postures possible in true prayer, the need for prayer, times when to pray.

The Princeton Study on Prayer

The Princeton Religious Research Center, 1994, asked 688 adults, ages 18 and over questions about their views on prayer.[22] Only ten per cent reported that they most often did not pray in a house of worship, even though the Church is called "a house of prayer." Twenty-three per cent claimed that they heard voices and saw visions as a result of prayer. Eighty-six per cent reported that prayer made them feel better. Ninety-five per cent of those queried asserted that their prayers were answered and claimed that as a result of prayer they have a feeling of more peace and hope after having prayed. That the individuals questioned by the Princeton researchers had erroneous views about prayer is obvious from the few responses just given. There is a difference between what people have established about prayer and what God in His Word has set down as the ground rules for God-pleasing prayer. Just like many people have created their own theology by ignoring what the Bible teaches, so the same holds true of many an individual's creation of the theology of prayer. What God has revealed through His inspired writers must determine a person's concept of prayer, to be correct and also acceptable to the Creator of all mankind. It would be instructive to ascertain what the Bible teaches about prayer.

1. Prayer and the Christian Life

Francis Pieper correctly pointed out the inseparable connection between the Christian life and prayer, when he wrote: "As soon as a Christian has been justified by faith and thus becomes God's child, he begins to commune with God. The personal conversing of the Christian with God is called prayer. It is altogether Scriptural to define prayer as 'the conversation of the heart with God' (Psalm 27:8), whether the heart alone communes with God without clothing the prayers in words of the mouth or whether the mouth utters the prayer of the heart."[23] J.T. Mueller claimed: "While the words of the mouth are not absolutely necessary to make a Communion with God's prayer. Is. 65:24; Rom. 8,26,27, yet they must not be regarded as superfluous. Acts 7:59; 16:25.[24] As long as a person remains in his natural state of sin and wrath, he fears and therefore flees God, Heb. 2,15; Gen. 3,6. But as soon as he by faith has entered into the new, he begins to commune with God. Rom 8:15."[24a]

2. Prayer Is Not a Means of Grace

In the Scriptures God has spoken and still speaks to human beings, but in prayer human beings speak to God. Prayer is not a means of revelation. A means of grace is that by and through which grace and forgiveness are offered and conveyed to people, but in prayer we ask for grace and blessings. The grace and forgiveness for which we ask in prayer is conveyed through the Word of God and the Sacraments. The latter are the means of Grace, not prayer. The prayers of the regenerate are not primarily a means of grace, but are an expression of the benefits of justification by faith.[25] Reu claimed that "the prayer of the regenerate is not primarily a means for appropriating the spiritual gifts of the heavenly realm, but rather the immediate and self-evident expression of the child-relationship between him and his heavenly Father (Psalm 19:14)."[26]

3. The Importance of Prayer.

Prayer is for the Christian life what breathing is for life. Stump is correct when he wrote: "Prayer is the active communion or conversation of the believing heart with God. Its necessity for the spiritual life is fundamental. There can be no Christian life without it."[27] By regeneration and justification the Christian has become a child of God and as such he is filled with love for God and trust in God and to this he gives most material expression in childlike conversation with the Father, in immediate approach to God and confident discussion with Him of all that moves the heart. Prayer is the evidence of this relationship, its natural expression. When the soul has become conscious of it, it turns irrevocably to God in prayer regardless of need to do so.[28]

In his writings, Luther has some interesting statements about prayer. He once said "that as the cobbler makes shoes and the tailor a coat, so shall the Christian pray, prayer is the Christian's handwork." On another occasion he averred about prayer that "it is the pulse beat of inner life."[29]

4. Prayer Not a Meritorious Act

According to the New Testament for many Pharisees prayer had degenerated into an **opus operatum** (i.e. something that worked mechanically). For them prayer was not basically communion with God, but it was the purpose of prayer to observe the correct form and also of praying at certain times. They made a show of their prayers, made broad their phylacteries and employed vain repetition (Matt. 6:5-7; 23:5). For these religious leaders of the Jews the content and the form of prayers were meticulously prescribed.[30] Therefore, prayer became a meritorious act. The effectiveness of prayer was determined by their length and number of repetitions. During the Middle Ages the Roman Catholic Church viewed prayer not so much as communion with God, as a meritorious act along with fasting and almsgiving. The mystics in the Church believed that the purpose of prayer was absorption with God. The Lutheran Reformation restored prayer to its proper place as consisting of communion with God by the restoration of the doctrine of justification by faith.[31]

5. Reasons for Christian Prayer

Christians should be moved to prayer because of a number of Biblical reasons. Above all, Christians will be moved by God's gracious invitation. "Seek you my face (Ps. 27:8)," "call upon me in the day of trouble (Ps. 50:15)."Through David God said: "Seek the Lord and His strength, see His face forever (1 Chron. 16:11)." Asaph in Psalm 50 encouraged: "Call upon Me in the day of trouble, I will deliver thee (v. 16)." Jesus told His disciples: "Ask, and it shall be given you, seek and you shall find, knock and it will be opened to you (Matt. 7:7)."

Another reason why Christians will want to pray is God's promise to hear us. Such promises are numerous as can be seen from Matt. 7:7-8, Ps., 145: 18-19; Ps. 50:15. Praying is not a futile exercise for Christians, because God has said: "O Thou that hearest prayer, unto Thee shall all flesh come (Ps. 65:2)." The healed blind man correctly stated a true fact, when he said: "We know that God does not listen to sinners, but that if anyone is God-fearing and does His will, to such he listens (John 9:31)."

Still another reason why Christians will wish to pray is their own as well as the neighbor's need. Trouble is a powerful motivation for praying, especially when God tells us to do just that. The prophet Isaiah recognized this when he wrote: "In trouble have they visited Thee, they poured out a prayer when chastening was upon them (26:16). Our own trouble, whether or not they are small or great, bodily, as the leper's (Luke 17:13), or spiritual, as the publican's (Luke 18:13) should prompt Christians to ask God for help. Abraham prayed for the righteous people in Sodom (Gen. 18:23-32) and as the Roman centurion did for his servant" (Matt. 8:5-6).

6. Biblical Conditions for Valid and Effective Prayer

Prayers to be Valid must be offered up to the Triune God. The Old and New Testaments forbid the offering up of prayers to idols or false gods.[33] In the days of the judge Samuel, Eli's successor, advised Israel: "If you return to the Lord with all your hearts, then put away the foreign gods and the Ashtaroth from among you, and prepare for the Lord and serve Him only, and He will deliver you out of the hands of the Philistines" (1 Sam. 7:2). The prophet Isaiah, speaking for the Lord, declared: "I am the Lord, that is My name, and My glory I will not give to another" (Is. 42:8). The apostle John closed his First Letter with the warning: "My little children, guard yourselves from idols." (1 John 5:21). When the people of

Lystra wanted to worship Barnabas and Paul as Zeus and Hermes, the two Christian evangelists refused such worship and called upon the Lystra people to turn from empty things to living God. Only Jesus and His Father and the Holy Spirit were to be worshipped. In the Pauline epistles there are many warnings about avoiding idols and idolatry.[34] To call upon the Supreme Being, or the Great Spirit, Allah, Brahma or any other God who is not the Scriptural one, means being guilty of idolatry. Acts 4:12, John 3:16; John 14:1; Matt. 28:20 require that prayer to be acceptable must be directed to the One True God.

Since Christ is the only Mediator between God and men, it is wrong to address angels or saints asking them to pray for them.[35] Acceptable prayer must proceed from faith. James warns: "But let him ask in faith with no doubt is like a wave of the sea driven and tossed by the wind. For let no man suppose that he will receive anything from the Lord, he is double-minded man unstable in all of his ways" (James 1:6-8). This faith which is essential for prayer to be acceptable is created by the Holy Spirit for as St. Paul asserted: "Likewise the Spirit helps in our weaknesses. For we do not know what we should pray for as we ought, but the Spirit Himself makes intercession for us with groanings which cannot be uttered" (Romans 8:26). Prayer addressed to the Triune God excludes by its very nature willful sin, a fact known by the Pharisees (John 9:3). Isaiah asserts: "But your iniquities have separated you from God, and your sins have hidden His face from you (Is. 59:2). Why will God not hear? For your hands are defiled with blood and your fingers with iniquity, your lips have spoken lies. Your tongue has muttered perversity" (Is. 59:2).

Acceptable prayer to the true God must be conditioned by the will of God. In Gethsemane, as Jesus faced the great crisis of His life, he prayed "not my Will be done but Thy will be done (Matt. 26:39)." John assured his readers in his First Epistle: "Now this is the confidence that we have in Him, that if we ask anything according to His will. He hears us" (1 John 5:14).

7. For Whom Should Christians Pray?

Prayer must be as wide as living mankind. Writing to a fellow laborer in the ministry, Paul instructed Timothy: "Therefore, I exhort first of all that supplications, prayers and intercessions and giving of thanks be made for all mankind (1 Timothy 2:1)." A Christian should offer up prayer for his neighbor who has troubles. The believer may also pray for himself as it pertains to spiritual matters and his earthly existence. *The General Prayer* lists people and causes for which the obedient child of God will send his petitions before the throne of grace.[36]

8. The Contents of Christian Prayer

What may be the subject of the Christian's prayers? Christ answered: "What things soever ye desire, when ye pray, believe that ye receive them (Mark 11:24)." Paul encouraged the Philippian congregation: "Be careful for nothing but in everything by prayer and supplication with thanksgiving let your requests be made known unto God (Phil. 4:6)." Koehler observed: "No matter, what may trouble and oppress us, we should not give way to anxious worry, but take it to the Lord in prayer. In 'everything,' things great and small, personal or general, temporal or spiritual, make your requests known to God. However, it would be wrong to ask for things which are sinful and are not in harmony with God's will." As already stated, Christian's prayers must be in harmony with the will of God, for the apostle John wrote: "This is the confidence that we have in Him, that if we ask anything according to His will. He heareth us" (1 John 5:14). It is God's will that Christians should ask for spiritual blessings (Luke 11:13). In a general way believers may request those things necessary for their temporal existence as we do in the Fourth Petition of the Lord's Prayer.

9. Prayer Exists in Many Kinds and Forms

Prayer has been expressed in many kinds and forms. It is interesting and instructive to note the different terminology employed by the holy writers in their discussion of the topic of prayer.[37] In the Old Testament the word **tephilah** is of frequent occurrence and chiefly refers to calling upon God, but also involves making intercession for someone. As a heading, it occurs in Psalms 17, 86, 102, and 142, also in Habakkuk chapter 3 (actually a psalm.) The word **sheelah** is employed for prayer in general, the word **todah** is used of special prayers of thanksgiving. However, there are many divisions, subdivisions of prayer, as various psalms clearly show. In the New Testament, St. Paul in 1 Timothy 2:1 indicates a number of different kinds of prayer: "I exhort therefore that first of all supplications, prayers, intercessions and giving of thanks be made for all men." This directive clearly shows that the Christians, the children of God, in observing the demands of the Second Commandment are required to bring their needs and their desires to the attention of the Heavenly Father, that they are to be in constant communication with Him.

10. The Old Testament Prayer Book

The Book of Psalms has been termed the "Prayer Book of the Old Testament." For over two thousand years the Old and New Testament believers have used the 150 poems of the Psalter as prayers.[38] In the Psalms one finds reflected all possible types of prayer. Thus there are psalms of confession of sins, laments by the individual, laments for the nation, intercessions for help, praise and thanksgiving. Moorehead has asserted about the Psalms: "The Psalms are a remarkably fruitful of experience. It would seem as if the Spirit of God had gathered together into these one hundred and fifty lyrics all the varied experiences of soul of which the redeemed have knowledge in the world. There is no state or exigency, no circumstance or act, set of circumstances of whatsoever, prosperous and adverse, bad and good, near and remote, but it may find a faithful expression in this inimitable book. Here is mirrored all that the saint desires and seeks, loves and hates."[39]

11. Prayer in the Old Testament

In the Old Testament beginning with Genesis there are depictions of God's children having personal intercourse with a powerful and holy God. With God, in proportion as a man was surrendered to Him, fellowship was the blessing of the covenant (Ex. 24:11).[40] Schultz summarized the blessing of the covenant like this: "In a word, they enjoy, in living communion with God, the highest and truest happiness man can enjoy—a happiness greater and more needful far than—any that earth can give."[41] In Genesis 5:22 it is stated that Enoch walked with God and later did not taste death. The earliest group fellowship is given in Genesis 4:26: "Then men began to call upon the name of the Lord." With Abraham and Isaac in the patriarchal period came the beginnings of the doctrine of prayer (Gen. 29:17; 25:21). Similarly related to prayer were Abraham's intercessions with the Lord on behalf of Sodom (Gen. 18:25-32). Eliezer went to find a wife for Isaac (Gen. 24:12-18; 22-24) he uttered a first prayer set down in the Bible. It was described as being a conversation with God and taking place in the heart (Gen. 24:45). Jacob's urgent plea, spoken before his meeting with Esau about 1909 B.C. was being brief but gives an inspired pattern for believing prayer.[42]

The first set prayers are found in the Mosaic legislation and are the following: Numbers 10:35,36, Psalm 68:1, which lists two sets of invocations for the journey of the ark. Deut. 21:7,8 records a prayer for community atonement. Deut. 28:5-10 gives the prayer to be spoken at the offering of the first fruits at the presentation of the third-year tithes.

The Old Testament gives two examples of believers who were weighty in intercessory prayer (Jeremiah 15:1). The first concerned Moses (Ex. 32:32). When the latter was willing to be blotted out of God's book in order to save the life of the idolatrous Israelites. For as God's Word declares that God would destroy them; if had not Moses stood before Him in the breach to turn away His wrath (Psalm 196:23). The second example was the judge Samuel whose prayer for Israel is written down in 1 Samuel 7:8,12,19. Amos' petition in the eighth century B.C. was of similar import (Amos 7:2,5). Jeremiah in the seventh century B.C. was warned not to pray for his hopelessly apostate people (Jer. 16:11,14; 14:11). During the Exile, Ezekiel was told that the greatest of God's saint, past or present, could accomplish their own deliverance but not that of anyone else (Ezekiel 14:14-26).

The Old Testament shows that fellowship with God, however, carried with it the promise of answered prayer. 1 Chronicles 4:10 states that God answered Jabez' prayer. The Lord responded to His people's request for the birth of children (Gen. 25:21, cf. 1 Sam. 1:11). When Israel fell out of fellowship with God, they discovered that He refused to listen to their pleas (Deut. 1:45). Moses' prayer to be allowed to enter Canaan was rejected because of Israel's great leader's sin (Deut. 3:25). When Saul was confronted by the Philistines at the battle of Gilboa (1 Sam. 28:6), God refused to answer Saul's request. David's first child by Bathsheba was not spared. When David asked for the child to be allowed to live (2 Sam. 12:16-18). Solomon in Proverbs 15:8 enunciated a great promise and principle: "The prayer of the righteous is his delight." Solomon at the beginning of his reign asked God for wisdom and it was granted him (1 Kings 3:9). By prayer Elijah raised the dead (1 Kings 3:17:20-21). By prayer he shut up the heavens for three and a half years. Kings Asa and Jehoshaphat were able to win victories by their prayers, who prayed: "Oh our God, we have no might against this great company that cometh against us neither know we what to do, but our eyes are upon thee (2 Chron. 20:12; cf. 14:11)." The prophet Isaiah enunciated a moral principle for answered prayer as the following shows: "When you make many prayers, I will not hear you, your hands are full of blood (Is. 1:15; c f 50:21)." By contrast God said through the same prophet: "Loose the bonds of wickedness and deal your bread to the hungry... Then shall you call and Yahweh will answer you; you shall cry and He will say: Here I am (Is. 58;6,7,9)." King Hezekiah was faithful to the Lord and because of it the Lord delivered him from the siege of Sennacherib (2 Kings 19:1,15) and also from his sickness which was to cause his death (20:2,3) by contrast Asa's sickness was great and in his disease he did not ask for help from the Lord, but sought the doctors (2 Chron. 16:12). The prophet Isaiah has one of the most interesting prayers about God answering prayer: "It shall come to pass that before they call, I will answer, and while they are yet speaking, I will hear (64:24)."

Concerning the forms of offering prayer, the Old Testament illustrates almost all of the bodily positions that might be taken: Whether standing, kneeling or even prostrate.[43] An interesting feature of Old Testament prayer was that the fact that the believers directed their prayer toward Jerusalem David directed his prayers to God's Holy Temple in Jerusalem. Solomon assumed that after the dedication of the Temple, that Jewish believers would direct their prayers to God's permanent sanctuary (1 Kings 8:30,35). Jonah likewise observed this geographical direction (Jonah 2:4,7). Daniel, in the Babylonian exile, faced Jerusalem three times a day when he prayed (Dan. 6:10).

12. What Christ Taught About Prayer

The nature of prayer is seen by studying the Four Gospels to see what Christ did.[44] Jesus life was one of constant and perfect communion with the Father. The references to His praying are frequent (Mark 1:35; Luke 5:16, 6:12; John 11:41,42; Matt. 11:25; John 17:1-26; Matt. 26:36-39; Luke 23:34; Matt. 27:46; Luke 23:46). Not only does the Bible reader find Jesus pronouncing blessing upon the food at the great feedings of the 5,000 and 4,000 reported in the Gospels, but His great Prayer in Gethsemane and on Calvary shows that Christ's relationship with the Father was of an intimate kind. Jesus gave His disciples an example by the fact that He often rested for solitary prayer (cf. Mark 1:35,45; John 6:15). On the evening before His death Jesus uttered the unique and great High priestly Prayer (John 17).

An example of a true and comprehensive prayer has been presented by Christ in the Lord's Prayer. Stump remarked about it: "It is given as a model not so much of form as of content. It expresses what all His disciples under all circumstances should pray for. It shows the spirit of childlike confidence in which we should approach God: Points out that the things of God—the hallowing of His name, the coming of the kingdom, and the doing of His will—should be our foremost concern for praying and that upon these petitions there fitly follow petitions for the supply of our own bodily and spiritual wants (Matt. 6:9-13). Because the Lord's Prayer is so all inclusive relative to what is important for the Christian the latter will add this prayer to their own. Luther in his two catechisms, the Small and the Large, has important discussions on Christ's Lord's Prayer."[45]

Christ brought to perfection the teachings of the Old Testament on prayer, by both precept and practice. He lived in constant communion with His heavenly Father. He repeatedly emphasized that men ought always to pray and faint not. Christ lived as a man who needed and enjoyed prayer, as He lived so He died with prayer upon His lips.

In the Book of Acts and in the remainder books of the New Testament, prayer played a very important role.[46] Throughout the New Testament prayer is seen as the sphere of the congregation (Eph. 5:19-20). After a prayer meeting the church was born at Pentecost. According to Acts 2:42 the Jerusalem congregation met constantly for prayer. Prayers were offered by the believers when the Apostles were persecuted and imprisoned. Prayer led to the vision that the Gospel was also meant for the Gentiles. After fasting and prayer the first missionaries were sent out by the congregation at Antioch. It was at a place of prayer that the Gospel was proclaimed in Europe for the first time. No observant readers of Paul's letter to churches and individuals can fail to notice how much Paul mentions prayer and what an important role it played in the life of the "apostle to the Gentiles." The first portion of most of the Pauline Epistles has a prayer of thanksgiving.[47] The early Christians saw themselves as spiritual priests who could offer the incense of prayer to the Triune God (Heb. 13:15). Paul enjoined Timothy, a coworker, to be engaged in offering: "Supplications, prayers, intercessions, and thanksgiving for all men (1 Tim. 2:1)." Christensen claimed: "The whole portrayal of the church's struggle finds its culmination in the triumphant prayer and worship of the Book of Revelation."[48]

13. The Manner of Praying

The Christian prayer must be on his guard to engage in endless babble and battologizing by the heathen and by Roman Catholics.[49] The Buddhists have their prayer wheels and the Roman Catholics emphasize numerous Lord's Prayers and Hail Marys, believing that they shall be heard for their much speaking (Matt. 6:7). Koehler contended that "the value of prayer does not depend upon their number or length nor on the language and grammar we use, but on this that we pray from the heart earnestly and sincerely (Psalm 145:18)."[50] True prayer must not be offered from Schleirmacher's feeling of "dependence upon God" or from Ritschl's "faith in the divine presence."[51] It is only because of Christ's vicarious satisfaction can Christians really pray with the confidence that God for Christ's sake will answer their prayers.

14. When and Where Prayers Are to Be Offered

The sanctuary or place where prayers are offered does not make individual prayers more acceptable. Paul instructed Timothy on this matter: "I will that men pray everywhere." Effective prayer may be offered in the home, the church, the street, the workplace. "Pray without ceasing (1 Thess. 5:17)." Christians should not make public show with their prayers as the Pharisees did in the time of Christ. On the Sermon on the Mount Jesus suggested that praying be done in private, at home, rather than showing off, prayer should be done in secret Matt. 6:5-6).

Christians should pray together with one another as is done in public worship (Psalm 26:12; Acts 1:14; 2:12). Those who worship other gods than the Triune God and thus adore idols, there should not be joint prayer with Jews, Mohammedans, Buddhists, with lodge members, that deny the Trinity.

While it is good to pray at any time of day or night, it is helpful to observe certain times for prayer. When we arise in the morning, at night when we go to bed, at meal times and at church services are desirable occasions for prayer.

15. Posture in Prayer

The posture should ordinarily be one which indicates a reverent and humble spirit; but the essential thing is that there be reverence and humility in the heart. The Church from the early days sanctioned standing during public prayers on Sunday, because Sunday is a day of rejoicing over the resurrection of Christ. Kneeling was recommended on fast days and days of humiliation.[52]

16. Ex Corde and Formulated Prayers

Since prayer is the spontaneous expression of the Christian's heart and of his child relationship to God, it is in the very nature of the case that the prayer of the Christian will be a matter of the heart. It will be highly personal prayer in which the believer brings his own individual needs and his own individual thanks to God. Reu believes that the earliest psalms were spontaneous utterances of the heart before they were formulated in written form. However, since the needs of Christians as well as their wants are the same and what other Christians have experienced and written down in a concise and beautiful manner, this can be appropriated by other Christians as found in prayer books. In fact, there is an advantage in the use of formulated prayers as found in prayer books, since the latter have the special advantage that they will keep the fundamental needs of salvation and the great objective facts of divine grace in the foreground and sometimes petty interests of his own little self and place the prayer in the time with the great congregation of believers. Printed prayers often will lead to more **ex corde** prayer.[53]

The Old and New Testaments give many examples of ready-made written prayers. Besides the Book of Psalm there comes to mind the prayer of dedication of the temple by Solomon (1 Kings 8:22-53). In the New Testament the high priestly Prayer of Jesus on Maundy Thursday or the prayers of Paul in a number of his epistles (1 Cor. 1:4-9; Eph. 1:3-14; Phil. 1:2-11).

17. The Biblical Prayers of Great Biblical Characters and of Leaders of Church History

The indispensableness of prayer will be realized when the Christian recalls the outstanding men in the kingdom of God have been fervent in prayer. Abraham, Jacob, Moses, David, Elijah, Hezekiah, Jesus, Paul, Peter, John and others and after the close of the New Testament canon, church leaders as Chrysostom, Augustine, Luther, some medieval mystics, Starck, George Mueller, of Bristol, Louis Harms of Hermansburg, Walther and a host of others.[54]

18. Means for the Preservation of the Christian Life

One Lutheran theologian phrased it this way: "Diligent use of the means of grace, constant communion with God in prayer, coupled with incessant watchfulness, those are the means for the preservation of the Christian life. Especially in the hour of temptation they must be used to fight the good fight and attain the victory."[55]

Footnotes

1. A. Kuyper, *Encyclopedia of Sacred Knowledge*, 1898, pp. 627-631; Edward A. Young, *An Introduction to the Old Testament* (Grand Rapids: Wm. Eerdmans Publishing Company, 1969), p. 15.
2. Rev. Franklin Weidner, *An Introduction to Dogmatic Theology* (Rock Island, III, Augustana Book Concern, 1888. 2nd Edition, p. 32.)
3. Martin Reu, *Lutheran Dogmatics* (Decorah, Iowa: Wartburg Theological Seminary, 1951) Revised Edition.
4. Joseph Stump, *The Christian Life - A System of Christian Dogmatics* (New York: The Macmillan Company, 1932).
5. Conrad Lindberg, *Christian Dogmatics and Notes of the History of Dogma*, English Translation from Swedish by Rev. C.E. Hoffsten, Second Revised Edition (Rock Island, III., Augustana Book Concern, 1926).
6. Heinrich Schmid, *Doctrinal Theology of the Evangelical Lutheran Church*, (Minneapolis: Augsburg Publishing House, 1966), Reprint Edition of 1889).
7. E. Hove, *Christian Doctrine* (Minneapolis: Augsburg Publishing House, 1930).
8. Henry Eyster Jacobs, *A Summary of Christian Doctrine* (Philadelphia: (General Counsel Publication House, 1905), pp. 16, 251-253, 289, 432, 317, 291.
9. Francis Pieper, *Christian Dogmatics* (St. Louis: Concordia Publishing House, 1955), III, pp. 76-89.
10. J.T. Mueller, *Christian Dogmatics* (St. Louis: Concordia Publishing House, 1955), pp. 428-434.
11. Paul Althaus, *The Theology of Martin Luther* (Philadelphia: Fortress Press, 1966, pp. 997,106, 119,225,289,291,318,323,333,345-348,375,403.
12. Adoph Hoenecke, *Dogmatik* (Milwaukee: Northwestern Publishing House, II, 274), III, pp. 426-431; 441.
13. J. Oliver Buswell, *A Systematic Theology of the Christian Religion* (Grand Rapids;

Zondervan Publishing House, 1967), 2 volumes. The work has scattered pages alluding to prayers but no separate discussion of prayer.

14. L. Berkhof, *Systematic Theology* (Grand Rapids: W. B. Eerdmans Publishing Company, 1941).

15. William T. Shedd, *Dogmatic Theology* (New York: Charles Scribner's Sons, 1889), 2 volumes.

15a. Heinrich Heppe, *Reformed Dogmatics,* Revised and Edited by Ernst Bizet English Translation by G. T. Thomson (London: George Allen & Umwin, 1950).

16. John Calvin, *Institutes of the Christian Religion* (Philadelphia: Presbyterian of Christian Education, no dates), Book III, Ch. 20.

17. Martin Reu and Paul H. Buehring, *The Christian Life, A Handbook of Christian Ethics* (Columbus: Wartburg Press, 1935), pp. 175-187.

18. Joseph Stump, *The Christian Life, A Handbook of Christian Ethics* (New York: The Macmillan Company, 1930), pp. 182-186.

19. Paul Zeller Strodach, *The Church Year* (Philadelphia: The United Luther Publication House, 1924), pp. 166-168.

20. *The Lutheran Hymnal* (St. Louis: Concordia Publishing House, 1941), Hymns: Numbers 454-459.

21. C.A. Behnke, "Prayer," Theodore Laetsch Editor, *The Abiding Word* (St. Louis; Concordia Publishing House, 1946), vol. I, pp. 2-47-200.

22. "Prayer, *The Importance of Prayer to Nearly Everyone,*" *The Reporter*, May 1994, p. 12.

23. Pieper, **op. cit.**, III, pg. 76-77.

24. Mueller, **op. cit.**, p. 429.

24a. **Ibid.**, p. 428.

25. Raymond F. Surburg, "Do Christians Receive Forgiveness of Sins through Prayer!" Lutheran Education, 91 (1955-56), 167-171.

26. Reu, *Christian Ethics*, **op. cit.**, p. 175.

27. Stump, *The Christian Life*, **op. cit.**, p. 182.

28. Reu, *Christian Ethics*, **op. cit.**, p. 175.

29. As cited by Reu, **Ibid.**, p. 376. For other statements of E.W. Plass, *What Luther Says*, (St. Louis: Concordia Publishing House, 1959), II, 1024-1101.

30. Stump, *The Christian Life*, **op. cit.**, p. 184.

30a. **Ibid.**

31. **Ibid.**

32. Edward A Koehler, *A Summary of Christian Doctrine* (Second Edition, prepared by Alfred Koehler, Detroit and Cleveland by L. H. Koehler and Alfred W. Koehler, 1952), pp. 165-170.

33. Mueller, **op. cit.**, p. 430.

34. *The Zondervan Expanded Concordance* (Grand Rapids: Zondervan Publishing House, 1968), cf. idols, idolatry, idolater.

35. "Saints, Worship," Erwin Lueker, *The Lutheran Cyclopedia* (St. Louis: Concordia Publishing House, 1954), p. 940.

36. As found in *The Lutheran Hymnal*, **op. cit.**, p. 23-24.

37. "Prayer," *The Lutheran Cyclopedia*, **op. cit.**, p. 835.

38. John H. Walton, *Chronological Charts for the New Testament* (Grand Rapids: Zondervan Publishing Company, 1978), W. Graham Scroggie, *Know Your Bible,* Volume I, *Analytica: The Old*

Testament (London: Pickering and Inglis. No date, p. 107.

39. W. C. Moorhead, *Outline Studies in the Books of the Old Testament* (Chicago: Fleming H. Revell and Company, 1895), p. 181.

40. **Ibid.** J. Barton Payne, *The Theology of the Old Testament* (Grand Rapids: Zondervan Publishing Company, 1962), p. 421.

41. Herman Schultz, *Old Testament Theology* (Edinburgh: T. & T. Clark, 1962), p. 30.

42. Payne, **op. cit.**, p. 432.

43. Cf. G.T. Lambert, "Prayer," James Orr, Editor, *The International Standard Bible Encyclopedia* (Grand Rapids: Wm. B. Eerdmans Publishing Company, 1939), IV, 2430.

44. Cf. Walton, **op. cit.**, p. 332.

45. Stump, *The Christian Life*, **op. cit.**, pp. 185-188.

46. Walton, **op. cit.**, p. 37-39.

46. "Prayer in the New Testament," H.W. House, *Chronological Charts and Background Charts*, (Grand Rapids: Zondervan Publishing House, 1981), pp. 38-39.

48. Christensen, "Prayer," Julius Bodensieck, *The Encyclopedia of the Lutheran Church* (Minneapolis: Augsburg Publishing House, 1965), III, 1973.

49. Pieper, **op. cit.**, III, p. 79.

50. Koehler, **op. cit.**, p. 185.

51. Mueller, *Christian Dogmatics*, **op. cit.**, p. 429.

52. Stump, *The Christian Life*, **op. cit.**, p. 185.

53. Johann Michael Reu in Conjunction with Paul H. Buering, *Christian Ethics* (Columbus: The Lutheran Book Concern, 1935), p. 185.

54. "Prayer," *The Lutheran Cyclopedia*, 1954, 835.

55. Reu-Buehring, **op. cit.**, p. 187.

Questions

1. How often does Calvin in his *Institutes* mention prayer? _____
2. Have LCMS theologians in their writings often mentioned prayer? _____
3. Which Sunday particularly calls attention to prayer? _____
4. When does a person begin to commune with God? _____
5. What are prayers for the Christian? _____
6. What is an **opus operatum**? _____
7. How did the Lutheran Reformation restore prayer to its proper place? _____
8. Why will a Christian want to pray? _____
9. Christians should be in constant communication with _____.
10. The Book of Psalms has been called _____.
11. The beginning of the doctrine of prayer began with _____.
12. Solomon at the beginning of his reign asked for _____.
13. What is recorded in Isaiah about God answering prayer? _____
14. What did Christ teach about prayer? _____
15. The value of prayer depends upon _____.
16. Effective prayer may be offered in _____.
17. Should there be joint prayers with those who deny the Trinity? _____
18. What is an **es corde** prayer? _____
19. What is an advantage of formulated prayers? _____

The Salutary Relation Between Christian Doctrine and Christian Life[1]

Christian News, October 10, 1994

The historical Lutheran Church has distinguished itself by her inculcation of Christian doctrine. In so doing she has obeyed the command of Christ: "Go and make disciples of all nations baptizing them in the name of the Father and the Son and the Holy Spirit teaching them to keep and preserve and do everything I have commanded you (Matthew 28:19-20)."[2] In his farewell address to the Ephesian elders Paul said: "That is why I declare to you today that I am innocent of the blood of any of you, because I did not shrink from telling you the whole plan of God (Acts 20:26-27)."[3]

It is a serious matter to reject and disobey the teachings of Christ, for Jesus declared: "The person who rejects ME and does not take to heart what I say has one that is condemning him; the word that I spoke will condemn him on the Last Day (John 12:48)."[4] The entire body of Christian truth and doctrine must be believed, accepted and practiced as set forth in Holy Writ.

In His day, Christ warned against false prophets, who came in sheep's clothing but inwardly they were ravening wolves. Paul warned the Ephesian elders: "I know after my departure fierce wolves will come among you, and they will not spare the flock, and that from among your number men will arise perverting the truth, to draw away disciples after them. So be on your guard (Acts 20:30-31a)."[5] Paul admonished Timothy "give heed to yourself and to your teaching. Persevere in these things for by so doing this you will save both yourself and your hearers (II Timothy 4:16)."[6] In the opening chapter of I Timothy, Paul said to his coworker in Ephesus: "Instruct certain individuals there not to be teaching heterodoxy, nor to be paying attention to myths and interminable genealogies, which tend to promote discussions rather than stewardship entrusted by God, a stewardship which is in faith (1:4)."[7] Peter instructed the congregations of Asia Minor: "If any one preaches, let him always preach as one who utters God's truth (1 Peter 4:11)."[8] In the last chapter of his Roman Epistle, Paul, referring to all the doctrines enunciated by him, in his letter, which sets forth the great doctrines of the Christian faith, said: "But I warn you, brothers, to keep an eye on those who cause divisions and temptations, quite out of harmony with the doctrine you have been taught, and keep away from them" (Romans 16:17).[9] The apostle John in writing to the elect lady, warned: "Whoever transgresses and does not abide in the doctrine of Christ does not have God. He who abides in the doctrine of Christ hath both the Father and the Son. If anyone comes to you and does not bring this doctrine, do not receive him into your house nor greet him (2 John 9-10)."[10]

In the past the Lutheran Church in general, and now only partially, has emphasized the indoctrination of children, sponsored confirmation classes, maintained day schools, high schools and colleges. "Train up a child in the way he should go, and when he is old he will not depart from it (Proverbs 22:6)." The earnest Christian steeps himself in Christian doctrine as a sure way to a vital Christian life. There are many in Lutheranism and in Protestantism who no longer believe that Christian doctrines and Christian beliefs are necessary for God-pleasing Christian living. "Away with creeds, give us deeds" has become the guiding star for many religionists today. Unionism and ecumenism have deemphasized Christian doctrine failing to distinguish between doctrine and erroneous dogmas.

In this time of doctrinal indifference, it is essential to demonstrate the vital relationship between Christian doctrine and Christian living. In the following discussion by Christian doctrine is meant God's truth as it is set forth for a person to learn, believe, defend and practice and refers to all doctrines derived from the Bible, God's Word. All sound teaching derived from the Bible is "Christian." All doctrine not taken from the Bible is not Christian. In this presentation the word "life" will be used in the sense of "Principle of Life," and manner of life—that is spiritual life that lives in the believer, and the spiritual life that is lived by the child of God. An analogy would be a fruit tree, the life that animates the tree and the fruit which is produced from the tree. By the term "salutary" is meant the sound, healthy wholesome connection or relation between doctrine and life so that Christian doctrine can flow unimpeded into the believing Christian.

I
Christian Doctrine Is the Sole Source of Christian Life

The spiritual life within the Christian is not obtained by his natural birth. Jesus told Nicodemus: "That which is born of the flesh is flesh, and that which is born of the Spirit in spirit (John 3:6)."[12] For a Christian to have true spiritual life he must experience regeneration, the new birth. "Man born of a woman is conceived and born in sin (Ps. 51:5)." All people are by natural birth spiritually dead (Ephesians 2:1). Through God's grace, as Paul wrote "you are alive. Who were dead in trespasses and sins (Ephesians 2:1)."[13] The new spiritual life is not the same as the natural life each person has by birth. Without repentance and faith in Christ, created by the Word of God through regeneration and justification, man alienated from God, cannot please God.

The Manner Christians Attain Spiritual Life

This cannot be achieved by mystical experiences with God. It is only through the Means of Grace (Baptism, the Word of God, spoken, read, heard, visualized) that the new birth is effected and cannot be achieved in ways that do not use Holy Scripture, Baptism, the Lord's Supper, the Holy Spirit only works through the means of grace to bring about the radical change every human being needs. Only the Word of God in its various forms, spoken, read, heard or visualized is able to create new life and also after its creation to sustain the same.

Baneful Effect of All Forms of Mysticism

Mysticism has had a baneful effect on Christian doctrine, because there have been those mystics who teach that God pervades the physical universe, just as the soul pervades the body. By establishing contact with God, a person can place himself in harmony with the universe about him.[14] When this happens life is supposed to flow into the individual and he becomes spiritually alive. But God's Word pricks this bubble by saying: "Be not conformed to this world (Romans 12:2)." In fact, the Bible says that the whole world lies in wickedness (I John 5:17). Any person who contends that he must have communion with nature, or have communion with God in a direct mystical way with God apart from the Word is placing himself or herself in rapport with the world, the Devil or with delusion. Union with anything or anybody, save the Triune God will result in a lack of spiritual life. By birth or by nature people do not possess eternal life but are destined to eternal death, unless the Triune God changes mankind's unspiritual life into spiritual life.

Christian Doctrine Conveys Spiritual Life

According to the Word of God it is the doctrines and teachings found in the Bible and associated with the sacraments, which are the conveyors of God's truth and the latter can only be apprehended by faith, because as Hebrews asserted: "Without faith it is impossible to please God." Genuine Christian faith immerses itself in God's Word, without detracting from the Word or adding to it.

Through Holy Writ, life that is eternal, expresses itself in Christian living and in good works. Through the Means of Grace,[15] the written, spoken word and the visualized Word in the sacraments of Baptism and the Lord's Supper faith is created, sustained and preserved. Life comes from the Trinity. John says: "For as the Father has life in himself, so he has granted the Son to have life in himself."[16] From God's Son life is passed on to the Christian. Jesus declared: "I tell you the truth, whoever hears my word and believes him who sent me has eternal life (5:24)."[17] In the Bread of Life chapter of John's Gospel, the Lord said: "For the Bread of God is what comes down from heaven, and gives life to the world" (6:33)."[18] In the same chapter 6, Jesus assures mankind: "Just as the living Father hath sent me, and I live by the Father, so also that man who feeds on me shall live by me (V. 57)."[18a] Again the Savior promised: "I have come that they have life, and that they may have it more abundantly (10:10)."[19] One of the outstanding I Am's of John's Gospel reads: "I am the way, the truth, and the life. No one comes to the Father except through me (14:6)."[20] In his first epistle, John declared: "The witness is this; that God has given us eternal life, and that this life is found in his Son. He who possesses the Son hath life indeed; he who does not possess the son of God has not that life (5:12)."[21]

The Means of Possessing Christ

James told the Jewish converts to whom he wrote: "Of His own will He brought us forth by the word of truth, that we might be a kind of first fruits of His creatures (1:18)."[22] Peter assured the congregations of Asia Minor: "Having been born again, not of corruptible seed but incorruptible, through the Word of God which lives and abides forever 1:23)."[23] Through baptism, a form of the visible Word, faith is begotten. "Now when we were baptized into His death, we were buried with Him so that, as Christ was raised from the dead by the glory of the Father, we too will live a new life (Rom. 6:4)."[24] The person hearing the words of institution: "Take eat, this the body of your Lord Jesus, given and shed for the forgiveness of sin," can learn that he is a sinner, that Christ died to obtain forgiveness for sinners and that the Words are for those addressed. The Lord's Supper produces and sustains faith in Christ, the life of the world.

The Word of God Nourishes and Sustains Spiritual Life

Just as God is the begetter of the new spiritual life, so He alone is its sustainer. Only by God's grace is a child of God reborn and endowed with a new life, new affections and new will power do obey God's commands. The God-created spiritual life is so unique that God is said to dwell within His Christian followers. The Bible says that the Triune God comes and dwells within His saved. Christ is said expressly to dwell in the believers. Paul assures of Christ's indwelling: "I was crucified with Christ, and I don't live anymore, but Christ lives in me. The life I now live in my body I live by believing in the Son of God who loved me and gave himself for me (Gal. 2:20)."[25] Without Christ in the person's heart there cannot be true spiritual life. Avers John: "He that hath the Son has life and he that hath not the Son hath not life (I John 5:12)."[26] Christ Himself taught that He is the Vine and the Christians the branches, but the branches that have no life are cut off (John 15:6).

The maintenance of the Christian life only occurs when Christians have God in their hearts. Jesus promised: "If anyone loves Me, he will keep My word, and My Father will love him, and we will come to him and make our home with him (14:23)."[27] It is for this reason that Peter encourages the congregations of Asia Minor: "As newborn babies, desire the pure milk of the word, that you may grow thereby (1 Peter 2:2)."[28] The Word of God, and it alone can nourish the growth of the spiritual life in human beings.

Christian Good Works and Activities
Are Motivated by God's Word

Genuine spiritual life is bound to express itself in spiritual life. "The new spiritual life in the believer is lived by virtue of the new power which the Holy Spirit has begotten in those reborn or regenerated." The new spiritual life, constituted by God, will produce good works. Paul is clear on this issue: "For there is nothing for any man to boast of for we are God's handiwork, created in Christ Jesus to devote ourselves to the good deeds for which God has designed us (Eph. 2:16)."[29] A Christian is like a good tree producing good fruit. The relationship between doctrine and Christian life has been well expressed by Paul in his last letter to Timothy; "All Scripture is inspired by God and is useful for teaching, showing what is wrong, improving and training in right living so that a man of God is ready and equipped for every good work (II Tim. 3:15-17)."[30]

The Word and Spiritual Life

All that God does for the spiritual life of man He does through the Word. The Word mediates God to man in the first place. When God begins His work in man, and it is by the Word that He begets spiritual life in man, nourishes it, and directs its activities. God does this in no other way. That this is so, is shown by the fact that Christ warned against human instructions and traditions. Purely human instruction is forbidden, as the Savior warned: "They worship me in vain, teaching for doctrine rules which are only human (Matthew 15:9)."[31]

II
Christian Doctrine Will Produce Life in the Measure in Which It Is Received and Placed Into Practice

When a physician prescribes a potent medicine for a patient in order to restore health, it is incumbent on the patient to take it, otherwise the medicine will do no good. So Scriptural Christian doctrine has the power to create, sustain and bring forth an abundant spiritual life, but in order to secure the abounding life, human beings need to receive and apply the life-bearing doctrine. Correct Christian doctrine possesses divine power. The unbeliever who does not know of or possess the Biblical doctrine does not have God's truth or power. Only that individual alone has the life-working truth who believes it and accepts it.

Mankind by nature does not possess the truth of Christian doctrine (I Cor. 2:14). Many people reject Christian doctrine because to them it is foolishness, going against their sinful natures or because it offends human reason. By nature human beings are enemies of God (Romans 8:7). Before the people addressed by Paul in Ephesians were converted, they were dead in trespasses and sins (2:1). But Christian doctrine has not only the power to produce spiritual life, but the measure of that life depends, first of all, on the measure with which it is received.

The Necessity of Knowledge of Christian Doctrine

Before Christian doctrine can be practiced, it must be known. Thus Paul asked: "And how shall they call upon Him in whom they have not believed? And how shall they believe in Him whom they have never heard? And how shall they hear without a preacher? (Rom. 10:14)."[32] Knowledge of Christian doctrine is a prerequisite for the Christian doing of good works. This requirement is stressed by Jesus: "Blessed are they that hear the Word of God and keep it (Luke 11:28)."[33] In the Great Commission Jesus stated: "Teaching them to observe all things I have commanded you (Matt. 28:20)."[34]

The Use of Christian Doctrine in the Church's Program

In the entire gamut of the church's activities the Word must constantly be employed. In preaching, teaching, evangelism, counseling, church administration, Christian doctrine must be used. The impartation of God's truth as expressed in doctrines is vital to the learning process. Doctrine shapes the individual's mind, affects his emotion and moves the will. If doctrines set forth clearly in the Bible are left out, then false human opinions will replace them. Thus the power for God-pleasing good works will be eliminated, if God's Word as expressed in Christian doctrine is ignored, then, man's speculations will be substituted as has happened in Eastern Orthodoxy, Roman Catholicism, and other religious churches.[35]

Various Outcries Against Christian Doctrines

Today in some sections of Lutheranism and in many Protestant denominations there is a definite aversion for Biblical doctrines to be taught and believed. Especially when insistence is made that the whole counsel of God be taught faithfully and accurately. There is first of all the mistake of the identification of Biblical correct doctrine with ecclesiastical dogma and the aberrations flowing them from. Secondly, there is the distaste of the human mind against revealed truth.[36] The Christian Church has no reason to fear sound doctrinal teaching, for its propagation is the only sure way to Christian life and the performance of God-pleasing good works.

In Protestant religious education, influenced by secular educational philosophy, the methodology has stressed the "pupil-centered" or "experienced centered" approach. Instead of God's Word controlling the educational process, it has made the pupil the dominant controlling feature of the pedagogical procedure, in which the Word of God is ignored, or watered down or changed to what people want in place of what God demands. Instead of teaching, preaching, teaching, evangelism and counseling being "Bible-centered," the objects of teaching now have become man-centered. Christ commanded:

Preach the Gospel to all creatures, teach all instructions that I have given you or will through my inspired apostles. Among the last instructions of Paul to his coworker Timothy was: "Preach the Word, be prepared in season and out of season; correct, rebuke, and encourage—with great patience and careful instruction. For the time will come when men will not put up with sound doctrine. Instead, to suit their own desires, they will gather around them a great number of teachers to say what their itching ears want to hear (2 Timothy 4:2-3)."[37]

However, true knowledge in itself is not sufficient to produce the Christian vibrant life, full of good works. There is a difference between head knowledge and a fruitful Christian spiritual life.

Conditions for Knowledge to Become Vital and Active

For the life-giving truth to become a life-giving power in human beings, it is necessary for the doctrine to be believed. Paul makes this clear to the Roman congregation, when he asserted: "I am not ashamed of the good news; for it is God's power for salvation to every believer, to the Jew first and to the Greek also." For God's righteousness is disclosed in it through faith and leading to faith, as it is written, "The one who is righteous through faith will live (1:16,17)."[38] The Apostle John wrote his Gospel: "But these have been recorded to help you believe that Jesus is the Messiah, the Son of God, so that through this faith you may have life in his name John 20:31)."[39] In his interpretation of The Sower and the Seed, Jesus explained: "But they on good ground are they, which in an honest and good heart; having heard the word, keep it and bring forth fruit with patience (Luke 8:15)."[40]

So the reason in the last analysis, as to why the Word of God or Christian doctrine brought forth spiritual fruit in some is because they believed and obeyed the Word, whereas in the case of the unfruitful, it is that they did not believe. Yes, Christian doctrine, accepted by faith created by the Holy Spirit, can work Christian activity and produce fruits in people's lives.

A number of corollaries flow from this general proposition. 1. If it is true that faith is the only way by which Christian doctrine can produce good works, it follows the stronger the faith, the stronger will be the spiritual life and more abundant will be the fruitage. A strong faith produces more life-giving power that does a weak faith. Since faith from the human side is the instrument, we usually speak of faith producing fruit in people's lives. So do the Holy Scriptures. On one occasion when Jesus was with His disciples crossing on the Sea of Galilee, a great storm arose and the disciples awakened Jesus so he would save them, Christ rebuked them: "You of little faith, why are you afraid?" (Matt. 8:26)[41] Jesus castigated His disciples when they could not drive out a demon, by saying: "Because you have so little faith, I tell you the truth, if you have faith as a mustard seed, you can say to this mountain, 'Move from here to there' and it will move. Nothing is impossible for You" (Matt. 17:20).[42]

Luke records in his church history, the Book of Acts: "and Stephen full of faith and (consequently of) power, did great wonders and miracles among the people" (Acts 6:8).[43] In his First Epistle John declared: "Because everyone has been born of God conquers the world, and this is the victory that triumphs over the world, the faith that we have" (5:4).[44] In Hebrews chapter 11, the great heroes of faith listed there, are men and women who had a great faith and by it accomplished remarkable things.

If a strong faith produces more of life in people, conversely, it must be true, that less of good fruits comes forth from a person possessing a weak faith. Now it is true that a man with a strong and a person with a weak faith have spiritual life. There is only one true faith that has Christ as its object. The measure of the strength of a strong faith would be measured by the amount of fruitage the Christian life produces. The weak faith necessarily brings forth less good works. Frequently unbelief enters the Christian's faith and he fails to achieve what God would have him accomplish. On another occasion involving Christ and His disciples on the Sea of Galilee and when Peter was trying to walk on the water, he began to sink, Jesus rebuked him: "O you of little faith, wherefore did you doubt (Matt. 14:31)."[45] Weak Christians should pray: "Lord, help my unbelief."

Misbelief Endangers Christian Faith and Productive Spiritual Life

The second corollary of the position earlier enunciated is this: If only Christian doctrine results in life, then misbelief of that doctrine will lessen its power to produce life. Linder contended that "in fact, the evidence is on every hand that many a person with an implicit faith in that part of doctrine which is pure has a more abundant life than the most orthodox believer who has a weak faith."[46] However, it is still true that impure, unhealthy doctrine cannot build genuine spiritual life. This is what St. Paul told the Corinthians who held erroneous doctrinal views, when he wrote: "For no one can lay any other foundation than the one that is already laid. If someone builds on this foundation with gold, silver, precious stones, wood, hay, or straw, what each one does will become evident. For that Day will show what it is, because fire will reveal it and test it to show what kind of work everyone has done. If what a person has built on the foundation stands the test, he will receive a reward. If this work is burned, he will lose something, but he himself will be saved, though it will be like going through a fire (I Cor. 3:11-15)."[47]

Unbelief Unable to Produce Spiritual Life

Another corollary flowing from the supposition earlier announced is this: If Christian doctrine produces life only when it is believed, then unbelief will be powerless to produce true spiritual life and the good works flowing therefrom. The helplessness of unbelief to produce spiritual life and good works was clearly explicated by Jesus, when He said: "I tell you the absolute truth, unless you eat the flesh of the Son of Man and drink His blood, you do riot have any life in you (John 6:53)."[48] Rejection of Christ as mankind's substitute for their sins and atonement for them, cannot have spiritual life. Unequivocally Jesus declared: "Without Me you can do nothing (John 15:5)."[49] Paul warned: "What is not of faith is sin (Romans 14:23)."[50] The writer of Hebrews who has made the God-man Jesus the central factor of his epistle declared "Where there is no faith it is impossible truly to please Him; for the man who draws near to God must believe that there is a God, and that He proves Himself a rewarder of those who seek God."[51] But it is only through Jesus that one can come to God (Hebrews 11:6).

To summarize: Christian doctrine will produce life in the measure in which it is received by faith. No faith, no spiritual life. A mixed faith means lessened life. A weak faith not so virulent a spiritual life, a strong faith results in abundant life and consequent good works.

Jesus taught that a healthy tree produces an abundance of fruit. This raises the important question: "How can a person acquire a strong faith?" Paul advised Timothy: "Let the word of Christ richly dwell within you, with all wisdom, teaching and admonishing one another with psalms, and hymns, and spiritual songs (Colossians 3:16)"[51a] so that you will "constantly be nourished on the words of faith and of sound doctrine which you have been following, but have nothing to do with worldly fables, fit only for old women. On the other hand, discipline yourself for the purpose of godliness, for bodily discipline is only of little profit, but godliness is to profitable for all things, since it holds promise for the present life and also for the life to come (I Tim. 4:6-8)."[52]

Exercising for Godliness

Paul taught his followers that faith needed to be exercised, which was profitable for all things. Spiritual life must express itself in Christian life or good works. The life of sanctification must follow justification.

People who believe Christian doctrine should also have spiritual life. The Christian's spiritual life must express itself in good works. The Bible also teaches that Christian doctrine informs believers what to do and not to do. Christian doctrine based squarely on the Word of God will bestow the incentive and empowerment to live God-pleasing lives in the God-intended ways.

Thus it can be asserted that a living faith will cause its possessors to live spiritual lives and will cause the Christian believer to be convinced that faith without works is dead. By the power mediated by the Word of God the Christian believer will thoroughly be furnished unto all good works. The Christian is under obligation to live his Christian doctrine according to God's directives given in the Scriptures. The Christian is under obligation to practice his God-given instructions as they apply to being prolific in good deeds.

Use It or Lose It

It is a universal law of human existence that whenever God's gifts are not used they atrophy and eventually are lost. The Parable of The Fig Tree and the Parable of the Talents teach this lesson very emphatically. In John 15 Jesus, the Vine, warned: "If a man abide not in me (i.e. by believing and practicing), he is cast forth as a branch, and withered and men gather them, and cast them into the fire and they are burned (15:6)."[53]

The Beneficent Results of an Active New Spiritual Life

And now it follows that the more a Christian uses his spiritual life active in good works, based on instruction laid down in Holy Writ as Christian doctrine, the more will be his ability and capacity to increase for living the life rich in good works. Justified Christians must do what Jesus instructed them to do: "In the same way your light must shine in the sight of men, so that, seeing, your good works, they may give praise to your Father in heaven (Matt. 5:16.)"[54] The justified Christian has the opportunity to be active in prayer for missionaries, in prayers for the welfare, and growth of the Church, in teaching in Sunday School, Christian day school, in counseling people in need, performing works of charity, in evangelistic efforts, in visiting the sick and prisoners in jails, participate in those projects of the church that promote its correct programs, singing to the glory of God and in every way that helps in the purpose of the church to seek to save that which was lost. Every Christian should endeavor to give expression to his Christian life. The more activities a

Christian participates in, this will make for an all-sided spiritual life. And he or she will be a symmetrical tree, in which not only a few branches will produce fruits.

Scripture and human experience testify to the fact that correct Christian doctrine will produce life in the measure it is believed and practiced. However, it must not be forgotten that the spiritual life is derived from God and thus all honor belongs to God for whatever the Christian is able to accomplish. Like St. Paul, the Fruit-bearing Christian must confess: "But through the grace that is granted me I warn each among you not to value himself more highly than he should, but to think soberly as God has measured out to each his portion of faith (Romans 12:3)."[55] What Paul wrote to the Corinthians is true of every Christian: "I wish all men were as I am, but each person has his own gift from God, the one in this direction, the other in that (I Cor. 7:7)."[56] No Christian has ever come near to exhausting the possibilities for spiritual life within his God-appointed sphere.

The Necessity of Good Works

Good works are necessary, because God asks them of his children (Matt. 5:16; 2 Cor. 9:6,8; Titus 2:14). They are furthermore the necessary fruits of repentance (Matt. 3:8), the inevitable product of faith (Gal. 5:6; John (15:5). Without them faith is dead (James 2:17). *The Epitome of the Formula of Concord* stated it this way: "The regenerate do good works from a free spirit, this is not to be understood as though it is at the option of the regenerate man to do or to forbear doing good when he wishes, and that he can nevertheless retain faith, if he intentionally perseveres in sin."[57] Good works are not necessary to give our faith strength and saving power, for faith trusts in the merits of Christ. Nor are they necessary to preserve faith in our hearts for this is done by the Holy Spirit.[58]

God's Own Instruction About Good Works

Through Christian doctrine, setting forth faithfully God's Word, God gives instructions as to how Christians are to exercise their spiritual lives. St. Paul taught that "all Scripture is God-breathed and is useful for teaching, rebuking, correcting and training in righteousness, so that the man of God may be thoroughly equipped for every good work (2 Timothy 3:16)."[59] God's Word is like a lamp for our feet, helping us to walk the narrow path.

There Old Adam does not delight in doing God's will, but "for it is God who works in you both to will and to do for His good pleasure (Philip. 2:13)."[60] Paul told us his coworker Titus that the Son of God "gave Himself as a payment for us to free us from all wickedness and to cleanse us to be His own people, eager to do good works (2:14)."[61] Since the Holy Spirit furnishes the enablement, the horn-again believer can say: "In my inner being I delight in God's law (Romans 7.22)."[62] And with the psalmist: "I delight to do Thy will, O my God (Psalm 40:8)."[63]

God Employs Examples of Love to Be Imitated

To encourage His followers to do good works, God uses love to persuade Christians by giving them examples of mercies shown to people in Bible times. God's undeserved mercies should cause Christ's followers to respond to the gracious mercies and benefits God in the past has bestowed on them.

The Promise of the Indwelling of Holy Trinity in Christians

Christ also promised His followers than the three persons of the Trinity will dwell in them. Jesus on Holy Thursday night promised: "If anyone loves Me, He will keep My word, and My Father will love him, and We will come to him and make Our home with him (John 14:23)."[64] Pieper claimed that "The Holy Trinity is present for the Scripture teaches that all three persons of the Holy Trinity make their abode in the heart of every man who has come to faith."[65]

The Holy Spirit will produce the fruits of the Spirit, such as love, joy, peace, patience, kindness, goodness, faithfulness, gentleness and self-control (Galatians 5:22-23). With Paul the believer can say: "I can do all things around Christ who strengthens me (Philippians 4:13)."[66] God makes the Christian like "a tree planted near running waters that yields its fruits in due season and whose leaf never fades, and whatsoever he does prospers."[67]

Sometimes God purges the branches by means of crosses and afflictions, that they may bring forth more fruit (John 15:2). With God's help the good works performing Christian can believe that being confident of that very thing, that He which has begun a good work in you will perform it to the day of Jesus Christ (Phil. 1:6).[68] In view of the help of the Triune God, Paul appealed to his followers: 'Therefore since we have these promises, dear friends, let us cleanse ourselves from everything that pollutes body and spirit and let us continually do what is holy in the fear of God (2 Cor. 7:1).[69]

God Employs Admonitions to Motivate Christians

Should the promises of God fail to persuade and motivate His followers. He utilizes admonitions to motivate them. Here are a few of the many found in Holy Writ: "But speaking the truth in love, may grow up in all things, to Him who is the head-Christ (Eph. 4:15)."[70] Again: "Abound in the work of the Lord (1 Cor. 15:15)." Again: "Increase in the knowledge of God (Col. 1:10)." "May the Lord cause you to increase and abound in love for one another and for all men (1 Thess. 3:12)."[70a] "Further, brethren, we beg and exhort you in the name of the Lord Jesus, as you learnt from us how you ought to live so as to please God, as indeed you do live, so to do even more thoroughly. For you know the commands which we gave you by the authority of the Lord Jesus (1 Thess. 4:1-2)."[71]

The Bible resorts to warnings and threats to arouse the consciences of Christians. Thus the author of Hebrews states: "Ever strive for peace with all and for the sanctification apart from which no one will see the Lord 12:14)."[72] Paul warned: "Do not be deceived: God cannot be mocked.

A man reaps what he sows. The one who sows to please his sinful nature, from that nature will reap destruction:

"They who sows to please the Spirit from the Spirit will reap eternal life (Gal. 6:7-9)."[73] Christ also warned: "Every branch in Me that beareth not fruit He taketh it away (John 15:2)."[74]

God Uses the Law to Arouse Consciences

Some Christians are inclined to fail to do what God has prescribed for them in His Holy Word. When this occurs, God often calls upon the conscience of the Church through its pastors, teachers, professors and dedicated lay people to preach the law to awake the consciences of the slothful by bringing about repentance so that these dormant Christians will realize their sinful slothfulness and inactivity. The Bible has many warnings, exhorting Christians to be active in good works. Paul directed the congregations of Asia Minor "So I tell you and call on you in the Lord not to live any longer like the Gentiles (Eph. 4:17)."[75] To the Corinthians Paul wrote: "And there is no limit to the blessing which God can send you—he will make sure that you will always have all you need for yourselves in every possible circumstance (2 Cor. 9:8)."[76]

Again in the First Corinthian Letter Paul commended these Greek Christians: "Always do more and more work for the Lord, since you know that in the Lord your hard work is not wasted (15:58)."[77]

God has recorded dire warnings for those who were negligent and who do not live lives filled with good works. The prophet Isaiah has characterized those who were remiss in living God—fearing lives as "dumb dogs, sleeping, lying down, loving to slumber (Is. 56:10)."[78] Paul admonished Timothy "I solemnly charge thee in the presence of God and of Christ Jesus who is to judge the living and the dead, and by His manifestation and His Kingdom— preach the Word, be insistent in season and out of season; convince, rebuke, exhort, with all forbearance and doctrine (2 Tim. 4:1-2)."[79]

Requirement for Successfully Practicing God's Precepts

What must Christians do to faithfully practice God's precepts? On the basis of Holy Writ, it can be said: 1. The Christian must accept God's gift of life together with the obligations to practice God's precepts. 2. The believer must take seriously God's pleadings of the Gospel as well as the exhortations of the Law. 3. The Christian believer must constantly make use of prayer. 4. Since the Means of Grace are the medium through which God creates and sustains faith, he must faithfully use Word and Sacraments, the visible Word. That these suggestions are true may be seen from the First Christian congregation at Jerusalem, of whom it is written: "and they continued steadfastly in the apostle's teaching and fellowship, in the breaking of bread and the prayers (Acts 2:42)."[80]

That believer who will follow the suggestions just listed (1 to 4) will discover that God has thoroughly furnished him to engage in good works. James encourages his Jewish readers: "But be doers of the word, and not hearers only, deceiving your own selves (1:22)."[81]

Why Do Christians Faith to Do Good Works?

Not only is the flesh weak, but it is also utterly opposed to what God wants His followers to do. Paul understood this for he explained: "For the flesh lusts against the spirit and the spirit against the flesh for these oppose each other lest whatever things ye wish, ye do" (Gal. 5:17).[82] It is a serious matter not to follow the Holy Spirit's urgings. "For if you live according to the sinful nature, you will die, but if by the Spirit of God you put to death the misdeeds of the body, you will live (Romans 8:13)."[83] If a Christian would maintain his spiritual life he must do what St. Paul told the congregations of Asia Minor: "Put off your old nature which belongs to your former manner of life and is corrupt through deceitful lusts and be renewed in the spirit of your minds, and put on the new nature, created after the likeness of God in true righteousness and holiness (Ephesians 4:22-24."[84] The Christian must follow Paul's advice by repenting of his former failures, by forsaking all evil and by diligently applying himself to the performance of good. In this effort the Christian needs God's assistance through prayer and the Word of God and victory will be bestowed.

Young and the Declension of Doctrine

In his monograph of *Isaiah Fifty Three* Edward Young already in 1952 wrote: "We are living in an age when doctrine is not popular. One reason for this lack of popularity is probably to be found in the fact that so few people know what doctrine is. It is very rare that one hears a sermon that can be called doctrinal. And that valuable institution the catechism class, has almost entirely vanished from the churches. If people knew something about doctrine they might make the astonishing discovery that, far from being dry and uninteresting and irrelevant, doctrine is the most interesting and relevant of all subjects."[85] Again the same scholar contended: "The fact is, nevertheless, that we are living in a day of doctrinal declension. In the churches men are very much interested in a program, and anything, such as doctrine, which might tend to interfere with the smooth working of that program, is looked at askance. Yet there is nothing more important than doctrine. The word simply means teaching, and surely it is important to know what teaching the Word of God contains. The greatest need of the day is a revival of doctrinal teaching and preaching."[86] The Westminster scholar believed that once men have understood the importance of Biblical doctrine, that there would come a revulsion from the shallowness of so much of modern religious life and a genuine return to the Word of the living God. May God hasten the coming of that day!

Addendum
Clarifying Note

In this essay the Gospel has been adduced a number of times when speaking about God's dealing with Christians who are believers. God uses both the encouraging words of the Gospel to motivate Christians to lives rich in good works, and also through the Law warns Christians as to what will happen to them if their lives are empty of good works. However, when dealing with unbelievers, the Law must first be preached to make them see their sinful ways, to cause them to repent, to experience the pangs of conscience and then the Good News of Christ must be offered to create faith in Jesus Christ, so that they also will become living branches on Christ the true Vine and produce much fruit. Nothing in this essay should be considered as promoting the Gospel-Law inversion.

Christ has clearly stated: "This is what is written: The Christ (Messiah) will suffer and rise from the dead on the third day; and on the basis of His Name, repentance and forgiveness of sins will be preached to all nations, beginning at Jerusalem. You will testify to these things (Luke 24:48-49)."

Footnotes

1. Abridgment, summarization and adaption of an essay by C.E. Linder, *The Salutary Relation Between Christian Doctrine and Christian Life*, published about 60 years ago. The Authorized Version is used throughout the essay. Most of these have been replaced by verses from 20th century translations. Surburg has made certain additions in harmony with the spirit of the essay. The introduction and conclusion are Surburg's.

2. *Holy Bible, New Testament, New Evangelical Translation* (Cleveland: NET Publishing, 1992), p. 66. Hereafter referred to as NET.

3. **Ibid.**, p. 271.

4. **Ibid.**, p. 200.

5. Helen Barrett Montgomery, *The Centenary Translation. The New Testament in Modern English* (Philadelphia: The Judson Press, 1924), p. 370.

6. **Ibid.**, p. 568.

7 **Ibid.**, p. 563.

8. **Ibid.**, p. 642.

9. Gerrit Verkuyl, Editor in Chief, *The Holy Bible, The New Berkeley Version in Modern English* (Grand Rapids: Zondervan Publishing House, 1969), Romans 16:17, New Testament, p. 128.

10. Holy Bible. *The New King James Version* (New York and Nashville: Thomas Nelson Publishers, 1982), p. 1198.

11. **Ibid.**, p. 638.

12. *Holy Bible Containing the Old and New Testament*, Set Forth in 1611. *The King James Version* (New York: American Bible Society, no date), p. 96.

13. *The New King James Version*, **op. cit.**, p. 1142.

14. Cf. L. Lueker, "Mysticism," *Concordia Cyclopedia* (St. Louis: Concordia Publishing House, 1954), p. 726.

15. Cf. Edwin Pieplow, "The Means of Grace," *The Abiding Word* (St. Louis: Concordia Publishing House, 1947), II, pp. 32-346.

16. *New International Version of the Holy Bible* (Grand Rapids: Zondervan Bible Publishers 1984), 754.

17. **Ibid.**, p. 574.

18. Montgomery, **op. cit.**, p. 258.

18a. **Ibid.**, p. 260.

19. *New King James Version*, **op. cit.**, p. 1045.

20. **Ibid.**

21. *The New English Bible With the Apocrypha* (Oxford and Cambridge Universities (oxford and Cambridge, 1970), NT, p. 309.

22. *New King James Version*, p. 1182

23. **Ibid.**, 1186.

24. NET, **op. cit.**, p. 286.

25. William Beck, *The Holy Bible, An American Translation* (New Haven: Leader Publishing Company, 1976), NT, p. 237.

26. *Holy Bible, King James Version.*

27. NET, **op. cit.**, p. 203.

28. *New King James Version*, **op. cit.**, p. 1187.

29 *The New English Bible*, **op. cit.**, NT, p. 246.

30. Beck, *An American Translation*, **op. cit.**, NT, p. 269.

31. **Ibid.**, NT, p. 20.

32. *New American Standard Bible*, (Philadelphia: A. J. Holman Company, 1973), p. 813.

33. *King James Version*, **op. cit.**, NT, p. 74.

34. **Ibid.**, NT, p. 34.

35. Th. Engelder, W. Arndt, Th. Graebner, and F. E. Mayer, *Popular Symbolics* (St. Louis: Concordia Publishing House, 1934, pp. 25; *Formula of Concord*, Th.D. Comp. Sum, 3.9; Apology IV, 107; III, 268.

36. *Formula of Concord*, Th. D., VII, 45; Apol. III, 175, VII and VIII, 27.

37. *New International Version*, **op. cit.**, p. 843b.

38. Berkeley, **op. cit.**, NT, p. 163

39. *Saint Joseph Edition of The New American Bible* (New York: Catholic Publishing Company, 1970). *King James Version*, **op. cit.**, NT, p. 68.

40. *The King James Version*, **op. cit.**, NT, p. 68.

41. *New International Version*, **op. cit.**, p. 686.

42. **Ibid.**, p. 695.

43. *King James Version*, NT., p. 127.

44. Berkeley, **op. cit.**, NT, p. 268.

45. *New King James Version*, **op. cit.**, p. 947.

46. Linder, *The Salutary Relation Between Christian Doctrine and Life*, **op. cit.**, p. 20.

47. NET, **op. cit.**, p. 308.

48. **Ibid.**, p. 308.

49. **Ibid.**, p. 204.

50. *King James Version*, **op. cit.**, NT, p. 167.

51. Richard Frances Wymouth, *The New Testament in Modern Speech* (Boston; The Pilgrim Press, 1943), p. 546.

51a. *New American Standard Bible*, **op. cit.**, p. 845.

52. **Ibid.**, p. 845.

53. *King James Version*, **op. cit.**, NT., p. 113.

54. Alexander Jones, (General Editor, *The Jerusalem Bible*, (New York: Garden City: Doubleday and Company, 1966), NT, p. 22.

55. Berkeley, **op. cit.**, p. 174.

56. **Ibid.**, NT, p. 183.

57. *Concordia Triglotta* (St. Louis: Concordia Publishing Rouse, 1921), *Formula of*

Concord, Art. IV, 11, p. 799.

58. **Ibid.**, p. 799. *Formula of Concord*, Epitome and Th.D. IV, pp. 787ff.

59. *The New International Version*, **op. cit.**, p. 1148.

60. *New King James Version*, **op. cit.**, p. 1148.

61. Beck, *An American Translation*, **op. cit.**, NT, p. 272.

62. NET, **op. cit.**. NT, p. 288.

63. *King James Version*, **op. cit.**, p. 540.

64. *New King James Bible*, **op. cit.**, 1052.

65. Francis Pieper, *Christian Dogmatics* (St. Louis: Concordia Publishing House, 1953), III, p. 274.

66. *King James Bible*, **op. cit.**, p. 264.

67. *The New American Bible* (New York: The Catholic Press, 1970), p. 448.

68. *New American Standard Bible*, **op. cit.**, p. 841.

69. NET, **op. cit.**, p. 336.

70. *The New King James Version*, **op. cit.**, p. 1144.

70a. *New American Standard Bible*, **op. cit.**, p. 847.

71. Weymouth, **op. cit.**, p. 486.

72. **Ibid.**, p. 550.

73. *New International Version*, **op. cit.**, p. 826.

74. *King James Version*, **op. cit.**, NT, p. 113.

75. NET, **op. cit.**, p. 360.

76. *The New Jerusalem Bible*, **op. cit.**, NT, p. 317.

77. NET, **op. cit.**, p. 326.

78. *King James Version*, **op. cit.**, p. 666.

79. Francis Aloysius Spencer, *The New Testament of Our Lord Jesus Christ* (New York: The Macmillan and Company, 1946), p. 578.

80. *The Holy Bible Containing the Old and New Testaments*. British Revised Version (Oxford: At the University Press, 1892). NT, p. 90.

81. George M. Lamsa, *The Holy Bible From Eastern Manuscripts, The Peshitta* (Philadelphia: A. J. Holman Company, 1951), p. 1208.

82. Alfred Marshall, *The International Version*, Interlinear Greek-English New Testament (Grand Rapids: Zondervan Publishing House, 1976), p. 755.

83. TEV, **op. cit.**. p. 880.

84. *The Revised Standard Version*, p. 689 in *The Layman's Parallel New Testament* (Grand Rapids: Wm. B. Eerdmans Publishing Company, 1952), 1970.

85. Edward J. Young, *Isaiah Fifty Three* (Grand Rapids: Wm. B. Eerdmans Publishing Company, 1952), p. 54.

84. **Ibid.**, p. 55.

85. **Ibid.**, p. 55.

86. *NET*, p. 171.

Questions

1. In the past the Lutheran church emphasized _____.
2. What has become of the guiding star for many religions today? _____
3. What is the sole source of Christian life? _____
4. For a Christian to have true spiritual life he must experience _____.
5. Mysticism has had a baneful effect on _____.

6. Life comes from the _____.
7. What sustains faith in Christ? _____
8. There cannot be true spiritual life without _____.
9. What must be constantly used in the entire Christian program? _____
10. What has become the dominant controlling feature in religious education? _____
11. There is a difference between head knowledge and _____.
12. No faith, no _____.
13. Faith without work is _____.
14. Use it for _____.
15. The Holy Spirit produces _____.
16. Edward Young wrote in 1952 _____.
17. Doctrine simply means _____.

Divergent Approaches to the Nature of the Holy Scriptures Determine Interpretation, Doctrine and Ethics

Christian News, November 27, 1978

The important question of religious authority is ultimately determined by the attitude with which a Biblical scholar and student approaches the Old and New Testaments. Basically there are two attitudes toward the Bible: the low view and the high view.

I. The Low View of Holy Scriptures

Under this class there are a number of variant positions that are somewhat different from each other, but the final result is that these approaches are inadequate and are not in a position to do justice to the claims which the Bible makes concerning itself.

There exist and have existed a number of scholars who have an extremely low view of the Bible. They have depicted the Bible as merely containing the national literature of the Jews as far as the Old Testament is concerned, and the New Testament as the religious teachings of a group of Jews who did not follow the mainline stream of Judaism, as may be seen from a study and reading of the Palestinian and Babylonian Talmud and other Jewish literature that came into existence between 70 A.D. and 500 A.D. The sixty-six books of the Holy Scriptures are portrayed as the literature of people whose religious literature is on a level with similar religious productions of other nations of antiquity. *The Epics of Homer*, the Iliad and Odyssey, *Gilgamesh* and *Enuma Elish Epics of the Akkadians*, and *Egyptian Book of the Dead, The Story of Wenamon, The Tale of the Two Brothers*, the *Kalevala of the Finns, The Niebelungenelied of the Germans*, and *Beowulf* are placed on a par with the Bible by these readers and would-be interpreters of the Bible. It follows that if the Bible is a purely human book, then it cannot be the Word of God. In the nineteenth and twentieth centuries, this was and still is the approach to the Bible by the school of comparative religious. In Great Britain Frazier, *The Golden Bough* in 12 volumes would be representative of this school of thought.

Concerning this school of thought E. J. Young asserted: "This potion is unsatisfactory because it is in basic error. It regards the Bible as a book of only human origins, whereas, as a matter of fact, this is basically a book of divine origin,"(*An Introduction to the Old Testament*. Eerdmans, 1969, p. 26).

The members of the school of comparative religion were motivated by the concept of the evolution of religion and as far as they were concerned, the difference between the Judeo-Christian literature and other religious writings is not one of kind but of degree. Those schools of thought who hold a low view of Scripture are forced to reinterpret the concepts of revelation and inspiration, terms which involve the divinity of the Scriptures. The Bible is a divine-human book; this means that the Bible is in a class by itself when compared with all other books that have been published and that will be written and published in the future.

Many would-be interpreters of the Bible claim that the only valid method that should be employed in the interpretation of the Bible is the scientific method. By the scientific method, they mean following an approach that ignores and refuses to recognize the supernatural element found intertwined through the Old Testament. In the Bible there are recorded over one hundred miracles; there are at least eighty miracles in the Old Testament. No interpreter can read the life of Jesus Christ and not notice the intertwining of the miraculous and supernatural in the books from which the church has derived its beliefs about the life and teachings of Christ God the Father's Only-Begotten Son.

Those who claim to be guided in their interpretation of the Bible by the use of what they believe is the scientific method, a method which they define as not permitting the existence of the supernatural or which permits God to interfere with the cause and effect relationship in which they conceive national and personal events to have occurred are holders of a low view of the Bible. Those who erroneously define the scientific method in this manner naturally are forced to advocate a low view of the Bible. Revelation ,inspiration, the occurrence of miracles, prophecy as prediction, are either rejected or ignored. When such views are held on these basic Biblical teachings it will lead consequently to a rejection or reinterpretation of the Biblical text. The miracle, for example, which the Book of Exodus ascribes to Moses are explained in a naturalistic way and are interpreted in a manner that contradicts the data of the Biblical text.

Many of the individuals who claim that they are employing the empirico-scientific method believes that they can justifiably ignore the question of divine revelation, inspiration and the divinity of the Scriptures and still have adequately dealt with all the data and factors contained in the Bible. Young declared about this view: "Let it be said with all positiveness that it cannot satisfactorily be done, and those who adopt such a method find themselves in essential agreement with those who badly assert that the Bible is only a human production and nothing more." Edward Young, *Introduction to the Old Testament* (Grand Rapids: Wm. Eerdmans Publishing Company, 1969), p. 26.

The empirico-scientific method properly used deals with all given factors in its investigation of a subject, and does not rule out in advance certain evidence, which it will find as not acceptable. Many proponents of the empirico-scientific method limit themselves to the evidences of the senses. That God exists and that God can act in history is rejected by these interpreters who claim that they are Objective, and because of their rejection of those factors in the Biblical data which are distinctive of the Bible, then refuse to accept its divinity. However, to deal realistically with all in the Bible, which purports to be a revelation from God to man, a true empirico-scientific approach considers all the factors and does not circumscribe what the Biblical interpreter may and may not find.

There is another school of Biblical thought which believes that it can approach the Bible in a neutral manner. These advocates claim that they wish to study the Bible as any other book. The Bible is to be subjected to the same tests as any other book. If the Bible can stand these tests and if it comes out of these tests as the Word of God, then well and good. The neutrality of this method claims that when miracles are found in any book in world literature, these miracles are unacceptable. If a book is found that makes predictions many years before the happenings have occurred, then those passages with predictions in them are said to be later interpolations. When stories from Greek and Roman mythology have the various gods doing all manner of supernatural thins, these are not considered by historians as historical. The Old and New Testaments have accounts where God the Father, God the Son and God the Holy Spirit appear in connection with supernatural events connected with the history of Israel, with the life of Christ and the activities of the apostles which modern historiography cannot accept as having actually occurred. Such interventions of God simply did not take place according to proponents of this kind of an approach to the Bible. Is it possible for a Biblical interpreter to approach the Bible in a neutral manner? By ignoring the divine character of the Bible and by the claim that anything that smacks after the supernaturalism to be ignored and thus rejected, such a stance cannot quality as being classed as neutral. This alleged type of neutrality amounts to a form of prejudice against the Bible, which claims to be the Word of God. "The so-called neutral attitude towards the Bible is in reality not neutral at all," asserts Young, "For it assumes that the human mind itself can act as judge of divine revelation. This is, in effect, to substitute the mind of man as ultimate judge and reference point in the place of God Himself" (p. 27).

The low view of Scripture inherent in the variant approaches to the Bible just described makes it impossible to set forth the teachings which historic Christianity has accepted for the last two thousand years of its existence. With the low view of the Bible there have been associated the different types of criticism which have appeared on the stage of Biblical studies, beginning the Age of Reason and Rationalism. The higher-critical methodology as expressed in a radical kind of literary criticism was followed by form criticism, then succeeded by redaction criticism, which in turn was then followed by tradition criticism, which was allied with content criticism. Redaction criticism in recent years has now been succeeded by structural exegesis which has resulted in a new set of rules being adopted for interpretation (usually referred to as part of the new hermeneutic) with a resultant reinterpretation of Biblical message. Traditional dogmatics has been made impossible and all major doctrines of the Christian faith have been emasculated of their Biblical content. With the rejection of the supernatural there could have been no directives given to Adam, Noah, Isaac, Abraham, Jacob, Moses, Joshua, Eli, Samuel, Saul, David Solomon, the prophets, any of whom are described as recipients of divine messages. It further means that many events have been described in the Bible, which in truth, so it is claimed never happened. The historical events before the time of David are largely suspect.

The promises of Messiah as found in Genesis 3:15; 12:3; 49:10; Deut. 18:15; Numbers 2:17; II Sam. 7:12-17; 23:1-7; Hosea 1:10; 2:14-24; 3:5; Isaiah 2:2-4; 4:2-6; 7:14; 9:27; 11:1-16; 32:1-6; 42:1-9; 49:1-6; 50:49; 52:13-53:12; 60:1-3; 63:16; Jer. 23:5-6; 33:15-16; 31-34; Ezek. 34 are not accepted as prophecies which were fulfilled in the New Testament.

The results of the historical-critical methodology involve the repudiation of Jesus as the God-man. His miraculous conception by the Holy Spirit, His miracles, His resurrection, His ascension and His promised Second Return are all repudiated.

The low view of the Holy Scriptures has resulted in the denigration of Christian doctrine and ethics; it has made for a constantly changing theology and has created uncertainty and skepticism among Christians and constitutes an insuperable hindrance for evangelization of the unconverted and has eventuated in a redefining of the true purpose and character of the Christian Church.

2. The High View

The high view of the Bible is the one that represents the position, which various books of the Old and New Testament Scriptures set forth and claim. The historic view of Christendom relative to the Sacred Scriptures was that it was the very Word of the God of truth. "Holy men spake as they were moved by the Holy Ghost" (2 Pet. 1:21b). Concerning the Old Testament God said through Paul: "All Scripture is 'God-spirited' or 'God-breathed.'" This assertion can also be applied to the New Testament. In the Old Testament God selected prophets like Moses, Isaiah, Jeremiah, Ezekiel, Daniel, Amos, Hosea, Joel, Micah, Nahum, Habakkuk, Zephaniah, Haggai, Zechariah, Malachi, David; individuals like Joshua, Samuel, Ezra, Nehemiah and other persons to be the human agents through whom He wished to reveal His will. Then in a mysterious fashion, the Holy Spirit worked upon His instruments to record what He wanted them to write in precisely the languages and words necessary to communicate God's message to men. In one sense, the Bible may be considered a human book. However, overshadowing the humanity of the Bible is the fact that God Himself is its author.

In the Bible, mankind has God's revelation of truth, without which man cannot know God. God revealed Himself before the inscripturated revelation through conscience and through His revelation in nature. In Romans 1:18-21, Paul speaks about God's general revelation as well as David does in Psalm 19:1-6. Examples of special revelation are found in Genesis 2:16 and Gen. 3:18-19. Oral revelations become lost if they are not recorded in written form. So God commissioned chosen individuals to write on various subjects.

Gleason Archer claims:

> If there be a God, and if He is concerned for our salvation, this is the only way (apart from direct revelation from God to each individual of each successive generation) He could reliably impart this knowledge to us. It must be through a reliable written record such as the Bible purports to be (*A Survey of Old Testament Introduction*, Chicago:

Moody Press, 1969, p. 15).

Two critical questions, which the Bible student and reader must face, are, how did the human authors know what God wanted them to write? And were their writings without error? Concerning these two questions there has been sharp theological disagreement. Here will be found the continental divide between current schools of interpretation that are basically opposed to each other relative to Biblical interpretation. The supernatural way in which God communicated to men His will and also caused His chosen vessels to write what He wanted them to is a mystery. 2 Timothy 3:16 claims the writings of the Bible are **theopneustia**, are "God-breathed." Peter claimed that the holy men of God were carried along by the Holy Spirit, that the Spirit undergirded their writings. These passages assure us that the Bible authors wrote what God desired them to put in writing, and that the words expressed perfectly and infallibly the truths and historical facts which God wanted mankind to have and know. Inerrancy and infallibility belong to the autographs. The original writings of the Biblical writers are accurate relative to matters of science and history as well as to the spiritual truths expressed in them. The high view eliminates the confusion and uncertainty which the various low views previously described foster, promote and defends. Confusion and theological destruction is the result of the destructive form of higher critical theories, part and parcel of the low view of Holy scripture.

Questions
1. If the Bible is a purely human book, it cannot be ____.
2. The only divine-human book is ____.
3. The Bible records over ____ miracles.
4. The so-called neutral attitude toward the Bible is ____.
5. With the rejection of the supernatural there could have been no ____.
6. The results of the historical critical method involve ____.
7. The assertion ____ can also be applied to ____.
8. Who is the author of the Bible? ____
9. Overshadowing the humanity of the Bible is the fact that ____.
10. Infallibility and inerrancy belong to ____.
11. Confusion and theological destruction is a result of ____.

Lent's Central Doctrine:
The Biblical Teaching of the Atonement

Christian News, March 18, 1996

Theologians claim that the Bible contains two kinds of doctrines: Non-fundamental and fundamental.[1] There are a number of Scriptural doctrines that a born-again and saved sinner can be ignorant of and still be saved. He could be ignorant of the doctrine of the angels or the seven day creation and still enter heaven at the end of life. The purpose of this division is not to deny such teachings or to claim that they are unnecessary. To do so would amount to contradicting Christ's instruction: "Teaching them to observe all things I have commanded you" (Matt. 28:19). The Apostle Paul asserted: "For whatever things were written before were written for our learning that we through the patience and comfort of the Scriptures might have hope (15:4).[2] This distinction between non-fundamental and fundamental doctrines helps theologians to recognize those doctrines which constitute the foundation of the Christian faith."[4]

The doctrine of justification by faith is the central fundamental doctrine of the Christian faith.[5] Luther has correctly declared: "The doctrine of justification by faith is the heart and cornerstone, which alone begets, builds up, preserves and protects the Church and without this doctrine cannot exist one hour."[6] In years past Lutheran and other Protestant theologians have denominated the doctrines of justification by faith in Christ and the vicarious atonement as the most fundamental of all doctrines.[7] Morris said this about the "atonement": "The atonement is critical, it is the central doctrine of Christianity. That does not mean that other doctrines (e.g. the incarnation) may be neglected. Each of the great Christian doctrines is important and has its place. But we must not minimize the centrality of the atonement."[8]

The Position of the Historic Confession of Protestantism

Until theological liberalism and theological modernism invaded the Christian Churches, all held to the Biblical doctrine of the atonement. Both Luther and Calvin,[10] the fathers of major Protestant Church bodies, held and taught the Vicarious Atonement, that Christ shed his precious blood for the sins of the world. The following Confessions or Statements of Faith set forth clearly the Biblical doctrine of the atonement: *The Second Helvetic Confession, The Belgic Confession, The Thirty-Nine Articles* of the Church of England, *The Irish Articles of Religion, The Westminster Confession of 1647, The New Hampshire Conference of 1833, The Confession of Freewill Baptists* of 1834 and 1868, *The Confession of the Wadenses* of 1855. *The Auburn (Presbyterian) Declaration of 1837, The Methodist Articles of Religion* of 1784, *The Reformed Episcopal Articles of Religion, The Augsburg Confession* of 1530, *The Apology of The Augsburg Confession, The Smalcald Articles* of 1537, both *The Epitome and the Solid Declaration* of the *Formula of Concord*. All these stress justification by faith and state that man is declared righteous because of the shed blood of Christ, who gave His life on Calvary's cross for the sins of the world.

P. E. Kretzman in chapter one of his monograph *For Us*, in which he cites from the various doctrinal declarations just cited, asserted: "From these quotations it is evident that the public confessions of the evangelical denominations are in essential agreement concerning the fact of justification, as a forensic act whereby the righteousness of God is imparted to unworthy sinners in view of the merits of Jesus Christ, the blessings of this justification being received by faith which is wrought in the heart of man by the message of redemption."[11]

Not only in the New Testament but also in the Old Testament is it taught that through the Messiah's substitutionary, sacrificial death mankind would be saved. By giving His life an offering for sin, the Savior was to fulfill not only what was foreshadowed in the redemption of Israel from Egypt, as well in the redemption in the actions performed in the cultic observances of the ceremonial law.[12]

The Hebrew Words For Atonement

The Hebrew words universally translated "atonement" in modern English are **kippur** (noun) and **kapar** (verb). The root **kapar** and its related words are used about 150 times in the Old Testament and are linked in the Bible with forgiveness of sin and with reconciliation to God.[13] It has been said that the idea expressed by **kappar** is related to the Arabic root, meaning "to cover" or "to conceal." If this supposition is correct, it would mean that the Old Testament would depict man's sin being covered and the sinner, therefore, enabled to approach God. Although in the Old Testament different objects and peoples were purified by atoning acts, and sins of commission and sins of omission could only be paid for by the sacrifice of an innocent animal, it can safely be asserted that atonement involves a sacrifice that in some significant and just way deals with the guilt of sin so that God extends forgiveness, reconciling the person or group to Himself.[14]

Weidner wrote: "That the intercession of the righteous for a sinful nation is factual, is a thought through the entire Old Testament from Genesis 18:23,24 and Ex. 32:32 onward."[15] In Weidner's Soteriology he devoted pages 40-54 to the various Old Testament passages and teachings of Psalm 22, to the various Servant pericopes and especially to the sufferings of the Messiah in Isaiah 52:13-53:12 and to relevant passages in Zechariah.[16]

The Place of the Atonement in the New Testament

Vernon Grounds correctly claimed "that according to apostolic preaching and doctrine, the significance of Jesus Christ does not lie supremely in His person or ministry or teaching: It lies supremely in His death upon the cross. In the NT, to be sure, that event is never viewed in isolation from His person, His ministry, and His teaching; nor is it viewed apart from His resurrection. His death exegetes His teaching and together with

His sin-free, miracle-working ministry of love, constitutes the active obedience of life without which the passive obedience or suffering would have been nugatory."[17] Yet it is His suffering upon Calvary's cross which constantly underscores as all-important His death, which was of a martyrdom or was it a miscarriage of justice, but the atoning death of Christ was planned for in eternity and was determined to be successful in redeeming mankind.

The Atonement-The Essence of Christ's Priestly Office

In the accomplishment of the world's redemption Christ is our great high priest who as the Mediator between God and man, has satisfied in full for us the laws of God. The priests of the Old Testament, and especially the high priest were types of Christ in His priestly office: They offered up sacrifices for the people.[18]

The Nature of Christ's Priestly Office

Biblical students have appropriately defined Christ's priestly office as constituting of two parts: Namely, Satisfaction and Intercession. The latter follows the Resurrection and Ascension of Christ. Satisfaction preceded the great Easter event. While the word "satisfaction" is not a Biblical word, it is associated with those words that speak of vicariousness and substitution. The New Testament declared that Christ came as a ransom, which He paid for men's sins end thus effected reconciliation. This fact can rightly be termed "satisfaction," because by His substitutionary death He satisfied for human beings all demands of divine justice.[19]

Christ's Atoning Activity

Stump defined the Priestly Office of Christ as follows: "The Priestly Office may be defined as that mediatorial activity or work by which, through His active obedience, He fulfilled for us and in our stead all the holy requirements of the divine moral law by which, through His passive obedience, He bore the full penalty of our sins; and by which is end will continue forever to be our Intercessor with God. By His twofold obedience He satisfied the full demands of divine justice for us; and His complete satisfaction of the divine law is imputed to all those who believe in Him."[20]

The Necessity for Atonement (At-one-ment)

In Eden God placed Adam and Eve, who were crested in the image and likeness of God, and who were at first holy and immortal. However, mankind's first progenitors cut themselves off from God and placed a middle wall of partition between themselves and God.[21] Adam and Eve broke the happy relationship that existed between God and them which resulted for Adam and Eve suffering all forms of death: Temporal, spiritual and eternal.

If this broken relationship was to be changed, God only could restore it. Mankind's enmity had to be removed, if the sons and daughters of

Adam and Eve, who were conceived and born in sin, were not to be permanently banished from the presence of God. Satisfaction for mankind's sins has to be made. The holiness of God and His righteousness demanded it according to Holy Writ.[22] God's anger, spoken of in both testaments, be appeased by a complete fulfillment of the Law, which mankind had not kept.

The Proof for the Need of Atonement

Consciences of men and women testify to the eternal law of righteousness. Sin involves guilt and demands punishment and there can, according to the demands of righteousness, be no forgiveness without expiation.[23] The essence of punishment is retribution. Retribution is a fundamental law of the universe. People who have never read Holy Writ's demand for punishment for sin, offer up sacrifices with the intent of appeasing the God they worship and trust that their sins will be atoned for and forgiven. Who so sheddest man's blood, by man shall his blood be shed—this is a universal belief, powerfully testifying to the fact that sins are to be paid for. The Code of Hammurabi powerfully shows that the ancient dwellers of Mesopotamia believed that violations of their laws were subject to punishment.[24] In its clearest and most adequate form the Bible testifies to the need for appeasing God for sins committed against both the First and Second Tables of the Law.

Mankind's Inability to Atone for Its Sins Against God

God's Word in Psalm 49:8-9 teaches: "None of them can by any means redeem his brother, nor give to God a ransom for him, for the redemption of their souls is costly and it shall cease forever, that he should continue to live eternally and not see the Pit."[25] The members of the human race cannot save themselves, since they are conceived and born in sin. The Bible's teaching says: "Whosoever shall keep the whole law and offend in one, is guilty of all." "The imagination of man's heart is evil from conception." Who would save his life shall lose it and "whosoever loses his life for my sake shall find it."

Only the individual who does not realize that a great gulf exists between him and God, can believe that he can please God, earn His salvation and receive the Almighty's approval.

Mankind's Status Before God

Before God the human race is nothing but dust and ashes. This is especially true when finally the representatives of humanity are deposited in the grave. The human race is like grass that withers or like a tale which is told. Mankind is vanity, in fact vanity of vanities. Man cannot by his own strength approach God. It was God who taught the Israelites how to approach Him and have their sins covered and forgiven. Sins of omission and sins of commission could only be atoned for by having an innocent animal take the place of the sinner and pay the punishment sin had deserved by giving its life. No sinner could approach God in the holy of holies. Only the high priest could enter on one day of the year, and that only if he followed God-given regulations before and during entrance. The sacrificial system outlined in Leviticus clearly shows that atonement could only be effected by the shedding of innocent blood.

In order to be acceptable to approach a holy God, those hoping to be right with God and acceptable to him had to be holy, as Leviticus 19:2 declared: "Be ye therefore holy as I the Lord your God am holy." The Third Book of the Pentateuch might be called "The Textbook on Holiness."[26] All who approach God, the priests who minister and the people who worship, must be holy. The redeemed must be holy because the Redeemer is holy. Priests, people, tabernacle, vessels, offerings and garments had to be holy, that is, separate not only from sins but from common usage. "Holiness and its cognates occur some 131 times in Leviticus. And such holiness is made possible by atonement. Holiness occurs 87 times; sacrifice, offering and oblation, some 300 times, the word atonement 45 times."[27]

Leviticus and the Epistle to the Hebrews

Leviticus is an indispensable book, and should be studied with Hebrews, its New Testament counterpart. Observed Lockyer: "It is the key to the New Testament teaching on salvation. The Epistle of the Hebrews is a book of illustrations on the way of salvation. The Epistle to the Hebrews is an inspired commentary on the book of Leviticus, from which we learn that the Hebrew ritual was the Gospel of Christ, exhibited in symbols and shadows to the Israelites. Carrying, then, a symbolic setting forth of the Gospel, being so full of Christ."[28]

Complete Self-Atonement An Impossibility For Mankind

Even if human beings could cleanse themselves of their present sins and live righteous lives, this present atonement would not be able to pay for past sins. The fact that a person is honest today, does not atone for past acts of dishonesty. The fact that a person pays his bills today, does not mean that past financial obligations are cancelled. The truth is that mankind cannot atone for past sins, as the heathen believe[29] or Roman Catholic theology claims when it contends that some saints have done so much, and those above the law's requirement can be deposited in a treasury of good works now available for use for such who need more good works to merit God's forgiveness.[30] It is possible that beneath the good works done by people that there lies self-righteousness, pride and even hatred of God.

Present Sorrow for Sins Cannot Atone for Past Sins

Sorrow for sins of the present cannot atone for past sins, as may be seen from a number of Biblical incidents, thus Cain, Saul and Judas come to mind as sinners who felt sorrow for past actions and yet found no peace or sense of forgiveness. The murderer who is sorrowful for his crime, cannot restore the life taken wrongfully. All the repentance cannot restore a human body which wrongfully has been damaged beyond repair.[31]

Impossibility of Atonement For Others' Sins

If human beings cannot atone for their own sins, it naturally follows that the same individuals cannot stone for other people's wrongdoings and misdemeanors. The Bible teaches that the atonement demanded by God presupposes the belief of the total inability of people to save themselves. No person can obtain atonement for his sins who does not recognize and believe the truth that by nature mankind is at enmity with God and therefore deserves God's wrath and punishment. This necessary precondition for man's forgiveness is brought about by the preaching of the law.

Complete and Total Atonement
Effected by Christ, the God-Man

The activities associated with the priestly office were done according to both natures, the divine and the human.[32] Wrote Stump: "In accordance with the **Genus Apotelesmaticum**, as we have seen, all His official acts are ascribed to the person of Christ. While, therefore, the sufferings were endured by Him according to His human nature, the divine nature participated in them because of the personal union, by willing and permitting the sufferings and by supporting the human nature under them.

The priestly work of Christ is, therefore, not a work of Christ according to His human nature alone, but a work of the person, and hence according to both natures. It is not as God nor as man that Christ is our great High Priest; but it is as the God-man, as God and man in one person, that He stands between God and men and offers sacrifices and intercession in order to effect reconciliation between them."[33]

The Factuality of the Atonement for Mankind's Reconciliation

The great comfort of Biblical teaching is that atonement is an indisputable fact. Paul, in his Epistle to the Colossians, assured: "And you, who were once strangers and hostile in mind doing evil deeds, he has now reconciled by his death, in order to present you holy and blameless and unreproachable before him"(1:21-22). The same apostle informed the Romans: "For while we were enemies we were reconciled to God by the death of his life" (5:10). John the Baptist told his followers that Christ, who was coming to be baptized by him, "was the Lamb of God that took away the sins of the world" (John 1:29).

The Sufficiency or Christ's Atonement for The World's Sins

The atonement which Christ achieved for all mankind is complete and totally adequate to cover the sins of all sinners who ever have lived, were then living and who would exist after the year A.D. 33, the year of Christ's crucifixion. The Scriptures do not countenance the ideas or theory that Christ's atonement was really inadequate, but that God graciously accepted it as a complete payment (This is known as the Acceptilation theory).[34] The death of Christ is an actual propitiation for the sins of the whole world. The question has been proposed: "How can the death of Christ sufficiently atone for the millions of people who have lived or will still live in the ages to come? How could the sufferings of one person effect so much?" Stump gave the following answer to this query: "To this it is to be replied that Christ suffered exactly as much as all the members of the human race would have suffered if punished for their sins, but that the sufferings of Christ have a value equal to or greater than those which men deserved to suffer. The sufferings of Christ were not, indeed, eternal, but were comprised within the period of His lifetime on earth; but their value and weight must be judged, not by the length of time during which they lasted, but by their intensity on the other hand and by the person of the sufferer on the other."[35]

It is beyond human comprehension to evaluate the intensity of Christ's suffering because who can fathom the nature of the sufferings of the Godman who never sinned[36] and at all times did the will of His Father. How can any person adequately understand the anguish of Christ suffered in Gethsemane or the terrible anguish when the Son of God exclaimed: "My God, My God, why have You forsaken me?" Certainly God's suffering as a man for the sake of mankind's sins was adequate to cause God to consider mankind's debt as paid and atoned for.

The Atonement and Christ's Resurrection
Paul, who made the preaching of the cross central in his preaching and missionary endeavors, declared that Jesus was put to death for our offenses and raised again for our justification (Romans 4:25).

The resurrection is the guarantee that the sins of the whole world have been forgiven by virtue of Christ's sacrifice on the accursed tree.[37] The resurrection removes all doubts of those who question the accomplished fact of Christ's reconciling death.

Reconciliation precedes faith on the part of the sinner. He who teaches that faith in justification precedes atonement cannot teach the Biblical doctrine of justification by faith, apart from the deeds of the law.[38] The Gospel does not set forth a demand that good works should precede faith in order for the sinner to become justified through faith which has as its objective the atoning death of Christ. The Gospel sets forth the truth that Jesus kept the law vicariously for mankind and that the God-man kept the law perfectly in thought, word and deed. Faith is the hand which accepts God's offer to forgive those who are repentant and believe Christ died for all people's sins.

Atonement Terminology in the New Testament
The word "atonement" is rare in the New Testament, found once in the Authorized Version (Romans 5:11) and not at all in many translations. In the *New International Version* "atonement" translates the Greek words **hilasterion** (Romans 3:25; Hebrews 9:5), **hilaskomai** (Heb. 2:17) and **hilasmos** (I John 2:2; 4:10), whereas *The New American Standard Bible* has "mercy seat" in Hebrews 9:5, and propitiation in other passages.[39]

The Means of Grace and the Doctrine of the Atonement

It is through the Means of Grace (i.e., baptism, The Lord's Supper, the written Gospel) that the truth of the atonement is made known to mankind. Since God effected reconciliation and total forgiveness, He must make it known. That God for Christ's sake forgives mankind's sins must be proclaimed and is the heart of the Gospel. The doctrine of the atonement must be central in preaching and pastoral care. This truth must be proclaimed with vividness and vitality and not be presented in a cold and dry manner.[40]

The objection has been made that preaching the atonement leads to false security. But the truth is that regeneration, as some urged should first be proclaimed, instead of constantly harping on the atonement, is brought about by the truth of the atonement or reconciliation. Men are really converted by the preaching of the atonement and leads to the living of pious lives.[41]

The Biblical Doctrine of The Atonement and Faith

How do individuals, male and female, young and old, become justified with God? The simple answer is: "Accept and believe what God has done for them through the shed blood of Christ" (2 Cor. 5:18-20).

Theories of the Atonement

In the history of Christianity the fact of the atonement was not questioned but **How** the atonement was achieved has been.[42] While there were good intentions to describe the method by Christ, a number of the explanations do not do justice about what the Bible teaches on this important doctrine. One theory advanced was called the Accidental Theory, claiming that Christ's death was unexpected as any other victims of man hatred (Modernism). But Christ atoning death had been determined with the counsels of the Trinity in eternity (decrees of predestination and redemption).

A second theory might be called The Martyr Theory, namely that Christ gave up his life for a principle, which went against the spirit of the day. But the Bible teaches that God sent His Son to redeem those who were held bondage to the law. This is the view of modernism. A third theory, known as the Declaratory Theory, advocated the idea that Christ died that men might see that God loved them (this was sponsored by Ritschl). A fourth theory is known as the Moral Example Theory, or the Moral Power View of the Atonement. According to this interpretation Christ died to influence mankind to seek moral improvement (thus the Socinians, Horace Bushnell). A fifth theory is as The Governmental Theory, namely, that God made Christ an example of sufferings to exhibit to every erring person that sin is not pleasing to the Father. Another version of this theory holds that God's government required God to show men His wrath against sin by having Christ killed (thus Hugo Grotius, New England Theology). A sixth theory has been denominated The Guarantee Theory, according to which reconciliation was achieved by His death but by Christ's guarantee that He would win followers and thus conquer human sinfulness (proposed by Schleiermacher, Kirn, Von Hofmann).[43]

J.T. Mueller in his article "Theories of the Atonement," pertinently wrote about all these anti- scriptural views: "As these and other man-made theories of the Atonement deny Christ's vicarious satisfaction and are based on the same leading thoughts of salvation through personal sanctification, stimulated by Christ's death."[44]

Twentieth Century Protestant Denials of the Atonement

Herman Otten, in his excellent book *Baal or God*, has a chapter dealing with Christ's Vicarious satisfaction and has shown how anti-Scriptural concepts of the atonement have been accepted by Lutheranism, the Reformed, the Methodists, the Anglicans and the attack of The Interpreter's Bible, which follows liberal theories on the atonement.[45]

Otten concluded his chapter with the Biblical teaching and shows how The Lutheran-Church Missouri Synod set forth and explicated the truth of Romans 3:24-25: "Being justified freely by his grace through the redemption that is in Christ Jesus, Whom God has set forth to be a propitiation through faith in His blood, to declare His righteousness for the remission of sins that are past, through the forbearance of God."[46]

Footnotes

1. John Theodore Mueller, *Christian Dogmatics* (St. Louis: Concordia Publishing House, 1955), p. 47; Francis Pieper, *Christian Dogmatics* (St. Louis: Concordia Publishing House, 1950), I, p. 80.
2. Pieper, **op. cit.**, II, p. 80.
3. Mueller, **op. cit.**, p. 48.
4. As cited by Mueller, **Ibid.**, p. 48.
5. *The Apology of The Augsburg Confession* IV, 1 (Tappert, *The Book of Concord*) (Philadelphia: The Fortress Press, 1959), p. 107; *Formula of Concord, Solid Declaration*, III, 6, Tappert, p. 540.
6. *D. Martin Luther's Saemtliche Schriften*, 23 volumes in 25, ed. Johann G. Walch (St. Louis: Concordia Publishing House, 1880-1913), XIV, 1680.
7. E. Hove, *Christian Doctrine* (Minneapolis: Augsburg Publishing House, 1930), p. 262 on justification and pp. 218-219 on the atonement.
8. L. L. Morris, "Atonement," S.B. Ferguson, D.E. Wright and J. I. Packer, *New Dictionary of Theology* (Downers Grove, IL; Inter Varsity Press, 1981), p. 54b.
9. Walter Albrecht, *The Theology of Luther* (Springfield: Concordia Mimeo Co, 1962), p. 20-21. Martin Luther, Smalcald Articles, XIII, 1-3. Tappert, **op. cit.**, p. 315.
10. *The Institutes of the Christian Religion* by John Calvin (Philadelphia: Presbyterian Board of Christian Education, no date) translated from the French by John Allen, II, pp. 3ff., cf. especially page 20.
11. Paul E. Kretzmann, *For Us* (St. Louis: Concordia Mimeo Company, no date), p. 3.
12. Lawrence Richards, *Expository Dictionary* (Grand Rapids: Zondervan Publication House, 1985), p. 82.
13. **Ibid.**, p. 82.
14. **Ibid.**, p. 82b.
15. Revere Franklin Weidner, *Soteriology of the Doctrine of the Work of Christ*

(Chicago: Wartburg Publishing House, 1914), p. 40.

16. **Ibid.**, pp. 40-42.

17. Vernon Grounds, "Atonement," in E. F. Harrison, C. W. Bromiley and Carl C. F. Henry (Grand Rapids: Baker Book House, 1960) *Baker's Dictionary of Theology*, p. 71.

18. C. E. Lindberg, *Christian Dogmatics* (Rock Island, IL: Augustana Book Concern, 1928), pp. 251-257.

19. Stump, **op. cit.**, p. 186.

20. David S. Bauslin, "Reconciliation," Henry Eyster Jacobs and John A. A. Haas, *The Lutheran Cyclopedia* (New York: Charles Scribner's Sons, 1899), p. 403b.

21. Stump, **op. cit.**, p. 186-187.

22. Grounds, **op. cit.**, p. 75b.

23. Weidner, **op. cit.**, p. 32.

24. Ira Maurice, Ovid R. Sellers and E. Leslie Carlson, *The Monuments of the Old Testament* (Philadelphia: The Judson Press, 1958), p. 184-185.

25. *The New King James Version* (New York: Thomas A. Nelson, 1982), p. 563.

26. Herbert Lockyer, *The Gospel in the Pentateuch* (Chicago: The Bible Institute Calportage Ass'n, 1939), p. 67.

27. **Ibid.**, p. 69.

28. **Ibid.**, p. 71.

29. Stump, **op. cit.**, footnote 1, p. 189.

30. "Works of Merit," L. Fuerbringer, Th. Engelder, P. E. Kretzmann, *The Concordia Encyclopedia* (St. Louis: CPH, 1927), p. 823-824.

31. Versoehnung, in C. Eckhardt, *Homiletisches Reallexicon nebst Index Rerun* (St. Louis Success Printings Company, 1917), V-Z, p. 183d.

32. A. L. Graebner, *Outlines of Doctrinal Theology* (St. Louis: Concordia Publishing Company, 1910), pp. 110-113.

33. Stump, **op. cit.**, pp. 188-189.

34. "Theories of the Atonement," Erwin Lueker, Editor, *Lutheran Cyclopedia* (St. Louis: Concordia Publishing House, 1954), p. 67b.

35. Stump, **op. cit.**, p. 194.

36. *On the Sinlessness of Jesus*, cf. Mueller, **op. cit.**, p. 259.

37. Mueller, **op. cit.**, p. 298, cf, especially the quotation by Calov on the results of the resurrection.

38. "Versoehnung," un Eckhardt, **op. cit.**, No. 6, Anmaerkung cf, p. 185d.

39. Richards, **op. cit.**, p. 83b.

40. Eckhardt, **op. cit.**, p 186d, No. 9.

41. **Ibid.**

42. Morris, "Atonement, *New Dictionary of Theology*," **op. cit.**, p. 55b.

43. Relative to the different theories of the atonement, cf. "Theories of the Atonement", *Lutheran Cyclopedia*, **op. cit.**, p. 67, Grouns, "The Atonement", *Baker's Dictionary of Theology*, pp. 71-76.

44. Mueller, **op. cit.**, p. 67.

45. Herman J. Otten, *Baal or God* (New Haven Leader Publishing Co., 1965), pp. 59-65.

46. **Ibid.**, pp. 66-70.

Questions

1. The priests of the Old Testament offered up ____.
2. By his substitutionary death Christ satisfied for human beings ____.

3. ____ for mankind's sin has to be made.
4. The members of the human race cannot ____.
5. The Epistle to the Hebrews in an inspired commentary on ____.
6. The resurrection of Christ is ____.
7. Faith is the hand ____.
8. The doctrine of the atonement must be ____.
9. How do individuals become justified with God? ____
10. Otten in his book *Baal or God* has shown how anti-scriptural concepts of atonement have been ____.

The Proper Use As Well As Misuse of The Law/Gospel Dichotomy In 20th Century Protestantism With Special Reference To American Lutheranism

I
The Proper Use of Law and Gospel in Historical Lutheranism

Galatians was one of Luther's favorite New Testament looks for understanding the plan of salvation. The Wittenberg Reformer "saw the root heresy of the Galatian churches transposed into a different key in the Catholic Church."[1] The Judaizers claimed that in order to be saved it would be necessary for all Jews and Gentiles alike; first, to be circumcised and secondly, to believe in Christ. For Paul, circumcision was the seal of the Old Testament Covenant while Christ was the center of the New Covenant. Luther held that there was a parallel between the Galatian false teaching about justification by faith and the method of salvation taught by the Roman Catholic Church, which taught that first one must do religious works, and secondly, belief in Christ would save. The Pauline doctrine of justification by faith consisted in this namely, that the sinner who repents and is caused by the Holy Spirit to believe in Christ as Sinbearer and Sin-atoner, that such a person's faith is accounted to him as righteousness. Because of what Christ did for him as a lost and condemned sinner and believing that fact, the sinner is declared righteous. The sinner is not held culpable for his sins, but his sin is forgiven and Christ's righteousness is placed to his account. Rome, on the other hand, held that grace is infused into the sinner and that grace becomes a habitude of the soul and with this new God-given power the sinner can keep God's commandments and laws and thus merit justification. The Roman Catholic Church confuses sanctification and justification and does not recognize the proper order of events in the plan of salvation.[2]

Luther in his writings therefore taught that the Biblical interpreter must carefully distinguish between Law and Gospel in the Bible; in fact, this became one of Luther's principal hermeneutical rules. Ewald Plass asserted about Luther's distinction between Law and Gospel as follows: "Few, if any, theologians have insisted more emphatically than did Martin Luther on the indispensable necessity of sharply defining the areas within which the Law and the Gospel were designed to apply, and probably no statement of the Doctor on this point is better known than his words in the New Year's sermon of 1532, on Gal. 3: 23-24, which was devoted to this subject."[3] Here is the view of Luther as uttered on the first day of 1532:

> This difference between the Law and the Gospel is the height of knowledge in Christendom. Every person and all persons who assume or glory in the name Christian should know and be able to state this difference. If this ability is lacking, one cannot tell a Christian from a

heathen or a Jew; of such supreme importance is this differentiation.

This is why St. Paul so strongly insists on a clean-cut and proper differentiating among Christians of these two doctrines, the Law and the Gospel. To be sure, both are God's Word: the Law, or the Ten Commandments, and the Gospel; the latter first given by God in Paradise; the former on Mt. Sinai. But everything depends on the proper differentiation of these two messages and on not mixing them together; otherwise one will know and retain the proper understanding of neither the one nor the other nay, while under the impression of having both, one will have neither. . .

Therefore place the man who is able nicely to divorce the Law from the Gospel at the head of the list and call him a Doctor of Holy Scripture, for without the Holy Spirit the attainment of this differentiation is impossible.[4]

In order that these two terms should be correctly understood and that his hearers would not labor under any misapprehension, Luther in the same sermon explained them as follows:

By "Law" we should understand nothing but God's Word and command in which He commands us what we are to do and not to do and demands are obedience and service (Werk) ...

The Gospel is such a doctrine or Word of God as does not demand our works or command us to do anything but bids us simply receive the offered grace of the forgiveness of sins and eternal salvation and be satisfied to have it given us as a present.[5]

Already as early as 1518 Luther was concerned that those who had read the 95 Theses should have a clear understanding of the terms Law and Gospel. In his elucidation of the 95 Theses Luther carefully explained their meaning. Thus he wrote:

According to the apostle, Rom. 1:1-3f., the Gospel is the message about the incarnate Son of God; who was given us without our merits for salvation and peace. It is the Word of salvation, the Word of grace, the Word of comfort, the Word of joy, the voice of the Bridegroom and the bride, the good Word, the Word of peace, as Isaiah says: "How beautiful upon the mountains are the feet of him that bringeth good tidings, that publisheth peace, that bringeth good tidings of good" (52:7). But the Law is the Word of perdition, the Word of wrath, the Word of sadness, the Word of pain, the voice of the Judge and the accused, the Word of unrest, the Word of malediction; for, according to the-apostle; the Law is the strength of sin (I Cor. 15:56), the Law works wrath (Rom. 4:15), and it is a law of death (Rom. 7:13).[6]

The importance of knowing the distinction between Law and Gospel is also set forth in the *Formula of Concord*. "We believe, teach and confess that the distinction between Law and Gospel is to be maintained in the Church with great diligence as an especially **brilliant light**, by which according to the admonition of St. Paul, the Word of God is rightly divided."[7]

The proper distinction between Law and Gospel was the subject of Article V of the *Formula of Concord*. The Law is defined as follows: "The

Law is properly a divine doctrine in which the righteous, immutable will of God is revealed, what is to be the quality of man in his nature, thoughts, words and works, in order that he may be pleasing and acceptable to God; and it threatens its transgressors with God's wrath and temporal and eternal punishments. For as Luther writes against the Law stormers: everything that reproves sin is and belongs to the Law, whose peculiar office is to reprove sin, and to lead to the knowledge of sins (Rom. 3:20; 7:7); and as unbelief is the root and wellspring of all reprehensible sins, the Law reproves unbelief also."[8]

The same article also defines the Gospel: "The Gospel is properly such a doctrine as teaches that man has not observed the Law; and therefore is condemned by it, is to believe, namely, that Christ has expiated and made satisfaction for all sins, righteousness that avails before God and eternal life."[9]

In the Age of Orthodoxy various Lutheran theologians were keenly aware of the teaching of the Lutheran Confessions on the proper distinction of Law and Gospel. Chemnitz, Hollaz, Baier, Quenstedt and other theologians show clearly in their writings that they knew the importance of the proper use of Law and Gospel in exegesis, teaching, preaching and pastoral practice.[10]

The Proper Use of Law and Gospel
In the Lutheran Church-Missouri Synod

II

When the Evangelical Lutheran Synod of Missouri, Ohio and other states was founded in 1847 in Chicago, its chief theologian, Carl Frederick Walther emphasized the distinction between Law and Gospel. One of the great classical writings of the 19th century was his *The Proper Distinction between Law and Gospel*.[11] In his treatise *The Evangelical Lutheran Church - the True Visible Church of God*, a book organized in terms of major theses, a number of them set forth principles for the interpretation of the Scriptures. Thesis XIV-XXI may be regarded as delineating the distinctive   interpretative principles of Lutheranism. Thesis XVIII reads: "The Evangelical Lutheran Church gives to each teaching of God's Word the place and importance it has in God's Word itself."

A. It makes the teaching- concerning Christ, or justification, the foundation and marrow and guiding star of all teaching.

B. The Evangelical Lutheran Church distinguishes sharply between Law and Gospel. Bible passages cited by Walther are John 1:17; Rom. 10:4 and 2 Tim: 2:15. From the Lutheran Confessions, Epitome V is given, and from the works of Luther, Vol. 9 of the St. Louis edition.

Between 1847 and 1947 the proper distinction between Law and Gospel was the subject of a number of doctrinal essays at the following district conventions: Eastern in 1877; Iowa in 1880 (Dr. F. Pieper the essayist); Kansas in 1892 (Dr. F. Pieper the essayist); the Nebraska in 1915

(W. Mahler the essayist). Professor F. Bente, a member of the St. Louis faculty prepared a study in connection with the 400th anniversary of the Reformation in 1917 entitled *Gesetz und Evangelium: Busse und Gute Werke* **(vornehmlich nach dem 4. 5. und 6. Artikel der Konkordienformel)**[12]; Dr. Francis Pieper devoted 31 pages of Volume III of his *Christian Dogmatics* to a discussion of "Law and Gospel."[13] Engelder, Arndt, Graebner, Mayer in 1943 set forth the relationship of these two different doctrines to each other in their *Popular Symbolics*.[14] In volume 33 of *Lehre und Wehre*, Dr. George Stoeckhardt published a series of articles on Law and Gospel immediately after Dr. Walther's death.[15] Former Professor Koehler of Concordia Teachers College, River Forest has a good section on Law and Gospel in his *A Summary of Christian Doctrine*.[16] When the Lutheran Church-Missouri Synod celebrated the centennial of the founding of the Synod, it issued two volumes, in which the fundamental doctrines of Lutheranism and Christianity were set forth, delivered by pastors and Professors of the Synod. Appropriately there was an essay on "Law and Gospel" by Walter Geihsler.[17] The Lutheran Cyclopedia of 1954 also presented the position of historic Lutheranism on Law and Gospel.[18] *The Revised Lutheran Cyclopedia* of 1975 also has a discussion of Law and Gospel. 18a Dr. J. T. Mueller's *Christian Dogmatics* also contains a pertinent discussion of these two fundamental doctrines of the Bible.[19]

In 1973 Concordia Publishing House issued an abridgment of Walther, *The Proper Distinction between Law and Gospel* under the title *God's No and God's Yes*, the condensation being prepared by one of Pieper's descendants, namely, Walter C. Pieper.[20] Walther had delivered two series at the Friday evening "Lutheran Hour" at Concordia Seminary, St. Louis, between September 12, 1884 and November 6, 1885. The first series on Law and Gospel was presented in 13 theses in 1878. The second series included 25 theses and was published in 1929. Of the effect of Walther's *The Proper Distinction between Law and Gospel*, Walter Pieper asserts: "That it is not easy to measure what its influence has been. It could be argued that it was his greatest contribution to the church, for within Lutheranism pastoral practice in preaching, counseling and evaluating the mission of the church have grown out of the understanding of the proper distinction between Law and Gospel."[21]

The Baptist scholar Bernard Ramm, who has given a good statement about the basic principles of interpretation as developed by Luther between 1512 -and 1522, has listed the Law/Gospel principle as one of Luther's important basic Lutheran principles of hermeneutics. Ramm wrote concerning this matter as follows:

> Luther taught that we must carefully distinguish Law and Gospel in the Bible, and this was one of Luther's principal hermeneutical rules. Any fusion of the Law and Gospel was wrong (Catholics and Reformed who make the Gospel a new law), and any repudiation of the Law was wrong (Antinomianism). The Law was God's word about human sin, human imperfection, and whose purpose was to drive us to our knees under a burden of guilt. The Gospel is God's grace and

power to save. Hence we must never in interpreting the Scriptures confuse these two different activities of God or teachings of Holy Scripture.[22]

Luther regarded both the errors of the Roman Church and of the Schwaermers as a result of a confusion of Law and Gospel. In the sixth decade of the twentieth century the Faith Forward Committee published a study on "Law and Gospel," authored by Dr. A. R. Kretzmann. In the introduction of this monograph the Committee claimed: "There is now a united front against the Lutheran distinction between Law and Gospel. The Pietists and Rationalists-Schleiermacher at the beginning of the 19th century and Ritschl at its end-and almost every theologian of stature in between Karl Barth, the prophet of dialectical theology, and Bultmann, the advocate of a demythologized Gospel-all agree in their rejection of the basic distinction between Law and Gospel."[23]

The Presbyterian G. Ernst Wright, in his evaluation of Bultmann's famous essay: "The Significance of the Old Testament for the Christian Faith" criticizes what he believes is Bultmann's preoccupation with the Lutheran "fascination with the Law/Gospel problem." Again Wright asserted: "Further, Bultmann's background comes out, perhaps, in the amount of space he gives to Law/Gospel problems. To one raised in another tradition, particularly the Reformed or Calvinistic, this problem does not assume the centrality it does in the Lutheran."[24]

It is the proper distinction between Law and Gospel with all of its ramifications that has and still means that there are major differences regarding the interpretation of many passages in the Old and New Testaments in Protestantism. These are differences which many Lutherans today are sweeping under the rug in their passion for religious fellowship with church bodies that do not correctly understand the Scriptures nor God's plan of salvation. C. F. W. Walther has pointed out what some of the serious consequences are when Law and Gospel are not properly distinguished:

> Even nature teaches that certain materials must not be mixed if they are to retain their salutary virtue. There are certain substances that are, by themselves, salutary; but when they are mixed, they turn into poison. That is what happens when Law and Gospel are mingled. Or take an instance from colors: when you combine yellow and blue, it is neither yellow nor blue but green. In like manner there arises a third substance (tertium genus), when Law and Gospel are confounded in a sermon. The new substance is entirely foreign to either original substance and causes both of them to lose their virtue.[25]

In the introduction to Thesis XII Walther wrote relative to effective preaching:

> To achieve this task, it is especially necessary to divide ... the Law and the Gospel from each other. When a person does not understand how to do this and always mingles either doctrine into the other his preaching is utterly futile and vain. More than this a preacher of this kind does harm and leads the souls of men astray; he leads them to a false faith, a false hope, a false contrition, makes them hypocrites,

and frequently hurls them into despair.[25a]

The Proper Distinction Between Law and Gospel For Present Day Biblical Interpretation

While the word "Gospel" in the New Testament sometimes means the entire record of the life of Christ (Mark 1:1), embracing all the teachings of Christ (Acts 20:21) its peculiar sense is the proclamation of the forgiveness of' sins and sonship with God through Christ. Upon the correct definition of "Gospel" the true conception of justification and its relation to sanctification depends. This is a distinction many of the early Christian writers failed to grasp; they did not understand the clear antithesis between Law and Gospel. A giant in theology like Augustine did not grasp the clearness with which the two doctrines, Law and Gospel, are enunciated in the Scriptures. Thus Augustine wrote that "in preaching of the Gospel there is taught us what we ought to love, to despise, to do, to avoid, and to hope" (Migne, Edition V., 1357).[26] Because of his intensive study of the Pauline epistles Luther came to a clear understanding of the function of these two forms of God's Word.

In 2 Timothy 2:15, Paul in writing to his coworker Timothy admonished him: "Earnestly seek to commend yourself to God as a workman who, because of his straightforward dealing with the truth, has no reason to feel shame." In the King James Version this same verse is translated: "Study to show thyself approved unto God, a workman that needed not to be ashamed, rightly dividing the word of truth." Luther in his German translation rendered the verse: "Berfleissige dich Gott zu erzeigen einen rechtschaffenen und undstraflichen Arbeiter, der da recht theile das Word der Warheit." The KJV and Luther renderings were responsible for using 2 Tim. 2:15 as a passage that stressed the holding there were two different words of God that must be properly used, namely Law and Gospel.[27] More correctly the Greek reads "orthtomounta ton logon," "cutting straight the Word of God." Cutting straight the Word of God certainly does involve a proper distinction between Law and Gospel, but the expression is broader and would also include other matters relative to Biblical interpretation.

The Difference Between Law and Gospel Is Not Found:
A. In their origin.

Both Law and Gospel are divine. Paul speaks of the divine character of the Law when he wrote: "While you take pride in the law, you dishonor God by breaking it" (Rom. 2:23, NEB).[28] "In my inmost self I delight in the law of God, but I perceive that there is my bodily members a different law that my reason approves and making me a prisoner under the law that is in my members, the law of sin" (Roman 8: 22-23).[29] The Gospel is of divine origin for Paul, writing to the Galatian congregation asserts: "I must tell you brethren, that the Gospel which I preach bears no human impress. For indeed it was not from man that I received it, but by revelation from Jesus Christ" (1:11-12).[30]

B. In their necessity

The Law prepares for the Gospel. This Paul asserts: "Before faith came we were perpetual slaves under the Law, in preparation for the destined faith about to be revealed. So the Law has been our tutor-slave (our pedagogue) to lead us to Christ, so that we may be justified by faith; but now that the Faith is come, we are no longer under a tutor-slave" (3:23-24).[31] On the other hand the Gospel saves, for Paul: "For I am proud of the Gospel. It is God's saving power for everyone who believes, for the Jew first, and also for the Gentile. For in it is being revealed a righteousness which proceeds from God, from faith unto faith" (Rom. 1:16).[32]

C. In the time they are in force:

Both Law and Gospel served their respective purposes during Old as well as New Testament times. One of the wrong notions found in theological literature of the past has been the idea that the Old Testament is Law and the New Testament is Gospel. This idea was expressed by Bultmann in his essay "The Significance of the Old Testament for the Christian faith."[33] According to the Scriptures both doctrines, Law and Gospel, are found in the Old and in the New Testaments. The Old Testament contains the Ten Commandments and many other laws. In fact Luther classified laws given by God to the Jews as being of three kinds: Moral, ceremonial and political. The Pentateuch, or Torah, contains many different kinds of law. The word nomos occurs hundreds of times in the New Testament. But the Gospel is also found in the Old Testament. Paul instructs his readers concerning this matter as follows: "But now, quite apart from any law, a righteousness coming from God has been fully brought to light, continually witnessed to by the Law and the Prophets. I mean a righteousness coming from God through faith in Jesus Christ, for all who believe" (Romans 3:21-22).[34] Concerning the Judaizers who were placing the yoke of ceremonial law upon the Gentiles, Peter declared: "Now, then, why are you tempting God by laying on the necks of these disciples a yoke which neither our forefathers nor we have been able to hear. On the contrary we believe that it is by the grace of the Lord Jesus Christ that we and they shall be saved."

D. In their duration, between the Fall and the Second Coming

Both Law and Gospel will be in effect until the day of judgment This, however, is a truth which is denied by the millennialists who hold that during the present dispensation, salvation by faith in Christ Jesus is the method of salvation. But when the return of Christ occurs for the establishment of his earthly rule, supposedly foretold in the Old Testament Scriptures, then the Jews will automatically embrace Jesus as their King. During the millennium the method of salvation that obtained during the dispensation of the church, or the dispensation of grace, will no longer be operative. *The Scofield Reference Bible*[35] and *The New Scofield Reference Bible* support this type of hermeneutics.[36]

There is a Difference Between Law and Gospel with Regard to:

A. Their Revelation

The Law was written in man's heart at the creation. St. Paul declares concerning this matter: "When people who are not Jews and don't have the Law do by nature what the Law says, they who don't have the Law are a law unto themselves. They show that what the Law wants them to do is written in their heart" (Romans 2:14-15).[37] Stump wrote about the revelation of the moral law as follows: "The moral law was written in man's heart at the creation. He knew without any external law what was morally right and wrong. Something of this original law still remains in the mind or heart of the natural man. The heathen give evidence, as Paul tells us, that the law is written in their hearts by the fact that to some extent they observe its requirements, and are accused by their own consciences of wrongdoing" (Rom. 2:14, 15).[38]

The Gospel was given by divine revelation. The New Testament emphasizes this fact in a number of passages. Thus Paul, at the conclusion of his Roman epistle declares: "No I commend you to Him who is able to keep you steadfast according to my Gospel, and the proclamation of Jesus Christ, whereby is unveiled the secret truth which was kept secret through immemorial ages, but now has been brought to light, and by command of the eternal God made known to the Gentiles by the scriptures of the Prophets, so that the Gentiles might hold obedience of the faith" (Romans 16: 25-26).[39] To the Corinthian congregation he states about his Gospel that it is not a philosophy of this present age, but it is the hidden wisdom of God which God had decreed before the world began. "None of the rulers of the present age understands it, for if they had, they would not have crucified the Lord of Glory." Nay, as it is written: "Eye has not seen, nor ear heard, neither have entered into man's heart the things which God has prepared for those who love him" (I Cor. 2:9-10).[40] To the Greeks this revealed Gospel was foolishness, but to those who are saved it is the wisdom of God.

B. Their Contents

The Law speaks of the deeds of men and says: Do this! Law and Gospel are opposite in what their contents are. In his Galatian epistle Paul has clearly depicted this difference: "And it is manifest that by the Law no man is justified in the sight of God: because the just shall live by his faith, and the Law has nothing to do with faith, but declared, The man that has done these things shall live therein" (3:11-12).[41]

When the lawyer asks Jesus what he has to do to inherit eternal life, Jesus replied: "What is written in the Law?" This was summarized by the lawyer in the words: "You must love the Lord your God with all your heart, and with all your soul, and with all your strength, and with all your mind; and your neighbor as yourself." To which Jesus replied: "You have answered right, do that, and you shall live" (Luke 10:26-28).

The Gospel, by contrast, says nothing about what man needs to accomplish, by what God has accomplished for man. "God so loved the world that he gave his only begotten son that whosoever believes in him should not perish but have everlasting life" (John 3:16).

C. Their Promise of Salvation

The Law promises eternal life on condition of a perfect balance, "This do, and thou shalt live," Lev. 18:5 declares: "You shall therefore Keep my statutes and my ordinances, by doing which a man-shall live: I am the Lord."

By contrast, the Gospel promise is free, gratuitous, unconditional. "Being justified freely by His grace (Rom. 3:24)," and in another passage in the same letter Paul writes by inspiration: "This is why righteousness is of faith, that it may be a free gift; so that the promise stands for all Abraham's posterity; not to his children of the Law alone, but also to the children of faith. For in the sight of God in whom he believed, who gives life to the dead, and call into being that which is not, Abraham is the father of us all" (4:16-17).[42] Again Paul says in 11:6: "But if it is by grace, it is no longer of works, or else grace is no more grace." In the Old Testament the same thought is expressed in Isaiah 1:18 and 43:25. There are "no strings attached" to the Gospel-promise. In this connection Koehler reminds his readers: "Faith is not a condition of the promise in the sense that thereby we earn or become worthy of the promised gift, but only in the sense that thereby we accept what the promise offers."[43]

D. Their Declaration

The Law threatens all men with the curse of damnation. In showing the great difference between Law and Gospel, Paul taught: "All who depend upon obedience to the Law are under a curse; for it is written. 'Cursed is everyone who does not abide by all the precepts of the Law and practice them.'" Here Paul was citing Deuteronomy 27:26. This means that both Testaments teach the same truth, namely, the Law promises punishment and condemnation to those who fail to live up to it. The Law demands 100% keeping of its requirements. "Whosoever shall keep the whole law and offend in one, is guilty of all".

While the Law threatens, the Gospel invites and promises forgiveness. "Come unto me all ye that labor and are heavy laden, and I will give you rest (Matt. 11:28)." In the Old Testament the Gospel invitation sounded forth as: "Ho, everyone who thirsts' come to the waters; and he who has money, come and buy and eat! Come, buy wine and milk without money and without price" (Is. 55:1). The contrast between the Law and the Gospel as to their respective kind of declarations, is succinctly set forth by Paul in his Galatian letter: "And the Law has nothing to do with faith. It teaches that 'he who does these things shall live by them' (Lev. xviii. 5). Christ purchased our freedom from the curse of the Law by becoming accursed for us (for Scripture says, 'Cursed is everyone who hangs on a tree' (Deut. xxi. 23), in order that in Christ Jesus the blessing of Abraham might come upon the Gentiles, so that through faith we might receive the promised Spirit" (Gal. 3:13).[44]

E. Their Effect

The Law kills because the Law reveals the wrath of God against all ungodliness and unrighteousness of man (Rom. 1:18); it works fear of punishment, sorrow and regret, despair, and hatred of God in the heart of man. While the Law demands love (Matt. 22:37), it cannot inspire love;

the law kills love. Paul teaches: "For sin, taking occasion by the commandment, deceived me, and by it slew me" (7:11). In another epistle Paul states this way: "He also made us competent servants of a new Covenant, which is not a written code but a Spirit; for the written code kills, but the Spirit gives life" (3:2).[45] The Law cannot make Christians of us (Gal. 3:2).

By contrast, the Gospel gives life. In Romans 5:1-8 Paul has described what flows from being justified by faith in Jesus Christ. To the congregations, to whom the Ephesian epistle is addressed, he declares: "To you also, who were dead through your offenses and sins, which were once habitual to you while you walked in the ways of this world and obeyed the Prince of the powers of the air, the spirits that are now at work in the hearts of the sons of disobedience to you God have given Life" (Eph. 2:1-2).[46]

F. Their Object

The Law is to be preached to secure sinners. The object of Law preaching was clearly outlined to Timothy by Paul: "Now we know that the Law is good, if a man uses it in a lawful way, and remembers that a law is not enacted for a righteous man but for the lawless and rebellious, the irreligious and sinful, the godless and profane — for those who strike their fathers or their mothers, for murderers, the licentious, sodomites, slave-dealers, liars, and false witnesses; and for whatever else is opposed to the wholesome teaching of the glorious Gospel of the blessed God with which I am entrusted" (I Tim. 1:8-10).[47]

The Gospel is to be proclaimed to terrified sinners. The Gospel comforts those who are depressed because of their sins (Is. 40:1-2). The Gospel works faith and trust in God (Rom. 10:17), love of God and the neighbor (I John 4:19,21), joy and hope (I Peter 1:3,6). The Gospel regenerates a person (I Peter 1:23), creating a new spiritual life and a willing obedience (John 6:63; Ps. 119:32).

G. Their Purpose

The Law was not given to save man. St. Paul made this clear to the Roman readers: "For no man living will be declared righteous before Him on the ground of obedience to the Law. Law simply brings a knowledge of sin."[48] (Romans 3:20) The same truth is affirmed in the Galatian epistle: "I do not nullify the grace of God; for if acquittal comes through the Law, then Christ died in vain."

The purpose of the Gospel was given and proclaimed that men might be saved. Romans 1:16, the theme of Romans, declared that the Gospel is the power of God unto salvation by faith in Christ Jesus. "The purpose of the Gospel is to tell men of the love of God, who sent His Son into the world" (Romans 5:8; John 3:16). It tells men that Christ made full atonement for our sins (Heb. 9:12) and reconciled us to God; "when we were enemies, we were reconciled to God by the death of His Son (Rom. 5:10)." The Gospel does not reveal a possible grace of God, a possible reconciliation and forgiveness, contingent on certain conditions we are to fulfill; redemption, reconciliation, forgiveness are revealed as accomplished facts, which are not affected by what we may or may not do (Rom. 3:3).

The Use of Law and Gospel After Conversion

The Law does not concern us in the matter of our justification and salvation. But relative to Christian living the regenerate still needs the Law, as a curb, mirror and as a guide. The *Formula of Concord* teaches: "For the old Adam, as an intractable, refractory ass, is still a part of them, which must be coerced to obedience of Christ, not only by the teaching, admonition, force, and threatening's of the Law, but oftentimes by the club of punishments and troubles" (F. C. Th. D., Art. VI, 24).[49] Concerning the Law as a mirror the *Formula of Concord* says: "Therefore, as often as believers stumble, they are reproved by the Holy Spirit from the Law, and by the same God, Spirit, are raised up and comforted again with the preaching of the Gospel"[50] (F.C. Th. D. Art. VI, 14). The Law also serves as a guide: "This doctrine is needful for believers, in order that they may hit upon a holiness and devotion of their own, and under pretext of the Spirit of God set up a self-chosen worship, without God's Word and command" (F.C., Th. D., Art. VI, 14).[51] Since the Law is God's will and holy and since the converted wants to place His God and live a life in harmony with the Divine Will, the Law is a welcome guide for the Christian, showing him in what kind of works he should exercise his faith. The Gospel is the power that enables the Christian to do the good works as shown in harmony with God's Law. The *Formula of Concord* correctly teaches that "so far as they have been born anew according to the inner man, do what is pleasing to God, not from coercion of the Law, but by the renewing of the Holy Ghost, voluntarily and spontaneously from their hearts" (F.C. Th. D., Art. VI, 24).[52]

The Great Importance of the
Distinction between Law and Gospel

Only where the proper distinction between Law and Gospel are understood and practiced can the Bible correctly be understood. Many Biblical interpreters and Bible commentators interpret the Sermon on the Mount as Gospel. The teachings of Christ as found there are often taught as to what a person must do in order to be saved. What has been given as instruction for living the life of a sanctified life of a member of Christ's kingdom is portrayed as Gospel and thus Law and Gospel are confounded; many exegetes make the directives and instructions as an instrument of salvation, but the Sermon on the Mount describes how the true member of Christ's kingdom will conduct himself on earth.

It is only as Law and Gospel are properly distinguished that a Christian can remain a Christian. The person who believes that he must constantly do good works to remain a child of God is confusing justification with sanctification. Instead of daily repenting of his sins and throwing himself on the mercy of God, the individual who believes that the performing of good works as a means of remaining in favor with God as in jeopardy of losing his salvation.

Only as Law and Gospel are properly distinguished can there be assurance of salvation, joy, strength to do good works and can a believer have comfort against the day of judgment. Only by being aware of their distinction can the true church be distinguished from false churches.

III
The Misuse of Law and Gospel in 20th Century Christianity

The Roman Catholic Church conceives of the Gospel as the "New Law." This results in making Christ a new lawgiver. The Gospel is not a new and better law. Jesus expounded the Law indeed, thus performing a "foreign work" (F.C., Ep. V. 10) but Christ did not amend it. If He had amended it, He would have broken it, (Deut. 12:33). *The Popular Symbolics* claims also that the so-called "evangelical counsels" of Rome are in part fictitious, not given by Christ at all; and in part they belong to Christ's exposition of the Law.[53] The commandment requiring perfect love is a commandment given by Moses, Matt. 22:37-40; Rom. 13:9; Deut 6:5; Lev. 19:18. Christ calls it a new commandment, John 13:45, because the Gospel produces the new powers needed for its fulfillment. Rome makes the Gospel a new and better code of morals for the observance of which insures salvation. But the Gospel and the Sacraments are means by which Christ confers and bestows His grace, but are not to be regarded as prescribing works for a Christian to perform.

Calvinism and Arminianism are also guilty of commingling Law and Gospel. F. E. Mayer wrote of Calvinistic theology that it is atavistic and therefore directs the Christian to seek the assurance of his wellbeing in the state of grace in a program of Christian activity rather than in the means of Grace. Mayer cites Question 86 of the *Heidelberg Catechism*: Why must we do good works? is answered: "That with our whole life we may show ourselves thankful to God for His blessings and that He may be glorified through us; then also that we ourselves be assured of our faith by the fruits thereof, and by our godly walk may bring our neighbors also to Christ."[54] Arminianism makes of the Sacraments legal ordinances and of faith a work, by means of which salvation is achieved.[55] Any person who emphasizes the Law as a means of pleasing God or as the basis for assurance of standing in the favor of God is doing what St. Paul accused the Judaizers in Galatia: "Christ is become of no effect unto you whosoever of you are justified by the Law; ye are fallen from grace" (Ga. 5:4).

The "social Gospel" of theological modernism with its doctrine of this worldliness, aiming as it does chiefly at the achievement of the temporal wellbeing through right living, completely obliterates the Gospel of Jesus Christ, and its doctrine of the forgiveness of sins, and other worldliness.[56]

Certain Gospel passages have been misunderstood as legal commands. For example, I John 3:23: "His commandment is this that we should believe in the name of His Son, Jesus Christ and love one another as he has commanded us to do" (I John 3:23). Or "Believe on the Lord Jesus Christ and thou shalt be saved" (Acts 16:32). "Come unto me all that are heavy laden and I will give you rest for your souls" (Mt. 11:28). These and similar passages are not to be understood as legal commands, but as gracious invitations, expressed in the most forceful manner, to accept the offer of the forgiveness of sins. Faith is described by the Gospel as the very opposite of human accomplishment (Rom. 3:28); (Eph. 2:8,9).

Rome makes the Gospel promises of eternal life conditional on condition of observing the commandments. Cognate with this same teaching is that of Arminianism "in its various species and varieties conditioning salvation on any work of man, or anything preceding or following faith, contrition or holiness of life, or on faith itself as an ethical act, nullify the Gospel and keep the sinner under the curse of the Law (Gal. 3:10,12,13; 5:4)."[57]

The Law does not produce faith. It is only the doctrine of faith that brings pure grace and makes men godly. Only the Gospel can create willing obedience to God's will. The legalism of the Roman Church and of all rationalistic systems make the Law of Moses as the means through obedience is to be produced and results making the Means of Grace a Law. The observance of many ordinances of historic Methodism, the observation of rules of conduct, cannot produce a genuine but only an unwilling obedience.

Many laws of the Old Testament in force from Mount Sinai to Mount Calvary are no longer binding on Christians since the completion of the atoning work of Jesus Christ. "Let no man therefore judge you in meat, or in drink, or in respect of an holy-day, or of the new moon, or of the Sabbath days; which are a shadow of things to come, but the body is of Christ" (Col. 2:16, 17). Besides these passages, the following New Testament passages: Acts 10:11f.; 15:15; Gal. 2:3-5, 12-14; 4:1f.; Heb. 7:11f.; 9:9f.; 10:1 emphasize that the Jewish state and the Temple have passed. The many ceremonial laws are now abrogated.

No church or any group of men have the right to insist on regulations and ordinances being kept that are not specifically commended either directly or by logical inference or deduction. Paul declares: "Stand fast therefore in the liberty wherewith Christ hath made us free and be not entangled again in the yoke of bondage" (Ga. 5:1). So also I Cor. 7:23 and Col. 2:16-23.

Those churches that teach that a Christian must observe one day as the Christian Sabbath, like the Roman Catholic, the Reformed, and others, are guilty of holding to an abolished ceremonial law. Thus *The Augsburg Confession* criticizes those that "judge that by the authority of the Church the observance of the Lord's Day instead of the Sabbath-day was ordained as a thing necessary, do greatly err. Scripture has abrogated the Sabbath-day, for it teaches that, since the Gospel has been revealed, all the ceremonies of Moses can be omitted" (A. C. XXVIII, 57f. 32)[58] To treat Sunday as if it were the Sabbath day is also a violation of Christian liberty. The New Testament has abrogated the sabbath and other ceremonial days of the ceremonial Law, (cf. Rom. 14:5f; Gal. 4:10f.; Col. 2:16-17). Thus Luther wrote concerning this matter: "If I receive Moses in one Commandment, I must receive Moses' entire; it would follow that, if I accept Moses as master and lawgiver, I would have to submit to circumcision, drinking, dress, and entire mode of life according to the laws given the Jews."[59] *The Augsburg Confession* discusses the Sabbath and Sunday in Article XXVIII under the general heading of "Ecclesiastical Powers."[60]

In the post-Reformation period, sabbatarianism came to play an important role.[61] In a general sense sabbatarianism denotes all those who hold that the Christian Sabbath should be kept on the seventh-day (Saturday), especially the Adventists, Seventh-day Baptists, and some scattered communistic societies. In a wider sense the term also signifies those that the Lord's Day among Christians should be observed in the same manner the Jews kept the Sabbath, or those who hold a strict view regarding keeping the Sabbath. The Puritans in the 17th century adopted a strict observation of the Sabbath and led to a controversy regarding the manner in which Sunday was to be observed. This concept was brought to America and was reflected in blue laws which were in force till recently in many American cities and towns.

IV
Problems with the Proper Use of Law and Gospel in American Lutheranism

1. The Third Use of the Law.

In 1556, after Luther's death, the Second Antinomian Controversy, which concerned itself specifically with the third use of the Law, developed. Poach, Otto, Neander, and Amsdorf contended that the teaching of the Law had no value for directing the Christian life. Theologians like Flacius,Moerlin, Wigand, Westphal entered a demurer. This controversy was settled in Article VI of the *Formula of Concord*:

> Accordingly we condemn as dangerous and subversive of Christian discipline and true piety the erroneous teaching that the Law is not to be urged, in the manner and measure above described, upon Christians and genuine believers, but only upon unbelievers, non-Christians, and the impenitent.[62]

American theologians have been influenced by Werner Elert who in his book, *The Christian Ethos*, has questioned the validity of the third use of the Law.

The following are quotations from this book which exhibit this viewpoint:

> If we mean by the third use that we can listen to the law without its threats, we indulge in pure fiction. There is never a situation when it does not function as accuser. For that reason we cannot distil an innocuous third use from that social use of the law which weighs upon our conscience.[63]

He further argues:

> But the new nature which needs to win out over the old is liberated nature which no longer requires the law. In fact it is new only insofar as it is in every respect removed from the law. The dangers of libertinism are not averted when the new man is once more placed under the domination of the law but only when he is "led by the Spirit." "If you are led by the spirit you are not under the law ..." All roads lead to that open space which is no longer restricted and hemmed in by

laws. These roads lead into the freedom of the new creature of God, especially when we understand that they originate in God.[64]

In still another page of this book, the following occurs:

It (i.e. the law) need no longer drive the regenerate because they do "without instruction, admonition, coercion, or impact of the law what they ought to do according to God's will ..." Note: "without instruction ..." In other words, there can be no law for the earthly life of the regenerate which serves purely as information, neither for the old Adam in him or for the actual performance of good works of the law.[65]

This supposedly is to be the interpretation of *Formula of Concord*, VI, 6. But as Eggold pointed out Elert failed to begin the quotation with the sentence that says: "If believers and the elect children of God were perfectly renewed in this life" ... [66] If Christians did not possess the Old Adam and after their conversion never sinned but were able to lead a life of complete sanctification, then the Christian would need no guide for the Law of God. However, inasmuch as Christians still have to battle their sinful nature, the Law cannot be dispensed with. The situation is portrayed by Paul in Romans 7:23-24: "I see another law in my members warring against the law of my mind, and bringing me into subjection to the law of sin which is in my members." Francis Pieper has noted that the flesh never becomes pious in this life but retains its characteristics throughout the life of a Christian.[67] Paul was constrained to cry out: "O Wretched man that I am, who shall deliver me from the body of this death" (Rom. 7: 24). Luther apprehended the situation correctly when he said: "A Christian is in two realms at once. So far as he is flesh, he is under the Law; so far as he is spirit, he is under grace."[68]

That the Christian man is a dual person must be recognized by the Biblical interpreter. Paul Althaus declared this fact in the following:

This new Ego, as surely as it is not an abstraction but a here and now reality of the concrete man..., is never simply identical with the empirical man. Until death, there will always remain also "flesh," the old man. The sign of the Holy Spirit's presence in man is therefore not the unity of a completely renewed ego which now need simply runs its course as self-evidently as a process in nature, but the sign of the Spirit's presence is precisely the quality, the conflict between the Spirit and man, as far as he is flesh.[69]

Because the Christian is also flesh, he needs the Law of God in its three uses: curb, mirror and rule.

2. The Use of The Law-Gospel Dichotomy to Deny That All Scriptural Truths and Facts Need to Be Accepted

In recent years various Lutheran scholars have pitted the Law-Gospel distinction against the **Sola Scriptura** principle of Luther and of historic Lutheranism.[70] It is contended that an interpreter can question the data of the text, but as long as these questionings and differing interpretations do not "impair the right understanding of the Gospel," that such differences should not be a matter of controversy.[71] The denial of certain Biblical miracles in both Testament is permissible, if such denial does not conflict with the Gospel. This stance permits finding many mistakes in the Bible, claiming that the Word of God contains contradictions, but simultaneously asserts that there is no reason to become upset, since they do not affect the Gospel. Clear statements of the Biblical text can be challenged but it in no way, so we are told, does their rejection endanger the Christian faith. To utilize the proper distinction between Law and Gospel as a method for the rejection of statements that are said to be the very Word of God is a completely wrong use of the Law-Gospel dichotomy as a hermeneutical principle. While the Gospel is the heart of the revealed Word of God, yet it must be remembered that its validity rests upon the same Scripture that certain Lutherans are willing to question and reject in many places of both the Old and New Testaments. The proper distinction between Law and Gospel as set forth by Luther, the Lutheran Confessions and Lutheran theologians since Reformation times rests upon deductions from numerous Bible passages. What if the basic passages, the sedes doctrinae, are challenged by critical scholars and shown by various types of criticism as false, then what happens to the proper distinction of Law and Gospel? If a theologian has the right to question the Pauline authorship of Ephesians, of the Pastorals, the six-day creation, the existence of the Devil and of good and bad angels, why cannot others challenge the very passages that are employed to support the Law-Gospel dichotomy?

Two recent sociology of religion studies, namely the *Kersten Study*[72] and *A Study of Generations*[73] indicate that American Lutherans have espoused views which seem to indicate that millions of Lutherans do not know how Law and Gospel should function in the Christian life. It was J.H.C. Fritz, a former dean of Concordia Seminary, St. Louis, who wrote: "Many sermons therefore, in spite of the fact that they abound in Christian phraseology, are nevertheless wrong throughout. A Christian pastor cannot too well learn the right use of the Law and the Gospel. Especially must the young pastor be on his guard in this respect he make most serious and disastrous mistakes."[74]

What has been asserted about preaching also holds true about religious educational materials. If it is true that the thinking of the rank and file of the members of a Lutheran congregation is influenced and formed by the preaching and religious instruction as contained in the Sunday School and other educational materials, then, judging by the attitudes and answers given by Lutherans in the Michigan, as shown by the *Kersten Study* and nationally in over three thousand congregations of the three major denominations of Lutheranism, according to *A Study of Generations*, the proper distinction between Law and Gospel is not being made and people are not being instructed in the proper use of the Law and the Gospel and shows wherein the differences between these two words of God consist.

Historic Lutheranism, following Paul and Luther, held that man cannot save himself. Furthermore, man can contribute nothing toward his salvation, the believer's salvation is due purely to the grace of God. Yet the *Kersten Study* shows some disconcerting evidence in this matter.

Thus, 60% in the Lutheran Church in America hold that people are saved by keeping the Ten Commandments, 59% in The American Lutheran Church, 54% in the Lutheran Church-Missouri Synod, and 46% in The Wisconsin Synod. Only 22% in the LCA believe that man plays no part in his salvation, 33% in the ALC; 73% in the Missouri Synod, and 93% in the Wisconsin Synod of the clergy. Thus Kersten wrote: "The responses to the question on the Ten Commandments reveal definite problems between the clergy and laity in interpreting the Lutheran concepts of salvation. More than half of the laymen think that people are saved by keeping the Ten Commandments. In contrast the clergy show great unanimity in holding to Justification by faith apart from the keeping of the Law."[75]

According to A *Study of Generations* 59% of those responded to the questionnaire stated that "the main emphasis of the Gospel is on God's rules for right living."[76] Nearly 60% of Lutheranism does not understand the true difference between Law and Gospel. The Gospel tells men and women what God has done for their salvation; salvation is bestowed 100% as the gift of God. The Gospel heart is what Christ has accomplished for mankind. By keeping the Law perfectly all his human existence in thought, Word and deed and by suffering the punishment that all people had deserved because of their sins, Jesus has reconciled the world to His Heavenly Father and has appeased the wrath of God. Those who are moved by the Gospel invitation to accept Christ as their Savior are declared righteous, their sins are forgiven. The Decalogue of God demands fulfillment of its moral requirements; failure to live up to the Law results in condemnation for failure to have kept all commandments of God. Therefore; all men need Jesus Christ as Redeemer and Savior. No person can come to God apart from Jesus. 64% of Lutheranism claim "that hard work will always pay off it you have faith in yourself and stick to it."[77] 50% or those responding in the study conducted by Strommen and associates believed that "God is satisfied if a person lives the best life he can."[78] Forty-two percent opined that "salvation depends upon being sincere in whatever you believe."[79] Thirty-one percent responded in the affirmative to the following question: "If I say I believe in God and do right, I will get to Heaven."[80] 72% of the respondents expressed the opinion that "although there are many religions in the world, most of them lead to the same God."[81]

Both the *Kersten Report* and *The Study of Generations* indicate a serious state of affairs in American Lutheranism. The great solas of historic Lutheranism are no longer known, or if they are known they are being rejected. **Sola Scriptura**, **sola fide**, **sola gratia** and **solus Christos** are no longer being emphasized in preaching and educational materials: Participation in the ecumenical movement, working with the National Council of Churches, sharing the endeavors of the World Council of Churches has led to a watering down, yea, even of the rejection of those teachings that were Scriptural and Lutheran.

Footnotes

1. Bernard Ramm, *Protestant Biblical Interpretation* (Third Revised Edition; Grand

Rapids: Baker Book House. 1970), p. 56.

2. F. E. Mayer, *The Religious Bodies of American* (St. Louis: Concordia Publishing House, 1956). p. 58.

3. Weimar Edition of *Luther's Works*, Vol. 360 pp. 25,29 as translated by Ewald Plass. *What Luther Says* (St. Louis: Concordia Publishing House. 1959), II, p. 732.

4. Weimar Edition of *Luther's Works*, Vol. 36, p. 30f., as translated by Plass, **op. cit.**, p. 732.

5. Weimar Edition of *Luther's Works*, Vol. I, p. 616, as translated by Plass, **op. cit.**, p. 733.

6. *Concordia Triglotta* (St. Louis: Concordia Publishing House. 1921), p. 801.

7. *Formula of Concord*, Th.D., Art. V, 17. *Concordia Triglotta*, p. 957.

8. **Ibid.**

9. Cf. quotations from the writings of these Lutheran theologians in Heinrich Schmid, *Doctrinal Theology of the Evangelical Lutheran Church* (Third Edition; revised. Translated from the German and Latin by Charles A. Hay and Henry E. Jacobs (Minneapolis; Augsburg Publishing House. 1189). pp. 508-520.

10. Dr. C. F. W. Walther, *The Proper Distinction Between Law Gospel* reproduced from the German edition or 1897 by W. H. T. Dau (St. Louis: Concordia Publishing House. 1929). 426 pages.

11. As given in Wm. Dallmann. W. H. T. Dau and Th. Engelder, *Walther and the Church* (St. Louis: Concordia Publishing House, 1938), pp. 122-127.

12. F. Bente, *Gesetz und Evangelium: Busse und Gute Werke* (St. Louis: Concordia Publishing House, 1917), 104 pages.

13. Pieper, *Christian Dogmatics* (St. Louis: Concordia Publishing House, 1953), III, pp. 222-252.

14. Th. Engelder, W. Arndt, Th. Graebner and F. E. Mayer, *Popular Symbolics* (St. Louis: Concordia Publishing House, 1943), pp. 8-82.

15. George Stoeckhart, "Gesetz and Evangelium nach ihren unterschiedlichen Wirkungen," *Lehre and Wehre*, 33: 154-169, 191-204; 244-248; 273-281, June, July, Aug., Sept., Oct., 1887.

16. Edward W. A. Koehler, *A Summary of Christian Doctrine* (Distributors: Rev. L. H. Koehler, Detroit and The Rev. A. W. Koehler, Oakland, 1939), pp. 194-197.

17. Theodore Laetsch, *The Abiding Word* (St. Louis: Concordia Publishing House, 1947)), I, pp. 105-103.

18. Erwin L. Lueker, *Lutheran Cyclopedia* (St. Louis: Concordia Publishing House, 1954), p. 575.

18a. Erwin L. Lueker, *Lutheran Cyclopedia* (Revised Edition: St. Louis: Concordia Publishing House, 1975), p. 463.

19. John Theodore Mueller, *Christian Dogmatics* (St. Louis: Concordia Publishing House, 1955).

20. C.F.W. Walther, *God's No and God's Yes* (St. Louis: Concordia Publishing House, 1973), 118 pages.

21. **Ibid.**, p. 6.

22. Ramm, **op. cit.**, p. 57.

23. Dr. A. R. Kretzmann, *Law and Gospel* (St. Louis: Publishing by the Faith Forward Executive Committee, The Lutheran Church-Missouri Synod, no date), 50 pages plus 3 pages bibliography and xiii pages in an appendix, p. iv of the introduction written by the committee.

24. G. Ernst Wright, "History and Reality: The Importance of Israel's 'historical' Symbols for the Christian Faith," in Bernard W. Anderson, *The Old Testament and the Christian Faith* (New York: Harper & Row, Publishers, 1963), p. 178.

25. Walther, *The Proper Distinction Between Law and Gospel*, **op. cit.**, pp. 34-35.

26. Migne edition, V, 1357.

27. Cf. Raymond F. Surburg, "The Pastoral Epistles and Sound Doctrine," *The Springfielder*, 24:26-30, Autumn, 1961.

28. *The New English Bible* (Oxford and Cambridge University presses, 1961), p. 258.

29. **Ibid.**, p. 266.

30. Richard Francis Weymouth, *The New Testament in Modern Speech* (Boston: The Pilgrim Company, 1943), p. 437.

31. Helen Barrett Montgomery, *The New Testament in Modern English. The Centenary Translation* (Chicago, Kansas City, Los Angeles: The Judson Press, 1944), p. 406.

32. **Ibid.**, p. 400.

33. Rudolf Bultmann, "The Significance of the Old Testament for the Christian Faith," In Anderson, **op. cit.**, pp. 14-17.

34. Montgomery, *The Centenary Translation*, **op. cit.**, p. 406.

35. *The Scofield Reference Bible*. C.I. Scofield, editor (New York: Oxford University Press, 1917). xvi & 1392 pages & 192 pp. & maps.

36. *The New Scofield Reference Bible*. C.I. Scofield, editor (New York: Oxford University Press, 1967), XVI and 1392 pages and maps.

37. William F. Beck, *The New Testament in the Language of Today* (St. Louis: Concordia Publishing House, 1964), p. 270.

38. Joseph Stump, *The Christian Faith - A System of Christian Dogmatics,* (New York: The Macmillan Company, 1932), p. 307.

39. Montgomery, *The Centenary Translation*, **op. cit.**, p. 436.

40. **Ibid.**, pp. 441-442.

41. **Ibid.**, p. 503.

42. **Ibid.**, p. 408.

43. Koehler, **op. cit.**, p. 195.

44. Weymouth, **op. cit.**, p. 440.

45. **Ibid.**, p. 420.

46. **Ibid.**, p. 451.

47. **Ibid.**, p. 499.

48. Weymouth, **op. cit.**, p. 358.

49. *Concordia Triglotta*, **op. cit.**, p. 969.

50. **Ibid.**, p. 967.

51. **Ibid.**, p. 967.

52. **Ibid.**, p. 969.

53. Engelder, Arndt, Graebner and Mayer, *Popular Symbolics*, **op. cit.**, p. 52.

54. Mayer, *The Religious Bodies in American*, **op. cit.**, p. 194.

55. Philip Schaff, *Creeds of Christendom* (New York: Harper and Brothers, 1919), III, p. 338.

56. F. E. Mayer, "Modernism," in Erwin L. Lueker (ed.) *Lutheran Cyclopedia* (St. Louis: Concordia Publishing House, 1954), p. 707.

57. Engelder et al. *Popular Symbolics*, **op. cit.**, p. 79.

58. *Concordia Triglotta*, **op. cit.**, p. 91.

59. St. Louis Edition of *Luther's Works*, III, p. 6.

60. *Concordia Triglotta*, **op. cit.**, pp. 91-92.

61. "Sabbatariaism," in *Lutheran Cyclopedia*, **op. cit.**, p. 922. O. Boettcher, Sabbath and Immersion (St. Louis: Concordia Publishing House, 1925), pp. 3-11.

62. "The *Formula of Concord*, Epitome," *The Book of Concord*, edited by Theodore G. Tappert (Philadelphia: Muhlenberg Press, 1959), IV, p. 8.

63. Werner Elert, *The Christian Ethos*, translated from the German by Charles J. Schindler (Philadelphia: The Muhlenberg Press, 1957), p. 298.

64. **Ibid.**, p. 294.

65. **Ibid.**, p. 298f.

66. Henry J. Eggold, "The Third Use of the Law," *The Springfielder*, 27:16, Spring, 1963.

67. Francis Pieper, *Christian Dogmatics*, translated from the German by F. W. Albrecht (St. Louis: Concordia Publishing House, 1953), III, p. 240.

68. St. Louis Edition of *Luther's Works*, ix., p. 452f.

69. Paul Althaus, *Der. Geist der lutherischen Ethik*, p. 29, as quoted by Edmund Schlink, *Theology of the Lutheran Confessions*, translated by Paul F. Koehneke and Herbert J. A. Bouman (Philadelphia: Muhlenberg Press, 1961), p. 109, n. 2.

70. Kent Knudson, "The Authority of Scriptures," *Concordia Theological Monthly*, 40:156, 1969; Gerharde Forde, *Theological Perspectives - A Discussion of Contemporary Issues in Lutheran Theology* (Decorah: Luther College Press, 1967).

71. Forde, **op. cit.**, pp. 55-56.

72. Lawrence L. Kersten, *The Lutheran Ethic. The Impact of Religion on Laymen and Clergy* (Detroit: Wayne State University Press, 1970).

73. Merton P. Strommen, Milo L. Brekke, Ralph C. Underwager, Arthur L. Johnson, *A Study of Generations* (Minneapolis: Augsburg Publishing House, 1972).

74. As quoted in Kretzmann, *Law and Gospel*, **op. cit.**, p. iii.

75. Kersten, **op. cit.**, p. 157-158.

76. *A Study of Generations*, **op. cit.**, p. 369.

77. **Ibid.**

78. **Ibid.**

79. **Ibid.**

80. **Ibid.**

81. **Ibid.**

Questions

1. Galatians was one of Luther's ____.
2. Rome held that grace is ____.
3. Who should be called a Doctor of Holy Scripture? ____
4. One of the greatest classical writings of the 19th century was ____.
5. Is the Gospel also found in the Old Testament? ____
6. What does the Scofield Reference Bible support? ____
7. The Gospel promise is ____.
8. Where can the Bible only be correctly understood? ____
9. Is the Sermon on the Mount Gospel? ____
10. The Roman Catholic Church conceives of the Gospel as ____.
11. Calvinism and Arminianism are guilty of ____.
12. How does Rome make the Gospel promises eternal life conditional?

13. The ordinances of historic Methodism cannot produce a ____.
14. These churches that teach that a Christian must observe one day as a Christian Sabbath ____.
15. Sabbatarianism denotes ____.
16. What was reflected in the blue laws? ____
17. Werner Elert questioned ____.
18. The Christian needs the law of God in its three uses ____.
19. *The Kersten Study* and *A Study of Generations* showed ____.
20. *The Great Solas* of historic Lutheranism are no longer ____.
21. What has led to a "watering down?" ____

The Domino Effect of the Rejection of One Doctrine Upon Other Doctrines of the Bible

Christian News, August 4-25, 1980

According to Webster's *New World Dictionary* the word "domino" has a number of different meanings.[1] The primary one given is that of "a loose cloak or robe with wide sleeves, hood, and mask worn at masquerades." The word is used in French and Spanish of hooded cloak worn by cathedral canons. Ultimately the French and Spanish domino goes back to the Latin "dominus," a "lord" or "master". After the meaning of "loose cloak" Webster cites as a second signification "a small mask for the eyes; a half mask that is generally black."[2] A third usage given by the *New World Dictionary* is that of "a person dressed in such a cloak or mask."[3] As a fourth meaning Webster lists, as coming from French through Spanish, the blackness of the piece, and has special reference to "a small oblong piece of wood, bone or plastic marked into halves, each half blank or having from one to six dots marked on it," and the last definition of domino or dominoes (constructed as singular) is that of a "game played with twenty-eight such pieces, which the players must match according to the number of dots on each half."[4]

When these dominoes are placed side by side in a vertical position and the last in the series is made to fall on the one standing next to it, this action will cause each adjacent one to fall and affect all the others in the series until all have been knocked down and they all have assumed a horizontal or flat position. The effect produced by one domino upon the other.

I. The Domino Effects of the Denial of One Doctrine Upon Other Christian Doctrine or Doctrines

In the areas of Christian theology one can speak of a doctrine as having a domino effect upon others. When a Biblical interpreter rejects one or more Christian doctrines, there occurs what might properly be called a domino effect upon other teaching constituting the corpus of Christian doctrine. One of the serious problems which has developed in European and American Christianity and in world Lutheranism is that important and basic doctrines have been surrendered, rejected or reinterpreted. By calling important Biblical doctrines into question, there has been a domino effect upon other vital Scriptural teachings.

Lutheran scholars in the past have distinguished between "the abstract analogy" and "the concrete analogy."[5] By the "abstract analogy" is meant the harmonious relationship in which all Scriptural doctrines stand to each other. The doctrines of Holy Writ are not to be regarded as disjoined members but as links in a chain, or as beams in a building or like a bell without flaws.[6]

The interpreter who falsifies one doctrine logically causes others to be affected. Thus the denial of original sin or inherited sin makes unnecessary the need for infant baptism. Proponents of the new hermeneutic have argued that the rejection of one or more doctrines does not of necessity have repercussions for other doctrines or teachings in the system of revealed Christian truth.

II. The Domino Effects of the
Denial of the Doctrines of the Trinity

According to Holy Writ, God is one in essence, but this God has revealed Himself in three distinct Persons, namely, as the Father, Son and Holy Spirit. Martin Luther expressed it like this: "Scriptura Sancta docet esse Deum simplicissime unum et tres, ut vocent, personas verrisme distinctas."[7] *The Augsburg Confession* (I), asserts: "Our churches with common consent do teach that the decree of the Council of Nicea CONCERNING THE UNITY OF THE DIVINE ESSENCE AND CONCERNING THE THREE PERSONS is true to be believed without any doubting; that is to say, there is one divine essence which is called God...; and yet there are three Persons, of the same essence and power, who are also coeternal, the Father, the Son and the Holy Ghost."[8]

The Bible asserts that God is one. "Hear, O Israel, the Lord our God is one Lord" (Deut. 6:4). Paul taught: "There is none other God but one" (I Cor. 8:4). All the so-called "gods" of the Gentiles are called "elelim" (Lev. 19:4), which means being without existence. The descriptions of idols in Isaiah 44:6-20; Jeremiah 2:26-28; Psalm 115:1-9; 135:15-17 reveal their non-existence according to these Old Testament inspired writers. With these Old Testament declarations Paul agrees when he wrote: "An idol is nothing in the world" (I Cor. 8:4). "There is only one true God." Paul encouraged the people of Antioch in Pisidia "to turn from these vanities, unto the living God" (Acts 14:15).

While the Holy Scriptures clearly teach the unity of God, yet simultaneously they also instruct its readers that this one God has manifested Himself in three persons, distinct and distinguishable from each other. The Bible distinguishes between God the Father, God the Son and God the Holy Ghost. Christ's command was: "baptizing them in the name of the Father, Son and Holy Ghost" (Matt. 28:20). At the Baptism of Jesus the three Persons of the Godhead were in evidence. The Son, the Second Person, was standing in the waters of the Jordan, the Father, the First Person spoke from heaven, saying: "This is My beloved Son, hear ye Him," while the Holy Spirit, the Third Person became visible as a Dove, which rested upon Jesus, the Godman. In concluding this Second Corinthian epistle, Paul wrote: "The grace of our Lord Jesus Christ, the love of God, and the fellowship of the Holy Ghost be with you" (II Cor. 13:14). In John 5:31-38 Jesus clearly teaches that God the Father had sent Him and also that the Father testified to His works. In the same Gospel Jesus declared: "I and the Father are one" (John 10:30). In Acts 5:3-5 Peter informed Ananias and Sapphira that when they lied to the Holy Ghost, they did not lie to men, but to God.

The truths of the unity and the trinity have been rejected in the early history of the church, just as they were in the post-Reformation period and as they have been since the beginning of the age of rationalism. Such monotheistic religions as Judaism and Mohammedanism have vehemently rejected the Christian doctrine of the Trinity. Both Jews and the followers of Islam have accused Christian believers in the Trinity as being polytheists and as advocates of an erroneous doctrine of God. Unitarians, humanists, modernists and theist have all repudiated the Trinity of the Godhead.[9]

The doctrine of the Trinity is a watershed doctrine. John declared that the person who denies the deity of Christ, thereby does not have the Father (I John 2:23). In the fourth Gospel John asserted: "He that hath not the Son hath not life" (5:12). Again the same thought was set forth on this wise:

"All men should honor the Son even as they honor the Father. He that honoreth not the Son honoreth not the Father which hath sent Him" (John 5:23). Therefore, to reject Christ as God's only begotten Son, means not worshipping the true God at all. Jesus clearly set forth the fact that there is a domino effect upon other revealed doctrines, when He is not accepted as the Logos, who existed from all eternity and through Whom the worlds were created.

The doctrine of the Trinity is interwoven with the doctrines of creation, predestination, redemption and sanctification. The doctrines of preservation, hamartiology, soteriology, ecclesiology, the Christian ministry, eschatology as enunciated in the Bible all presuppose the work and activity of the Three Persons of the Godhead. The plan of salvation cannot be grasped, understood and believed apart from a correct understanding of the doctrine of the Trinity.[10] To adopt a modalistic interpretation, which means that God has revealed Himself in three different modes, sometimes as Father, other times as the Son and again at still others as the Holy Spirit, will have a domino effect of making it impossible to faithfully deal with the many passages which distinguish between the different Persons of the Trinity and result in confusion in explicating the work of the Triune God relative of the **opera and extra**, as the activity of God relates to the works of creation and preservation, redemption and sanctification. The repudiation of the Three Persons of the Godhead has also a domino effect when endeavoring to describe the relationship of the Father to the Son and of the Son to the Father of the procession of the Holy Spirit from the Son and the Father. The **opera ad intra** become impossible from the perspective of a unitarian idea of God.[11]

III. The Dommo Effects of the
Denial of the Divinity or Deity of Christ

It is generally agreed that the locus of Christology is the central locus of Christian theology. As a result of the employment of the historical critical method so-called Christian theologians affiliated with the Roman Catholic, the Protestant and Lutheran Churches have questioned, yea, even rejected the Virginal Conception and Virgin Birth of Jesus Christ.[12] Matthew 1:18-25 and Luke 1:32-35 clearly teach that Jesus, God from all eternity, was caused by the Holy Spirit to assume human life in the womb of the Virgin Mary. The domino effect of not accepting this clear teaching on the manner according to which God's Son began His prenatal experience, has serious repercussions for the sinlessness of Jesus.[13] The New Testament proclaims the important truth that Christ entered this world sinless and also left it without having sinned. Peter said of Jesus: "He did no sin, neither was guilt found in his mouth." Pilate exclaimed: "I find in him no fault at all." The malefactor on the cross testifies: "This man has done nothing amiss." The captain under the cross cried out: "Certainly this was a righteous man and the Son of God." And Judas, the traitor, standing before the chief priests and elders, and throwing the blood money upon the floor of the council chamber, exclaimed: "I have sinned in that I have betrayed innocent blood." If there has been a flaw in the spotless armor of Jesus, the Jews would have found it. But none of them was able to answer on His challenge, "which of you convinceth Me of sin?" The Apostle Paul claimed in his second letter to the Corinthian Church: "God hath made Him who did not know sin to be sin for us to make us God's righteousness in Him" (II Cor. 5:, Beck). If Jesus as mankind's substitute was to keep the demands of the law perfectly in thought, word and deed, it was imperative that He be pure and sinless. To make Joseph the earthly father of Jesus, as Moffatt has suggested in his New Testament translation, is to jeopardize, yes repudiate the sinlessness of Jesus.[14] Those who insist that the Scriptural account disagrees with the science of genetics, refuse to bow before the authority of the Word of God. It is further motivated by the presupposition that the Creator of man, can never intervene in the laws he has placed in nature and man. The Virginal Conception and the Virgin Birth were predicted by the prophet Isaiah when he announced to Ahaz: "Therefore the Lord himself will give you a sign: Look the virgin will conceive and have a son, and His name will be Immanuel" (Is. 7:14). This was a prophecy Isaiah uttered in connection with the events connected with the Syro-Ephraimitic War of 735-734 B.C.[15]

By the rejection of the Virgin Birth,[16] negative Biblical criticism has removed from the corpus of Christian teaching a doctrine which is foundational for a number of other teachings and whose denial has a domino effect on a number of Christological teachings set forth in the great creeds of Christendom, as well as in the denominational creeds of major Christian denominations. Negative critical scholars regard the Matthean and the Lucan accounts as myths or as fabrications. The suggestion has even been advanced that Christ was born out of wedlock. The domino effects of the rejection of the Virgin Birth may be stated as being: (1) the account in Scripture is false; (2) Jesus had a human father, and (3) Jesus was a mere man and not God.

IV. The Domino Effect of the Denial of the
Doctrine of the Vicarious Atonement

Those interpreters, who do not believe that man born of woman is conceived and born in sin and therefore spiritually speaking dead, logically reject the teaching that Christ as men's sinless substitute died in the sinners' place. Peter, however, asserted that Jesus bore man's sins in his own body. Many moderns do not believe in a vicarious atonement, because they are convinced that man can save himself by his character. It is their contention that man has the ability to live a morally acceptable life. The domino effect of such a stance is that Christ's vicarious or substitutionary atonement is repudiated and Christ's death is explained in such a way as to deny the Bible's revealed statement about the purpose of Christ's death. The domino effect of the rejection of the deity of Christ has resulted in the contention of the enemies of the Gospel that no human being can redeem his fellowman.[17] By their denial of the vicarious atonement the objectors of this teaching that have called the truthfulness of all those passages into question that clearly and unmistakably teach the importance of the substitutionary atonement. The prophet Isaiah in one of the greatest passages of the Old Testament has announced at least seven hundred years before Christ's death on Calvary about the Messiah: "But surely He will take on Him our suffering and carry our pains, but we will think God afflicts Him, strikes Him, and makes Him suffer. He is pierced for our transgressions and crushed for our sins; He is punished to make us happy and wounded to heal us. We have all gone astray like sheep, every one of us has turned to go his own way, and the Lord has punished Him for the sins of all of us" (Is. 53:4-6). (Beck) Paul taught the same truth in II Corinthians: "He hath made Him to be sin, that we might be made the righteousness of God in Him."

It is a clear teaching of God's Word that there is only one road to heaven; the Bible sets forth a salvation only through Christ's atoning blood. It was the claim of the world's Redeemer: "I am the Way, the Truth and the Life, no man Cometh unto the Father, except by Me" (John 14:6). Peter agreed with Paul, when he wrote the congregations of Asia Minor: " Knowing you were freed from the worthless life you inherited from your fathers, not by a payment of silver or gold, which perish, but by the precious blood of Christ, the Lamb without a fault or spot" (I Peter 1:18-19, Beck). That is the Gospel. There is no salvation by character.

V. The Domino Effects of the
Denial of Christ's Corporeal Resurrection
The Apostle Paul has clearly shown how the rejection of the doctrine of Christ's bodily resurrection effects a number of important Biblical truths. Paul declared: "If we preach that Christ rose from the dead, how can some of you say, the dead don't rise?" "If the dead don't rise, Christ didn't rise. And if Christ didn't rise, our preaching means nothing and your faith means nothing. And we stand there as men who lied about God, because we testified against God that He raised Christ, whom He didn't raise if it is true that the dead don't rise. You see, if the dead don't Christ didn't rise. But if Christ didn't rise, your faith can't help you, and you are still in your sins. Then those who have gone to their rest in Christ have perished. If Christ is our hope only for this life, we should be pitied more than any other people" (I Cor. 15:12-19, Beck).

The denial of Christ's corporeal resurrection according to Paul has the domino effect upon a number of Christian doctrines and beliefs. Those proponents of the new hermeneutic, who follow Rudolf Bultmann, reject the resurrection of Christ as an historic event that occurred in calendar time.[19] Liberal Biblical scholarship does not accept the events recorded as truly happening which occurred between Good Friday and the day of Christ's Ascension as described in Matthew 28, Mark 16, Luke 24, and John 20-21. A number of biographies of Christ have been written, which terminated their lives of Christ with His burial, for example, as Edgar Goodspeed does.

Paul informed the Corinthian congregation, some of whose members had questioned man's resurrection, that if Jesus Christ, whom the Roman crucified, but whom God raised from the dead, had actually remained in the grave, then the Christian faith was a fraud and a deception. If the grave means the termination of man's aspirations and hopes and there is no continuing of human personality beyond the grave, then the exercise of the Christian religion is futile. Then people might wisely adopt the philosophy of Epicureanism, one version of which held: "Eat, drink, and be merry for tomorrow we die." If there is no judgment and future accountability, which sinners must give before the judgment seat of God, then why endeavor to lead a virtuous life or make sacrifices for other members of the human race? Why spend millions, yes even billions to support religious institutions and all their humanitarian projects? Why send missionaries into all the world (as Christ commanded) to proclaim a message which has no relationship to reality whatsoever), if there is no resurrection of Christ? If the resurrection of Christ, which is referred to some two hundred times in the New Testament, and which was foretold in the Old Testament, is not a true fact, then every Biblical passage asserting this truth, is false and its writers are liars, deceivers and prevaricators. This means that all those Scriptural writers were wrong who so boldly averred that Christ had arisen from the dead. If they were in error on such an important and vital doctrine as the resurrection, what shall we say about the other teachings advocated by them?

By telling people that Christ arose from the dead, when actually He molded away in the grave, and teaching Biblical readers that because of Christ's resurrection they also can look forward to their own personal resurrection from the grave, when such will never be the case, the New Testament writers thereby have given their readers a false hope. Furthermore, another domino effect of the denial of Christ's resurrection would be, that Christ held forth as man's Savior and Redeemer from sin, is not true. Still another domino effect the denial of Jesus' corporeal resurrection will have is to remove the possibility that believers will again see their loved ones who have died as believers in Christ. Thus in I Corinthians 15 Paul has effectively shown the importance of Christ's resurrection for man's future happiness.[21] The denial of the factuality of our Lord's resurrection on the third day after His crucifixion, death and burial has a number of domino effects on an important range of vital Christian teachings.

VI. The Domino Effect of the
Denial of Christ's Ascension Into Heaven

Those Biblical interpreters who refuse to accept the corporeal resurrection and who claim that the deposit of Christ's lifeless body into the tomb of Joseph of Arimathea marked the end of the life of Christ, consequently cannot accept the accounts in the Gospels which give information about the forty post-resurrection days of Jesus.[22] The period between Easter day and the day of the Ascension is not considered as reporting true historical events and actual conversations between Christ and His disciples. The domino effect of denying Christ's bodily ascension necessitates not recognizing those comforting doctrines that flow from the Ascension. The Scriptures teach that Jesus ascended on high to prepare a place for His followers, also to intercede for His own as Advocate before the Father and to rule and govern the world in the interest of His church. These three activities, a source of great comfort to Christ's followers, cannot happen if Christ remained in the grave and never ascended into heaven. The Christian Church in its ecumenical creeds has confessed for centuries the belief that Christ will return from heaven to judge the dead and the living. But it would be a domino effect of the rejection of the ascension that there will not be a world judgment, as Christ taught in the Mount Olivet Discourse, Matthew 25:31-46 or as depicted by John in Revelation 20:11-15. In fact the rejections of Christ's resurrection, ascension, session at God's right hand and the coming for world judgment affect the all Biblical doctrines dealing of the Last Things (eschatology).

VII. The Domino Effects of the Denial of the
Personality and Deity of the Holy Spirit

Those who refuse to recognize the separate personality of the Three Persons of the Godhead are logically forced to deny or explain away the clear assertions of the Bible about the Holy Spirit.[23] The distinction between the Three Persons is evident from a considerable number of Biblical passages.[24] Thus the author of Hebrews, in speaking about Christ asserted: "Christ, who through the eternal Spirit offered Himself without spot to God, purge your conscience from dead works to serve the living God" (Heb. 9:14). A clear distinction is made between the Three Persons of the Godhead. In His Farewell Discourse, Jesus told the disciples on the way to the garden of Gethsemane: "I've told you this while I'm still with you. But the Comforter, the Holy Spirit, whom the Father will send in My name, will teach you everything and remind you of everything 1 told you" (John 14:25-26, Beck). In Psalm 139:7-10 the psalmist clearly sets forth the truth that there is no place on the universe where the Holy Spirit cannot be found.

Those who reject the existence of the personality and the deity of the Third Person of the Trinity logically cannot teach, as the Bible does, that the Holy Spirit, like the Father and the Son, was involved in the creation of the world, for Psalm 33:6 asserts: "The Lord made the heavens by His Word, and all the stars by the Breath (Spirit, Ruach, in Hebrew) of His mouth."

The refusal to accept the distinct personality of the Holy Spirit, as separate from the Father and the Son, has the domino effects of making impossible the conversion of the sinner, dead in trespasses and sins, by the Holy Ghost. St. Paul wrote by inspiration: "No man can call Jesus Lord, except by the Holy Ghost" (I Cor. 12:3). In baptism according to the teaching of God's Son the Holy Spirit is active; for "except a man be born of water and the Spirit, he cannot enter into the kingdom of God." The Holy Spirit brings about the acceptance of the truths of the Bible.

The denial of the existence of the Holy Spirit as one of the Three Persons in the Godhead has the domino effect of not making it possible to recognize the part played by the Holy Spirit in conversion and regeneration. "But a natural man doesn't welcome the things of God's Spirit. He thinks they are foolish and can't understand them, because you must have the Spirit to see their real value. If you have the Spirit, you can find out the real value of everything, but nobody can know your real value" (I Cor. 2:14-15, Beck).

The rejection of the separate personality of the Holy Spirit has the domino effect of rejecting both the work of sanctification in the narrower and in the wider sense. The important part played by the Holy Spirit was stated by Paul like this: "But you have been washed, you've been made holy and righteous by the name of the Lord Jesus Christ and by the Spirit of our God" (I Cor. 6:11, Beck). That person who has been justified, sanctified by the Holy Spirit, also will find that it is through the activity of the Holy Spirit that he is kept in hope (Rom. 15:13).

Those Biblical interpreters who are Unitarian in their approach to the doctrine of God or those who adhere to the ancient heresy of modalism cannot do justice to and adequately understand many Biblical doctrines in which the Holy Spirit is involved. The Old Testament Scriptures are described by Paul in the Greek text as being "theopneustos" i.e. "God-spirited." Jesus promised His disciples the Holy Spirit, Who would bring back all things to their remembrance when they proclaimed Christ and when they wrote the Word down.

VIII. The Domino Effects Involved in the Rejection of the Bible as God's Inerrant and Infallible Word

Theological modernism, neo-orthodoxy, both of which have invaded and infiltrated Protestantism, Roman Catholicism and Lutheranism, have attacked the foundation and very heart of God's revelation and which constitutes the very source of Christian doctrines and ethical directives.[25] By resorting to the use of the historical-critical method the contents of the Bible present day scholars are emphasizing the fact that the Bible has a divine as well as a human element. With this no sound scholar would quarrel.[26] But an inordinate emphasis has been placed on the humanity of the Bible as opposed to its divinity. It is a common place stance in higher critical circles to argue that to be human, is to err (*Errare est humanum*). Since the Bible was penned by human writers, it is argued that it is logical to find errors and mistakes in it. Critical scholarship seems to delight in belittling the Bible by concentration on its alleged errors, inaccuracies and use of confusing sources.

It is the contention of Biblical scholars, wholeheartedly committed to the historical-critical method that the Bible is no exception when compared with other human books, that like other books the Scriptures contain errors, mistakes, inaccuracies and contradictions.[28] Thus it becomes necessary when dealing with the sixty-six canonical books to distinguish within them between what is truly God's Word and what is the fallible word of man. Those portions of the Bible classified as "the word of man" are therefore, subject to evaluation and where man's conclusions do not agree with the assertions of the Bible, the latter may be rejected or changed, which ever suits the spirit of the times. If the Bible is in conflict with either the presuppositions or conclusions of such sciences as evolution, geology, astronomy, prehistoric archaeology, ethnography, linguistics, history, paleontology, physics, biology, genetics, archaeology (especially Near Eastern) or any other science developed by man, (even though the sciences are constantly changing their views), then God's Word is rejected or reinterpreted. When non-Christian psychologists and psychiatrists disagree with the declarations of the Bible, it is argued that the latter need not be followed or accepted. When certain sociologists question the teachings of the Bible on the family, divorce, sex, the relationship of the church to society, the conclusions of unbelieving sociologists are to be preferred. The economics of Marx and of communistic economists are chosen over against Biblical teachings which deal with the same areas of economic concern.

Only those teachings which do not come under the jurisdiction and purview of philosophy and humanistic ethics, as well as the whole range of the sciences just enumerated and which do not conflict with theories, teachings and views of scholars, may be accepted and used. Otherwise, there is much in the Bible which supposedly is outmoded, dated, and useless. However, when Biblical critics proceed with such an hermeneutical approach, it has a serious domino effect on many Biblical doctrines and ethical teachings. To reject, reinterpret or explain a passage, paragraph or chapter or book in a manner not intended by the text, violates the instruction of the Word of God itself. Christ gave His disciples the command that they were to teach man everything which He had told them Matt. 28:20). Paul in the last chapter of his great theological letter admonished the Roman congregation: "I urge you, fellow Christians, to watch those who cause disagreements and make people fall by going against the teaching you have learned. Turn away from them. Such men are not serving Christ, our Lord, but their own bellies and by their fine and flattering talk are deceiving innocent people" (16:15). John toward the very end of the Book of Revelation admonished the recipients: "I warn everyone who hears what the prophecy of this book tells him: If you add anything to this, God will add to you the plagues written in this book. And if you take away any words in the book of this prophecy, God will take away your share in the tree of life and in the holy city that are   described in the book" (22:18-19, Beck).

IX. Domino Effects of the Denial of the Bible In the Area of Ethical Concerns

God has given clear directives concerning the use of sex by men and women. God endowed human beings with sex so that they might propagate the human race and also enjoy sex as a part of conjugal bliss. The use of sex by the unmarried, outside of wedlock is prohibited.[29] Both the Old Testament and New Testament denounce the illegitimate employment of sex as either adultery or fornication. One of the commandments of the Decalogue states: "You shall not commit adultery." Adultery at one time was severely punished. Abnormal forms of sexual behavior were warned against. Bestiality and incest were forbidden in the strongest terms.

Modern critical Biblical scholarship has rejected the Biblical teaching on sex's proper use and had advocated sexual freedom.[30] The Decalogue has been described as social laws adopted and conceived by the Hebrews, and although those commandments which belong to the moral code are repeated in the New Testament, liberal theologians among Jews, Roman Catholics, Protestants and Lutherans have relegated all Biblical sexual commands to the outmoded past and now advocate free love. Modern situation ethics has repudiated and replaced the teachings on sex as given by God in both testaments. The Word of God for many modern Christians no longer furnishes the guidelines for ethical conduct. By claiming that the Bible in its entirety is not the Word of God and by arguing that Paul's ethical directives were conditioned by first-century culture and sociological views, Roman Catholic, Protestant, and Lutheran scholars, pastors and lay people have accepted God-dishonoring views and practices, as advocated by humanists and naturalists relative to sex and marriage. While the New Testament prohibits divorce (except for adultery and desertion), divorce has become generally acceptable among church people, for reasons the Word of God does not recognize. More and more Christians are securing divorces; in fact, the clergy is becoming guilty of violating the Biblical teaching on divorce and thereby setting a bad example for the members of their flocks and for the world at large.

Today Christian theologians, yea, even entire denominations are condoning homosexuality and lesbianism.[31] In the first chapter of Romans Paul has spoken out in the strongest possible terms against unnatural sex practices. Paul claims to be an apostle of Jesus Christ, who received his teachings by revelation from Jesus Christ. In warning the Roman congregation. about the perversions of the Gentile world, he wrote: "God in heaven shows He is angry at all the ungodliness and wickedness of people who by their wickedness hold back the truth" (1:18, Beck). Forms of wickedness listed and warned against are given in chapter 1:24-28: "And so God, letting them follow the lusts of their hearts, gave them up to live immorally and dishonor their bodies because they traded the true God for a lie, worshipped and served what was created instead of the Creator, who is blessed forever — Amen! That is why God gave them to shameful lusts. Women have changed their natural way to an unnatural way. And men likewise have given up the natural relation with a woman and burnt lust for one another, men doing the shameful act with men

1725

and for their error getting punished in themselves as they must" (Beck).

To be a lesbian or a homosexual according to Paul is to be subject to God's wrath, unless these sinners change their lifestyle and repent of such sins. Unless repentance for these sins takes place and these sexual practices abandoned, such individuals are not in a state of grace. In his letter to Corinth Paul wrote: "Don't be mistaken about this: nobody who lives in sexual sin or worships idols, no adulterers or men who sin sexually with other men, who steal, are greedy, get drunk, slander, rob will have a share in God's kingdom" (I Cor. 6:8-10, Beck).

A wrong view about Paul's apostleship, as a spokesman for Christ, as the utterer of God's will, has the domino effect of advocating ethical teachings that are diametrically opposed to Clod's teachings.

Footnotes

1. Webster's *New World Dictionary of the American Language* (Cleveland and New York: The World Publishing Company, 1964), p. 433.
2. **Ibid.**
3. **Ibid.**
4. **Ibid.**
5. Cf. C. Eckhardt, *Homiltetische Realexikon nebst Index Rer um* (St. Louis: Success Printing Company, 1909), I, pp. 134-148.
6. **Ibid.**
7. John George Walch, *Dr. Martin Luther's Sammtliche Werke* (St. Louis: Concordia Publishing House, no date), X, 176f.
8. *Augsburg Confession*, Article I, *Concordia Triglotta* (St. Louis: Concordia Publishing House, 1921), p. 43.
9. John Theodore Mueller, *Christian Dogmatics* (St. Louis: Concordia Publishing House, 1955), pp. 150-153.
10. Francis Pieper, *Christian Dogmatics* (St. Louis: Concordia Publishing House, 1950), I, pp. 406. Pieper wrote "Scripture established an indissoluble nexus between the doctrine of the Trinity and soteriology (Rom. 16:25f.)."
11. **Ibid.**, pp. 406-427.
12. Th. Engelder, *Popular Symbolics* (St. Louis: Concordia Publishing House, 1934), pp. 394, 397, 428.
13. Henry Eyster Jacobs, *A Summary of the Christian Faith* (Philadelphia: General Council Publication House, 1905), p. 129.
14. James Moffatt, *The Bible - A New Translation* (New York: Harper Brothers, Publishers, 1935), N.T., p. 1. Here Moffatt translates: "And Jacob the father of Joseph (to whom the Virgin Mary was betrothed) the father of Jesus, who is called the Christ." This is the view of Joseph Klausner, *Jesus of Nazareth, His Life, Times and Teaching* (New York: The Macmillan Company, 1925), p. 232, where Klausner states that Joseph was the real father of Jesus.
15. Vernon Grounds, "Virgin Birth," Merrill C. Tenney, *The Zondervan Pictorial Bible Dictionary* (Grand Rapids; Zondervan Publishing House, 1963), pp. 882.883.
16. Millar Burrows, *Jesus in the First Three Gospels* (Nashville: Abingdon 1977). p. 24; Edward E. Hindson, *Isaiah's Immanuel* (Nutley, N. S. Presbyterian and Reformed Publishing Company, 1978), 100 pp.
17. Cf. C. L. Milton, "Atonement," *The Interpreter's Bible Dictionary of the Bible,*

George A. Buttrick, editor (Nashville and New York: Abingdon, 1962), I, 312.

18. A G. Hebert, "Atone, atonement," Alan Richardson, *A Theological Word Book of the Bible* (New York, The Macmillan Company, 1951), p. 26a.

19. Rudolf Bultmann, *Theology of the New Testament*. Translated by Kendrock Grobel (New York: Charles Scribner's Sons, 1951), 1, p. 305. Burrows, **op. cit.**, p. 278.

20. Edgar Johnson Goodspeed, *A Life of Jesus New York*: Harper & Sons, 1950) p. 226.

21. Charles R. Erdman, *The First Epistle of Paul to the Corinthians* (Philadelphia: Westminster Press, 1928), pp. 157-158.

22. Charles M. Laymon, *Christ in the New Testament* (New York and Nashville: Abingdon Press, 1958), p. 126.

23. Th. Engelder, W. Arndt, Th. Graebner and F. E. Mayer, *Popular Symbolics* (St. Louis Concordia Publishing House, 1934), pp. 335-36.

24. Cf. George Johnstone, "Spirit," in Richardson, **op. cit.**, pp. 233-246, in which Johnstone never refers to the Holy Spirit as a separate person of the Godhead.

25. Claus Westermann, *Our Controversial Bible* (Minneapolis: Augsburg Publishing House, 1969), 139 pp.

26. Cf. Gerhard Ebeling, "The Significance of the Historical Method for Church and Theology," in Gerhard Ebeling, *Word and Faith* (Philadelphia Fortress Press, 1963), pp. 1742.

27. Cf. Paul Bretscher, *After the Purifying* (River Forest: The Lutheran Education Association, 1975), pp. 86-93.

28. Arthur C. Piepkorn. "What Does 'Inerrancy' Mean?," *Concordia Theological Monthly*, (September, 1965), pp. 577-593; John D. Frey, *Is the Bible Inerrant* (Published by the author John D. Frey. 4718 West 80th Street, Prairie Village, Kansas 66208, 1976), 43 pp.

29. Joseph Stump, *The Christian Faith* (New York: The Macmillan Company, 1930), p. 221.

30. Wayne Oats, "Sex," Carl F. Henry, Editor, Baker's *Dictionary of Christian Ethics* (Grand Rapids: Baker Book House, 1973), p. 619.

31. David A. Noebel, *The Homosexual Revolution* (P.O. Box 45200, Tulsa, Oklahoma, 1979), 191 pp. Also cf. the articles by E. L. Hebden Taylor, "Should Homosexuality Be Legalized and Discrimination against Homosexuals Be Outlawed?" (*Christian News,* June 30,1990), p. 7.

Questions

1. What is the "Domino Effect?"____
2. Who has vehemently rejected the doctrine of the Trinity? ____
3. The use of the historical-critical method has led to ____.
4. What is the vicarious atonement?____
5. There is only one ____ to heaven.
6. What is Epicureanism? ____
7. Modernism and Neo-orthodoxy have invaded ____.
8. The use of sex by the unmarried is ____.
9. Modern situation ethics has ____.
10. Who is condoning homosexuality and lesbianism today? ____

The Removal of Satan or the Devil from the Old Testament by Modern Lutheran Theologians

Christian News, July 17, 1978

In a number of previous issues of *Christian News, Affirm, The Spring-fielder* and *Concordia Theological Quarterly* it has been pointed how that there are significant differences for Christian theology and religion that result from the use of the historical-critical method (HCM) as compared with the employment of the historical-grammatical method (HGM). The devastating effects of the HCM on theology have been shown in previous issues of *Lutheran News* at the Dallas Convention of the Lutheran Church-Missouri Synod (LCMS), held in July, 1977, a resolution was passed rejecting the HCM as a valid interpretative methodology for the understanding of the Bible. The HCM is not consonant with principles of interpretation employed by Luther, the Lutheran Confessions and by the theologians, teachers and pastors of the LCMS since 1847, except in the case of those in the LCMS who were influenced by modern negative higher critical views.

One of the results of the application of the HCM to theology has been the denial of the existence of the Devil or Satan in the Old Testament before the Persian period of Biblical history (539-331 B.C.). The Lutheran Confessions associate Satan with the very beginning of human history as a powerful spirit, who as a personality had existence. Article XIX of *The Augsburg Confession* states: "Nevertheless, the cause of sin is the will of the devil and of men turning away from God, as Christ said about the devil" (John 8:44), "When he lies he speaks according to his own nature" (Tappert, *The Book of Concord*, p. 226). The article on "Original Sin" of *The Formula of Concord* asserts: "Hence, they say, we must preserve the distinction between the nature and essence of fallen man (That is, between his body and soul, which are God's handiwork and creatures in us even after the Fall) and original sin" (which is a work of the devil by which man's nature has become corrupted). (Tappert, p. 509). Again in the *Solid Declaration of the Formula of Concord* it is declared:

> The source and cause of evil is not God's foreknowledge (since God neither creates nor works evil, nor does he help it along and promote it), but rather the wicked and perverse will of the devil and of an, as it is written, "Israel, thou has plunged thyself into misfortune, but in me alone is thy salvation" (Hos. 13:9). Likewise, "thou are not a God who delights in wickedness" (Ps. 5:4). (Tappert, p. 617).

In a number of places the Lutheran Confessions quote the New Testament statement that "the devil was a liar and a murderer from the beginning."

Genesis 3 is the first place in Holy Writ where the personality of Satan manifests itself by the use of the serpent through whom he spoke and tempted Eve. Luther believed in the literal accuracy and the truthfulness of the Genesis account and was convinced that in the garden of Eden the real Devil spoke to Eve through a real serpent. He did not believe that Genesis 3 was to be understood poetically or symbolically. For Luther there was no poetic personification or primitive myth or folklore to be found in Genesis 3. His understanding of this crucial chapter was stated in a sermon of 1523 on Genesis 3:1-6. Here is the Reformer's interpretation as given by Plass, *What Luther Says* (St. Louis: Concordia, 1959), I, p. 393.

The first thing Moses here describes is how the serpent spoke with the woman. We cannot escape that fact. We must, as I constantly say, allow Scripture to retain the simple, plain meaning supplied by the words and must provide no comments. For it does not behoove us to explain God's Word as we please. We must not direct it but must allow ourselves to be directed by it and accord it the honor of being put down better than we can express it. We must, therefore, let it stand that what the woman saw with her eyes was a real, natural serpent....But the devil dwelt in it, because Moses says that it talked with her. For speaking is not an endowment of any animal, but only a man. Thus Moses makes it clear enough for our understanding that the devil in the serpent spoke through its tongue. And this should not surprise anybody, for the devil is a powerful spirit. God has not forbidden him to deal with physical things. We still see that he is the lord and prince of the world and speaks not only through animals but also through human beings, nowadays for the greater part through the latter (Weimar edition, 24, 82f.)

Luther, however, found in Genesis 3:15, in the protevangelium, an announcement of God's declaring that from the woman, whom Satan had deceived, there would come a Descendant who would crush the Devil's head (Weimar, 42, 144). Historical Lutheran theology has taught that the fall of the Devil and of the evil angels occurred between the end of the sixth day of creation and the time of the temptation in Genesis 3.

The Lutheran Cyclopedia, in both the 1954 and 1975 editions states: "Satan himself, Eph. 2:2, an opponent of the kingdom of God. He is the tempter of the faithful, 1 Pet. 5: 8ff., **who led Eve into sin** and so became the originator and king of death, Heb. 2:14. Originally created good, evil spirits, through their own fault, fell, 2 Pet. 2:4, and are destined to a fearful sentence" (p. 209 of 1954 edition; p. 233 of 1975 edition), (emphasis supplied).

Modern Lutheran Theologians and Satan

In the last three decades certain Lutheran interpreters and theologians have been influenced by negative higher criticism and have removed the Devil or Satan from most of the Old Testament. Professor Hals of The Lutheran Seminary of the ALC at Columbus, Ohio in his article on "Satan and Evil Spirits" in *The Encyclopedia of the Lutheran Church* (Minneapolis: Augsburg Publishing House, 1965), III does not refer to the presence of Satan in Genesis 3. For Hals, Satan is not a fallen angel but an idea which he claims goes through development in the Old Testament. For Hals, Satan "was used to refer to a particular one of the divine creatures who fulfilled the function of a public prosecutor before the heavenly court." In Job 1,2 Satan is not a proper name nor is he a proper name in Zechariah 3:1. Professor James Kallas has written a book, entitled. *The Real Satan - From Biblical Times to the Present* (Minneapolis; Augsburg Publishing House, 1975). In discussing the role of Satan in the Old Testament, Kallas claims two words characterize the evidence in the entire Old Testament: "(1) Satan in the Old Testament is **insignificant**; and (2) Satan in the Old Testament is a **servant** of God, not an enemy but a servant" (p. 15). CF. also page 25 for the same assertion. Lutheran professor Richard S. Hanson, *The Serpent Was Wiser* (Minneapolis: Augsburg Publishing House, 1972), in chapter 2, "The Snake and I" rejects the traditional and historical Lutheran understanding of Genesis 3 as recording the real fall of Eve and Adam. On page 43 writes "But who is this creature, the serpent? The devil in disguise or the devil without disguise? **No, not the devil at all**" (Emphasis supplied), (p. 43). A few pages later in the same chapter Hanson asserts: "A more productive question with which to undermine our traditional notion of original sin is to ask (as we have) after the identity of the serpent. An early sect of gnostic Christians, the Ophites, revered the serpent as the one who showed man the **gnosis** that makes him like God, and they may have not have been the first and were not the only ones to see the wisest of all God' s creatures as a hero rather than a villain. What if the serpent actually spoke for God? Would this cause problems? Or would this throw light on the human situation?" (p. 47).

These views raise the serious question about the actuality and the Devil as a reality, as existing as a powerful living spirit. The idea of the Devil being associated with the snake according to Norman Habel, former St. Louis Seminary professor of the Old Testament, occurred in the period between the Testaments. In his controversial monograph. *The Form and Meaning of the Fall Narrative* (St. Louis: Concordia Seminary Print Shop, 1965), Habel writes:

> The snake of Genesis 3 is first associated with the devil (with whom Satan is later identified) in the intertestamental period. In Enoch 69:6 it is the angel Gadreel (apparently identified with one of the satans) who is said to have led Eve astray. The Wisdom of Solomon 2:24 states that, "It was through the devil's envy death entered the world." This passage suggests that the devil was the first murderer because he robbed Adam of "life." Moreover this designation of Satan as a "murderer from the beginning" is employed by John in juxtaposition with the epithet "father of lies" (John 8:44; Cf. Rom. 5:12). The accumulation of apocalyptic imagery in Rev. 12, 9, 20, used to describe the devil as Satan, as the chaos dragon, as the ancient serpent is derived from passages such as Isaiah 27:1 as well as Genesis 3 and thereby makes further points of identification which are not explicit in the Old Testament. The description of Satan as "the deceiver of the whole world" probably reflects the prevalent identification of Satan with the snake of Genesis 3. In general it seems that the identification of the snake with the devil, made first in the inter-testamental period, is reflected

in the New Testament and made explicit in subsequent generations of the Christian Church. This fact, however, does not demand that the ancient Israelite listener also made this identification; God spoke to him through the text of Genesis 3, not through the New Testament (p. 14).

Habel's position is in direct contradiction to the inspired New Testament scriptures. John writes: "The devil sinneth from the beginning" (1 John 3:8), and that he is the father of lies (John 8:44). Paul clearly teaches that it was the Devil or Satan who tempted Eve (2 Cor. 11:3).

Views similar to those views thus far advocated by Hals, Kallas, Hanson and Habel are also to be found in the recent book on Christian anthropology, *Our Cosmic Journey, Christian Anthropology in the Light of Current Trends in the Sciences, Philosophy and Theology* (Minneapolis: Augsburg Publishing House, 1977), pp. 176-183. The author of this book is Professor Hans Schwarz of The Lutheran Seminary of the ALC at Columbus, Ohio. According to Schwarz there is only one passage in the Old Testament where the word Satan (which means in Hebrew: the opponent or adversary) is a proper name, namely, 1 Chron. 21:1: "Satan stood up against Israel, and incited David to number Israel." However, earlier in 2 Samuel 24:1 it was said; "Again the anger of the Lord was kindled against Israel, and he incited David against them saying: 'Go number Israel and Judah.'" The difference between these two versions of the cause for David's census of Israel, is explained by Schwarz that originally God was depicted as the cause of both good and evil. But by the time of the Chronicler, however, it was felt that to blame God for evil and sin was not proper and so a cause outside of God and humanity had to be found and thus "Satan was selected and blamed." The ALC professor rejects the idea of Kluger that "the figure of Satan represents the result of a process of development within the divine personality itself" (p. 182). But avers Schwarz: "Not the divine personality underwent a developmental change, but the Israelite understanding of God was gradually clarified. This process is reflected in God's ongoing self-disclosure, culminating in Jesus Christ" (p. 182). Schwarz believes that Zoroaster, the founder of Zoroastrianism, had an influence on bringing about a change in the conception that became evident in Judaism in the Persian period (p. 184). Kallas, Habel, Hals and others credit the intertestamental period as being the time span during which the existence of the belief in the Devil was developed, as may be found in certain pseudepigraphical writings and it was from the intertestamental literature that early New Testament Christianity took over the notion of the existence and activity of Satan or the Devil.

If the concept of the Devil was a development of Israelite thinking, then the frequent New Testament teachings must be considered as setting forth teachings which are not a matter of divine revelation and also simultaneously one must assume that beliefs are advocated which are not true. Jude informs us that Michael, the Archangel, when contending about the body of Moses with the Devil did not dare to pronounce sentence for blasphemy, but said, "The Lord rebuke you." Was the Devil or Satan already there in the days of Moses? If the Evil One was not a reality before the intertestamental period, then the New Testament is misinforming Christians. There are many New Testament passages which are nonsensical, if the Devil or Satan did not exist before Genesis 3. (Heb. 2:14; 1 John 3:8; John 14:30.)

Questions
1. The 1977 Dallas convention of the Lutheran Church-Missouri Synod rejected ____.
2. The Lutheran Confessions associate Satan with ____.
3. What did Luther believe about Satan? ____
4. Who are some Lutheran professors who reject what the Bible teaches about Satan? ____
5. There are many New Testament passages that are nonsensical, if the Devil or Satan did not ____.

The Biblical Doctrine of the Angels
(An Essay to Commemorate
St. Michael and All Angels, Sept. 29)

Christian News, no date

In the liturgical calendar of a number of Christian denominations, September 29 is dedicated to St. Michael and All Angels. The historic Christian Church has together with Christ and the Apostles believed in the existence of angels, both good and bad. Both the Old Testament and New Testaments have many passages that describe the activities of angels as well as divulging facts about their nature and creation.[1] Major angels are mentioned by name, such as Michael (both in Daniel and Revelation) and Gabriel (Daniel and Luke) in connection with the events associated with the coming of Christ.

The Roman Catholic Church, the Eastern Orthodox Churches, the Anglican Church and the Lutheran Church in their church calendars list September 29 as the day the church members should recall Michael and all the angels.[2] Feasts in honor of angels developed particularly in the East. After the time of Constantine many churches were dedicated in honor of St. Michael the only archangel in Scripture (Daniel and Revelation).[3] In the Apocrypha other angels are mentioned by name, namely, Raphael[4] and Uriel.[5] September 29 was the date for the dedication in the fifth century of a small basilica on the Via Salaris, six miles from Rome, the first church in Italy in honor of St. Michael.[6]

The feast which commemorates this dedication eventually was regarded as honoring Michael, who then was considered as representing all angels. The observance gradually spread throughout the West. In A.D. 813 the Council of Mainz introduced it. The "warrior saint" became very popular in the West as is evidenced by the large number of churches which carry the archangel's name. In A.D. 1019 King Ethelred established the feast in England. The term "All Angels" is an Anglican addition made at the time of the Reformation. Since the calendar Reform of 1969 the Roman Catholic Church has also added Raphael and Uriel angels to be remembered (Cf. "Michaelmas," *Encyclopedia Americana*, 1987 edition, vol. 10,19).

The Existence of Angels Questioned

Although it is admitted by critical scholars that Christ and the Apostles believed in angels, with the coming of rationalism, the ego-theology and the higher critical method of Biblical interpretation, the existence of the angels, and especially the Devil and the evil angels, has been questioned, yes, even denied.[7]

The Source for the Doctrine of the Angels

The doctrine of the angels cannot be known from reason or from a study of nature, but can only be ascertained from the Holy Scriptures, where their existence is clearly taught.[8] Stump has set forth the traditional Lutheran position when he wrote: "They are actual beings, and not the mere personifications of the attributes of God or of the life forces of nature. They we not the departed spirits of human being."[9] Angels are being of a particular kind. Their very existence postulates evidence for the fact that they are creatures of God. Martin Reu claimed that when God called forth the universe out of nothing, that this includes also the host of spirits or angels which invisibly surround us. Thus he averred: "Their existence is no less real than that of the visible world in which we live. And it is stupid when Sadducees—ancient and modern—deny their existence, change them into souls of departed men, or let them be more poetical conceptions or personifications of natural powers of extraordinary interferences of God in the order of nature."[10] Critical scholars claim the angel and Satan concepts were borrowed from Zoroastrianism.[10a]

Misconceptions about Angels

According to Luke 1:19 angels are persons. Gabriel speaks in the first person; in I Peter 1:18 they are said to desire to look into the great teachings being divulged to human beings. Angels are not human beings in another existence. In Matthew 25:41 and Ephesians 6:12 there is a sharp distinction made between "men" and "angels." Unbelief already characterized New Testament times relative to angels as well as the Devil's existence. Since angels cannot be seen, rationalism and theological liberalism have consigned the belief in angels to the realm of myth and fantasy.[11] In his defense before the Sanhedrin Paul distinguished between the Pharisees who believed in spirits and the Sadducees "who maintained there is no resurrection, and neither angel, not spirit" (Acts 23:8). Ancient and modern Sadducees labelled the belief in angels, good and bad, as a superstition. When one approaches Holy Writ with the presupposition that the supernatural is impossible and that the Bible must satisfy the demands of reason, the doctrine of angels logically must be surrendered and repudiated. The Churches at the time of the Reformation, whether Roman Catholic, Lutheran, Calvinistic or Armenian, believed in angels. Luther by contrast, included in the petition, found at the conclusion of both the morning and evening prayers: "Let thy holy angels be with me that the wicked foe may have no power over me."[12] (*Small Catechism*) It is also in his *Large Catechism* Part III, 80;[13] *The Augsburg Confession*, article XIX speaks about angels as does the *Apology* of *The Augsburg Confession* in article XIX.[14] In our day, Christian Science rejects the reality of angels. Swedenborg claimed the angels were the spirits of good men. The Shakers erroneously ascribed sex to angels, despite the fact that Jesus taught that angels do not marry and therefore do not have offspring, one of the main purposes of God-endowed sex in human beings. The Roman Catholic Church prays to angels, a practice nowhere enjoined in Holy Writ. One of the tenets held by Spiritism is the supposed fact that there can be communication between beings now on earth and angels.[15]

The Creation of Angels

When God by his creative power brought the universe into existence among the created being were all angels, who surround us, even though they are not apparent to the human eye. Reu claimed that "The universal fear of this spiritual host, man's deep-rooted interest in the angelic beings, and above all, the fact that Scriptures treats the devil and his kingdom as a reality, the great enemy and principle opponent of God — all this is proof for the reality of this grim, fateful, unseen world."[16] Now it is true that the creation of MALAKIM or BENE ELOHIM is nowhere stated in the Old Testament, not even in Nehemiah 9:6 which states: "Thou art Yahweh, even thou, alone: thou hast heaven, the heaven of heavens, with all their hosts, the earth." In the New Testament only in one passage, viz., Colossians 1:16, where Paul by inspiration of the Holy Spirit wrote: "Since in Him was created everything you can see and cannot see in heaven and on earth thrones, Lords, rulers, or powers — everything was created by Him and for Him."[17] However, all Scripture presupposes their creation. Already in Genesis 1:26; 3:22; 11:7 the angels are associated with God; and when God is called Yahweh Sebaoth — not always but often this expression designates Lord of heavenly spiritual beings or hosts.[18]

Like the world and all living creatures the angels were created before man. Cf. Job 38:7 which states that "while the creation of the earth took place" the morning stars sang together and all the sons of God shouted for joy."[19] "The angels were not created before the original substance of the world, for only God existed before foundation of the world.

The French 19th century theologian and exegete Godet attempted to prove that angels exist. Thus he wrote: "We know of three kinds of being: plants, animals, and man. Our thought requires a fourth series. Among plants there exists only the species, for which reason we speak of specimens. Among the animals the species are essential, but the individual appears. The animals are governed by instinct. The individual lives but as if bound by the fetters of the species. In man the species is found because we speak of the human race. Instinct is found, but it is not dominant. Man bursts open the prison door of species and instinct, because he is a distinct person. Should there not be a found a fourth series of living beings to complete the system? In a mathematical proportion the fourth term can be ascertained when the three are known. May it not be that the angels must be the living beings that complete the system of creation?"[20]

Genesis 1:1 informs the Biblical reader that in the beginning God created the "heavens and the earths," an expression Leupold considered equal to the Greek "cosmos," the universe.[21] After Genesis 1:1, Genesis is concerned with the planet earth. At the end of the six-day creation, "all was very good" (Gen. 1 :31).

The Purpose of the Creation of the Angels

Why did God create the angels? It would be best to relate the act of the angel's creation to the certain fundamental attributes of God, His love and it might also be added that God created the angels that they might share His life and love.[22]

Biblical Terminology for Angels

The word "angel" means "messenger." According to Lindberg the word occurs in at least a threefold significance. According to this Swedish theologian it is "Used in the broadest sense the word angel may apply to the powers of nature and natural phenomena." Who maketh winds his messengers, flames of fire his ministers (Ps. 104.4). "In the broad sense it may apply to human beings, such as priests, prophets and pastors. In the narrow sense however, the word 'angel' has reference to those personal spirits who are specifically called angel."[23]

The Nature of Angels

Angels, though spirits, who possess no body, are like men persons and were created with self-consciousness and self-determination.[24] Because they are spirits (Hebrews 1:14) they are invisible, at least to the human eye. However, in the course of human history, they assumed materiality and were seen like human beings by men. Angels conversed with men. This was the case with angels appearing to Abraham and Lot (Gen. 18:19). The ascription of wings to angels is simply a poetic device. It is simply a figure of speech.[25]

The Angels are Not A Race

God created millions and millions of angels. Unlike men and Women, who are a race and have the ability to propagate, this is not the case with angels. Two people were originally created by God, Adam and Eve, the rest of mankind, past and present and future, are their offspring. However, in the case of the angels, the aggregate group was the direct creation of God. Jesus told His disciples that the angels neither marry nor are given in marriage (Matthew 22:30).

The Attributes of Angels

Since angels do not possess, like men and women, bodies, they are endowed with the attributes of individuality, immutability, illocality and agility.[26] Because the angels are simple beings, they are immutable and immortal. They cannot change or decay, so they are immutable and immortal.[27] They are not subject to the limits of space and are therefore illocal. But angels like God are not omnipresent. They are agile and can move with great speed. As creatures of God are not independent but are dependent on God. According to Matthew 24:36 they possess much knowledge and also great power (2 Kings 19:35). They are finite beings and do not have omniscience and the omnipotence of their Maker.[28]

The New Testament speaks about archangels (I Thess. 4:16; Jude 9), seraphim (Is. 6:2), cherubim (Gen. 3:24). In Colossians 1:16 and Romans 8:38, Ephesians 3:10 Paul refers to THRONOI, KYRIOTTEETES, ARCHAI, EXOUSIA, DYNAMEIS (usually rendered thrones, dominions, princedoms, powers)[28a] to indicate their varying office and endowments.

The author of the short article in Harper's Dictionary of the Bible (1973 edition) claims these designations in Colossians 1:16 refers to "fallen angels,"[29] which is not a correct explanation of that Pauline text! In the Book of Daniel we read of the archangel Michael who communicated revelations as well as interpretations to Daniel.

The Frequency of the Mention of Angels in Scripture

There are but few books of the Bible — such as Ruth, Nehemiah, Esther, the Epistles of John and James — that make no mention of angels at all.[30] With regard to the angels' existence and their nature, one finds the same development in Holy Writ as one discovers relative to other Biblical doctrines.[31] It is evident that the doctrine of the angels becomes more detailed and clearer in the later books of the Old Testament and is more full in the New Testament, relative to their significance and importance.[32] Angels appear more often and conspicuously in connection with the life of Jesus Christ, the promised Messiah of the Old Testament.[33]

Harmony of Teachings Concerning Angels in New Testament

There is harmony on the subject of angels between the teachings of Christ and the Apostles and those of Scripture generally. Many questions that can be raised about angels are not answered for us in the Bible. In the New Testament the Devil or Satan is mentioned with considerable frequency. Both good and evil angels are referred to as realities to be believed in and to be taken seriously and not summarily dismissed as modern unbelief has done and is doing at the present time.

The Original Status of God's Created Angels

The angels when they were created were holy and perfect. The statement, occurring six times that everything that God made was good and at the conclusion of the six-day creation, "behold everything was very good," also implies that there was only one class of angels, namely, the good ones. As to when they were created, Berkhof claimed: "The only safe statement seems to be that they were created before the seventh day."[34]

Beginning with Genesis 3 there appears the Tempter who according to the New Testament used the serpent to tempt Eve. Good and evil spirits exist side by side during most of Man's existence upon earth. Stump wrote as follows about the original status of the angels: "Endowed with freedom of the will as personal beings they were meant voluntarily to choose the service of God and to preserve in it. Their original perfections were to be developed and increased by the practice of the right."[35] Many of the angels employed their freedom to do God's will alone, thus fulfilling the purpose for which they had been created. Others, unfortunately, misused their freedom and acted contrary to God's will. Because of their rebellion led by Satan, the evil angels have been condemned and confirmed in this status.

The History of the Angels

The history of the angels, good and evil, may be divided into three periods: 1. The State of Innocence; 2. The State of Glory; 3. The State of Misery. Numbers 1 and 2 apply to the good angels; Number 1 and 3 to the evil angels.

The State of Innocence of the Good Angels

The State of Innocence is that state when all created angels enjoyed the same status, being sinless and living in harmony with their Creator. The State of Glory is that state to which those angels who did not rebel were assigned by God everlastingly to love and serve Him. The State of Misery was that state to which those angels were assigned and were confirmed in, who had rebelled against God's authority. Stump described the relationship of the two classes of angels as follows: "In the State of Innocence they were able to sin and able not to sin (posse peccare et posse no peccare). In the state of Glory the good angels are not able to sin (non posse peccare). In the State of Misery the bad angels are not able to sin (non posse non peccare) that is, they are not able to do otherwise but sin."[36]

The History of the Good Angels

In their original state all angels had the ability and right to choose either good or evil. No angel needs to do anything contrary to the will of God. All were perfect, there was no moral defect in them.[37] On the basis of John 8:44 it might be asserted that the first sin was self-originated. Why Satan, who had no evil principle from without to tempt him, revolted against God is a mystery. While we live on this earth the question why the Devil sinned will always be a mystery. Still it is clear from Holy Writ that the Devil or Satan did fall and host of angels followed in his footsteps. How many fell and what the proportion of the original angelic hoot was, is not revealed in God's Word.

The State of Glory of the Good Angels

In the State of Glory the good angels have been advanced to a position, where they can never rebel or fall away from God.[38] (Cf. Matthew 18:10). They have been advanced to a closer relationship with God as compared when they first were created by the Almighty. There has been a law which God has established in connection with personality, and which therefore holds in the angelic as well as human world, according to which good or evil become eventually fixed. So according to this principle the good angels were confirmed in their bliss so that they can no more sin. They are enabled to choose, but never again will they chose evil.[39]

The Occupation of the Good Angels

The functions of the good angels are to praise and glorify God, to exercise their will in carrying out His commandments, and especially to serve the believers.[40] All of God's creatures should praise and glorify their Creator and this also holds true of the good angels. Thus in Psalm 103:20 we read: "Bless the Lord, ye his angels, that excel in strength, that do His commandments, hearkening unto the voice of His Word." Cf. also Psalm

148:2; Isaiah 6:3; Luke 2:13.

Hove wrote about this aspect of the angels' functions as follows: "When the angels praise God, they do not do this because they are compelled to do it. But they do this because they, who see God's face, see Him as He is, rejoice in Him, love Him, admire Him, feel pleasure in His presence. God is the chief source of their bliss, and they praise Him spontaneously, as, when a person sees a beautiful sight or is spontaneously impelled to expressed his joy. The praising of God by the angels is the natural expression of the joy that is felt."[41]

The good angels also serve God. Psalm 103:21 says: "Bless ye the Lord all ye His hosts, ye ministers of His, that do his pleasure." The angels serve God as messengers and execute his commandment! In the world they help promote the establishment and growth of the Kingdom of God. Throughout the history in God's kingdom, angels are met from time to time, especially in great Biblical epochs.[42]

The mighty wonders of creation moved the angels to glorify God, as it is stated in the first Yahweh speech in the Book of Job (ch. 38:7). Angels were placed by Yahweh Elohim at the entrance of Eden to prevent Adam and Eve from having access to the tree of life after their fall (Gen. 3:24). Angels, as has already been mentioned, appear in the lives of the Patriarchs. At Mt. Sinai in the establishment of the Old Covenant God made use of the angels as His servants (Acts 7:53; Gal. 3:19; Deut. 33:2).

In the Old Testament in connection with the lives of the prophets angels are met with frequently. An angel announced the birth of John the Baptist and the conception and birth of Jesus Christ. A great multitude of the heavenly host sang the night Christ was born. At the time of Christ's temptation angel appealed to strengthen Him as also happened some time later in the Garden of Gethsemane. At the Savior's resurrection they were present; first rolling the stone away and then as announcers to the women that He was risen and also informing them to tell the disciples that they should meet the risen Lord in Galilee. As He left this earth on the day of the ascension, two angels were present, telling the disciples that Christ would return in the same manner as He had left the earth. Finally, on the last day the angels would accompany the Son of Man when He returns to judge the world. The angels will awaken the dead, gather all men, living and dead, before the judgment, seat and accompany the righteous into the Kingdom of Glory (Matt. 13:41,49; 16:27; 24:31; 25:31; Mark 8:38; 2 Thess. 1:7; I Thess. 4:16,17).

The angels also follow the growth and history of God's Kingdom with interest and sympathy.[43] They rejoice over every sinner who repents (Luke 15:10). They are also present at the assemblies of believers (I Cor. 11:10; I Timothy 5:21). The angels are also concerned about the revelations which God gives for man's salvation (Phil. 3:10; I Pet. 1:12). According to Daniel 10:13, 2 Kings 19:35; Genesis 24:1 the good spirits help to promote whatever is good in the world, to promote truth and righteousness in the state, the Church and the home.

The angels also serve individual believers, they accompany the followers of Christ, help them and preserve them from harm. They are like an invisible army fighting for Christians against the spiritual hosts of evil. From the cradle to the grave angels minister to Christ's followers. They watch over children (Matt. 18:10). They protect and keep the children of God. Psalm 34:7 assures us: "The angel of the Lord encamped round about them that fear him, and delivereth them." 1 Samuel 91:11,12 has this comforting promise: "For He shall give His angels charge over thee to keep thee in all thy ways. They shall bear thee up in their hands, lest thou dash thy foot against a stone." Here are some Biblical examples how angels served God's followers and often delivered them: Lot is saved from Sodom (Gen. 19); Daniel's three companions are protected in the fiery furnace (Dan. 3:25-28); Joseph together with Mary and Jesus were saved from the murderous designs of Herod the Great (Matt. 2:13,19); the apostles were freed from prison (Acts. 5:19); Peter was delivered by an angel (Acts 12:7).

Just as the angels guard and protect Christians during their lifetimes, so they are with them in death; Lazarus was carried into Abraham's bosom by angels (Luke).

Angels Are Not to Be Worshipped
The good angels are not to be worshipped (Rev. 19:10), because they are all creatures as human beings are themselves.[44] Stump claimed that the distinction made by the Roman and Greek churches between invoking the aid of angels and worshipping them is untenable, since such invocations assumes the possession of attributes which belong to God alone.[45]

The History of the Evil Angels
The Nature of the First Sin
What the original sin was in the angel-world cannot be positively determined. The most common assumption is that it was pride. This conclusion is based upon what St. Paul wrote in I Timothy 3:6; where it is stated "that a bishop should not be a 'novice' (one lately converted), lest being lifted up with pride, he fall into the condemnation of the devil." Hove in commenting on the meaning of this verse wrote: "The condemnation of the devil is here probably the judgment, the punishment incurred by the devil when he sinned, and was cast down to hell. The condemnation of the devil is accordingly a punishment for being puffed up, for being lifted up with pride. Pride is, according to this interpretation, the original sin."[46]

Satan Has Become the Leader of Other Bad Angels
The fall of the Devil and the evil angels must have occurred before Genesis 3. Exactly when the fall of Satan occurred has not been revealed to mankind in the Bible. Relative to the evil angels, a passage in Jude informs Biblical readers that "the angels which kept not their first estate, He hath reserved in chains that are everlasting, in darkness, for the great day of judgment (Jude 6)." The number of those who fell was great. Possibly, when Satan fell, he persuaded others to follow him.

The Bible teaches that there is a real kingdom of evil. The Devil is the prince of darkness. In Ephesians 6:12 Paul warns the readers of the congregations of Asia Minor: "Put on the complete armor of God, so as to stand against all the stratagems of the devil. For ours is not a conflict with mere flesh and blood, but with the despotisms, the empires, the forces that control and govern this dark world — the spiritual hosts of evil arrayed against us in the heavenly warfare."[47]

The Devil, the Great Enemy of God and Man

Before discussing the activity and lot of the evil angels, this presentation will first discuss the Biblical teaching about man's great archenemy. Satan is not an evil principle but a person, a fact which is clear from many passages in both Testaments, but especially from the New.[48] On the basis of a number of New Testament passages the Christian Church has understood the temptation by the Serpent in Genesis 3, as actually being Satan who employed the serpent as the means of temptation.[49] He suggested to Eve that God was trying to withhold from her and Adam the state of being God. The Devil called God a liar. Jesus said that the Devil is a liar and a murderer from the beginning.

Passages that Allegedly Tell of Satan's Fall

The Scofield Research Bible and many who follow its interpretations, list two passages which supposedly tell how Satan fell from his original state and how he became guilty of rebellion against God, namely, Isaiah 14:12-20 and Ezekiel 28:11-19.[50] An examination of these two passages will reveal that Satan is not mentioned in either of them. The New Testament nowhere refers to these passages as in anyway referring to Satan or the Devil. Isaiah and Ezekiel pericopes state that two heathen kings will be punished because of their pride and sins. These two Scriptural set of verses do not speak of the manner of Satan's fall.[51] Isaiah 14:8ff describes the fact that the king of Babylon who exalted himself over Yahweh would be received in Sheol and Ezekiel 28:11-19 describes the punishment and the reason the king of Tyre will be punished.[52] Unfortunately, Isaiah 14:12 has been translated in the King James or Authorized version as follows: "How you have fallen from heaven Lucifer, son of the morning, how art thou cut down to the ground, which didst weaken the nations!" The word "Lucifer" which has come to be employed as a term for the Devil or Satan is a mistranslation of the Hebrew "helal," which should be rendered as "day star," or "son of the morning," a designation for the goddess Ishtar, worshipped by the Babylonians as Slotki remarked: "Ishtar was worshipped by the Babylonians and Nebuchadnezzar's days of power and glory are well represented by their comparison with the shining star."[53] Scofield, Unger, Hiebert and many fundamentalists, claim the two passages in the major prophets must refer also to someone much higher.[54] Finding Satan referred to in Isaiah is not exegesis but eisegesis, that is reading an idea which is not found in the text. The same judgment must be made about Ezekiel 28:11-19, where the reader will find only a "Lamentation for the King of Tyree."[55] Again in this passage Satan is not mentioned or is this pericope ever referred to in the New Testament.

The Hebrew word "satan" means "opponent" or "adversary." But most of the times when used with the article it is a proper noun.[56] There are critical scholars who claim that Satan is not a bad angel or spirit but rather is a helper of God. Critical scholarship claims that Satan appears only a few times in the Old Testament and that the doctrine of the Devil developed in the Intertestamental period of Hebrew history.[57]

The Doctrine of the Satan or Devil in Both Testaments

The doctrine of the Devil is found in its fullest form in the New Testament.[58] Genesis 3 (on the authority of the N.T.), Job 1-2, where Satan appears as Job's adversary and accuser, 1 Chronicles 21:1, where Satan instigates David to sin, Zechariah 3:1-2 show that he is a personality. Hiebert is correct when he wrote: "The teaching concerning evil and a personal devil finds its full presentation only in the N.T."[59] In the N.T. the term Satan, transliterated from the Hebrew, always designates the personal Satan (But cf. Matt. 16:23; Mark 8:13).

In the New Testament mankind's malignant foe appears under other names and descriptive titles. He is frequently called the "devil" meaning "slanderer" (Matt. 4:1; Luke 4:2; John 8:44; Eph. 6:11; Rev. 12:12). In the Authorized version "devil" should properly have been rendered "demons." Other titles descriptive designations used of the Devil are "Abaddon," or "Appollyon," (Rev. 9:11), "Accuser of the brethren" (Rev. 12:10), "Adversary," "antidikos" in Greek (1 Pet. 5:8) , "Beelzebub," (Matt. 12:24), "Belial," (II Cor. 6:15). "The deceiver of the whole world" (Rev. 12:9)," "the great dragon," (Rev. 12:9); "the evil one" (Matt. 13,19,38; I John 2:13; 5:19) "the father of lies;" (John 8:44); "the god of this world" (II Cor. 4:4); "a murderer" (John 8:44); "the old serpent" (Rev. 12:9); "the prince of this world" (John 12:31; 14:31; 14:30); "the prince of the power of the air" (Eph. 2:2; "the tempter" (Matt. 4:5; I Thess. 3:5).[60]

The person who takes the New Testament seriously cannot ignore the Devil, just as Christ had to battle him and ultimately defeated him by His death and resurrection. It is for this reason that Christians are advised to put on the whole armor of God so that they may be victorious over Satan. The Devil sometimes appears an as angel of light to delude people (II Cor. 11:14); at other times he comes "as a roaring lion seeking whom he may devour (I Pet. 5:8)." Christians must be constantly vigilant of his presence and attacks. The Devil also attacks the Church and its Means of Grace. Sometimes it appears that he threatens the very existence of the Church. However, Christ has promised his followers that the Devil will not prevail against her (Matt. 16:18).[61]

The History of the Evil Angels

It is evident from Scripture that angels originally created good, like Satan was, fell and as a result they lost their heavenly glory and their endowment of grace was lost forever. Just like the good angels have distinctive attributes, so the evil spirits, called often "demons" in the New Testament passages[62] have their evil attributes heightened. Although their knowledge is still great, the keeness of their intellects have deteriorated because of their apostasy and their reasoning became defective. Thus the Devil was thwarted in his attempts to cause Jesus to sin (Matt. 4:1-12), and he appears to have entertained the notion that he could thwart God's plan by crucifying Christ (I Cor. 2:7,8). The Devil is not stupid, an idea propounded in the Middle Ages, nor is he easily outwitted. No, the Devil is resourceful and still possessed of great intelligence, cunning, and resourcefulness (II Cor. 11:3,14) Peter warns Christians in his first epistle: "Be circumspect, and be on the alert. Your enemy, the Devil, is going about like a roaring lion to see whom he can devour. Withstand him, firm in your faith" (5:8).

The power of evil angels is great but God has placed a boundary beyond which they may not overstep. They desire man's destruction as may be seen from the Book of Job, chapters 1-2, where Satan afflicted Job and his family with woes, tragedies, death and sickness. Yet the Devil and his evil angels cannot hurt the souls of believers.

The State of Misery of the Evil Angels

Because of the rebellion of the evil angels came under the wrath of God and His condemnation (2 Peter 2:4) and they will receive to the utmost measure of punishment. They will be punished eternally on Judgment Day. The evil angels cannot be saved, unlike evil men who are able to repent and be saved even in the eleventh hour of their lives. The Son of Man took on Himself the nature of man but not of angels (Heb. 2:16). Stump opinioned as follows as to why there can be no Salvation for the evil angels: "Since God is a God of infinite love, it is a fair assumption that He would have sought to save some of the fallen angels if they had been savable. There must have been something in their apostasy from God radically different from the sin of man."[63]

The evil angel's entire disposition toward their creator is absolute and persistent hostility. They work together in the kingdom of darkness to frustrate God's gracious promises toward fallen man (Matt. 13:19: II Cor. 4:4). The malignant design of the evil angels finds its chief representation in their leader, the Devil.

The Activity of the Evil Angels

Just as the good angels, so the evil angels are active in the world. However, the objective of their activity in the world is to harm, to corrupt, to destroy, wherever they can, in the Church, in the state, and in the private lives of individuals. The Scriptures calls the evil angels "the spiritual hosts of wickedness." Satan is the prince of these evil powers. This presupposes a bond or union between the Devil and the evil angels. How can there be a union between them? How can there be cooperation between them? The bond of union between them is their hatred of God. The power of their sinister beings is very great. The powers of these world rulers is so great because of men's sins.

The evil angels above all endeavor to destroy the Church, by either corrupting it or even destroying it. The enemy, the Devil, taught Christ, sows tares among the wheat (Matt. 13:24-30, 36-43). The devil and his evil angels spread false doctrine II Tim. 4:1-2; 2 Thess. 2:8,9). They hinder the preachers of the Word from properly discharging their duties (I Thess. 2:18). They hinder the hearers from properly receiving the Word (Luke 6:12). The evil angels stir up persecution against the Church (I Pet. 5:8,9).

The evil angel, led by their leader, also try to corrupt and destroy the state and the home by endeavoring to create dissensions and disturbances by arousing all kinds of evil passions, and engendering all manner of sinful intrigues and plots (I Kings 22:21-23; I Cor. 7:5). The Scriptures show in a number of places that the devil and his iniquitous hosts try to harm and corrupt individuals in body and soul (Job 1:12-22; 2:7-13; Luke 13:11; 22:11; 1 Peter 5:8,9).

The Part the Evil Angels Play In the Physical Possession of Human Beings

The New Testament gives a number of cases were the devils, also called "demons," took physical possession of human beings, male and female. "Demonical possession is spoken as two kinds: physical and spiritual. Spiritual possession is a state in which the evil spirit has gained such a power over the spirit of man that he controls it according to his will" so claims Hove.[64]

Henry Eyster Jacobs asserted the following about demonical possession: "A special temporary bodily possession, permitted by God, in Testament times, particularly those of the visible ministry of Christ as a factor in the struggle of the powers of darkness with the Son of God for the control of the human race. After principalities and powers were spoiled in our Lord's resurrection from the dead, we can find no bodily possession like that described in the Gospels."[65] There are those who would explain the phenomenon of demonical possession as another way of describing illnesses, such as insanity, epilepsy, or some similar disease.[66] Demonical possession seems to have been quite numerous in Christ's time. The New Testament distinguishes between various diseases and demonical possession. In Mark 1:32 the text states: "They brought to him all sick people . . . and those that were possessed of evil spirits." Matthew 8:16 informs the readers: "He cast out spirits . . . and healed all diseases." "Lunatics" are especially distinguished from those demon possessed (Matthew 9:32,33). Driving out devils from people was known as exorcism.[67]

For the comfort of Christians the statement of Hove should be noted: "While the evil angels themselves only intend evil, yet they must, against their will, help to further the purposes of God, as the history of Job and the crucifixion of Jesus show."[68]

The Value of the Doctrine of the Angels

While the doctrine of the angels is a non-fundamental doctrine of Holy Writ, of which a Christian could be ignorant, yet it is an important doctrine and cannot be denied or explained away without rejecting the inspiration, correctness and truthfulness of God's inscripturated Revelation.[69]

Here are some values of knowing and believing the doctrine of the angels:

1. They show us the importance of realizing that God created a variety of living beings.
2. The fact that Christ is superior to the angels helps Christians to realize that Christ is to be worshipped and not the angels.
3. Angels give us somewhat an attractive conception of what the supernatural world is like.
4. The angels set before Christians the example of joyous and perfect fulfillment of God's will. "Thy will be done on earth, as it is in heaven."
5. They put to shame the great indifference men manifest toward the plan of salvation. "There is joy in heaven over one sinner who repents."
6. They broaden our view of God's great mercies, Who sent forth the angels as ministering spirits for the benefit of those who are to inherit salvation. Hebrew 1:14; Cf. Heb. 12:21.[70]

The Teachings on Angels and Satan in Twentieth-Century Lutheran Theology

Already earlier in this century Francis Pieper in his *Christian Dogmatics* pointed out that theologians of the nineteenth and twentieth centuries were undermining the Biblical doctrine of the angels and the Devil by claiming that what the Bible taught on the subject of angelology and satanology was unimportant or even not true.[71] It was contended that it was improper to speak of a "doctrine of the angels." Thus Nitsch-Stephan wrote: "The existence of angels may be possible, but there is no convincing proof of it at all; at all events, the existence of a personal devil cannot be sustained."[72] Kirn does not want the teachings about angels to be given a dogmatic reality. Asserted Kirn: "Since the angels have no inner necessary connection with the saving truth and the experience of salvation, it is not the business of dogmatics to set up a particular doctrine of angel."[73] Karl Hase, an aesthetic rationalist, relegated the doctrine of angels to the sphere of poetry, superstition, and church art.[74] Schleiermacher claimed that must be taken as components of the world order of Jesus and the Apostles and thus not applicable to our times.[75]

Lutheran theologians have taken ambivalent attitudes on the doctrine of the angels, good and bad. While Werner Elert does not deny the existence of angels, he devoted one page to the subject of angelology in his *Der Christliche Glaube*.[76] Again he does not deny the Existence of Satan, but does appear to do justice to the New Testament's teaching of the Devil, as other Lutheran dogmatics earlier in this century have done.[77]

Paul Althaus, a Lutheran dogmatician, defended the existence of angels, although he does not devote the amount of space to the subject as previous Lutheran scholars have done.[78] Both Elert and Althaus do not present "the doctrine of angels," in the systematic form usually given as, for example in Luthardt-Weidner,[79] or as Stump, Hove, Pieper, E. Jacobs, and M. Reu have. Althaus believes in the existence of the Devil and discusses him in the chapter entitled "Das Boese."[80]

The Swedish dogmatician Regin Prenter says very little about angels in his work, *Creation and Redemption*. He has only one statement of significance about angels: "The Creator, in other words, does not only create directly, but indirectly through servants, He has surrounded himself with a host of servants who carry out his will."[81] On page 204 Prenter appears to accept the existence of the Devil. In his opinion, the Devil is the opponent of Christ and manifests his hostility over against Christ. There are supposed to be nineteen references in his work alluding to the Devil. Yet the readers will not find much substantive teaching about the Devil or Satan.[82]

The most recent Christian Dogmatics is that of six Lutheran scholars belonging to those Lutheran Churches that will become a new functioning church January 1988. This dogmatics was edited by Carl E. Braaten and Robert Jenson, who also contributed major sections, together with Gerhard Forde, Philip Hefner, Hans Schwan, and Paul Sponheim.[83] In comparing this major two-volume dogmatics of 1180 pages with earlier works coming from the same Lutheran Churches, one will find that these scholars have accepted the historical-critical method and have adopted the conclusions flowing from such an interpretative methodology, which have been incorporated in all areas and loci of theology.

The Creation of Angels

The Fourth Locus, "The Creation" is presented by Philip J. Hefner in Volume 1, pp. 269-358. While former dogmatics had a special section under "Creation" in Hefner's presentation, it is completely ignored. The Index of this two-volume dogmatics lists 28 references to "angels."[84] A reading of those pages will show there is nothing substantive or normative which the authors of this *Christian Dogmatics* hold about God's created spiritual beings. The new Lutheran *Christian Dogmatics* in its two volumes has many references to the Devil, to Satan. At least 40 references to the Devil and 21 to Satan.[85] Unlike previous Lutheran orthodox dogmatics, there is no special section on the Devil or Satan. Again the same observation must be made the statements on this Evil Spirit are not substantive or normative. One wonders whether writers of this dogmatics believed in a real personal Devil.

Implications Flowing from the Denial of Angels and Satan

There are a number of serious implications that flow from the rejection of angels, good and evil. Those who deny the clear assertions of the Bible on angels and the Devil, do this because they have adopted the historical-critical method of Scriptural interpretation, which is opposed to the historical-grammatical, the system used in the Bible itself. The historical-critical method only accepts those teachings which make sense or which can be defended sociologically and psychologically. If an exegete is permitted to substitute his own predilections for those of God's Word, then the hundreds of passages that speak of angels, demons, and Satan become unclear and often meaningless. What does this do to the Biblical teachings about inspiration and revelation? Did the Holy Spirit inspire wrong and false ideas and concepts? If the Bible cannot be trusted when it speaks on unessential doctrines, how can it be trusted when it gives instruction on matters which pertain to salvation and eternal life? What does it do to the reliability of Jesus Christ our Savior, and St. Paul, who claimed to be a recipient of revelations from Christ? Did not Jesus promise His disciples the Holy Spirit or Paraclete who would guide His disciples into all truth?

In answer to those who claim the doctrines of the angels and Satan are unimportant and could be ignored, Francis Pieper correctly asserted: "But when a man becomes a Christian and reads the Bible, he will find from Genesis to Revelation, the doctrine of the angels, side by side with the central article of Christ. And it certainly requires a great deal of inconsistency to accept the doctrine of Christ and reject the doctrine of angels."[86]

Footnotes

1. Cf. Nave's Topic Bible. *A Digest of the Holy Scriptures* by Orville J. Nave, Revised by S. Mazwell Coder (Chicago: Moody Press, 1974), pp. 54-57.
2. *The Lessons*, Series A (Minneapolis: Augsburg Publishing House, no date), p. 113. The New Lectionary System prepared by the Inter-Lutheran Commission on Worship is the same as that of the Roman Catholics, the Episcopalians and Presbyterians and Methodists.
3. Luther Reed, *The Lutheran Liturgy* (Philadelphia: Muhlenberg Press, 1947), p. 507.
4. Tobit VIII, 2 and xii, 15 The Apocrypha of the Old Testament. Revised Standard Version (New York: Thomas Nelson & Sons, 1957), p. 59.
5. Qsdras 5.20, *The Apocrypha of the Old Testament, Revised Standard Version*, **op. cit.**, p. 26.
6. Reed, **op. cit.**, p. 507.
7. Francis Pieper, *Christian Dogmatics* (St. Louis: Concordia Publishing House, I, pp. 497-498.
8. Edward W. A. Koehler, *A Summary of Christian Doctrine* (Second Revised Edition Prepared by Alfred W. Koehler (Detroit and Oakland, 1939), p. 44.
9. Joseph Stump, *The Christian Faith* (New York: The Macmillan Company, 1932), p. 88.
10. Martin Reu, *Lutheran Dogmatics* (Decorah: Iowa: Wartburg Theological Seminary, 1951), p. 78.
10a. L. Fredricksen, "Angels and Demons," *Encyclopedia Britannica*, 15th Edition.
11. G. W. Bromiley, "Angels" in Walter A. Elwell, Editor, *Evangelical Dictionary of Theology* (Grand Rapids: Baker Book House, 1984), p. 47b.
12. Theodore G. Tappert, *The Book of Concord* (Philadelphia: Fortress Press, 1959), pp. 352-353.
13. **Ibid.**, p. 423.
14. **Ibid.**, p. 226.
15. Based on information given in Th. Engelder, W. Arndt, Th. Graebner and F. E. Mayer, Popular Symbolics (St. Louis: Concordia Publishing House, 1934), pp.40.

397, 418,476.

16. Reu. **Op. cit.**, p. 78.

17. William Beck, *The Holy Bible - The New Testament* (New Haven: Leader Publishing Company, 1976), p. 252.

18. H. B. Kuhn, "God Names Of," *Zondervan Pictorial Bible Encyclopedia* (Grand Rapids: Zondervan Publishing House, 1975), II, 76.

19. Beck, **op. cit.**, *Old Testament*, p. 616.

20. F. Godet, *Biblical Studies*, pp. 2-3, as cited by Conrad Emil Lindberg, *Christian Dogmatis and Notes on the History of Dogma* (Rock Island: Augustana Press, 1928), p. 127.

21. H. C. Leupold, *Exposition of Genesis* (Columbus: Lutheran Book Concern, 1942), p. 41.

22. Stump, **op. cit.**, p. 88.

23. Lindberg, **op. cit.**, pp. 126-127.

24. Stump, **op. cit.**, p. 90.

25. **Ibid.**, p. 89.

26. Heinrich Schmid, *Doctrinal Theology of the Lutheran Church*. Third Edition Revised. Translated from the German by Charles A. Hay and Henry Jacobs (Minneapolis: Augsburg Publishing House, 1961), p. 196.

27. A. J. Graebner, *Outlines of Doctrinal Theology* (St. Louis: Concordia Publishing House, 1910), p. 49.

28. John Theodore Mueller, *Christian Dogmatics - A Handbook of Doctrinal Theology* (St. Louis: Concordia Publishing House, 1955), p. 198.

28a. Richard Francis Weymouth, *The New Testament in Modern Speech*, Fifth Edition (Boston: The Pilgrim Press, 1943), p. 474.

29. Madeleine Miller and J. Lane Miller, *The New Harper's Bible Dictionary* (New York: Harper & Row, 1973), p. 18.

30. Merrill F. Unger, *Unger's Bible Dictionary* (Chicago: Moody Press, 1957), p. 52.

311. **Ibid.**

32. Cf. James Strong, *Exhaustive Concordance, Complete and Unabridged* (Nashville: Broadman Press, 1979), Reprinted, pp. 64-65.

33. **Ibid.**, Unger, **op. cit.**, p. 52.

34. L. Berkhof, *Systematic Theology* (Grand Rapids: Wm. B. Eerdmans Publishing Company, 1941), p. 144.

35. Stump, **op. cit.**, p. 90.

36. **Ibid.**, p. 91.

37. Koehler, **op. cit.**; Mueller, **op. cit.**, p. 199.

38. Mueller, **op. cit.**, p. 200.

39. This reasoning is advanced by Stump, **op. cit.**, p. 92.

40. Cf. the passages given by Graebner, **op. cit.**, pp. 51-53.

41. E. Hove, *Christian Doctrine* (Minneapolis: Augsburg Publishing House, 1930), p. 104.

42. **Ibid.**, p. 105.

43. **Ibid.**

44. Cf. *The Smalcald Articles*, Part II, Article II, Tappert, **op. cit.**, 297, paragraph 28.

45. Stump, **op. cit.**, p. 93.

46. Hove, **op. cit.**, p. 102.

47. Weymouth, **op. cit.**, p. 458.

48. L. L. Morris, "Satan," *New Bible Dictionary*, J. D. Douglas, Revised Edition (Wheaton: Tyndale House, 1982), p. 1074.

49. Leupold, **op. cit.**, cf. p. 141.

50. *The Scofield Reference Bible* (New York: Oxford University Press, 1917), p. 727 (Isaiah passages); p. 871 (Ezekiel passages).

51. Paul E. Kretzmann, *Popular Commentary* (St. Louis: Concordia Publishing House, 1922), Old Testament, Vol. II, pp. 312-33 (Isaiah verses); pp. 561-562 (Ezeliel verses).

52. North P. Sherrill, *The Various Interpretations of Isaiah* 14:12-33. M. D. M. Div. Dissertation (Fort Wayne: Concordia Seminary, May 1978).

53. I. W. Slotki, *Isaiah, Soncino Books of the Bible* (London: The Soncino Press, 1949), p. 69.

54. Merrill F. Unger, *Unger's Bible Handbook* (Chicago: Moody Press, 1966), pp. 319, 374 M.F. Unger, "Satan," Walter A. Elwell; Editor, *Evangelical Dictionary of Theology*, **op. cit.**, p. 972.

55. Cf. Mark F. Schaarschmidt, *The Various Interpretations of Ezekiel 28:11-19*. M. Div. Dissertation (Ft. Wayne: Concordia Seminary, Ma., 1979).

56. "Satan," *Zondervan Pictorial Bible Encyclopedia*, Merrill F. Tenney, General Editor (Grand Rapids: Zondervan Publishing House, 1975), V. p. 292a.

57. James Kallas, *The Real Satan* (Minneapolis: Augsburg Publishing House, 1975), pp. 27-48.

58. Morris, **op. cit.**, p. 1074.

59. D. E. Hiebert, "Satan," *The Zondervan Pictorial Bible Encyclopedia*, **op. cit.**, p. 755.

60. Hiebert, "Satan," in Merrill C. Tenney, *The Zondervan Pictorial Bible Dictionary* (Grand Rapids: Zondervan Publishing House, 1963), p. 755b.

61. Cf. T. H. Gaster, "Satan," G.A. Buttrick, General Editor, *The Interpreter's Dictionary of the Bible* (Nashville; Abingdon Press, 1062), V., pp. 226, 227.

62. Cf. "daimonin," in G. Abbott-Smith, *A Manual Greek Lexicon of the New Testament* (New York: Charles Scribner's Sons, 1929), p. 97.

63. Stump, **op. cit.**, p. 94.

64. Hove, **op. cit.**, p. 112.

65. Henry Eyster Jacobs, *A Summary of the Christian Faith* (Philadelphia: General Council Publication House, 1905), p. 88.

66. J. S. Wright, "Demon-Possession," in the *New Bible Dictionary*, **op. cit.**, p. 279.

67. D. E. Aune, "Exorcism," *The International Standard Bible Encyclopedia*, G. W. Bromiley, General Editor (Grand Rapids; William B. Eerdmans Publishing Company, 1982), II, p. 244.

68. Hove, **op. cit.**, p. 112.

69. Cf. F. Pieper, *Christian Dogmatics* (St. Louis: Concordia Publishing House, 1950), I, pp. 80-81.

70. *Unger's Bible Dictionary*, **op. cit.**, p. 52b.

71. Pieper, *Christian Dogmatics*, **op. cit.**, I, pp. 497-498.

72. Nitsch-Stephan, *Lehrbuch der Dogmatik*, 3rd edition, 1912, pp. 441ff., cited by Pieper, **op. cit.**, p. 497.

73. Kirn, *Evangelische Dogmatik*, 3rd edition, p. 72 as cited by Pieper, p. 497.

75. Friedrich Schleiermacher, *Der Christliche Glaube* (Berlin: Walther de Gruyter, 7th edition, 1960.

76. Werner Elert, *Der Christtliche Glaube. Grundlinien der Lutherischen Dogmatik* (Hamburg; Furche-Verlag 1956), p. 260.

77. **Ibid.**, pp. 26-269.

78. Paul Althaus, *Die Christliche Wahrheit Lehrbuch der Dogmatik* (Guetersloh: Bertelmann, 1949), II, pp. 57-69.

79. Revere Franklin Weidner, *Theologia, The Doctrine of God, Outline Based on Luthardt* (New York: Franklin H. Revell Company, 1902), pp. 108-129).

80. Althaus, **op. cit.**, pp., II, pp. 152-161.

81. Regin Prenter, *Creation and Redemption*, Translation by Theodore I. Jensen (Philadelphia: Fortress Press, 1966), p. 203.

82. **Ibid.**, pp. p. 128f, 204, 279f., 331f., 355, 359, 377, 384, 396, 410, 468, 474, 487, 517, 530, 546, 562, 574.

83. This new Lutheran dogmatics is published by Fortress Press of Philadelphia, 1984.

84. Braaten and Jenson, *Christian Dogmatics* (Philadelphia: Fortress Press, 1984), II, p. 603.

85. **Ibid.**, II, pp. 606, 617.

86. Pieper, *Christian Dogmatics*, **op. cit.**, I, 498.

Questions

1. St. Michael and All Angels Day is commemorated on ____.
2. The higher critical method of Bible interpretation has led to the ____ of angels.
3. What is the only source for the doctrine of angels? ____
4. Which church prays to angels? ____
5. "Angel" means ____.
6. The ascription of wings to angels is ____.
7. The functions of the good angels are to ____.
8. The good angels are not to be ____.
9. Who is the great enemy of God and Man? ____
10. "Lucifer" in Isaiah 14:12 should be translated ____.
11. The Hebrew word "Satan" means ____.
12. What is the activity of the evil angels? ____
13. What is exorcism? ____
14. *Christian Dogmatics* edited by Carl Braaten and Robert Jenson, accept the ____ approach toward the Bible.

The Descent Into Hell
What Happened Between Christ's Burial and His Physical and Bodily Resurrection Appearances on Easter Morn?

Christian News, March 28, 1998

Holy Week, which commemorates the last earthly days of Christ during the State of Humiliation, reaches its climax with the death, and burial in the tomb of Joseph of Arimethea. Most Christians probably believe that the first important event of Easter morn was Christ's resurrection from the grave. But that is not quite accurate. Both the Apostles' Creed[1] and the Athanasian Creed[2] place the statement "He descended into hell" between the burial and the physical resurrection and bodily appearances of Jesus to the women and disciples. The descent by Jesus into hell occurred on the third day after his crucifixion and burial. The technical term for this first happening before the bodily resurrection is called "descensus ad infernos" or "descensus ad inferna." In German it is called "die Hoellenfahrt Christi."

Christian theologians when describing the earthly life of Christ speak of various steps that characterize the State of Humiliation and the different steps that occurred during the State of Exaltation.[3]

What is the difference between these two states? "Christ's State of Humiliation consisted in this, that according to His human nature, Christ did not always and fully use the divine attributes communicated to His human nature."[4] By contrast the State of Exaltation consists in this that according to His human nature, Christ always and fully uses the divine attributes communicated to his Human nature.[5] Historic Lutheran theology, beginning with Luther, believes that the descent into hell was the first step in the State of Exaltation.

There are a number of Bible passages that refer to what is commonly known as "the descent into hell."[6] The main passages for the descent of Christ is found in 1 Peter 3:18-20. Weymouth in his *New Testament in Modern Speech* translated 1 Peter 3:18: "He was put to death in the flesh, but made alive in the spirit, in which He also went and preached to the spirits which were in prison, who in former times had been disobedient, when God's long suffering patiently waited in the days of Noah during the building of the Ark."[7]

Dealing with the same event is Colossians 2:15, which reads: "He stripped rulers and powers of the armor and made a public show of them as he celebrated His victory by the Cross."[8] This Pauline verse may refer to the descensus. Again Paul's remark, when he declared about Christ: "Now what can He went up mean that He also has gone down into the lower earthly regions?" Some scholars contend that Acts 2:27, where it is stated, that God would not allow Christ's body to remain in hades and that this is what is referred to about Christ's descent into hell and therefore belongs to the last step on the State of Humiliation. However, the world "hades," in Acts 2:27: "refers to the grave and not to hell." *The New*

International Version renders Acts 2:27: "Because you will not abandon me to the grave, nor will you let your Holy One see corruption."[9]

It is true that 1 Peter 3:18 has seen different translation given by Biblical scholars. Hove, a professor of Luther Theological Seminary, St. Paul, in the thirties of this century, wrote about the descent into hell as follows: "The doctrine concerning Christ's descent into hell is by no means a peculiarly Lutheran doctrine. The doctrine was regarded so important in ancient times that it was incorporated into the Apostles' Creed and has been confessed by the Christian Church down through the ages. It is evident that according to the creeds Christ descended into hell is not to be identified with His suffering or with death or with His burial as some contend."[10] When Christ declared on the cross: "It is finished," that meant that His work of redemption and His suffering were complete. With the seventh Word from the cross: "Father I commend My spirit into Thy hands," Christ meant that His soul would go to paradise, while His body was placed into the tomb of Joseph of Arimethea. The days that Jesus' dead body was in the grave could not be a part of that which was involved by His "descent into hell."

The Interpretation of 1 Peter 3:18

The passage is considered as the seat of the doctrine for the descensus. The descent was preceded by the revivication of the dead body of Christ. Jesus exercised "the power to take it" (His life again, John 10:18). All three Persons of the Trinity are spoken of as causing the dead body of Christ to become alive again. According to body and soul, the God-Man descended into the prison of the damned, which would include the Devil and his evil angels.[12]

Many different interpretations have been given 1 Peter 3:18, especially to the first part of the verse which reads: "He was put to death in the flesh (Greek: sakri) and made alive in the spirit (Greek: pneumati). Some translations render 'pneumati' with a capital letter and thus understand the word to be the Holy Spirit. The New King James thus has: 'made alive by the Spirit.'"[13] *The Berkeley Version* renders "being put to death physically, but being made alive in the Spirit, in Whom He went and preached to the spirits in prison."[14] By contrast Dedward Koehler interpreted the first part of I Peter 3:18 like this: "The term 'in the flesh' refers to the days of His flesh" (Hebrews 5:7), to His earthy life, which began with His conception and ended with His death and burial. To be put to death, therefore belonged to that part of life which He lived in the flesh. "In the spirit" does not mean the Holy Spirit made Christ alive, but that it was Christ Himself who did this (John 10:18). "In the spirit" is here used in contrast to "in the flesh," and it denotes that the new life which began with His vivification, and which never ends. Hence, that Christ was put to death and buried happened to Him in His earthly life, but that He was quickened and descended into hell, belongs into the new life "in the spirit."[15]

Professor Hove interpreted the opening words of 1 Peter 3:18 in this way: "The contrast between 'the flesh' and 'the spirit' here is therefore not the contrast between His body and His soul, nor is it simply the contrast between His human and His divine nature but between two different modes in which His human nature existed and its exalted, super terrestrial super mundane, glorified mode of existence. Only if so understood can the text be consistently translated." Hove further explains his understanding: "He was put to death according to His earthly mode of existence. He was made alive again according to another higher mode and in this mode He went and preached to the spirits in prison. He the entire person, who had both a human and divine nature went forth with a glorified human body."[16]

Kretzmann understood 1 Peter 3:18 in this way: "Christ died, not according to His divine nature, although this was truly and separately united with His human nature also in death, but in the flesh, that is in His fleshly, natural mode of existence, in which He lived in the days of humiliation. Thus the entire Christ, the God-man, was put to death in the flesh. This same Christ, so the apostle proceeds to tell us, after His death resumed life in the grave. He was quickened, made alive, in the sepulcher. This quickening was made in the spirit, or with respect to the Spirit, that is, the new glorified state, in which Christ, in His transformed and glorified body, lived, acted, and moved about, came and went as a spirit. In this spirit, in this new spirit-life, glorified and exalted, Christ, the God-man, according to His soul and body, retaining His flesh and blood in a glorified form, went forth, as our triumphant champion, into the abode of the damned of the devils there proclaimed His victory to the spirits in prison, in hell, to those who are further described in verses 19 and 20."[17]

The Reformed View of the Descent Into Hell

L. Berkof stated that the usual Reformed view has that the words refer not only to the sufferings on the cross but also to the agonies of Gethsemane.[18] Berkhof categorically stated that Christ could not have descended into hell, because his body was in the grave. Calvin interpreted the phrase metaphorically, as referring to the penal sufferings of Christ upon the cross.[19] This was also the stance of the Heidelberg Catechism. However, the Westminster Confession states that the phrase means more than Christ died, and for three days remained under the power of the grave.

The Roman Catholic Teaching Relative to the Descent

The Roman Catholic teaching on this article of the Apostles' Creed was, that after the death of Christ, He went to the **Limbus Patrum**, where the Old Testament saints were waiting the revelation and application of redemption, preached the Gospel to them, and brought the O.T. saints out to heaven. [20] According to chapter 11 of Hebrew the Old Testament believers had true saving faith, because they believed the promises about the Messiah, especially as set forth in Isaiah 53. The Roman Catholic interpretation is a product of human tradition but has no evidence in the Scriptures.

The Views of Higher Criticism on the Descent Into Hell

In our days, the fact in the belief in demons and the activity of Satan has been given up by the majority of higher critics, has greatly influenced the attitude toward the descent into hell. They reject that such an event ever happened. They conclude their lives of Christ with the burial. Some scholars have gone so far as to change the Greek text. According to these pundits the passage 1 Peter 3:18 would begin with the words: "It was in the Spirit that Enoch also went and preached to the imprisoned spirits." The passage is then explained according to the apocryphal book of Enoch as follows: "In the days of Jared certain angels descended and married some of the daughters of men, children being born out of this unlawful union. Enoch was sent by God to pronounce sentence of condemnation upon the transgressors, who were eternal, immortal beings. Thus it followed that those spirits were bound in prison. About this interpretation Kretzmann declared: "Such attempts at solving the mystery of the Word of God are foolish and dangerous approaching the blasphemous."[21]

To What Place Did Christ Descend
According to His Glorified Divine Human Nature?

Some have called the place to which Christ went "hades," although I Peter 3:18 called the place "a prison." Reformed scholars have interpreted Acts 2:38 which The New American Standard renders: "Therefore my heart was glad and my tongue rejoiced. Moreover my flesh also shall dwell in hope, because Thou wilt not leave my soul, in Hades."[22] Peter, in his Pentecost sermon, quoted Psalm 16:9-10. Verse 10 reads: "For thou wilt not leave my soul to Sheol, neither wilt thou suffer thy holy one to see corruption." In Acts 2:26 hades is the rendering for the Sheol.[23] In Psalm 16:10 David is predicting that God would not permit the Messiah's body to decay. The word "hades" has different meanings in the New Testament depending on the context in which it occurs.[24] Only the body of Jesus was given burial, for Christ had committed his soul or spirit into the hands of the Father. Jesus had also promised the dying thief, that today (on Good Friday) that his soul would be with Him in Paradise (Luke 23:43).

Who Was In the Prison to Which Christ Descended?

The people who had been disobedient in the time of Noah and had rejected God's offer of salvation were the subjects of Christ's preaching. The prison (Greek: **phulake**) designates the abode of the wicked ones, for the use and meaning of **phulake** in the New Testament see Rev. 18:2,20:7; 1 Peter 3:18.

The Nature of Christ's Preaching in Hell

The Apostle Peter tells the Christians of Asia Minor that Christ preached to the disobedient people who were in "prison." Jesus became a **Kerux**, a herald, who is depicted as engaging in **kerussein**. The Greek verb does not necessarily denote the preaching of salvation. The verb **kerussein** is a vox media, which stands either for the preaching of the law or the proclamation of the Gospel. **Euanggelizo** is the Greek verb for the setting forth of the Gospel of salvation. **Kerussein** is employed for the preaching of the law as in Matthew 3:1; Acts 15:21; Rev. 5:2, Luke 12:3. The context of 1 Peter 3:18 shows that Christ came as a Herald, to bring the proclamation of His victory to such as had rejected His message. He went to those in the **phylake, hades**, used a number of times of the place of eternal punishment, Hell. John Theodore Mueller, averred: "That this is the meaning of Christ's appearing in hell is proved by the very scope of the text, for in the preceding verses the Christians are exhorted to bear suffering at the hands of the ungodly, trusting in the righteous Judge, who will mete out dire punishment to all enemies of His Church at His second coming."[26]

The Interpretation of 1 Peter 4:6
and the Preaching of Salvation

1 Peter 4:6 which reads: "Yes, it was for this reason that the dead also once heard the Gospel, so that they might be judged like human beings in the flesh." This verse has been adduced as proof that Christ preached the Gospel so that they might be saved. Origen went so far as to argue that there will be a complete restoration or **apokatastasis** for mankind. Others have argued, as some church fathers and modern theologians, that those who have not heard the Gospel in this life will be given a later opportunity after their deaths.

This interpretation of 1 Peter 4:6 is not correct, for in this verse Peter speaks of men who are not dead, but to whom during their lives on earth the Gospel was preached. This follows from the clause of purpose that "they might be judged according to men in the flesh." 1 Peter 4:6 does not teach a probation after death or that the lost will be given a second chance for salvation.[26]

The Teaching of the *Formula of Concord*
on the Descent Into Hell

After the death of Luther in 1546 and before the writing of the *Formula of Concord*'s several questions arose in regard to the descent, as to the time of the occurrence, as to whether it belonged to the State of Humiliation or to the State of Exaltation.[27] Of Article Nine "Of the descent into Hell" Little declared: "This is the shortest of all the Articles in the *Formula of Concord*, yet because of the divergent views of the Reformed on this subject it is an article of considerable importance."[28] Article IX avoids going into details and simply contents itself with quoting from Luther's sermon at Torgau in 1533, where after citing the Apostles' Creed, he says: "For in this Confession the burial and the descent of Christ into hell are distinguished as different articles; and we simply believe that the entire Person, God and Man, after the burial descended into hell, conquered the devil, destroyed the power of hell, and took from the devil all his might."[29] Luther warns against curious inquiry as to how this occurred. Later Lutheran theologians developed the doctrine further.

Twentieth Century Lutheran
Teaching on the Descent Into Hell

As a result of the invasion of the historical critical method in the Lutheran Church in America and the continuation of this method in the Lutheran denominations that formed The Evangelical Lutheran Church in America (ELCA) there has occurred a rejection of historic Lutheran teaching on the descent of Christ into hell. Thus Waltemeyer in New Testament Commentary explained 1 Peter 3:19: "He went and preached to the spirits in prison," as meaning that Peter was affirming the universal scope of the saving work of Christ. Men are not to be condemned without an opportunity to hear the Gospel."[30] Waltemeyer does not explain 1 Peter 3:18-19. The Lutheran Roth in his presentation of 1 Peter in *The Biblical Expositor* completely ignores a discussion of 1 Peter 3:18-19 but said: "Some interpreters say that 1 Peter 4:6, together with Ephesians 4:9 and others indicate that Christ preached in the realm of the dead to those who had not heard the Word in their previous existence in the flesh."[31]

Doctor Theodore Engelder wrote a series of articles which set forth the views of many modern theologians on the erroneous views of Protestant and Lutheran theologians who have been advocates of what he called "the hades Gospel" and the **apokatastasis** Gospel, the Gospel of a second chance.[32]

The Braaten-Jenson Christian Dogmatics
The Latest Lutheran Teaching on the Descent

The Braaten-Jenson Christian Dogmatics devoted one page to "Jesus' descent into hell." Braaten, the author of the locus on "The Person of Christ," opines that the descent belongs to the State of Humiliation and not to the State of exaltation as the *Formula of Concord* held. Braaten[33] depicted the theological significance as being twofold, first it stresses the depth-dimension of His suffering and humiliation, and secondly "insofar as we confess Christ's descent to hades as the realm of the dead, we are claiming that his work of salvation is universal and reaches beyond the limits of those who preach and hear the Gospel in this life. Nations and generations of people who lived before the coming of Christ and who have never been confronted with the preaching of salvation in his name are not eternally lost. Christ even goes to the dead, so that he might be acclaimed the Lord of the living and the dead."[34]

The view that Christ preached the word of salvation to those who died without faith in Christ contradicts Holy Writ, which clearly teaches: "It is appointed unto men once to die and then the judgment . . . (Hebrew 9:27)." Christ taught that the rich man, who showed no concern for Lazarus, went to Hades, where he was in torment (Luke 16:23).

The Significance of the Descent Into Hell

"If Christ had made the descent while His body was in the power of death, it would not have been a triumphant descent. But being made alive after His soul had returned to His body. His descent into hell pro-

1756

claimed that the grace would not be able to hold Him, that He was the One who had the keys of death and hell and was alive forevermore."[35]

The descent of Christ into hell is a fitting prelude to the miracle of Easter morning, when Christ showed his disciples that He was truly the Son of God and that His enemies failed to accomplish their nefarious plans to kill Him forever.

Footnotes

1. *Die Bekenntnis schriften der evangelish lutherischen Kirche* (Goettingen: Vandenhoek & Ruprecht, 1952), p. 21.

2. **Ibid.**, p. 30.

3. Francis Pieper, *Christian Dogmatics* (St. Louis: Concordia Publishing House, 1951), 11, p. 280.

4. *A Short Explanation of Dr. Martin Luther's Small Catechism*, (St. Louis: Concordia Publishing House, 1943), Question and Answer 134, p. 109.

5. **Ibid.**, Question and Answer 148, p. 116, *A Hoenecke, Dogmatic* (Milwaukee Northwestern Publishing House, 1910), II, p. 132-133.

6. John Schaller, *Biblical Christology* (Milwaukee: Northwestern Publishing House, 1981), p. 163; v. Stump, *The Christian Faith* (New York: The Macmillan Co., 193, p. 172.

7. Richard Frances Weymouth, *The New Testament in Modern Speech* (Boston: The Pilgrim Press, 1943), p. 574.

8. "Descent Into Hell," in L. Fuerbringer, The. Engelder, and P.E. Kretzmann, *The Concordia Cyclopedia* (St. Louis: Concordia Publishing House, 1927), p. 205a.

9. *The Holy Bible - New International Version* (Grand Rapids: Zondervan Bible Publishers, 1988), p. 771b.

16. E. Hove, *Christian Doctrine* (Minneapolis: Augsburg Publishing House 1930), pp. 197-198.

11. Colossians 2:12; Acts 2:24; Rom. 8:11; John 10:18; 2:18.

12. Cf. Hoye, **op. cit.**, Thus Hollaz taught, cf. Heinrich Schmid, *The Doctrinal Theology of the Evangelical Lutheran Church* (Minneapolis: Augsburg Publishing House: 1961). Reprints of 1875 and 1889 editions, p. 398.

13. Holy Bible, *The New King James Version in Modern English* (New York: Thomas Nelson Publishers, 1977), p. 1188.

14. Holy Bible, *The New Berkeley Version in Modern English* (Grand Rapids: Zondervan Publishing House, 1969), p. 259.

15. Edward A. Koehler, *A Summary of Christian Doctrine* (Detroit and Oakland: 1952), pp. 106-101.

16. Hove, **op. cit.**, p. 198.

17. P.E. Kretzmann, *Popular Commentary, New Testament* (St. Louis: Concordia Publishing House, 1924), II, p. 533.

18. L. Berkhof, *Systematic Theology* (Grand Rapids: Wm. B. Eerdmans Publishing Company, 1941), p. 382.

19. **Ibid.**, p. 342.

20. *Katholischer Kurz-Katechismus* (Koenigstein Ev., Albertus Magnus Kolleg, 1982), pp. 14-15.

21. Kretzmann, **op. cit.**, II, p. 343.

22. *New American Standard Bible* (Philadelphia: A. J. Holman Company, 1922), p.

781b.

23. **Ibid.**, p. 398a.

24. A. L. Harrison, "Hades," *The Wycliffe Bible Encyclopedia* (Chicago: Moody Press, 1975), I, pp. 746-741.

25. John Theodore Mueller, *Christian Dogmatics* (St. Louis: Concordia Publishing House, 1955), p. 297.

26. Koehler, **op. cit.**, p. 161.

27. George Fritschel, *The Formula of Concord* (Philadelphia: The Lutheran Publication Society, 1916), p. 213.

28. C. H. Little, *Lutheran Confessional Theology* (St. Louis: Concordia Publishing House, 1943), p. 166.

29. **Ibid.**

30. Wm. C. Waltemeyer, "The First Epistle of Peter" in Herbert C. Alleman, Editor, *New Testament Commentary* (Philadelphia: Board of Publications of the United Lutheran Church in America, 1937),p. 634.

31. Robert Paul Roth, "1 Peter," *The Biblical Expositor,* Carl F. H. Henry, (Philadelphia: A. J. Holman Company, 1976), p. 426.

32. Theodore Engelder, "Hades Gospel," *Concordia Theological Monthly* 16:293-366, May 1945. "The Evil of the Hades Gospel," *Concordia Theological Monthly,* 16:591-615, September 1945. "Catholic-Protestant Limbus Patrum," *Concordia Theological Monthly,* 17:561-583, August 1946. "Hades Gospel and the Apocatastasis Gospel." *Concordia Theological Monthly,* 17:641-676, September 1946.

33. Carl E. Braaten and Robert Jensen, *Christian Dogmatics* (Philadelphia: the Fortress Press, 1986), 1, p. 54.

34. **Ibid.**, p. 549.

35. Engelder, Fuerbringer and Kretzmann, *Concordia Cyclopedia,* **op. cit.**, p. 205b.

Questions

1. When did the descent of Jesus into Hell occur? ____
2. What is Christ's State of Humiliation? ____
3. Christ's State of Exaltation consists in ____.
4. Where is Christ's descent into Hell taught in the Bible? ____
5. What is Rome's Limbus Patrum? ____
6. What do higher critics of the Bible generally teach about the decent into Hell? ____
7. Will the lost be given a second chance of salvation? ____
8. Who are some modern Lutherans who reject what the Bible teaches about Christ's decent into Hell? ____

Jesus Is God
The Variegated Witnesses and Testimonies to the Deity of Christ as Set Forth in John's Gospel

Christian News, October 24, 1994

Most of what we know about the earthly life of Christ Jesus is found in the Four Gospels. Paul has preserved one saying not recorded by any of the evangelists, namely, "it is more blessed to give than to receive,"[1] Paul , John, Peter, and other New Testament writers corroborates statements found in the Gospels about Jesus Christ.[2] The Four Gospels may be divided in two groups, namely, the Synoptics and the Johannine.

Matthew, Mark and Luke most likely were written before the fall of Jerusalem in A.D. 70, while the Fourth Gospel was composed after the destruction of Jerusalem, which Jesus had predicted in the Mt. Olivet Discourse.[3] The First Three Gospels describe the life and activities of Christ from the same viewpoint and therefore are termed the "Synoptic Gospels," while the Fourth Gospel contains 93% new material when compared with the writings of Matthew, Mark and Luke treating Christ's life.[4] Each of the four evangelists makes a significant contribution to Christ's life and work, and the world would be much poorer, if one of them had been lost. Scroggie claimed "It is difficult to classify the Gospels as literature. They are not history, nor are they biography as we commonly understand these terms, and yet they are more than miscellaneous notes concerning Jesus' life, teaching and work. Perhaps Memoirs is a good designation as any."[5]

There Were Always Four Gospels
There always have been four gospels recognized and considered canonical. As early as A.D. 150 Tatian, a Syrian, made a harmony of the events recorded in the Four Gospels. There is a translation of this work extant.[6] It has been suggested that the reason for the Four Gospels is to be found in the needs of mankind. Matthew's Gospel is especially intended for the Jew, Mark's for the Romans, Luke's for the Greek and John for the world. Christ is presented as meeting the needs of all mankind. Christ is depicted especially as the Sovereign in Matthew, the Servant in Mark, the Man in Luke and as God in John.[7] In addition to these characteristics and emphases, it has been suggested that Matthew is especially related to the Past, Mark to the Present, Luke to the Future, and John to all eternity.[7] Scholars have compared the Cherubim of Ezekiel to characteristics of the Four Gospels: Matthew represents the Lion, Mark the Ox, Luke the Man, and John the Eagle. To distinguish the four evangelists, Matthew is depicted as the Preacher, Mark as the Chronicler, Luke as the Historian and John as the Philosopher.

Estimates of John's Gospel
Origen said, "This Gospel is the consummation of the Gospels as the

Gospels are of all the Scriptures."[8] Jerome averred: "John excels in the depths of divine mysteries."[9] Luther made this evaluation: "It is the unique, tender, genuine, chief Gospel, far preferable to the other three . . . Should tyrant succeed in destroying the Holy Scripture and only a single copy of the Epistle to the Romans and the Gospel according to John escape him, Christianity would be saved."[10] W. T. Davidson declared: "The fourth Gospel is unique among the books of the New Testament. In its combination of minute historical details with lofty spiritual teaching, in its testimony to the Person and Work of the Lord Jesus Christ and in its preparation it makes for the foundations of Christian doctrine, it stands alone. Its influence upon the thought and life of the Christian Church has been proportionately deep and far-reaching. It is no disparagement of other inspired Scriptures to say that no other book of the Bible has left such a mark at the same time upon the profoundest Christian thinkers, and upon simple-minded believers at large."[11] Dr. A. T. Pierson gave this evaluation of the Fourth Gospel: "It touches the heart of Christ. If Matthew corresponds to the Court of Israel, Mark to the Court of the Priests, and Luke to the Court of the Gentiles, John leads us past the veil into the Holy of holies. Here is the inmost temple, filled with the glory of God."[12]

Some Specific Characteristics of John's Gospel

John, the son of Zebedee, the author shows: 1. A great understanding of the Old Testament and Jewish tradition. There is a great emphasis on feasts (2-23; 6:4; 13:1; 7:2; 10:22) and customs and traditions (2:6; 7:37; 8:12) are looked at with comprehension. 2. The simplicity is only exceeded by the profound theological themes. John deals with such abstract themes as light, life, love, truth, Son. 3. While Mark is characterized by action, John's is noted by its comparative emphasis on the discourses of Jesus. 4. While John's Gospel, compared with Mark's which emphasizes action, in John journeys are recorded (2:12; 3:22; 4:3; 5:1; 6:1; 7:1; 10:40). The twenty-one chapters of John abound in narrative material. 5. The Gospel abounds in non-parabolic teaching. 6. It dwells at great length on the events and discourses which belong to a period of less than twenty-four hours (chapters 13-19). 7. It records with special emphasis the promise of the coming of the Holy Spirit (4:6; 17:26; 16:13,14). 8. This Gospel far more than others records Christ's words in Judea. 9. It is emphatically the spiritual Gospel, whose aim is to show who Jesus is, and with this there is a practical purpose (John 20:31).[13] Hence, much of what is found in the Synoptics is here omitted, and on the other hand much material is added, the type of material which brings into clear focus the glory of the Lord: His Messianic office and deity.

The Special Prominence of the Deity of Christ in John's Gospel

The divinity or deity of Christ is given special prominence in the Fourth Gospel. Christ is presented as greater than the Torah (1:17), the Temple (2:10,21), the Shekinah glory (1:14), and the significance and satisfaction of the feasts (7:37-39). According to Tenney: "It is a curious fact that the Fourth Gospel of all the Gospels presents the clearest case for the deity of Christ as expressed in his own words."[14]

Denials of the Deity of Christ by Liberal Theology

Ever since the age of Rationalism and higher criticism certain prominent unbelieving New Testament scholars have attacked the deity of Christ. Prior to the efforts of the Jesus Seminar, notorious for its rejection of the deity of Christ, there were a number of attempts to find the historical Jesus. Either unbelieving savants have rejected the reliability of the textual data itself or they have rejected the facts as they are stated as mythical and unbelievable. Formerly, the enemies of the Christian faith were those outside the Christian Church, but now its most vocal opponents come from within the Christian Church.

No person reading the text of the Fourth Gospel can state that it does not teach the divinity of deity of Christ in many different ways and in many different passages. What could be clearer than the statement of John in chapter 20:31: "There were many more signs which Jesus performed in the presence of his disciples which have not been written in this book, but these have been written that you may believe in the Christ the Son God, and that believing you may have eternal life in His name."

"Believe," a Key Concept in the Fourth Gospel

One of the key words on the Fourth Gospel is the word "believe," in Greek "pisteuoo," used 98 times by the Son of Zebedee.[15] Samuel Miller has produced an outline of John's Gospel in which he showed the development of belief versus unbelief during the three years of Christ's ministry. Chapters 1-12 show the development of belief and unbelief, and chapters 13-21 the culmination of belief and unbelief.[16] Faith in Christ, the Son of God is absolutely necessary for salvation. To refuse to believe in Christ as God's Son, Who died for the sins of the world, leads to the loss of eternal life.

The Method Employed by John to Prove the Deity of Christ

John uses various witnesses in establishing the Godhead of Mary's Son. He proves it by different witnesses. Leon Morris stated: "One of the distinctive categories of the Fourth Gospel is witness. John has the noun fourteen times compared to three times in Mark and once in Luke (it does not occur in Matthew); he also has the verb thirty-three times, while Matthew and Luke have it one each and Mark does not have it at all. John in fact uses both noun and verb more often than anyone else in the New Testament. Thus we can clearly see how important it is to him that there is ample testimony to the central truths he is writing about."[16a]

The Testimony of John, the Apostle

At various places in his Gospel narrative John the Evangelist testifies or witnesses to the deity of Christ. The Prologue, that remarkable introduction of the Fourth Gospel, a number of times witnessed to the deity of our Lord. In the Prologue the Evangelist clearly and powerfully testified to the deity of Christ. "In the beginning was the Word (Logos) and the Word was face to face with God and the Word was God."[17] In verse 14 John asserted "and the Word became flesh and tented among us and we gazed on his glory-glory as of the Father's only Son, full of grace and truth" (v. 14).[18] In John 3:16 John stated: "God so loved the world that He gave his only begotten Son, that whosoever believes in Him should not perish." If the Father is God, so His Son must be God.

Morris and others have pointed out that John the Evangelist is far from being the only one who bore witness to Christ's deity. "There is a sevenfold witness: In addition to the witness of John, there is that of the Father, of the Son, of the Holy Spirit, of Scripture, of Jesus' works, and of people who responded to Jesus' ministry. That is an impressive list and shows that the Evangelist saw ample testimony to Jesus. There is no excuse for not believing."[19]

The Testimony of John the Baptist

John the Baptizer, whose coming and activity had been predicted by Isaiah and Malachi and was called the "waypreparer" for the Messiah,[20] claimed that he was not the Messiah. John the Baptist directed his disciples to follow Jesus, saying to them, as he pointed to Christ, "Behold, the Lamb of God that takest away the sins of the world" (1:29). Relative to John the Baptist the Evangelist, recorded the Baptizer as saying: "I saw the Spirit like a dove descend from heaven and rest upon Him, but He who sent me to baptize in water said to me, the One on Whom you see the Spirit descending and resting is He who baptizes in the Holy Spirit. This I have seen and I am becoming a witness to the fact that He is the Son of God."[21]

The Witness of God the Father to the Son's Deity

Christ acknowledged the testimony of John the Baptist but simultaneously claimed that the testimony of God the Father was greater. How is this true? Christ's response was: "But I have a testimony greater than that of John; for the work which the Father has given me to bring to completion—the work which I am doing bears testimony concerning me, that the Father hath sent me. And the Father who sent me has himself borne testimony concerning me. None of you have heard his voice at any time or see him, nor has his word dwelling within you, because you do not believe him whom he sent" (5:36-38).[22]

Chapter 5:10-18 and 19-29 have a unique description of the relationship of Jesus to the Father, which presuppose Christ's deity. The distinctive teaching relative to Jesus and the Father may be outlined as follows: 1. The Son's relation to the Father; 2. The Father's relation to the Son; 3. The equality of Son and Father. In chapter 5 the Son is depicted as being equal of the Father. The Jews understood the teachings of Jesus' claims to being God. Thus 5:18 states: "For this reason the Jews continued to seek the more eagerly to put him to death, because not only was he breaking the Sabbath, but he was actually speaking of God as his own Father, thus making himself God's equal."[23]

The Testimony of the Holy Spirit

The Fourth Gospel writer reported the historical event of Christ's baptism when Jesus was thirty years old. After John has baptized Jesus with water, the Holy Spirit descended on Jesus and He was baptized with the Holy Spirit and power. In a parallel to John's report of Christ's baptism, Mark reported: "And immediately coming out of the water, He saw the heavens open and the Spirit of God descended upon Him and a voice from heaven came: 'Thou art My beloved Son, in Thee I am well pleased' (Mark 1:9-11). Because of the descending from heaven of the Holy Spirit, John wrote: "This I have seen and I am become a witness to the fact that He is the Son of God (John 1:23-24)."

The Witness of Christ Himself

Morris wrote: "There is a great deal about the witness of Jesus, and this is of central importance, for in this Gospel the truth is emphasized that Jesus is the Revealer. It is in him that we see what God is like. He is 'from above': He is not 'of this world' (8:23). He lets us see what God demands of us; He reveals the truth of God and what that means in our lives and in our lives on earth and in our hopes of the life to come. His place is central and his witness brings this out."[24]

On the first occasion that Jesus mentions His witness, He associated his followers with Him as he assured Nicodemus: "We speak what we know and bear witness to what we have seen and you people do not receive our witness" (3:11). Jesus had been speaking of the new birth and now assured His hearers that what He had said is soundly based. Jesus is not teaching any fantasies with no basis in fact. A little later he said that people did not receive the testimony of Him "who comes down from above." And again there is the affirmation that He spoke out of knowledge (w. 31-32). This failure of the people to believe in Him is a sad fact to which John comes back again and again. Jesus came from God, with the revelation of God, and had been sent by God, but people would not listen.

Jesus's Self-Testimony

Of the four Gospels, that of John contains more sayings and teachings than Matthew which contains six major sermons or discourses. Distinctive of the Fourth Gospel are the well-known "I AM's." In addition to these I AM's John reports that the Jews wanted to kill Jesus, "because he said, 'I am the Son of God'" (10:36).

The Seven I AM's assume as a foundational truth that He is God.[25] Here are these remarkable assertions and claims of Christ: 1. "I am the bread of life" (6:35); 2. "I am the light of the world" (8:12); 3. "Before Abraham was I am" (8:58); 4. "I am the Good Shepherd" (10:11); 5. "I am the resurrection and the life" (11:25); 6. "I am the true vine" (15:1); 6. "I am the door of the sheepfold" (10:17); 7. "I am the Way, the truth and the life" (14:6). In these I AM's Christ made claims which God alone could assert and keep. No religious leader in world history and in the history of religions has ever made such claims.

Tenney in *John: The Gospel of Belief* has some interesting and significant observations on the statement of Jesus to the Pharisees: "Before Abraham came into being, I am" (8:58). He wrote: "The same contrast of verbs is used that appears in 1:1 and 1:14. 'Came into being' involves a crisis in time when the Son was not. 'Am,' like the other form of the same verb in 1:1, means timeless being. There never was a time when the Son was not. He could always assert, 'I Am.' Three times in this context I am is used in the absolute sense: In verse 24, 'Except ye believe that I Am He, ye shall die in your sins'; in verse 28, 'When ye have lifted up the Son of man, then shall ye know that I am He,' and in verse 58, 'Before Abraham was born, I Am.' In no one of these passages does the third personal pronoun he follow the I am in Greek text. The italicized forms show that it has been inserted by the translators to complete the meaning of the English. In actuality the phrase I am is an assertion of absolute, timeless existence, not merely of a personal identity as the English equivalent would suggest."[26]

There is no doubt that the "I AM's" of John's Gospel should be connected with Exodus 3. Much the same terminology is used by Yahweh in His appearance to Moses in the burning bush occurrence. God, in commissioning Moses (3:14) said: 'Thou shalt say unto the children of Israel, I AM hath sent me to you.[27] When the Jews heard Jesus say, "Before Abraham was born, I am," they took the statement to mean not priority to Abraham, but an assertion of deity. To them it was blasphemy, and they picked up stones to cast at him (59).

The Works of Christ Testify to His Deity

In the Prologue (1:1-14), John by revelation from God described the preexistence of Christ. Prior to assuming human flesh Jesus, God in eternity created the universe, not only did Christ (the LOGOS) create the world, he also upholds and sustains it. "All things came into being through him, and apart from him nothing that exists came into being. In him was life, and the life was the light of men" (v. 3). Verse 10 declares: "He was in the world, and the world through him came into being, yet the world knew him not."

An outstanding feature of Christ's public ministry were his miracles. Of the 35 miracles recorded by the Evangelists, 8 are in the Gospel, 7 of them being wrought before Christ's death, and 1. After His resurrection. Of these eight, six are peculiar to John's Gospel. The following are only found in John: 1. Turning water into wine (2:1-11); 2. Healing a Nobleman's Son (4:46-54); 3. Healing an impotent man (5:1-9); 4. Giving sight to a man born blind (9:1-7); 5. The raising of Lazarus from the dead (11:17-44); 6. The draught of fishes (21:1-14); 7. Feeding of the five thousand (6:1-14); 8. Walking on the sea (6:16-21). The miracles of Christ were so powerful that they produced faith in those who witnessed them. John reports in chapter 2:28: "Now when he was in Jerusalem at the feast of the Passover, many believed in his name, when they beheld the signs which he did" (2:23-24). In chapter 20:31 John said about Christ's miracles: "But these are written that you may believe that Jesus is the Christ, the Son of God, and that by believing you may have life in his name."[27a]

The Old Testament Scriptures Testify to Christ

In His controversy with the Jews, Jesus reminded them that their Scriptures testified to Him. If His countrymen would follow the Old Testament which spoke of Him as life giver, they could have life, a gift which God only could bestow. Jesus unequivocally declared that the Old Testament wrote about him. "Because they refused to accept Moses' words, how could they believe His words?" (6:46-47).

The Testimony of Certain Disciples and Believers
1. Nathaniel's Testimony to Christ's Deity

The first chapter of the Fourth Gospel reports how Jesus' first disciples recognized Jesus as God. As a result of the testimony of John the Baptist: "Behold, the Lamb of God which takes away the sins of the world," (1:29) two disciples, Andrew and Simon, followed Jesus. In Galilee, the third of the first group of disciples accepted the Messiahship of Jesus confessed: "Rabbi, you are the Son of God" (1:49).

2. The Witness of the Samaritan Woman

John alone reports the journey of Christ through Samaria, probably in A.D. 26, where the Master met the Samaritan woman. After Jesus had revealed to the woman her past life and responded to the question as to where the true God was to be worshipped and that He was the promised Messiah, she informed her town's people that this was the Christ. The people of Sychar told the Samaritan woman: "We no longer believe what you said, for we ourselves have heard him, and we know that this is certainly the Savior of the world" (4:42).

3. The Testimony of Martha

When Jesus came to raise Lazarus from the dead, he was met by Martha, sister of Mary and Lazarus, to whom Jesus said: "I am the resurrection and the life, and everyone who believes in me, shall never die. Do you believe this?" To the latter question Martha responded: "Yes, Master, I have come to believe that you are the Christ, the Son of God, who has to come into the world" (John 11:27).

4. Peter's Great Confession

After the feeding of the 5,000 Jesus went to Capernaum, whither the Jews followed Him wanting to make Jesus a Bread King. As a result of His "Bread of Life" Sermon most of His listeners deserted Him. When Jesus asked the Twelve whether they would also forsake Him, Peter responded: "To Whom should we go, Master? You have the words of eternal life; and we have learned to believe and we know that you are the Holy One of God (6:68)." This confession reminds the Bible reader of another declaration Peter made at Caesarea Philippi: "Thou art the Christ, the Son of the Living God" (Matthew 16:16).

5. The Testimony of Thomas

One of the Twelve, Thomas not present on Easter evening when Christ appeared to the Ten Disciples and others present was there a week later. When Jesus gave doubting Thomas evidence of His physical resurrection, Thomas declared: "My Lord and my God" (20:28).

6. The Testimony of Jesus' Enemies to Christ's Deity

John chapter 5:1-16 reports how Jesus healed a cripple and how he asserted the necessity of the Jews to believe in Him (v. 24). "Solemnly, I tell you that the hour is coming and now is, when the dead shall hear the voice of the Son of God, and those shall hear shall live" (5:19). The response of the Jews testifies to the fact that they understood Jesus' claim to be God. The result was: "Therefore the Jews sought the more to kill Him, because He said also that God was His Father making Himself equal with God" (v. 18). What John has penned provokes the question: "Did Jesus really make Himself equal to God?"[28] Sidlow Baxter gave seven particulars which show that Jesus did just that. Baxter showed that in the following declarations of Jesus this was done. 1. **Equal in working**. "What things soever the Father doeth, these also the Son doeth likewise" (v. 19). 2. **Equal in knowing**. "For the Father loveth the Son and showeth Him all things that He Himself doeth" (v. 20). 3. **Equal in resurrection.** "For as the Father raiseth up the dead, so the Son quickeneth whom He will" (verses 21, 28-29). 4. **Equal in judging**. "For the Father judgeth no man, but hath committed all judgment unto the Son" (w. 22,27). 5. **Equal in honor**. "That all men should honor the Son as they honor the Father" (v. 23). 6. **Equal in regenerating**. "He that heareth My word and believeth in Him that sent Me is passed from death unto life" (w. 24-25). 7. **Equal in self-existence**. "For the Father hath life in Himself, so hath He given to the Son to have life in Himself."[29]

To be added to the list of those who professed the deity of Christ, according to Mark, were even the demons who possessed people bodily as they were confronted by Jesus confessed His deity. Thus in Mark 5:7 the reader is told: "The evil spirit said: 'Jesus, Son of God most high, what business have you with me? I adjure thee by God, torment me not!'"

Machen's Statement About Christ's Deity

"Thus Jesus, according to all the Gospels, presents Himself as the object of a truly religious faith. Well, who is the object of a truly religious faith? The answer is very simple. He is God. The way in which, in all the Gospels and even in the sources supposed, rightly or wrongly, underlie the Gospels, Jesus presents Himself as the object of faith is a tremendous testimony by Jesus Himself to His own deity. That testimony does not appear merely in individual passages. It is a kind of atmosphere that pervades the whole picture, or, to change the figure, a foundation that sustains the whole building. If you ignore it, the whole account which the Bible gives of Jesus becomes a hopeless puzzle."[30]

Footnotes

1. The Book of Acts 20:35.

2. William Arndt, *New Testament History* (St. Louis: Concordia Publishing House, 1940), pp. 18-19.

3. St. Matthew 24:1-3.

4. H. Wayne House, *Chronological and Background Charts of the New Testament* (Grand Rapids: Zondervan Publishing House, 1981), p. 95.

5. W. Graham Scroggie, *Know Your Bible*, Vol. 1, *Analytical* (London: Pickering and Inglis, no date), pp. 22-23.

6. A. Baumstark, *Geschichte der Syrischen Literatur* (Bonn: A. Marcus und E. Webers Verlag Dr. Jur. Albert Ahn, 1922), pp. 19-20; Anton Baumstark, Die Christliche Literaturen des Orients (Leipzig: G. J. Goeschen'sche verlagahandiung, 1911), 1, pp. 54ff.

7. Scroggie, **op. cit.**, p. 95.

8. As cited by D. A. Hayes, *John and His Writings* (New York: The Methodist Book Concern, 1917), p. 77.

9. **Ibid.**, p. 77.

10. **Ibid.**, p. 77.

11. W. T. Davidson in Hasting's One Volume *Bible Dictionary of Bible*, p. 477.

12. A. T. Pierson, *Keys to the Words*, p. 103 as cited by Hayes, **op. cit.**, p. 77.

13. Merrill C. Tenney, *The Zondervan Pictorial Bible Dictionary*, 1963), p. 44.

14. Cf. "Quest of the Historical Jesus (The); Leben Jesu Forschung, Liberal Lives," in Richard N. Soulen, *Handbook of Biblical Criticism* (Atlanta, John Knox Press, 1957), pp. 159-161.

15. Leon Morris, *New Testament Theology* (Grand Rapids: Zondervan Publishing House, Academic Books, 1986), p. 228.

16. Samuel Miller, *The Gospel of John* (Minneapolis: Lutheran Bible Institute, 1928), Chart at end of the volume.

16a. Morris, **op. cit.**, p. 238.

17. Helen Barrett Montgomery, *The New Testament in Modern English* (Philadelphia: The Judson Press, 1924), p. 241.

18. **Ibid.**, p. 241.

19. Morris, **op. cit.**, 239b; Hayes, **op. cit.**, p. 107.

20. Isaiah 40:3; Malachi 4:5-6.

21. Montgomery, **op. cit.**, 343.

22. **Ibid.**, p. 255.

23. **Ibid.**, p. 254.

24. Morris, **op. cit.**, p. 239.

25. Cf. Morris' discussion of the "I AM's" sayings, pp. 235 a-238b.

26. Merrill C. Tenney, *John The Gospel of Belief* (Grand Rapids: Wm. B. Eerdmans Publishing Company, 1948), pp. 149-155.

27a. F. W. Weidner, *Biblical Theology of New Testament* (Burlington, Iowa Lutheran Literary Board, 1891) I, pp. 38-39.

27. **Ibid.**, p. 150.

28. Scroggie, *A Guide to the Gospels*, **op. cit.**, p. 202.

29. J. Sidlow Baxter, *Explore the Book* (Grand Rapids: Zondervan Publishing House, 1967), "The Gospel According to John (3)," Lesson Number 123, p. 309.

30. J. Gresham Machen, *The Christian Faith in the Modern World* (Grand Rapids: Wm. B. Eerdmans Publishing Co., 1947), p. 158.

Questions

1. The Four Gospels may be divided into ____.
2. Matthew's Gospel is intended for ____ Mark's for ____ Luke's for ____ and John's for ____.
3. Matthew represents the ____, Mark the ____, Luke the ____, and John

the ____.

4. John deals with such abstract themes as ____.

5. Mark is characterized by ____.

6. What is given prominence in the Gospel of John? ____

7. The most vocal opponents the Christian faith are now come from ____.

8. ____ is one of the key words of the fourth Gospel.

9. What is absolutely necessary for salvation? ____

10. If the Father is God, so His Son must be ____.

11. Why did the Jews seek to put Christ to death? ____

12. Distinctive of the Fourth Gospel is ____.

13. There never was a time when the Son ____.

14. The I Am's of John's Gospel should be connected with ____.

15. What was the testimony of Thomas? ____

ELCA and the Jesus Seminar
The Resurrection of Christ
A Lutheran Attack on the Resurrection of Christ by a Defender of Jesus Seminar's Rejection of Christ's Corporal Resurrection
(A Biblical Refutation)

Christian News, May 1, 1995

Clark Morphew, a columnist for a St. Paul newspaper and a clergyman of the Evangelical Lutheran Church in America (ELCA), has given vent to his theological liberalism in his column written for Easter Sunday, entitled: "Believers should ignore diatribe on resurrection."[1] His latest attack on the reliability of Holy Writ defends and lauds the devastating conclusions of the Jesus Seminar relative to the historicity of Christ's resurrection. Morphew has correctly summarized the conclusions of the Protestant and Roman Catholic scholars who have attacked the very foundation of the Christian faith when he wrote: "Yes, this time the group of biblical scholars has pontificated about the resurrection, which has been considered the central event of the Christian story. In other words, if the resurrection didn't happen, you can kiss the Christian faith good-bye."[2]

The Jesus Seminar has selected one of the well-known explanations for explaining away the fact of the miracle of Christ's resurrection, namely, the Vision Theory. A former Lutheran professor and at one time president of Northwestern Theological Seminary, a defender of Christ's resurrection, described the Vision Theory as follows: "The Vision Theory maintains that the disciples, by brooding over Christ's death and His promised resurrection, became the victims of hallucinations, in which they imagined that they saw Him risen from the dead. The conditions necessary for such hallucinations, however, were not present. There was no glowing faith in the promised resurrection which would incline them to imagine that it had taken place. There was no lapse of sufficient time for such supposed brooding to produce hallucinations. It is utterly unlikely, if not impossible, that an identical hallucination should exist on the part of so many different individuals, or that five hundred brethren should simultaneously have the same visual delusion; or that such hallucinations, if they existed, should all cease among all the disciples at the end of forty days."[3]

According to Morphew, if a photograph had been taken at the grave on Easter morn, that his camera could not have captured the words spoken or the flashes of lightning.[4] However, there still would have been evidence, for if a picture had been taken, it would have shown the empty tomb and angels in human form. If the photographer had waited later he would have recorded the fact that a number of women looked into the empty tomb.

Morphew has no patience with books currently published discussing the identity of Jesus and is annoyed by those attacking the unbelief and misrepresentation of the Christian Gospel. The St. Paul ELCA clergyman commends the Jesus Seminar scholars for acquainting people in the pew with the higher criticism set forth in liberal theological seminaries, which is currently being done by professors in the ELCA's seminaries.[5] Morphew justifies this unsettling of the laypeople's faith by stating "Preachers know this stuff, but people sitting in the pew don't have a clue that biblical material is anything but a myth."[6]

Those Christian scholars who have opposed and still do reject the soul-destroying negative criticism of higher criticism are castigated by the ELCA clergyman because "the Jesus Seminar scholars are simply pointing out that the Bible was written by people who were capable of mistakes and who often had an axe to grind."[7]

Morphew informs his readers that the devastating critique of the Seminar need not change people's faith. The wonder of Easter is that in America, "the right of inquiry and bold thinking cannot be repressed."[8] Even though Jesus rotted in the grave, the believer may take great comfort and take a great leap of faith and say: "I believe in the resurrection of the body and life everlasting."[9] Even though there is no factual evidence for these beliefs according to the Jesus Seminar, people can believe truths which are mythical and fictional. The higher criticism which Morphew commends is known to use reason to debunk the Bible. Yet now Morphew is willing to abandon the use of logic and reason and tells his readers they can believe in events that never occurred. Ordinarily, when individuals imagine events that never occurred and then insist on their historicity and actuality, they are said to have mental problems and are even confined to a mental institution.

Since Morphew does not obtain his religious views from the Bible, he has to resort to philosophy and human speculation. Here the ELCA cleric has adopted Kierkegaard's "leap of faith" concept. Ramm in his book, *Handbook of Christian Theology* stated: "Kierkegaard introduced the concept of the leap into theology. In discussing the proofs for the existence of God, he states that the proofs do not seem to prove anything as we work them out. But when we let go of them God suddenly exists. In that moment we have leaped. . . Since fact is not the product of rational thought but a decision in the face of personality, it is a leap.[10] Kierkegaard is the father of neoorthodoxy. Similar statements can be found in Brunner,[11] Bultmann[12] and Barth[13] expressed—similar views about 'the leap of faith.'"

Biblical Doctrine of the Resurrection of Christ

The doctrine of the physical resurrection of Christ from the grave is central to the New Testament.[14]

All four evangelists give accounts of Christ's resurrection and declare that during the forty-day period He appeared at least ten different times.[15] Jesus appeared to 1. Mary Magdalene (Mark 16:9-11; John 20:11-18); 2. To the other women (Matt. 28:9-10). 3. To Simon Peter (Luke 24:33-35; 1 Cor. 15:5); 4. The two disciples on the Emmaus Road (Luke

24:13-32; Mark 16:14). 5. To the Ten Apostles and others (Mark 16:14; Luke 24:36-43; John 20:19-25). These five appearances occurred on the resurrection. 6. Appearance to the Eleven Apostles (John 20:26-31; 1 Cor. 15:5). 7. Appearances to the Seven Disciples (John 21:1-22). 8. Appearance to the Apostles and over Five Hundred Disciples in Galilee (Matt. 28:16-20; 1 Cor. 15:6). 9. Appearance to James, the Lord's Brother (1 Cor. 15:7; Mark 16:19-20). 10. Appearance for the last time to the Apostles (Luke 24:44-48; Acts 1:3).

An Analysis of the Post-resurrection Appearances[16]

Jesus did not appear to unbelievers or the leaders of the Jewish people, to the high priest or the Jewish Sanhedrin which had condemned Him to death. However, the followers of Jesus did see Christ alive who had died and been buried in Joseph of Arimathea's tomb. Christ appeared to both sexes. Women have the honor of having seen Him first. Mary Magdalene, a number of women, two disciples on the Emmaus Road, ten Apostles, the Eleven Apostles, with Thomas present, Peter, Thomas, Nathaniel, James, John and two other disciples, the eleven Apostles and five hundred disciples, James, finally again the Eleven.[17]

An analysis shows that Jesus appeared in order to one, a group, one, two, the eleven, seven, eleven, and 500, one and eleven. Scroggie asserted: "Three times. He appeared to eleven of the Apostles; once to ten of the Apostles, once to ten of them, and once to five of them. Two of the appearances, the first two, were to women. Three of the appearances were to individuals, Mary, Peter and James. Six of the appearances were to non-Apostles, the women, Emmaus disciples, the two disciples who were with the five Apostles, the five hundred disciples, and James, Jesus' brother. Concerning the variegated character of the appearances, to male and female witnesses. Bishop Westcott said the resurrection is one of the best attested facts of history. Twenty-seven years after the resurrection Paul claimed that there were 250 persons living who had seen the Lord in Galilee."[18]

The Scenes of the Appearances of Christ

Six out of the ten appearances were made inland around Jerusalem one road leading from Jerusalem to Emmaus; three were made in Galilee, if the meeting of Jesus is placed in the north, but it may have been in the south.[19] The appearances around Jerusalem to Mary, to the other women and Peter occurred out of doors. The three to the Apostles were made in the upper room, and on Mount Olivet. Of the two appearances in Galilee, one was on a mountain, the other by the Lake of Galilee (John 21). The first six appearances were made in the south, the next three, in the north (if that to James be included), and the last in the south again.

The Manner of the Appearances

Stump in his discussion of the resurrection, of Christ, the second step in the State of Exaltation, said this about the body of Christ: "The body with which Christ arose and appeared to his disciples was not a seeming body temporarily assumed, but a real body which had flesh and bones (Luke 24:34), and which was the same body which was crucified. It was recognized by the disciples and had the marks of the nails and spears (John 20:27). But it had undergone a great change, so that it was also a new and different body. It had now new powers and properties. During the forty days after Easter Jesus appeared to His disciples, His body was manifestly no longer hampered by limitations of the body in its natural state. Jesus was able to pass through closed doors and to appear and disappear at will in widely-separated places."[20]

The natural and supernatural are strangely blended. The natural features are visible, physical body, with marks of the nails and the feet. His references to his "flesh-and-bones" and eating "a piece of broiled fish" show he had a real body. Jesus first convinced the Apostles of His identity and then of His corporeality.

The Teachings of the Appearances

The passages which are instructive relative to the theological teachings taught, set forth and implied by these ten post-resurrection appearances are the following: (1) John 20:17; (2) Luke 24:25-27; (3) John 20:21-31; (4) John 21:15-22; (5) Matt. 28:18-29; (6) Luke 24:44-49; Acts 1:1-11. From these verses the Christian can deduce the following teachings: 1. When Jesus appeared unto Magdalene (John 20) He told her that there could no longer be tangible demonstrations toward Him, that is what is implied when He said to her: "Touch me not." When later He allowed the other women to touch Him, it was not accepted as an expression of affection but as an act of worship. Thomas was invited to touch the wounds caused by the crucifixion; Thomas was allowed to put his fingers in Jesus' wounds in order that Thomas would become convinced of His corporeality. In His conversation with His followers, the Lord distinguished their God and His Father. This he did on two occasions.

2. Jesus proved to the Emmaus disciple, to Cleophas and his friend, that He was the promised Messiah of the Old Testament and that the purpose of the Old Covenant Scriptures was to testify to Him, especially His death and resurrection.

3. Christ saw in the Apostles the future of Christ and gave them a mission to make disciples of all nations (Matt. 28:18). They were to continue the mission Christ had come to do, except that Christ had limited His activity to Palestine, Syria and the Decaplois. He further gave His followers who would constitute the Church the power to forgive and retain sins (John 20:23; Matt. 18:18).

4. In John 21:15-19 the Lord gave Peter, one of His under shepherds three progressive charges, including the whole pastoral office: "feed my sheep" and "feed my lambs." These commands covered the whole range of a Christian church's program. Christ also indicated that Peter would die a violent death.

5. The Great Commission of Matthew 28:18-20 given on a Galilee mountain is the most profound and wonderful of all post-resurrection teachings of Jesus. It contains three important teachings:

1772

A. All authority has been given me in heaven and in earth.

B. Go therefore go and make disciples of all nations by baptizing them in the name of the Father and of the Son and of the Holy Spirit, teaching them to observe (or obey) everything I have commanded you.

C. Surely I will be with you always, to the very end of the age.

6. Elements of the previous utterances are in Luke 24:44-49. Christ the fulfillment of the Old Testament Scriptures, preaching to all nations, and the endowment of the Holy Spirit (cf. Luke 24:25-27; Matt. 28:19; Luke 24:22-23; Acts 1:4-5).

7. The last appearance of Christ on the Mount of Olives is noteworthy, because in taking physical leave of His disciples, he repeated the Great Commission in these words: "And you are to be my witnesses both in Jerusalem, and in all Judea, and in Samaria, and to the very ends of the earth." The last appearance also predicted the outpouring of the Holy Spirit, a prophecy fulfilled ten days later on Pentecost. Christ also corrected a misconception the disciples had at this time relative to the true nature of God's kingdom. At this time the disciples had a carnal conception of God's kingdom instead of giving them hope for an establishment of an earthly kingdom, Christ directed His Apostles to the real Messianic kingdom.

Post Ascension Appearances of Christ

Luke, doctor and historian, records the fact that when Stephen, one of the deacons of the Jerusalem Church, as he was being stoned to death, said: "Look, I see the heavens open, and the Son of man standing on the right hand of God" (Acts 7:56).[21] In connection with the miracle of the conversion of St. Paul, Paul claimed that Christ appeared to him and spoke with him (Acts 9:3-9). In his defense before the Jewish mob who wanted told Paul, Paul reported the same facts as given by Luke's account of his conversion (Acts 22:3-16). Paul repeated the same account of his conversion before King Agrippa, stating that Christ appeared to him on the Damascene Road. John, in his apocalyptic writing, presents Christ appearing to him on the Island of Patmos (Revelation 1:12:16).

The Centrality of the Resurrection of Christ

The resurrection holds a central place in the Christian religion. It proves Jesus to be the Son of God and the Savior of men, and guarantees our own resurrection from the dead on the last day. Christianity either stands or falls if the resurrection did or did not occur. For this reason the four resurrection accounts in the Gospels have been under attack. A number of theories have propounded by the enemies of the Christian faith. The principal ones have been the Swoon or Vision Theories. The Jesus Seminar chose the latter, one of which we already have shown its fallaciousness. The Swoon Theory contends that the body of Jesus revived in the tomb and rejoined its disciples. But the theory is simply discredited in the face of the clear facts of Christ's crucifixion and death and of the certainty that the complete change in the disciples, after they were assured of the resurrection, could not have produced by the appearance among them of a crucified man who had been resuscitated from the

Swoon and would necessarily be a weak and pitiable object to look at.[21]

Truths Flowing from Christ's
Physical Resurrection from the Dead

Christ claimed to be the Son of God and this declaration was proved by the fact that God the Father, the Holy Spirit and the Son raised the dead Jesus.[22] Otherwise Christ would have been shown to be an impostor. The resurrection on Easter morning proves further that He was not an impostor. Jesus had predicted: "Destroy this temple, and in three days I will raise it again." The resurrection guarantees the sufficiency and actuality of Christ's work of redemption, because he paid the ransom for us. Christ's resurrection guarantees the Christian's resurrection. Now His followers can believe the Savior's promise: "I go to prepare a place for you (John 14:1)." If Christ had not been raised the Apostles would not have the message of power and persuasion which they had during their missionary efforts.

Paul's Refutation of Jesus Seminar's
Rejection of the Resurrection

Some members of the Christian Corinthian church had been declaring that there was no resurrection of the dead, a view held by Greek philosophy and religion. Paul in his first letter to the Corinthians, in chapter 15 dealt with this error and false teaching showing the fact that Christ's resurrection underlies the very existence of the Christian faith. In Chapter 15, one of the most important chapters in the New Testament, which Paul penned under the guidance and inspiration of the Holy Spirit states that the Gospel of Christ's resurrection from the dead implies the resurrection of Christians; for if the dead do not rise than Christ is still dead, the preaching of the Gospel is useless, and the Apostles are false witnesses (vv. 12-15). If Christ has not been raised, then faith in Him is empty. Christians are yet in their sins, those who have died in Him have perished, and Christian life is a pitiful delusion (w. 16-19).

The Apostle Peter's Hymn of Praise for Christ's Resurrection

In his "Epistle of Hope" Simon Peter opens his first letter to the congregations of Asia Minor: "Blessed be the God and Father of our Lord Jesus Christ who according to His abundant mercy has begotten us again to a living hope through the resurrection of Jesus Christ from the dead to an inheritance incorruptible and undefiled and that does not fade away, reserved in heaven for you, who are kept up by the power of God through faith for salvation ready to be revealed in the last time" (1:3-5).[23]

The Letter to the Hebrews Easter Doxology

Now may the God of peace who brought up our Lord Jesus from the dead, that great Shepherd of the sheep, through the blood of the everlasting covenant make you complete in every good work, working in you what is well pleasing in His sight, through Jesus Christ, to whom be glory forever and ever" (13:20-21).[24]

Value Judgments about Christ's Resurrection for the Christian Faith

John Theodore Mueller rendered this judgment: Holy Scripture, however, affirms that the denial of the resurrection involves the denial of the entire Gospel of Christ, 1 Cor. 15:12-19. It unqualifiedly condemns those who deny resurrection as having made shipwreck of their faith and erred concerning the truth, 1 Tim. 1:19-22; 2 Tim. 2:17,18. Hymenaeus and Alexander, who denied the resurrection, were delivered by St. Paul "unto Satan that they may learn not to blaspheme." The denial of the resurrection is therefore tantamount to blasphemy of Christ. It is for this reason we classify the doctrine of the resurrection among the fundamental doctrines of the Christian faith.[25]

Haberman correctly averred: "That Jesus Christ died and afterward rose from the dead is both the central doctrine of Christian theology and the major factor in a defense of its teachings. This was true in the earliest church and remains so today."[26]

Footnotes

1. *Summit Magazine*, April 15, 1995, p. 15, as found in *The Fort Wayne News Sentinel*, April 15, 1995.
2. **Ibid.**, p. Su. 15, Column A.
3. Joseph Slump, *The Christian Faith* (New York: The Macmillan Company 19321, p. 177.
4. Morphew, **op. cit.**, Column B.
5. **Ibid.**, *Summit Magazine,* Su. 15.
6. **Ibid.**
7. **Ibid.**
8. **Ibid.**
9. **Ibid.**, Column C.
10. Bernard Ramm, *A Handbook of Contemporary Theology* (Grand Rapids: William B. Publishing Company, 1966), p. 79; Martin J. Henecken, "Soren Kierkegaard," *A Handbook of Christian Theologians* (New York and Cleveland: World Publishing Company, 1965), pp. 143-157.
11. Emil Brunner, *The Philosophy of Religion*, p. 29.
12. Ramm. **op. cit.**, p. 79; John Macquarrie, "Rudolf Bultmann," in Martin Marty, *A Handbook of Christian Theologians*, **op. cit.**, pp. 445-463.
13. Karl Barth, *Church Dogmatics,* 1/2, 23 ff. in Marty, **op. cit.**, pp. 396-408; Daniel Jenkins, "Karl Barth."
14. Walther Kuenneth, *The Theology of the Resurrection* (St. Louis: CPH, 1965), p. 294.
15. Cf. Adam Fahling, *A Harmony of the Gospels* (Grand Rapids: Zondervan Publishing Company, no dale), pp. 216-225; Adam Fahling, *The Life of Christ* (St. Louis; CPH, 1936), 687-711.
16. W. Graham Scroggoe, *A Guide to the Gospels* (London: Pickering and Inglis, 1948), p. 609.
17. **Ibid.**, p. 610.
18. **Ibid.**
19. **Ibid.**, pp. 610-611.

20. Slump, **op. cit.**, p. 177.

21. Cf. The discussion on the three accounts of Paul's Conversion, in William Arndt, *Bible Difficulties and Contradictions*, Revised edition by Robert G. Hoerber and Walter Roehrs (St. Louis; CPH, 1987), p. 129.

22. Cf. Stump, **op. cit.**, p. 176; for the Father: Col. 2:12; Acts 2:24; for Holy Spirit: Romans 8:11 and by Christ's own act: John 10:18; 2:19. The explanation that all three persons of the Trinity were involved in the resurrection of Christ is found in the fact that the Father, the Son and the Holy Ghost are one Triune God.

23. *Holy Bible New King James Version* (New York: Thomas Nelson Publishers, 1982), p. 11.

24. **Ibid.**, p. 1181.

25. John Theodore Mueller, *Christian Dogmatics* (St. Louis: CPH, 1955), pp. 51-52.

26. G.R. Haberman, "Resurrection of Christ," Walter A. Elwell, Editor, *Evangelical Dictionary of Theology* (Grand Rapids: Baker Book House, 1984), p. 928b.

Questions

1. Who was Clark Morphew? ____

2. What is wrong with the vision theory of the Resurrection? ____

3. What is currently being taught by ELCA professors about the Resurrection? ____

4. Can an honest person believe that an event that did not happen is a historical fact? ____

5. Kierkegaard is the father of ____.

6. The doctrine of the physical resurrection of Christ is ____ to the New Testament.

7. What are some post resurrection appearances of the resurrected Christ? ____

8. The resurrection of Christ proves ____.

9. What is wrong with the Swoon Theory? ____

10. What is one of the most important chapters in the New Testament? ____

11. The denial of the resurrection in tantamount to ____.

God's Word to the Nations Bible Society's GOD'S WORD
Justification "By Faith" or
Justification "Because of Faith" or
Justification as "The Result of Faith?"

(A Study for The Luther Days, October 31 till November 11)

Christian News, November 6, 1995

There are three slogans that are said to set forth the heart of the Lutheran and Protestant Reformations.[1] They are SOLA SCRIPTURA (Scripture Alone), SOLA GRATIA (By Grace Alone) and SOLA FIDE (By Faith Alone). Some would add also: SOLUS CHRISTUS (Christ Alone). Apart from Christ, the Word of God teaches there cannot be salvation for any person (Acts 4:12; John 14:6). Without Christ these other solas would be meaningless. The core and essence of Roman Catholic theology involves a difference of understanding of these four solas. It is in the areas of these four theological assertions that the differences between Rome and true Biblical Christianity are to be found.

These four solas are based upon Holy Writ and not on human tradition or ecclesiastical speculations. These four solas are often denied or misrepresented. Such is the case with the phrase "justification by faith." Two recent versions of the New Testament have rendered verses that deal with justification by faith in a manner which can be misunderstood; these translations render "because of faith" or "in view of the faith" that the justification of the sinner before God occurs, and appear to deny or vitiate the truth that faith is the apprehending hand that is caused by the Holy Spirit to accept God's grace and trust in His Son as the redeemer from sin and damnation.[2]

Translations Which Present a
Problem on Justification by Faith

Thus *God's Word: Today's Bible Translation That Says What It Means*, published by World Publishing, Inc., Grand Rapids, Michigan has some readings that at best make the doctrine of justification by faith fuzzy and unclear, some would go so far as to claim these rendering vitiate the doctrine as to how justification is made possible.[3] This World Publishing Bible was the continuation of the *Holy Bible, New Evangelical Translation (NET)* Net Publishing Company, Cleveland, Ohio (1992).[4] The latter was the work of 25 scholars who worked on NET, using Beck's AAT as a base. The majority of translators were Lutheran Church-Missouri Synod scholars and thus one could say it was a Lutheran translation. The 1994 World Publishing Bible made some significant changes in its rendering of justification, in fact, it avoids the word "justify" and speaks of man "winning approval."[5] Thus the reader of *God's Word, Today's Bible Translation That Says What It Means* has these renderings of the Greek text in Romans 1:17; thus chapter 1:17 has: "God's approval is revealed in this Good News." This approval begins and ends with faith as Scripture says, "The person who has God's approval will live because of faith."[6] Romans 3:28 is translated: "We conclude that a person has God's approval because of faith not because of his own efforts."[7] In chapter 5:1 this same mistranslation occurred: "Now that we have God's approval because of faith, we have peace with God."[8] In Galatians 3:24 the reader is informed: "Christ came so that we would receive God's approval because of faith."[9] Yet Ephesians 2:8 the same version translated: "God saved you through faith as an act of kindness."[9a] Why these changes were made between the 1992 and 1994 editions has puzzled many who worked on the original Beck revision.[10]

Another recent version to challenge the traditional rendering of justification by faith is The American Bible Society's newest venture to make the Word of God available to the common people.

It is called *Holy Bible, Contemporary Version* (1995). Here are some of the verses from Romans. Chapter 1:17 is translated: "It is just as the Scripture says, 'The people of God accepts because of their faith will live.'"[11] A footnote gives this alternative possibility: "but only those who have faith," or "And faith is all that matters." Romans 3:30 reads like this: "There is only one God, and he accepts Gentiles as well as Jews because of their faith."[12] In 3:22 the reader is informed: "God treats everyone alike. He accepts people only because they have faith."[13] Romans 5:1 is made to read: "By faith we have been made acceptable to God."[14] Galatians 3:7 is translated: "Long ago the Scriptures said that God would accept the Gentiles because of their faith."[15]

These renderings in the two recent versions are actually not new, for a number of translations have similar interpretations. Thus Weymouth rendered Romans 3:21: "But now a righteousness of God has been brought to light apart from any law, both Law and Prophets bearing witness to it—a righteousness of God conditioned on faith in Jesus Christ for all who believe."[16] Schoenfeld, *The Authentic New Testament* translated Romans 5:1: "So being exonerated on a basis of faith, enjoy peace with God through our Lord Jesus Christ."[17]

Also *The New World Translation* (of The Jehovah Witnesses) understands Romans 5:1, thus giving the impression that faith is the reason why man is justified,[18] making it the true reason for forensic justification. *The Centenary Translation of the New Testament* rendered Romans 5:1: "since we stand justified as the result of faith, let us continue to enjoy peace through our Lord Jesus Christ."[19] Galatians 3:8 in The New World Version reads: "Now the Scripture, seeing in advance that God would declare people of, the nation's righteous due to faith."[20] Verse 11 of the same chapter renders the thought of this verse: "Moreover by the law no one is declared righteous with God is evident because the righteous one will live by reason of his faith."[21]

Webster's Dictionary "On Because"

Webster's *World Dictionary of the American Language* defines "because, as for the reason of," or "because that," "on account of the fact that."[22] All the examples in *God's Word* and *The Contemporary Version of the American Bible Society* and others cited previously appear to make faith the reason why God justifies human beings, thereby denying that God's act of the justification of the sinner is totally a gratuitous act of God's grace and mercy. The rendering of justification in all versions mentioned heretofore vitiates what Paul wrote in Ephesians: "For it is by grace that you have been saved through faith —and this not of yourselves, it is the gift of God—not by works, so that no one can boast" (Ch. 8-9).[23]

Crediting a person with contributing to his justification, impinges on the forensic character of justification. Thus J.T. Mueller, asserted: "When we speak of justification as a forensic, or judicial, act, we must, note however, that there is a distinctive difference between the judgment of the civil courts and that of God. The civil courts justify, or declare righteous, the just and condemn the wicked. Those who justify the wicked and condemn the just are an abomination to the Lord, Pov. 17,15. But God, in the act of justification, justifies the ungodly, Rom. 4,5, and this on the valid ground that Christ by His perfect obedience has paid the debt for the wicked. Is. 53,5,6; 2 Cor. 5:21."[24]

The Relationship of Faith to Justification

The Reformed scholar L. Berkhof has this insightful correct observation: "Scripture says that we are justified **dia pisteos, ek pisteos**, or **pistei** (dative), Romans 3:25,28,30; 5:1; Gal. 2:16; Phil. 3:9. The preposition **dia** stresses the fact that faith is the instrument by which we appropriate Christ and His righteousness. The preposition **ek** indicates that faith logically precedes our personal justification, so that this, as it were originates in faith. The dative is used in an instrumental sense. Scripture never says that we are justified **dia ten pistin**, on account of faith. This means that faith is never presented as the ground for justification. If this were the case, faith would have to be regarded as a meritorious work of man. And this would be the introduction to the doctrine of justification by works which the apostle opposes consistently, Rom. 3:21,27; 4:3,4; Gal. 3:16,21; 3:11."[25]

Greek Grammars Support Justification by Faith

A perusal of Greek grammars support the traditional "by" "or" through faith understanding. A study of **ek pisteos** and **dia pisteos** in Greek grammars supports the "through," or "by" translation, as does also the use of the dative as instrumental, helps in the rendering of "by faith," Chamberlain in An Exegetical Grammar of New Testament Greek asserted that the Greek particle **"dia"** with the genetive has as its primary idea the meaning of "through."[26] On the top of page 18 he gives an example **"dia Pisteos"** (Ephesians 2:8), "by means of faith."[27] However, he also pointed out that **dia** with the accusative expresses the ground or reason for an act, with the idea of "because of," "for the sake of," "on account of."[28] A. T. Robertson in *A Grammar of the Greek New Testament in the Light of Historical Research* claimed: "The agent may also be expressed by **dia**. This function was performed also in ancient Greek, though, when it means or instrument was meant, the Instrument was commonly employed. **Dia** is used with animate and inanimate objects, of course the agent is conceived as coming between the non-attainment and the attainment of the object in view."[29]

Relative to the preposition **ek** (eks) Chamberlain asserted as follows: "This preposition is used only with the ablative. It means 'out of,' 'from within.'"[30] Dana and Mantey, *A Manual of the Greek Grammar of the New Testament* claimed that the preposition **dia** means, "two, between, through."[31] As a remote usage: "By." The same grammar asserts about the preposition "**ek**" that it means "from within." Dana and Mantey also listed as meaning for "**ek**" that it means, "By means of."[32] Romans 1:17, in Greek **pisteos Tsesetai** means "saved by means of faith." In Romans 3:30 we have "who will justify **ek pisteos**."[33] George Milligan *Greek Papyri* stated that there are four places were **dia** means "by."[34] Other Greek Grammars may be consulted which will confirm the foregoing.[35]

Greek Lexica on Justification by Faith

Souter in his Pocket Lexicon of the Greek New Testament defined **dia** with genitive as "through." "By instrumentality."[36] Abbott-Smith in *Manual Greek Lexicon of the New Testament* devoted nearly a whole page to the New Testament usage of **dia** and lists (1) the meaning "through," employed among other usages of the genetive of things and persons, citing among other texts Romans 3:30.[37] Gingrich in *Shorter Lexicon* lists **dia** as "through."[38]

New Testament Word Study Books and Justification by Faith

Wuest translated Romans 3:28 like this: "Indeed God's righteousness through faith in Jesus Christ to all who believe."[39] Romans 3:28, the same exegete rendered: "For we have come to a reasoned conclusion that a man is justified by faith, apart from the works of the law."[40] Wuest translated Romans 5:1: "Having therefore been justified by faith, peace we are having with God through our Lord Jesus Christ.[41] Marvin Vincent's well-known *Word Studies in the New Testament*[42] in Romans and in Galatians gave ample evidence that **dia** (through, or by) as well, as **ek** should be translated the way it traditionally has been done."[43] In Galatians 3:11 "Vincent rendered the Greek **ho dikaios ek pisteos tsesetai** as "the righteous shall live by faith."[44] A. T. Robertson in his *Word Pictures of the New Testament*, in both Romans and Galatians, translated faith as occurring "through faith."[45]

Nineteenth and Twentieth-Century
Translations Supporting Justification by Faith

The following versions render **dia pisteos** and **ek pisteos** and **Pistei** "by faith" or "through Faith." *The British Revised Version*,[46] *The New King James Version*,[47] *An American Translation of the University of Chicago*,[48] *The American Standard*,[49] *The New American Standard*,[50] *The New Berkeley Version in Modern English*,[51] James Moffatt, *A New Translation*,[52] *The Revised Standard Version*,[53] Beck's *An American Transla-*

tion,[54] *The New English Bible* (cf. Romans 1:17; 3:12;5:1)[55] Phillip's *Modern English* (Cf. Romans 1:17,5:1),[56] *New International Version* translates the preposition **dia** and **ek** by "through" and "by."[57] *The Good News for Modern Man,*[58] the paraphrase The Living Bible.[59]

Roman Catholic Versions Translating Justification by Faith

Francis Alossius, O.P., rendered Romans 3:28: "for we argue that a man is justified by faith." Romans 5:1 like this: "Having been justified by faith, we have peace with God."[60] *The New American Bible,* produced by The Confraternity of Christian Doctrine of the American Bishops, translated Romans 3:28: "For we hold that a man is justified by faith apart from works, apart from the observance of the law." Romans 5:1 like this: "Now that we have been justified by faith, we are at peace with God."[61] *The New Jerusalem Bible* rendered Romans 1:17: "Or as the scripture says, the upright man finds life through 'faith,' or Romans 5:1: 'So far then we have seen that through our Lord Jesus Christ, by faith we are judged righteous and at peace with God.'"[62]

Justification by Faith According to the Ancient Versions

In the Septuagint Ambakoum (habakkuk) 2:4 reads: "**Ho de dikaios ek pisteos tsesetai,**" "the just shall live by faith."[63] This passage is repeated three times in the New Testament (Romans 1:17; Gal. 3:11; Hebrews 10:38). The *Peshitta* translated Romans 3:28 and 5:1 "the just shall live by faith."[64]

The *Vulgate* rendered Romans 1:17: "Justus autem ex fide Vivi" (The just shall live by faith) and Romans 3:28: "Arbitramus enim justificare hominem per fide." "Therefore we conclude that a man is justified by faith." Romans 5:1 reads in the Vulgate: "Justificare er go ex fide pacem habeamus ad Deum per Dominen Iesum Christum."[65]

European Versions That Translate "Justification by Faith"

Luther in Romans and Galatians translated justification as occurring "durch den Glauben," "by faith."[66] Such is the case in Romans 3:21,28; 5:1; Galatians 2:16;3:8. In an Italian version Giovanni Diodati rendered **dia pisteos** by "per fede," that is "by faith."[67] This is the case in Romans 1:17;3:22; and 5:1. A Norwegian Bible of 1943 translated Romans 3:28: "For vi holder for at mennesket blir Keferdiggjort av troe (by faith)." We hold that a man is justified by faith, and this uten lov-gjernigers (and without good works).[68] Romans 5:1: "da vi nu altsa or erettferdiggjort av troen (by faith) har vi fred med Gud ved Herre Jesus Kristus."[69] The Spanish Bible, Santa Biblia of De Valera, revision of 1960, translated Romans 3:28 as follows: "Concluimos pues, que el hombre es justificado por fe (by faith) sin las obras de la ley."[70] And Romans 5:1: "Justificados, pues, por fe (by faith) condios por medio de nuestro Senor Jesucliristo."[71] The French Bible translation of Louis Segond reproduced Romans 1:17 like this: "Le juste vivra par la foi" (par faith).[72] Segond rendered 3:28: "Car nous penson que le homme par la foi (by faith), sans les oevres del la lois."[73] Romans 5:1 is given as: "Etant done justifies par la foi (by faith) nous avont la paix Jesus-Christ."[74] A Dutch Bible published in 1921 translated Romans (Romeien in Dutch) 3:22, 28,5:1 by the preposition door which means "through."[75] Salkinson- Ginsburg's *Hebrew New Testament* rendered Romans 1:17; 3:22; 3:28; 5:1 with *be almunah* (by faith).[76]

The Lutheran Confessions and Justification by Faith

Both *The Augsburg Confession* and *The Apology of The Augsburg Confession* deal with the various elements involved in the Biblical doctrine of justification, termed as the "chief doctrine of the Christian faith." In the Tappert edition of *The Book of Concord* the defense of this doctrine received in *The Apology*, Article IV, pp. 107-168. In *The Augsburg Confession* not quite six lines are devoted to it. The latter's statement is a classic for succinctness and brevity. It reads as follows: "Our churches also teach that men cannot be justified before God by their own strength, merits or works but are freely justified for Christ's sake through faith when they believe that they are received into favor and that their sins are forgiven on account of Christ, who by his death made satisfaction for our sins. This faith God imputes for righteousness in his sight (Rom. 3,4)."[77]

The Apology of The Augsburg Confession has a number of places in Article IV where it states that justification by faith is clearly taught. Thus in the Tappert's *Book of Concord*, consult page 117, par. 73; page 474, par. 10, page 540, par. 7; page 545, par. 36; page 547, par. 43; page 548, par. 53 and page 551, par. 2.[78]

Footnotes

1. F. E. Mayer, *American Churches, Beliefs and Practices* (St. Louis: CPH, 1961), pp. 1, 4, 6,9.
2. P. E. Kretzmann, *Excursus* on "Justification." In *Popular Commentary* (St. Louis: CPH, 1923), II, p. 20.
3. *God's Word: Today's Bible Translation That Says What It Means* (Grand Rapids: World Publishing, 1995).
4. *Holy Bible. New Evangelical Translation* (Cleveland: NET Publishers, 1992.
5. *God's Word*, **op. cit.**, p. 1413 Romans 3:20.
6. **Ibid.**, p. 1410.
7. **Ibid.**, p. 1413.
8. **Ibid.**, p. 1415.
9. **Ibid.**, p. 1415.
10. William F. Beck, *The Holy Bible, An American Translation* (New Haven: Leader Publishing Company, 1976), New Testament Romans 1:17 (p, 191; 3:25,29, (p. 194; 5:1, (p. 195).
11. *Holy Bible, Contemporary English Version* (New York: The American Bible Society, 1995).
12. **Ibid.**, p. 1365.
13. **Ibid.**, p. 1365.
14. **Ibid.**, p. 1417.
15. **Ibid.**, p. 1415.

16. Richard Francis Weymouth, *The New Testament in Modern Speech* (Boston: The Pilgrim Press, 1943).

17. Hugh J. Schonfield, *The Authentic New Testament* (New York: Mentor Books, 1958), p. 302.

18. *New World Translation of Holy Scripture* (New York: Watchtower Bible and Tract Society, 1961), p. 1223.

19. Heien Barrett Montgomery, *The New Testament in Modern English - The Centenary Translation* (Philadelphia; The Judson Press, 1924), p. 409.

20. *New World Translation*, **op. cit.**, p. 1261b.

21. **Ibid.**, p. 1261b.

22. *Webster's New World Dictionary of the American Language* (New York: The World Publishing company, 1966), p. 1683.

23. *New International Version of the Holy Bible* (Grand Rapids: Zondervan Bible Publishers, 1988), p. 827.

24. John Theodore Mueller, *Christian Dogmatics* (St. Louis: CPH, 1955), p. 375.

25. L. Berkhof, *Systematic Theology* (Grand Rapids: Wm. B. Eerdmans Publishing House, 1941), pp. 520-521.

26. William Douglas Chamberlain. *An Exegetical Grammar of New Testament Greek* (New York: The Macmillan Company, 1941), p. 117.

27. **Ibid.**, p. 118.

28. **Ibid.**, p. 118.

29. Published by Broadman Press; Nashville, Tennessee, 1934, p. 582.

30. Chamberlain, **op. cit.**, p. 120.

31. Dana and Mantey, *A Manual Grammar of New Testament Greek* (New York: The Macmillan Company, 1927), p. 101.

32. **Ibid.**, p. 101.

33. **Ibid.**, p. 103.

34. George Milligan, *Greek Papyri*, pp. 39-40 as cited by Dana and Mantey, p. 102.

35. Cf. Blass and Debrunner, *A Greek Grammar of New Testament Greek*. Translated by Robert W. Funk (Chicago: The University of Chicago Press, 1961). Cf. section on "preposition;" J. H. Moulton, *A Grammar of New Testament Greek* (Edinburg: T. & T. Clark, 1919), Vol. II. Parti, p. 300, 308.

36. (New York, Oxford University Press, 1917), p. 61.

37. G. Abbott-Smith, *A Manual Greek Lexicon of the New Testament* (New York: Charles Scribner's Sons, 1929), p. 105.

38. F. Wilbur Gingrich, *Shorter Lexicon of the Greek New Testament* (Chicago: The University of Chicago Press, 1957), p. 48. James Hope Moulton and George Milligan, The vocabulary of the Greek New Testament, Illustrated from the Papri and Other Non-Literary Sources (Grand Rapids; Wm. B,
Eerdmans Publishing Company, 1930), p. 145, **ek**, p. 190.

39. Wuest's *Word Studies From the Greek New Testament* (Grand Rapids; Wm. B. Eerdmans Publishing Company, 1955), I, p. 59.

40. Vol. I, **Ibid.**, p. 63.

41. **Ibid.**, p. 77.

42. Published by Wm. B. Eerdmans Publishing Company, Vol. III, "The Epistles of Paul."

43. **Ibid.**, III, Rom. 1:17 (by faith), p. 42. Rom. 3:24; 3:28, p. 50.

44. Vincent, "Galatians," Vol. IV, p. 117.

45. A. T. Robertson, *Word Pictures in the New Testament* (Nashville: Broadman Press, 1931), IV, The Epistles of Paul, p. 355.

46. *The Holy Bible Containing the Old and New Testaments* (Oxford: At the University Press, 1892), New Testament, Rom. 1:17 (p. 114), 3:22 (p. 116), 3:28 (p. 116z), 5:1 (p. 117).

47. *Holy Bible, The New King James Version* (Nashville: Thomas Nelson, Inc., 1979), Rom. 1:17 (p. 1098), 3:22 (p. 1100), 3:28 (p. 1101), Gal. 3:10 (p. 1139.

48. *The Bible, An American Translation* (Chicago: The University of Chicago Press 1931), N.T. Rom. 3:28 (p. 255), 5:1 (p. 256).

49. *The Holy Bible contains Old and New Testaments, American Standard* (New York: Thomas Nelson & Sons, 1901), New Testament: Rom. 1:17(p. 159), 3:22 (p. 161), 3:28 (162), 5:1 (p. 163).

50. *New American Standard*, Student's Edition (Philadelphia: A. J. Holman Company, 1973; New Testament: Rom. 1:17 (p. 807), 3:22 (p. 808), 3:28 (p. 809), 5:1 (p. 809).

51. *Holy Bible. The New Berkeley Version in Modern English* (Grand Rapids: Zondervan Publishing House 1969), New Testament: Rom. 1:17 (p. 163), 3:35 (p. 166); 3:28 (p. 166), 5:1 (p. 167).

52. James Moffatt, *The Bible. Containing the Old and New Testaments* (New York and London: Harper & Brothers Publishers 1922, 1935) New Testament: Rom. 1:17 (p. 187), 3:28 (p. 190), 5:1 (p. 191).

53. *The New Testament: Revised Standard Version and the King James in Parallel Columns* (New York: Thomas Nelson & Sons 1964). 1:17 (p. 307), 3:22 (p. 311), 3:28 (p. 311), 5:1 (p. 313).

54. William Beck, *The Holy Bible, An American Translation* (New Haven: Leader Publishing Company, 176). New Testament; Rom. 1:17 (p. 191), 3:28 (p. 191), 5:1 (p. 195).

55. *New English Bible With the Apocrypha* (Oxford and Cambridge: At the University Presses, 1961,1970), New Testament Romans 1:17 (p. 191) 3:28 (p. 194), 5:1 (p. 196).

56. *The New Testament in Four Versions. Phillips Modern English* (Washington: Christianity Today, Inc., 1963), Romans 1:17 (p. 4511), 5:1 (p. 463).

57. *Holy Bible, New International Version* (Grand Rapids: Zondervan Bible Publishers, 1983), Rom. 1:17 (p. 796), 3:22 (p. 797), 3:28 (p. 797), 5:1 (p. 798).

58. *The Good News for Modern Man* (New York: American Bible Society, 1966), New Testament: Romans 1:17 (p. 340)3:22 (p. 344), 5:1 (p. 346).

59. *The Living Bible Paraphrased* (New York: Doubleday & Company, distributors for Tyndale House Publishers, Wheaton, IL. 1971), has in 3:28 by faith (p. 899) and 5:1 (p. 900).

60. Francis Alossius, *The New Testament of Our Lord Jesus Christ* (New York: The Macmillan Company, 1946), Rom. 1:17 (p. 414), 3:22 (p. 419), 3:28 (p. 419), 5:1 (p. 421).

61. *Saint Joseph Edition of The New American Bible* (New York: Catholic Book Publishing Co., 1970), New Testament; Rom. 1:17 (p. 181), 3:22 (p. 183), 3:28 (p. 183b), 5:1 (p. 184b).

62. Alexander Jones, General Editor, *The Jerusalem Bible* (New York: Garden City, N.Y.; Doubleday & Company, 1966), New Testament: Rom. 1:17(p. 269), 3:22 (p. 271), 3:28 (p. 272), 5:1 (p. 274).

63. *The Septuagint Version of the Old Testament With An English Translation* (New

York: Harper and Brothers, No Date), p. 1107.

64. *The Syriac New Testament According to The Peshitto Version* (London: Samuel Bagster and Sons No Date), pp. p. 324, 326.

65. *Augustinus Merk. Novum Testamentum Graece Et Latine* (Romae: Suumptibus Institute Biblici, 1951), pp. 511, 517, 517, 520.

66. *Neues Testament Und Psalmen Nach der Uebersetzung Martin Luthers* (Stuttgart Wuerttembergische Bibelanstalt 1973), Romans, 3:22; 3:28 (p. 232; 5:1.

67. Giovanni Diodati, *II Nuovo Testament Del Nostro Signore E Salvtore Gesu* (Societa Biblica Americana, 1916), p. 377, pp. 382, 384.

68. *Bibelen EllerDen Hellige Skrift* (New York: Del Amerikanske Bibelselskap, 1943. New Testament, p. 192.

69. **Ibid.**, p. 194.

70. *La Santa Biblia Antiguo Y Nuevo Testament* (Mexico; Sociedades Biblicas 1960), p. 1041.

71. **Ibid.**, p. 1041.

72. Louis Segond, *La Sainte Bible Qui Comprend L'Ancien Et Le Nouveau Testament* (Paris: 20 Rue De Tournon, 1911), New Testament: p. 114.

73. **Ibid.**, p. 116.

74. P. 116. *The Biblia detaer All den Heliga Skrift* (Stockholm Suenska Bibelsaellskapet, 1898).

75. *Bijbel Dat Is De Gansche Heilige Schrift Al De Kanonieken Boeken Des Ouden En Nieuwen Testaments* (London: British and Foreign Bible Society, 1921), Romans 3:22; 3:28; 5:1, New Testament, pp. 200, 201, 202.

76. Salkinson-Ginsburg, *Hebrew New Testament* (New York: J. Freshmann, 17 St. Mark's Place, 1891), Romans 1:17 (p. 299), 3:22 (p. 303), 3:28 (p. 303), 5:1 (p. 305).

77. George G. Tappert, *The Book of Concord* (Philadelphia: Fortress Press, 1959), p. 30.

78. **Ibid.**, p. 682.

Question

1. What are the four solas? ____
2. How did the God's Word translation make justification by faith fuzzy? ____
3. The God's Word translation avoided the use the term ____.
4. What impinges on the forensic character of justification? ____
5. Is faith a meritorious work of man? ____
6. *The Apology of The Augsburg Confession* teaches that justification is ____.

The Holy Spirit

The Person and Activities of the Holy Spirit As Set Forth in the Scriptures of the Old and New Testaments

Christian News, June 3, 1996

Pentecost or Whitsunday is the third great festival of the church year. The word "Pentecost" means "Fifty." The first Christian Pentecost occurred on the Jewish festival of Pentecost.[1] The Jewish Pentecost was observed 50 days after the Pascha. In Christ's time Pentecost was observed by the Jews as the festival of "wheat harvest." It was also called the "feast of weeks." Later the Hebrew nation also commemorated the giving of the Law on Mount Sinai and the establishment of the Jewish Church.[2]

In fulfillment of the prophecy of Joel (2:28-32; in Hebrew 3:1-4) and also that prophecy of Jesus that He would sent His Holy Spirit, the latter was sent from heaven and the result was that three thousand Jews and proselytes were baptized and were brought to saving faith in Christ Jesus. No person can read Luke's Book of Acts and not be impressed with the frequency with which the Holy Spirit is mentioned and the part He played in the organization and spread of Christianity in the Roman Empire through the apostles and their followers.[3]

Pentecost is also known as Whitsunday, a name peculiar to the English Episcopalian Church and those who were influenced by *The Book of Common Prayer*.[4] The original word "Pentecost" is retained by Roman Catholic Churches in Latin lands. Whitsunday is held by some to be a corruption of the German Pfingsten, but this is more than doubtful.[5] About the year 1200 the English spelling was Hwitesundel and later Wittesonday. The reference may be either to the wearing of white robes by candidates for baptism on the feast,[6] or else to the gift of "wit," an old Saxon word for wisdom (as in "witan," wise man), by the outpouring of the "spirit of wisdom" (Eph. 1:17), in fulfillment of Christ's promise (John 16:13).[7]

According to modern liturgiologists, Pentecost was a unitive festival, commemorating both the Ascension of Christ and the descent of the Holy Spirit. In the course of the fourth century it was resolved into two distinct parts, into two distinct commemorations. Eventually the Ascension of Christ was celebrated prior to and separately, ten days later Pentecost.[8]

Reed claimed that the celebration of Pentecost is very early. Hippolytus knew of it.[9] Gwynne also averred that this festival was mentioned by Origen in the third century and by Gregory Nazianzen in the third century and by Chrysostom.[10] The 50 days between Easter and Pentecost were observed as continuous festival days without fasting or kneeling.

The Association of the Christian Pentecost with the Jewish Pentecost

The association of the earlier Jewish festival would of course blend with the Christian festival of Pentecost, especially "the Feast of Harvest," now fulfilled in the baptism of three thousand converts and also in the first fruits of the great harvest of souls all over the world. The giving of law on Mt. Sinai, the making of a great nation, could be associated with the founding of the Christian Church in Jerusalem.

Current Christianity and the Holy Spirit

Some years ago a Lutheran professor wrote a book called "The Half Known God, [11] in which he deplored the lack of information on the Holy Spirit." However, since the growth of Pentecostalism, with its speaking in tongues and miraculous gifts, there has been an overemphasis on the activity of the Third Person of the Trinity.[12] The anniversary of the outpouring of the Holy Spirit is an opportune time to determine what both the Old and New Testaments teach about the Person and work of the Holy Spirit.

The Holy Spirit, A Member of the Trinity

Stump claimed: "The doctrine of Trinity distinguishes the Christian religion from all others. The natural religions do not have it."[13] Mohammedanism and Judaism reject it. The doctrine of the Trinity is accepted and taught solely on the basis of revelation which God made of Himself in His word. It is clearly taught in Holy Scripture and is fundamental to the plan of salvation.[14]

The Deity of the Holy Spirit

Four lines of proof may be developed from Scriptures that the Holy Spirit is not merely a power or influence, but a Person, one of the Three Persons of the Trinity.[15]

1. Distinctive characteristics are given the Spirit of God. There are three distinctive marks of personality-knowledge, feeling and will.[16] Any living being that knows, feels, and wills is a person.[17]

Thus Paul declares that the Holy Spirit knows the things of God and that is particularly what the Spirit does (I Cor. 2:11, Revised version). Will is ascribed to the Holy Spirit (I Cor. 12:11), mind (Rom. 8:27). Paul told the Roman Christians that the Holy Spirit loves the children of God (Rom. 15:30). Loving is a characteristic of a person. Out of love the Holy Spirit seeks out individuals in the world to bring them to saving faith in Christ Jesus. By the Gospel the Holy Spirit brings them to Christ by the creation of faith, prepared for by the condemnation of the Law. The New Testament claims that the Holy Spirit can be grieved. Only a person can be grieved! Both testaments teach the deity of the Holy Spirit.[18]

2. Divine Acts are ascribed to the Holy Spirit.[19] Thus He is said to search "the deep things" of God (1 Cor. 2:10). John in Revelation portrays the Holy Spirit as "speaking" (2:7).The Holy Spirit, dwelling in the believers hears cries of "Abba, Father." Paul assures believers that the Holy Spirit makes intercessions for them (Rom 8:26), He bears witness about Christ (John 15:26-27; 14:26). The Holy Spirit furthermore leads and directs the work of the Church by calling, converting and by the work of

sanctification in the lives of Christians.

3. Activities directed against the Holy Spirit emphasize the truth of the personality of the Holy Spirit. Both the Old Testament and the New Testament testify to the fact that the children of God rebelled against the Holy Spirit (Is. 63:10). The Holy Spirit's call can be resisted and it is possible to apostatize and so grieve God's Spirit. Thus Ananias and Sapphira lied to the Holy Spirit (Acts 5:3) nor can one blaspheme against the Holy Spirit (Matt. 12:31-32), if the Holy Spirit were not a person.

The Holy Spirit is clearly distinguished from the Father and the Son.[19] The three persons of the Holy Trinity appear at the baptism of Christ (Mark 1:10; Luke 2:21-22). And they are coordinated in the baptismal command (Matt. 28:19), and in the apostolic blessing (II Cor. 13:14). There is an historical order of revelation, according to which the Father comes first, the Son second, and the Holy Spirit third. Yet this does not mean simply any subordination or lack of equality, for thus they are coordinated in the baptismal command (Matt. 28:19) and in the apostolic benediction (II Cor. 13:14).[20]

The Divine Internal Acts of the Godhead

The Old Testament and the New Testament proclaim the Father as begetting His Son (Psalm 2:7 Heb. 1:5). Christ the Savior in John 15:26 proclaimed: "But when the Paraclete comes whom I will send to you from the Father, the Spirit of Truth who proceeds from the Father, He will testify of Me" (Surely, a clear passage for the Trinity).

The historical, though not ontological subordination, follows from the fact that the Holy Spirit comes to complete the work of Christ (John 11:26; 15:26; 16:14).

Divine works and Attributes Ascribed to the Holy Spirit

The deeds of God are ascribed to the Holy Spirit, He creates (Gen. 1:2), He works miracles, He inspired the Prophets of the Old Testament and Apostles of the New. The Spirit is called everlasting in Hebrews 9:18 and according to Psalm 139:7 the Holy Spirit is said to be omnipotent, omnipresent and omniscient.[21]

The Holy Spirit and the Inspiration of Holy Writ

Speaking of the Old Testament's origin, it is described by Paul as "theopneustos," that is, "God- breathed," or "Spirit breathed".[22] The author of Hebrews begins his letter this way: "God who spoke in times past, has now in a final form spoken by His Son" (1:1). St. Peter assured the congregations of Asia Minor that "holy men of God were moved by the Holy Spirit (II Peter 2:21)." "No Scripture is of any private interpretation, for holy men spoke as they were being carried along by the Holy Spirit."[22] Paul assured the Corinthians: "we speak, not in the words which man's wisdom teaches, but which the Holy Ghost teacheth" (I Cor. 2:13). No interpretation of the Bible can make the Holy Spirit a mere influence or attribute of God.

Areas in Holy writ Containing Material About the Holy Spirit

There are five main areas in Scripture that yield material for a summary of Biblical teaching on the person and work of the Holy Spirit. 1. The Spirit in the Old Testament; 2. The Spirit in the synoptic Gospels; 3. The Spirit in the Fourth Gospel; 4. The Spirit in Acts; and 5. The Holy Spirit in the Pauline Epistles.[23]

The Holy Spirit in the Old Testament

According to Genesis 1:2 the Holy Spirit was brooding over the abyss and was active in creation. The work of creation was the work of the Tri-une God: it was the word of the father (Heb. 11:3), who created in and through His Son (Hebrews 1:2), and by the Spirit (Gen. 1:2). The Psalmist declares that the Spirit was active in creation (Psalm 33:6) and in all natural processes (Psalm 104:30). God has not merely left the world merely to the out-workings of laws and principles.

He sustains and ordered all things by His 'Spirit', so indeed, there is a real sense in which one may say: "see God in nature" (natural theology), (cf. Romans 1:19-20).

A number of passages are concerned with the Spirit's relationship to mankind. The first Biblical reference is concerned with moral and religious conditions in Noah's time. "My Spirit shall not always strive with man (6:3)."[24] The text reference is the testimony of Pharaoh concerning Joseph as a man in whom the Spirit of God is (Gen. 41:8). The Egyptian ruler recognized the wisdom and the "spirit" which distinguished Joseph from other Egyptians. So here early in divine revelation the Holy Spirit is shown as bestowing gifts and graces which were on a higher level than the noblest natural endowments.

The next reference to the activity of the Spirit is found in Exodus 31:3, where Bezaleel is filled with the Spirit of God, in wisdom and in understanding and in knowledge and in all manner of workmanship.[25] Although Bezaleel was a skilled craftsman, an artist, a genius, Yahweh granted him a special ability for his craft in connection with the building of the tabernacle. The Spirit does not merely inspire with words, but also can give skill and enablement to ordinary people.

The period of the Judges (1375-1075 B.C.) was a time when the Holy Spirit was active according to data in Judges, and I Samuel. The Holy Spirit came upon certain individuals to judge the certain tribes.[26] Thus Judges reports that the Spirit came upon Othniel (Judges 3:10-11). Another judge upon whom the Spirit came was Gideon, with whom the Spirit clothed Himself and so the latter "wrought mighty deeds through Gideon" (Judg. 6:34). The same Holy Spirit came upon Jephtha (Judg. 11:29), used Samson (Judg. 14:6,19; 15:14). Saul, the first king of united Israel, felt the overpowering power of the Spirit, so that he prophesied (I Samuel 10:6,10), but later the Spirit of God left Saul (16:34), and from that time forward the same Holy Spirit came upon David.[27]

Nehemiah 9:20, 30 sums up the dealings with God's people, like this: "Thou gavest also Thy good Spirit to instruct them . . . and testified against them by Thy Spirit in Thy prophets." So here the believer is introduced to the prophets, who proclaimed the oracles of God by the Spirit of God. In one such utterance Joel predicted the outpouring of the Holy Spirit on Pentecost (Joel 2:28; Acts 2:10). Micah, contrasting the bounteous resources of God with the sorry condition of the people of Israel, asked: "Is the Spirit of the Lord straitened?" Then Micah went on to tell people: "But truly I am full of power by the Spirit of the Lord" (Micah 2:7, 3:8). Finally, in the Exilic period of Judaism, Zechariah, speaking regarding the building of the Temple, laid down the principle: "Not by might, nor by power, but by My Spirit, says the Lord of Hosts" (Zech. 4:6). Especially, it should not be forgotten that the Holy Spirit would come upon the Messiah as Isaiah predicted in a number of the Servant Passages (Is. 11:2; 42:1; 61:1).[28]

The Holy Spirit in the New Testament

In the Gospels, as in the Old Testament, the Holy Spirit came upon certain individuals for special purposes: John the Baptist and his parents, (Luke 1:15, 41, 67), Simeon (Luke 2:25-27) Jesus, as a man (Matt. 1:18; 3:16; 4:1; Mark 1:8,10).

Stevenson declared: "In the New Testament, the unveiling of the Personality is one of the major themes, but the persistent use of the term 'the Spirit of God indicates the continuity of His work, and links the fuller New Testament revelation with all that has been given in the Old.'"[29]

The Synoptics and the Holy Spirit— The Holy Spirit and Christ's Life

The Holy Spirit was the active agent in the miraculous conception of Jesus (Luke 1:34f; Matt. 1:18). Mary's pregnancy was effected by the Holy Spirit. The Holy Spirit replaced the human paternity of Jesus. It is Christ's miraculous conception with which Jesus' sinlessness is connected (Luke 1:35). In Jesus' baptism the Spirit of God was active (Matt. 3:13-17). Under the symbol of the descending dove the Holy Spirit was present and Jesus was anointed with the power of the Spirit. Peter announced to Cornelius and his household that God anointed Jesus of Nazareth with the Holy Ghost and power (Acts 10:38). At the beginning of Christ's public ministry it was the Holy Spirit who drove Christ into the wilderness, where Satan would tempt the Savior (Mark 1:12). The Holy Spirit furnished the dynamic, by means of which He would fulfill His Father's vocation. In Nazareth's synagogue Jesus declared that "the Spirit of the Lord is on Me" (Luke 4:18-21).[30]

Jesus' Teachings About the Holy Spirit

For the most part the statements about the Holy Spirit in John's Gospel are assertions that Christ made about the Spirit of God. Christ taught that the Holy Spirit is the agent for bringing about the new birth and regeneration (3:22f). No individual can say that Jesus is Lord but by the Holy Spirit, (1 Cor. 12:3). It is impossible for human beings to convert themselves and accept Christ, except by baptism—thus Jesus informed Nicodemus. According to John 4:14 and 7:37-39 for the born-again person, the Holy Spirit is an inexhaustible spring of living water welling up in the baptized person as rivers of water. Before the Ascension of Christ, the Age of Spirit could only come when Christ had left this earth on the fortieth day after Easter and ascended upon high (7:39). What the Spirit's coming would mean, is set forth in the Farewell Discourse of Christ, reported by John in chapters 13-17.[31] The Spirit's nature is also described in three different names which Jesus called Him: Paraclete (14:16), who would sustain, and comfort the disciples. The second name "Spirit of truth" reveals his nature and that He would guide the apostles in the truth (14:17; 15:26; 16:13). Holiness is the third element in the Spirit's nature, Who has as one of His goals to make and keep people holy (The work of sanctification).[32]

Function of Holy Spirit Relative to People

According to the Johannine Gospel the Holy Spirit has certain functions toward people, which depend upon the fact whether or not individuals are Christians or non-Christians.[33] The ministry of the Spirit is to teach believers (16:12-15). He guides Christians into truth (14:26): Examples of this activity are also found in 2:2; 12:16; 14:26; Luke 24:8). The Third Person of the Godhead fosters the Christian's devotional life (cf. 14).

Relation to the non-Christian, the Spirit's function is described in (16:8-11). The Spirit convinces unbelievers of sinfulness for not believing in Jesus Christ's triumph over sin, by which God declares the sinner righteous. The Holy Spirit declares judgment by revealing the relation between Christ's death and resurrection and the judgment of the world. The instrumentality by which this is achieved is through the Christian's witness of Christ (John 15:26f; Acts 2:37; 5:33; 7:54). While it is true the Christian witness to Christ is made by the Holy Spirit, He does this through the preaching of the law, to bring about repentance and through the Gospel to effect faith in the atoning work of Christ. Christians are given the Holy Spirit to use the God-ordained ways of effecting salvation in lost sinners (John 20:21f).[34]

The Holy Spirit in the Book of Acts

In the great apostolic missionary history and manual for missions, the Holy Spirit plays an important and significant role. Correctly Scroggle has said: "The Acts is essentially a record of the activities of the Holy Spirit, and here He is seen related to every aspect of the believers and the Church's life and work."[35] An examination of the 28 chapters in Acts reveals the fact that in at least 19 chapters, the Holy Spirit is active in guiding and building up churches.

Here are the facts about the Spirit of God revealed in Acts. Thus it is seen that the Holy Spirit is the Spirit of Promise (ch. 1), of Power (ch. 2), of Healing (ch. 3), of Boldness (ch. 4), of Judgment (ch. 5), of Administration (ch. 6), of Steadfastness (ch. 7), of Evangelism (ch. 8), of Comfort (ch. 9), of Guidance (ch. 10), of Prophecy (ch. 11), of Deliverance (ch. 12), of Missions (ch. 13), of Protestation (14), of Councils (ch. 15), of Restraint (ch. 16), of Opportunity (ch. 17), of Revelation (ch. 18), of Purpose (ch. 19).[36]

In Acts the Holy Spirit is very prominent.[36a] Correctly Scroggle has written "The Acts is the record which dominates the whole story. The Acts is the record of a Spirit-begotten, Spirit-filled and Spirit-guided Church of God."[37] The Acts of the Apostles would be better referred to as "The Acts of the Holy Spirit," because only four apostles are involved in the spread of Christianity from Jerusalem to Rome.

The Holy Spirit in the Pauline Epistles

There are many passages in the 13 Pauline Epistles that refer to the Holy Spirit and especially His activity in the lives of believers.[38] They constitute the fifth major area of information about the Third person of the Trinity. Because of the plethora of passages in the Pauline corpus the writer will be selective in his choice of references and illusions to the Holy Spirit. Swete, in his The Holy Spirit in the New Testament, pp. 223-253 limited himself to the Philippian, Colossian and Ephesian Epistles.[39]

1. For Paul, one cannot be a Christian without receiving the Spirit (Gal. 3:2). To have Christ's spirit is to belong to Christ (Rom. 8:9). The Christian life is life in the Holy Spirit (Gal. 5:16). In fact what the keeping of the law could not achieve, the Holy Spirit does (Rom. 8:11-4).

2. The Holy Ghost is "the Spirit of Christ" (f. II Cor. 3:17; I Cor. 6:17; Gal. 4:6; Rom. 8:4ff). That means that nobody can speak against the Christ and at the same time speak in the Spirit (I Cor. 12:3). This does not mean that the son and Spirit are one, but that both have the same purpose.[40]

3. The deity and personality are taught by St. Paul. The Holy Spirit is the Spirit of God (Rom. 8:9) cf. also I Cor. 3:16 and II Cor. 6:16. The personal activities of the Holy Ghost are prominent in the Pauline Letters, as they are in Acts. Thus for example, it is the Spirit's prerogative to bestow gifts (I Cor. 12:4-10 "as he will" (v. 11), and reveal the way in which the Spirit makes known the Father's will (1 Cor. 2:10-12), teaches the Christian followers (v. 13), and blesses the Christian witness (v. 4; I Thess. 1:5).

4. The Nature of the Holy Ghost's relationship receives considerable attention. The Holy Spirit greatly helps the Christian in his warfare against "the flesh," which endeavors to obtain a foothold in the believer. Not to put under the sinful flesh would grieve the "Spirit of God" (Eph. 4:30). Paul encouraged the Roman Christians to mortify the deeds of the body (Rom. 8:13) through the Spirit (Rom. 8:3). The important part of the Holy Spirit plays in the believer's life is the comforting truth that the Holy Spirit brings the tyrannical reign of sin to an end (Rom. 6:12-14) and also brings about in the Christian the effects of Christ's death and resurrection. It is solely through the Holy Spirit that moral transformation is effected (II Cor. 3:18) and it is by means of the Holy Ghost that believers are set free to walk not after the flesh but after the Spirit (Rom. 8:5-8). Through the Third Person of the Trinity Christ's followers become "servants of righteousness" (Rom. 6:15ff).

5. Paul in his Epistles places emphasis in what God's Spirit does for and within the community of believers. The Spirit sent in larger manner

1792

of Pentecost and energized the Christian community (Phil 3:3; I Cor. 14:15) so that her worship (Phil. 3:3; I Cor. 14:15), fellowship (Eph. 4:3; Phil. 2:1), gifts (I Cor. 12:13) are vital. For a Christian church to carry out its mission, it needs the Holy Spirit as an energizing presence.

6. Paul also connects the Holy Spirit and baptism (Rom. 6:1-4). Thus Thomson asserted: "Baptism implies Christ's death, burial and resurrection, and parallels the believer's own death to sin, and resurrection to newness of life which the baptism of the Spirit involves."[41]

A most significant passage about the Spirit's activity in the Christian life was set forth in I Corinthians 6:11: "But ye are washed, but ye are sanctified, but ye are justified in the name of the Lord Jesus, and by the Spirit of our God . . ." The words "washed . . . sanctified" "justified . . ." embrace our entire experience from regeneration to full Christian maturity—and all this effected through the redemption wrought for us by Christ and made effectual in our experience by the Spirit. "He is who takes the things of Christ, and reveals-unveils and imparts them to us (John 16:15). All that we are and have in Christ is ours in and by the Spirit of God."[42]

In his Second Letter to the Corinthians Paul describes the members of that Greek congregation as "our epistle written in our hearts . . . not with the Spirit of the living God" (2 Cor. 3:3) and Peter in his First Epistle to the churches of Asia Minor, who were passing through fiery trials, he encouraged with the thought that "the Spirit of Glory of God rested upon you" (I Peter 4:14). The title "spirit of glory" is a worthy final enlargement for the Old Testament title of the Third Person of the Holy Trinity.

The Holy Spirit is mentioned in 20 of the 27 books of the New Testament.[43] No person can understand the teachings and theology of the New Testament apart from New Testament statements about the Person and work of the Holy Spirit.

Footnotes

1. Cf. E. M. Blaicklock, "Pentecost," Merrill F. Tenney, Editor, *The Zondervan Pictorial Bible Dictionary* (Grand Rapids: Zondervan Publishing House, 1963), pp. 634-635.

2. **Ibid.**, p. 635.

3. Cf. in Acts, chapters 2:6:2; 8:4-8; 9:38; 10:44-48; the three missionary journeys Cf. also Robert Young, *Analytical Concordance to The Bible*, Twentieth Edition by Wm. B. Stevenson (New York

Funk & Wagnells Company, no date), p. 488.

4. Walker Gwynne, *The Christian Year - Its Purpose and Its History* (New York: Longmans and Green and Co., 1915), pp. 70-72; Paul Strodach, *The Collect for the Day* (Philadelphia: The United Lutheran Publication House, 1939), p. 143.

5. Alfred Jeremias, *Leben im Kirchenjahr* (Leipzig; Adolf Klein Verlag, 1928), pp. 60-63.

6. Strodach, **op. cit.**, pp. 142-143.

7. Gwynne, **op. cit.**, p. 72.

8. A. A. McArthur, "Pentecost," in J .G. Davies, *The Westminster Dictionary of Worship* (Philadelphia: 1972), p. 310.

9. Luther D. Reed, *The Lutheran Liturgy* (Philadelphia: Muhlenberg Press, 1947).

10. Gwynne, **op. cit.**, p. 90.

11. Lorenz Wunderlich, *The Half-Known God* (St. Louis: Concordia Publishing House).

12. F.E. Mayer, *The Religious Bodies of America* (St. Louis: Concordia Publishing House, 1956) pp. 317-320.

13. Joseph Stump. *The Christian Faith* (New York: The Macmillan Company, 1932), p. 45.

14. Theodore Tappert, *The Book of Concord* (Philadelphia: Muhlenberg Press, 1959), pp. 28, 217.

15. Cf. Raymond F. Surburg, "The Doctrine of the Holy Spirit in the Old Testament," *Christian News*, May 16, 1994, pp. 8-9.

16. Griffith Thomas, *The Holy Spirit* (Grand Rapids: The Kregels Publications, 1976), ch. 1; Leon woods, *The Holy Spirit in the Old Testament* (Grand Rapids: Zondervan Publishing House, 1976), p. 16.

17.

18. Francis Pieper, *Christian Dogmatics* (St. Louis: Concordia Publishing House, 1952), I, p. 377.

19. Stump, **op. cit.**, p. 51.

20. "Trinity," in Lueker, *The Lutheran Cyclopedia* (St. Louis: Concordia Publishing House, 1954), p. 1069.

21. J. Theodore Mueller, *Christian Dogmatics* (St. Louis: Concordia Publishing House, 1955), p. 149.

22. A. T. Robertson, *Word Pictures of the New Testament* (Nashville: The Broadman Press, 1931), p. 627.

23. Thomson, **op. cit.**, p. 493b.

24. Cf. Norman H. Snaith, *Notes on the Hebrew Text of Genesis I-VII* (London: Epworth Press, 1947), p. 44, notes on chapter 4:6; Benjamin B. Warfield, "The Spirit of God on the Did Testament," in *Biblical and Theological Studies* (Philadelphia: The Presbyterian and Reformed Publishing Company, 1952), p. 136.

25. Herbert F. Stevenson, *Titles of the Triune God* (Westwood, N. J. Fleming H. Revell, 1956), p. 172.

26. Warfield. **op. cit.**, p. 139.

27. G. Walters, "Holy Spirit," in J. D. Douglas, Editor, *New Bible Dictionary* (Grand Rapids: Wm. B. Eerdmans Publishing Company, 1962), p. 531b.

28. **Ibid.**

29. **Ibid.**

30. Thomson, **op. cit.**, p. 494.

31. H.D. McDonald, *Living Doctrines of the New Testament* (Grand Rapids: Zondervan Publishing House, 1971), pp. 58-59.

32. C. Hove, *Christian Doctrine* (Minneapolis: Augsburg Publishing House, 1930), pp. 236-237.

33. Thomson, **op. cit.**, p. 495.

34. **Ibid.**, p. 495.

35. W. Graham Scroggle, *Know Your Bible*. Volume II, Analytical, The New Testament (London: Pickering and Inglis, no date), p. 76.

36. **Ibid.**, p. 76.

36a. Raymond F. Surburg, "Teachings about the Holy Spirit in the Book of Acts," *Christian News Encyclopedia*, v p. 3640.

37. **Ibid.** p. 76.

38. Henry Barclay Swete, *The Holy Spirit in the New Testament* (Grand Rapids: Baker Book House, 1910), cf., pp. 169-173.

39. **Ibid.**, pp. 223-253.

40. Cf. T. S. Culley, "Holy Spirit, "in Walter A. Elwell, Editor, *Evangelical Dictionary of Theology* Grand Rapids: Baker Book House, p. 523.

41. Thomson, **op. cit.**, pp. 4496-497.

42. Stevenson, **op. cit.**, p. 174.

43. James Strong, *Strong's Exhaustive Concordance, Complete and Unabridged* (Nashville: Broadman Press, 1979). p. 489.

Questions

1. The word "Pentecost" means ____.
2. Whitsunday may be a reference to ____.
3. The growth of Pentecostalism led to ____.
4. The doctrine of the Trinity is taught in ____.
5. Loving is a characteristic of a ____.
6. What is ascribed to the Holy Spirit? ____
7. Where did the three persons of the Holy Spirit appear? ____
8. What divine works and attributes are attributed to the Holy Spirit? ____
9. Where is the Holy Spirit mentioned in the Old Testament? ____
10. The Holy Spirit was the active agent in the miraculous ____ of Jesus.
11. Who brings about the new birth? ____
12. How often is the Holy Spirit mentioned in Acts? ____
13. In how many New Testament books is the Holy Spirit mentioned? ____

The Lord's Supper
Past and Current Teachings About the Lord's Supper in Three Divergent Religious Traditions
(A Study for Maundy Thursday)

Christian News, March 17, 1997

The Thursday of Holy Week is observed as the anniversary of the Lord's Supper.[1] While it is God's will that all Christians should hold the same views about Baptism, the Lord's Supper and worship the same Biblical Christ, this unfortunately is not the case. At present there are at least three different religious traditions concerning the Lord's Supper: The Roman Catholic, the Lutheran and the Reformed.[2] Besides these certain religions sponsor aberrant views about the purpose, frequency and of observing the sacrament instituted on the night of Christ's betrayal.[3]

It is important that the meaning, purpose and usage of the Lord's Supper should periodically be reviewed in Lutheranism on the basis of God's infallible Word. In the Lutheran Church in America (ELCA) and in The Lutheran Church-Missouri Synod (LCMS), Holy Communion has been challenged.[4] Since Vatican II, the Roman Catholic Church has made certain changes relative to the Eucharist.[5]

In the days of the Reformation Luther and his fellow theologians had much to say about the Lord's Supper. All the Symbols or Confessions of the Lutheran Church, as found in the Book of Concord of 1580, have much to say about the three current religious traditions concerned with the Lord's Supper and in them they have taken issue with Rome and Geneva's understanding and practice of Christ's last will and testament.[6] Weidenschilling in his discussion of the Lord's Supper wrote: "If we can prove from Scripture that the Lutheran position is the only correct one, then it follows that all other denominations do not have the true sacrament. It is certainly important that we know the true Biblical facts about Holy Communion."[7]

Different Names for the Lord's Supper in Theological Literature

Paul in I Corinthians 11:20 calls the second sacrament "the Lord's Supper," because the Lord instituted it on the night He was betrayed by Judas Iscariot, now called (Maundy Thursday). The Apostle Paul in 1 Corinthians 10:21 also called it "The Lord's Table," because He has prepared a table for our souls (Psalm 23:5). The terms "breaking of bread" (Acts 2:42) was employed by early Christians because in the celebration of the Lord's Supper bread was broken. The bread after the breaking was distributed to the communicants. It has also been called "the Holy Supper" to distinguish it from ordinary meals. The designation "Eucharist" is derived from the fact that Christ gave thanks for the elements left over from the Passover Meal (Luke 22:17; 1 Cor. 10:16; 11:24).The Eucharist (Derived from Greek verb: euchariteo) was most widely used in the Early

Church. In 1 Corinthians Paul has suggested the name "Holy Communion," because there was a communion (Greek: koinonia) between the bread and body and the wine and the blood of Christ.[8]

The Lutheran Confessions also call the Lord's Supper, **Mass, Missa**, which is a term developed from the custom of the Early Church to dismiss from the common service those who were not entitled to partake of the Holy Supper.[9] Koehler opined: "As long as no heterodox ideas are connected with any of these names, we should not quarrel with them."[10] However, because of the wrong doctrines associated with the Roman Catholic Mass, Lutherans now for confessional reasons avoid the use of the word "mass."

The Lutheran Versus the Roman Catholic's Concept of What a Sacrament Is

When one analyzes the rites of Baptism and the Lord's Supper, it is found that both have three features in common: 1. The divine institution by Christ; 2. visible earthly means, in Baptism water, in the Lord's Supper bread and wine; 3. the promise of forgiveness of sins. The term "sacrament" is not a Biblical term. Originally it signified an oath or engagement, the military oath of a soldier. Koehler noted: "Because in the Early Church swore allegiance to Christ, which vow was really a 'sacramentum,' the term was applied to Baptism itself, and later also to the Lord's Supper. In church parlance the sacraments are visible means of spiritual blessings, religious rites instituted by Christ."[10]

The following rites of the Roman Catholicism do not meet these three criteria: 1. Confirmation; 2. Holy Wedlock; 3. Holy Orders; 4. Penance; and 5. The Last Rites. These five superary Roman Catholic Sacraments lack one or more of these three characteristics of Baptism and the Lord's Supper. If the Roman Church wished to call them sacraments, there should be no objection as long as it is realized that the Roman and Lutherans define the concept of "sacrament" differently.[11]

The Lord's Supper to Be Observed Till Christ's Second Coming

The Sacrament of the Altar, used by Luther, because the Last Supper was celebrated at altars when once churches were built after A.D. 313, was to be observed until His Second Return. Specifically the Institutor of the Lord's Supper instructed His followers that they should observe it till He come back (1 Cor. 11:26). Further, it was to be celebrated in memory of Christ's sacrificial death. To reject the fact that the Lord's Supper was to be a permanent rite as the Quakers and others do nullified the command of Christ (cf. Gal. 3:15) and frustrates His gracious provision for receiving personally forgiveness by the repentant sinner. The claim that the use of external means is not compatible with the spirituality of Christianity, such a stance is not supported by such passages as Rev. 19:17; Col. 2:16 and Rev. 3:20, which have no reference to the Lord's Supper and in effect charges Christ with lack of spirituality.

The Biblical Data for the Lord's Supper

The doctrine of the Lord's Supper is based upon passages recorded in Matthew 26:26-28; Mark 14:22-25; Luke 22:19-20 and 1 Corinthians 10:14-15 and 1 Cor. 11:23-29.[12] Here are four different accounts by four different writers, two of whom were Apostles (Matthew and St. Paul). Of the four writers one was present at the institution, namely, St. Matthew. All four wrote under the influence of the Holy Spirit. That one did not copy from the other is seen in the different wordings. Yet all four writers agree in the essential words which make every Lord's Supper a sacrament, namely, "Take eat this is My body," and "Take drink this is My blood." Stump observed about these three accounts of the Gospels: "There are many variations in these records which constitute the nature of the Sacrament. The records of Matthew and Mark on one hand and those of Luke and Paul in I Corinthians, on the other hand, are quite similar." The observant reader will also notice that these two writers have "blood of the new testament" and two speak of "new testament in My blood." Probably Jesus used both terms and so there would not be an essential difference. Jesus referred to "new testament" to point out the differences between what Christ had established and what preceded it in the Old Testament. The Old Testament sacrifices were a shadow of the shedding of Christ's blood, which cleanses from all sins (1 John 1:7). In different ways Christ spoke of his body and blood shed for the forgiveness of Sins.

Reu claimed that "the basis for establishing the true essence of the Lord's Supper is by no means found in John 6, as Zwingli and many of his disciples contend." The same Lutheran scholar contended that "the Lord's Supper as first observed in the Christian Church was not at all based upon John 6, but obviously upon the words of institution as recorded in the synoptic gospels and 1 Cor. 11."[13]

There are proponents in the Lutheran Church-Missouri Synod who claim to represent "high Lutheranism" (i.e., those emphasize extremely-oriented liturgical practice) who argue for the view that John 6:26,52 were referring to the body of Christ and was a Lord's Supper reference, thus mentioned a year and a half before its formal institution by Christ. This is advocated despite the fact that the Lutheran Confessions at least twice reject this theological interpretation. The Epitome of the *Formula of Concord* states that the body of Christ is not eaten with the teeth in a Capernaitic manner.[14] The Epitome of the *Formula of Concord* affirms: "This presence is not a mundane or Capernaitic, although it is true and essential as the words of Christ declare: 'This is My body, etc.'"[15]

Christ's Eating With Emmaus Disciples:
A Lord's Supper?

There are some in the LCMS who claim that the meal Jesus had with the Emmaus disciples was a celebration of the Lord's Supper. An examination of Luke 24:28-31 shows that only the bread is mentioned, but no wine and that this meal made possible the forgiveness of Sins. Here one has an instance where the Sacramentarians are reading an interpretation into the text which is exegetically unwarranted.

The Earliest Account of the Lord's Supper's Institution

The earliest written account would be Paul's statements about the Lord's Supper's institution, recorded in I Corinthians chapter 11:23-26, a letter penned during Paul's second missionary journey (following the Ephesian captivity theory for the four Christological Letters), and that would be A.D. 54. However, the actual historical event of the Last Supper's institution was in A.D. or A.D. 33 (if one follows Hoehner's date). In I Corinthians Paul is merely confirming what the three Evangelists have recorded. In 1 Corinthians 1:14-15, the apostle interprets for his readers what actually was involved in participating in Holy Communion, how bread and body, wine and blood are received.

What Paul wrote in I Corinthians 11 was known to him three years after the formal institution of the Eucharist. Paul's account was given in an apologetic context where he berates those, who at the **agapes** (love feasts) was making it impossible for believers to receive the body and blood of the Lord worthily.[16]

The Circumstances Under Which the Lord's Supper Was Instituted

One might call Baptism the first sacrament by which infants entered the kingdom of God, then the Lord's Supper would be the second one. Christ ordained the Lord's Supper celebration in connection with the Passover. Christ as paschal lamb is connected with the Passover lamb. Reu wrote:

The Old Testament paschal meal, in connection with which Christ instituted the Lord's Supper, was the divinely appointed type and preparation of the Lord's Supper.[17] The Passover meal, instituted at the time of Israel's exodus from Egypt, was a sacrificial meal and preceded by a sacrifice, as appears from the manner of its repetition and pertinent regulation, Ex. 12, Num. 9, Ex. 34:35. The blood which was offered represented the undefiled life of the sacrificial animal and covert the Israelites so that the angel, of death "passed over their houses." It also purified the members gathered for the meal. Averred Reu: "The meat of the expiating offering was consumed by all members of the family, thereby not only the communion among members of the family was demonstrated but also communion with God, who had by way of prefiguration been established through sacrifice."[18]

The paschal lamb was a type of Christ (I Cor. 5:6). It pointed forward to the sacrifice which He, the "true Lamb of God" (John 1:29) was to offer to God for the redemption of the world. On the Thursday of Holy Week Jesus was to begin carrying out the sacrifice promised in type and prophecy. The observance of the Passover was therefore no longer necessary and in its place Christ instituted the Sacrament of the Altar in remembrance that He had given His life as a sacrifice for mankind's sins.

Why Observe the Jewish Seder?

In recent years some Lutherans have been observing the "Jewish Seder," the feast commemorating the exodus of the Jews in the fifteenth century B.C. from Egypt, when the angel death passed over those houses that had the passover lamb's blood on the door posts. It was the beginning of the exodus from the 430-year Egyptian bondage. Since this is one of the great feasts of Judaism one wonders why Christians should hold Seders? The last legitimate seder occurred before Christ instituted the Lord's Supper. Paul told the Colossians "that they were not to regard important Jewish feast days or new-moons or sabbaths, because these were a shadow of things to come, but the substance belongs to Christ" (2:16-17). The apostle to the Gentiles told the Corinthians that in the future they should observe Easter by putting away malice and vice but with the unleavened bread of sincerity and truth, because "Christ Our Paschal Lamb has been sacrificed for us (1 Cor. 5:6)."

The Earthly Elements Used in the Eucharist
The earthly elements are bread and wine. Using the **Matzots** (unleavened bread) and the fruit of the vine, that is wine, Jesus specified their use in Matthew 26:26-29; Luke 22:18-10. Water is not to be substituted for wine or any other liquid. Since at Passover time only wine was employed, that is what Christ used and that rules out grape juice.

The Nature of the Bread to Be Distributed
Lutheran theologians claim, whether wheat or rye, leavened or unleavened, or its form, whether fragments of a loaf are used, are adiaphora, because Matthew 26:26 and Corinthians 11:26 use the general term for bread. The Eastern Orthodox Catholic Church insists on the use of **leavened** bread, the Roman Catholic Church insists on unleavened bread. Both positions go beyond the Biblical text.[19] The Reformed oppose the use of wafers, claiming that bread needs to be broken. As to what kind of bread is employed, the Lutheran stance is that this belongs to the article of Christian liberty (1 Cor. 7:23; Gal. 2:4ff; 5:1).

The Breaking of Bread Not
Essential to the Validity of the Sacrament
According to the *Solid Declaration of the Formula of Concord* the breaking of the bread into pieces does not belong to the Sacramental action, but the distribution is necessary not its mode. *Popular Symbolics* asserted: "The Reformed, with some exceptions, make it an essential feature, commanded by Christ as symbolizing the rending of His body on the cross. Christ did not command it. He broke the bread indeed, but that was only incidental to the distribution."[20] However, according to John 19:31-36 Christ's body was not broken. Weidenschilling observed about the word "broken." "Only in 1 Cor. 11:24 does our English translation of the Bible (Authorized Version) has this is "My body which is broken for you," but this expression probably kept into the Greek text used by the translators, other Greek texts have also "given," as in the Gospels.[21]

The mode of distribution is an adiaphoron. However, because the Reformed have made the mode of administration a doctrinal issue and a visible demonstration of the alleged absurdity of the real presence, it no longer can be an indifferent ceremony.[22]

The Necessity of the Sacramental Action as Constituting the Essence of the Supper

"Take eat this is My body," "take drink this is the blood of the new testament" must be spoken to the communicant who in a supernatural manner receives the body and blood of Christ.[23]

The Solid Declaration of the *Formula of Concord* stated: "Apart from this use, when the papistic Mass the wine is not distributed, it is not to be regarded as a Sacrament. If the institution of Christ be not observed as appointed, there is no Sacrament."[24] Not only the bread, but the wine must be distributed. In Luther's time and for over four hundred years the wine in the cup was withheld from the laity, the priests alone drinking the wine. Vatican II has restored the cup also to the laity, so communion in one kind is no longer the dogmatic rule.

The Real Presence of Christ in the Lord's Supper

Luther, Melanchthon and the writers of *The Formula of Concord* held on the basis of the Biblical text that in the Lord's Supper the body and blood are truly, and essentially present and are given to the communicants under the bread and wine.[25] According to the words of institution the communicant receives the bread and the body and also is given the wine and the blood of Jesus.

The Oral Eating and Drinking

The eating and drinking of the bread and wine is known as the oral eating and drinking of Christ's body and blood, because it occurs in and through the same act by which bread and wine are partaken. With the bread the body of Christ is received, and with the wine the blood of Christ are given the communicant. All attending the Lord's Table, whether contrite sinners or unbelieving people receive the four elements.

Also the unbelieving and the unworthy receive the body and blood of Christ, otherwise Paul could not say that whosoever eats the bread and the wine unworthily is guilty of the body and blood of Christ. The unworthy become guilty of sinning against the body and blood of Christ (I Cor. 11:27-29).[26]

This eating which takes place in the Lord's Supper is called "sacramental eating" and only occurs in the Lord's Supper. "Take eat this is My body," "take drink this is the blood" of the New Testament only occur in the sacrament of the altar. St. Paul told the Corinthians that there is a **koinonia**, a union between bread and body and a **koinonia** exists between the wine and the blood of Christ. Holy Writ does not tell us, nor could we grasp with our minds, how this **koinonia** (fellowship) takes place (1 Cor. 10:16). It is not a natural eating, physical union, but a supernatural, one peculiar to the sacrament, hence called "the sacramental union." Therefore, the historic orthodox Lutheran Church teaches the Real Presence of Christ. A number of Lutheran Confessions or Symbols set forth the teaching of the Real Presence *The Augsburg Confession X, The Apology of The Augsburg Confession X, the Smalcald Articles of Luther*, 2f. *The Large Catechism, V*, 8f. *The Formula of Concord, Solid*

Declaration VIII 2f, 92f. affirm this theological truth.

Rationalists question the Real Presence and contend that the body and blood are absent. When bread and wine are distributed,[27] Zwingli held that the verb "is" means represents or symbolized the body of Christ. Reformed theology claims that inasmuch as Christ is enclosed in heaven. He cannot be present thousands of places in the world. The problem with this is that human reason is pitted against Scripture's clear words, the Bible asserts the Omnipotence of God (Luke 1:37) and His Truth (Psalm 33:4). Those who oppose the teaching of the Real Presence ignore the Word of God, which ascribes full omnipresence to the human nature, described in Mark 16:19, Ephesians 4:10 and the omnipresence of the divine nature (Jer. 23:23f).

Calvin, Zwingli, Beza Oecolampadius all claim that the words of institution, setting forth the Real Presence are not to be taken literally and therefore not seriously. When the Reformed assert Christ's presence in the Lord's Supper, they think of a spiritual presence. Krauth *Conservative Reformation* claimed that there was no unity among the Reformed as to what "spiritual" means, he counts some twenty different interpretations in the Reformed camp.[29] *The Heidelberg Catechism* and the *Westminster Confession* are very clear in that they reject the Real Presence of Christ in the sacrament of the Altar.[30] Chapter XXIX, 7 of the Westminster Confession, declares that Christ's body and blood are "not corporally with and under the wine, yet as really, but spiritually, present to the faith of believers in that ordinance as the elements themselves are to their outward senses."[31]

Over against this figurative interpretation of the words of institution, and Luther with him the loyal Lutherans, have steadfastly maintained that the words of Christ "This is My body" and "This is My blood" must be accepted as they stand, in their literal sense.[32]

Reasons for the Literal Interpretation of "Is"

1. Christ Himself calls His Holy Supper His testament a designation which St. Paul has preserved: "This cup of the New Testament in My blood," and in the phrases that Matthew and Mark report, Jesus said "This is My blood of the New Testament." When a person writes a last will he uses the clearest and unmistakable words that he can find, in order to avoid any chance for ambiguity, and later when the will is read, the words are taken in their literal sense. Jesus certainly did not intend that His last will and testament be uncertain as to what he would have his believers believe and do. Jesus said that He is the Truth (John 14:6).

2. Holy Communion is a Sacrament of the New Testament. Zucker in his article on "The Lord's Supper," claimed: "If we were to set aside, reject, the proper sense of the words and teach that bread and wine only signify the body and blood of the Lord, that they are only types and symbols, we should be going back into Old Testament times and manners of speaking; speaking of the Old Testament the Bible says (Heb. 10:1) that it has a shadow of good things to come" and which are "a shadow of things to come but the body is of Christ." The Old Testament has figurative lan-

guage, symbolic actions and happenings; signs and types, prophecies of better things to come in the future; but the New Testament reports the actual fulfillment of types and prophecies.[33] The Passover meal was typical, the supper which the Lord had just celebrated with His disciples was fulfilled when He instituted the Lord's Supper, and thus appointed for centuries to come the holy meal to be celebrated till the Lord returns. Christ gave His disciples flesh and blood. If the actions at the Last Meal were to be merely symbolical, it would mean that the Old Testament believers had more than those of the New Testament, for the Israelites had the Paschal lamb with its actual flesh and blood, and that would mean that the Jews had a more impressive symbol than a symbol of bread and wine. Humanly speaking Christ would then have left his devotees no more than the Passover of the Jews.

3. The words of institution should be taken in their proper sense and nowhere is there an indication that they should not be interpreted literally but in a figurative sense. Nowhere is there an indication that the Lord's Supper's "Eat My body", and "drink the wine" are to be understood metaphorically.

4. Paul in 1 Corinthians 10:16 shows how the words of institution are to be understood.[34]

Misconception About The Real Presence

Luther in trying to discuss how Christ is present, used the expression "with, in and under" to indicate that somehow the communicant in a supernatural manner receives Christ's body and blood. The historic orthodox Lutheran Church has never recognized "consubstantiation," namely, that the body and blood are combined with the bread and wine into a third substance. Further the Lutheran Church does not teach "impanation" or of "subpanation" that is, that the body and blood are locally included in the bread and wine, or are located under them.[35] "The Lutheran expression of "in," "with" and "under" was adopted to reject substantiation and not to define the indefinable or to explain the Real Presence in terms of physics.

The Cessation of the Sacramental Union

With the last distribution at the communion rail the sacramental union ceases. Nothing has the nature of a sacrament apart from the use instituted by Christ. Thus asserts *Formula of Concord, Solid Declaration*, VII 15. 108. Rome and high Episcopalians defend and require the reservation of the host on the basis of transubstantiation. The body and blood are present during the administration, as the officiant uses God's Word and says: "Take eat, this is the body of the Lord," and "take drink this is the blood of the new testament." Without the Word of God one only has bread and wine in the Holy Supper. Both before the distribution and after it, only bread and wine are found on the altar.[36]

Unworthy Reception of The Lord's Supper

Those who are unrepentant communicants, who reject the real presence, receive the body and blood of Christ because Christ's body and blood are inseparately connected with the physical eating and drinking, they all constitute one action. In I Corinthians Paul warns the Corinthians that the unworthy participants take the body and blood to their damnation (Ch. 11:27-29).[37] According to Reformed theology the unbeliever who goes to the Lord's Table does not receive the Lord's body.[38]

Bread and Wine Are Not Changed
Into the Lord's Body and Blood

The Roman Catholic Church teaches officially since the Council of Constance AD 1215 that once the priest blesses the bread it is changed into the body of Christ and when he blesses the wine it is changed into the blood of Christ.[39] The priest performs a double miracle, as great as that when God assumed human flesh and blood. The bread looks like and tastes like bread but is the body of Christ. The wine looks like wine and tastes like wine yet is the blood of Christ. Until the time of Vatican II the laity only received the bread but not the wine in the cup, because it was argued that a piece of flesh has in it also blood (Called communion in one kind). This is known as transubstantiation, a doctrine which has been challenged by some Dutch Roman Catholic theologians.[40]

The Roman Catholic dogma of transubstantiation contradicts I Corinthians 11:26f. Paul states that the unworthy communicant who received the bread and wine is guilty of the body and blood of Christ. The same apostle also assured the Corinthians that there exists a fellowship between the bread and body and a fellowship (koinonia) between the wine and blood.

The *Concordia Cyclopedia* states: "While the person of Christ is present at the Lord's Supper, as indeed He is everywhere, it is not Christ whole and entire (thus Council of Trent) that constitutes the heavenly element, as Rome declares but as Christ distinctly states. His body and blood, all ratiocinations aside."[41]

The Adoration of the Host

The adoration of the host is a concomitant of transubstantiation and is a perversion of the Holy Eucharist, according to Matthew 26:26 is not to be reserved and adored and such action is tantamount to idolatry. When Roman Catholics adore the host, they are praying to bread, a creature. The *Formula of Concord*, Epitome Con. 4 describes this as a part of the false worship introduced by the Papacy and also a piece with the idolatry denounced in Romans 1:25. The papistical Mass, in which the priest sacrifices Christ in an unbloody manner "for the sins, penalties, and satisfactions of the living and dead," has nothing in common with the Holy Supper instituted by Christ, Matt. 26:26 or I Cor. 11:26. The words are addressed to the living and not to the dead. The sacrifice of the mass is a denial of the all-sufficiency of the sacrifice offered on Calvary (Hebrews 9:12,10:1,12,14,18; I Peter 3:18; John 19:30). The "unbloody" sacrifice of the Mass conflicts with Hebrew 9:22. The theological teachings relative to the sacrifice of the Mass contradict the doctrine of justification by faith, being instead accomplished by the priest and the devout.

The doctrine of substantiation serves the glorification of the priesthood, the priest effecting transubstantiation by virtue of powers conferred by holy orders, performing a miracle comparable to the Incarnation.

When Is Christ's Body Really and Essentially Present in the Eucharist?

Many believe that the consecration places Christ's body and blood in the Lord's Supper. Hove expressed the true Lutheran teaching when he wrote: "When the minister recites the words of institution, he thereby publicly declares that he is about to celebrate the Lord's Supper according to the Lord's institution, not to act according to his own pleasure, but as a steward of the mysteries of God. Thereby the bread and wine are set apart from their ordinary uses, and ordained for sacramental use. Thereby it is testified that Christ according to his promise is present in the solemnity of the Lord's Supper and by virtue of His institution He communicates His body and blood together with the bread and wine which are blessed, distributed, and received."[42]

The Words of Consecration Misunderstood

Hove wrote: "The recital of the words of institution must not be misunderstood. His pronunciation of these words must not act like a magical formula, must not be regarded as having the mystic power of conjuring the body and blood of Christ in the Lord's Supper. It is Christ who causes the union of His body and blood with the bread and wine in the Lord's Supper. He has willed and ordained it and what in this case He has willed he continues to will. His will is expressed in His Words, which are just as true and powerful today as at the first Lord's Supper."[43]

Holy Communion and Christian Fellowship

Because the communicant receives the body and blood of Christ, he or she enter into close communion with Christ by receiving the one bread (1 Cor. 10:17), and drinking that one cup which Christ has ordained, we also enter into fellowship with our Christian brethren, who eat and drink at the Lord's Table.[44]

The Purpose of the Lord's Supper

Holy Communion, one of the two visible Words of God (i.e. baptism and the Eucharist) was instituted by Christ for the remission of sins. In the Lord's Supper the forgiveness of sins is made personal and direct as the officiant says to the recipient: "Given and shed for your sins." The giving of the body and the blood assures the penitent communicant as a pledge of Christ's forgiveness.

Subsidiary purposes of Holy Communion are: (1) that Christians are to be witnesses to the death of Christ and (2) that by common participation the hand of fellowship among Christians is to be strengthened (1 Cor. 11:26; I Cor. 10:17; I Cor. 12:13).[45]

Who Should Be Admitted to the Communion Table?

As participation in the Lord's Supper may become harmful, taking the Holy Supper to one's damnation and not a blessing, and as, according to Scripture the Communicant should examine himself before partaking Holy Communion (1 Cor. 11:28), that would exclude certain individuals.

The Lord's Supper is only intended for true believers, who have the right understanding of what transpires at the celebration and participation in the Holy Supper. Therefore, 1) those who are ungodly should not be given the Lord's Supper; 2) those who have given offense and are knowingly unreconciled with fellow Christians; 3) those who can't examine themselves, children, people in a coma; 4) those belonging to churches that have erroneous views about the Lord's Supper. J.T. Mueller, asserted: "The Sacrament must be withheld from all who are connected with erring churches and unchristian and antichristian cults, Eph. 4:1-6; 5:7-11; 2 Cor. 6:14-18. Baptism is administered first to converts, then later the Lord's Supper."[46]

Closed Communion in Conservative Lutheranism

All former members of The Lutheran Synodical Conference, the Wisconsin Synod, the Evangelical Lutheran Church, a number of smaller Lutheran conferences and the Lutheran Church-Missouri Synod practice closed communion. In a letter sent out by Samuel H. Nafzger, February 22, 1993, the Executive Director of the Commission on Theology and Church Relations, wrote: "The Lutheran Church Missouri Synod believes, together with Lutherans from the time of the Reformation and in agreement with Christians from New Testament times, that the Scriptures teach what has traditionally been referred to as the practice of close(d) communion."[47] He further wrote in this letter: "This practice, which seeks to prevent both harmful reception of the Sacrament as well as a profession of unity in confession where this unity does not exist, means that ordinarily the pastors and congregations of the Synod commune only those individuals who are members of the Synod or of a church body with which the Synod is in altar and pulpit fellowship."[48] Here was being restated what had been set forth in **A Report of the Commission on Theology and Church Relations, The Lutheran Church-Missouri Synod**, May, 1983.[49]

Frequency of Communion Attendance

Mueller claimed: "While all Christians should frequently attend the Lord's Table in the manner which Scripture prescribes 1 Cor. 11:26-29, we cannot speak of **an absolute** necessity of the Lord's Supper. The spiritual eating of Christ's body, John 6:53, or faith in Christ (sola fide), is indeed absolutely necessary for salvation, but the sacramental eating is not absolutely necessary. Also here the words of St. Augustine apply: Not the privation, but the contempt of the Sacrament condemns."[50]

Not to attend the Lord's Supper frequently represents indifference or contempt and is tantamount to apostasy. In his *Large Catechism* Luther wrote: "Such people as deprive themselves of, withdraw from, the Sacrament so long a time are not to be considered Christian" (42ff.).

Sacrament of the Altar Not a Sacrifice

Sacraments must be distinguished from sacrifices. In a sacrifice man offers something to God, it is an act by which man deals with God. The *Apology*, however, states: "A Sacrament is a ceremony in which God presents to us that which the promise annexed to the ceremony offers. A sacrifice, on the contrary, is a ceremony or work which we render God in order to afford Him honor." The sacraments are acts, applying water and eating bread and drinking wine to which God's Word is added. "Accedit verbum ad elementum, et fit sacramentum. Sacraments are signs and tokens of grace; they are means through which God offers and assures His grace to man."[51]

The Validity of the Sacrament

When is a sacrament really valid? The validity does not depend on the piety and faith of him who administers it (Matt. 23:3,4), nor on the opinion and faith of him who receives it (Rom. 3:3-4). The nature and value of the Sacrament of the Altar depends upon the Word of God. The divinely intended sense of the Holy Communion can only be determined by what the Scriptures intended to say. It is not theologians, or church bodies who determine the intent of any sacrament. It is important to distinguish between the nature and purpose of the Lord's Supper and the benefits and blessings of the Holy Supper.[52]

The Power of the Sacrament

Both in the case of Baptism and the Lord's Supper it is none other than the Gospel that gives power to these two sacred rites. While the sermon which publicly proclaimed is heard by many individuals, in Baptism and the Lord's Supper God deals individually with people and the recipients of these two sacred actions have God's promise connected with water and with bread and wine. It is not water or bread and wine which effect the blessings, but the Word of God connected with them.[53] Without God's Word, the elements in both sacraments, are only water, bread and wine. It is the promise of God which conveys these blessings, and in the Sacrament this promise of grace by Christ's command definitely links up with the visible elements.

Does the Sacrament of The Altar Automatically Bestows Its Blessings?

Roman Catholic theology teaches the Holy Eucharist bestows blessings automatically. Luther in the *Small Catechism* said: "The words 'for you' require all hearts to believe." *The Augsburg Confession* asserts that on the basis of 1 Cor. 11:26-29, "the faith of those who use the Sacrament should remember what benefits it receives through Christ."[54]

The Roman Catholic teaching asserting that the Sacraments profit without faith on the part of the recipient (**ex opere operate**) turns them into pagan rites and subverts the fundamental article of the Christian religion that faith justifies and saves.[55]

Lord's Supper Views of Eastern Orthodoxy

Although this article has not explicated on the Lord's Supper theology of The Holy Oriental Catholic and Apostolic Church, a brief presentation should be made because of its views that differ somewhat from those of Rome. In Eastern Orthodoxy the Eucharist is viewed both as a sacrament and as a sacrifice. Wrote Mayer: "Until the Reformation various views concerning the real presence of the body and blood of Christ were entertained, and agreement seems to exist only on the use of the term **metousiosis**. No attempt is made to explain the mystery of the change which takes place."[56]

Unlike the Roman Catholic practice of limiting the laity to just the bread (supposedly turned into the body of Christ) the Greek Orthodox Church gives the laity both bread and wine. The elements are distributed by intinction, i.e., the particles of the consecrated bread are dipped into the wine.[57] Because the Eastern Church believes that according to John 18:28, Christ instituted the Eucharist on the 13th of Nisan, unleavened bread is required. The Lord's Supper is given to infants in contrast to Roman Catholic and Protestant theologies. Infant communion is practiced because it is held that the Eucharist is necessary for salvation. Eastern Orthodoxy believes that in the Eucharist, Christ as Priest and Victim offers His body and blood to the Father under the forms of bread and wine.[58]

Books for Further Reading

Martin Chemnitz, *Ministry, Word, and Sacraments, an Enchiridion*, translated by Luther Poellet (St. Louis Concordia Publishing House).

Martin Chemnitz, *The Lord's Supper*, translated by J.A.O. Preus (St. Louis Concordia Publishing House, 1979).

Herman Sasse, *This Is My Body* (St. Louis: Concordia Publishing House).

Herman Sasse, *We Confess; Volume II The Sacraments*, one of the three volumes of the set: *We Confess*; Volume I *Jesus Christ* and Volume III *The Church*.

Footnotes

1. Luther Reed, *The Lutheran Liturgy* (Philadelphia: Muhlenberg Press, 1947), p. 460. For other names by which the Thursday of Holy Week was called cf. Paul Zellar Strodach, *The Church Year*

(Philadelphia: The United Lutheran Publication House, 1924), p. 341.

2. L. Fuerbringer, Th. Engelder, and P.E. Kretzmann, *Popular Symbolics* (St. Louis: Concordia Publishing House, 1927), "Lord's Supper," pp. 415a-417.

3. **Ibid.**, pp. 513-514.

4. "A Declaration of Eucharistic Understanding and Practice" *Celebrate*, Pentecost, 1996, p. 4. John Johnson, "Close Communion . . . One View," Foreword, April, 1996. p. 4. Robert G. Hoerber, "Exegesis of 1 Corinthians 11:29," *Christian News*, December 6,1993, pp. 20-21.

5. Cf. Matthew Kohmescher, *Catholicism Today: A Survey of Catholic Beliefs* (Mahwah, N.J.: Paulist Press, 1991).

6. Theodore Tappert, *The Book of Concord* (Philadelphia: Fortress Press, 1959), cf. (General Index, pp. 685b-686b.

7. J.M. Weidenschilling, "The Sacraments," in *The Bible Student* (St. Louis: Concordia Publishing House, p. 47).

8. **Ibid.**, p. 47; *A Short Explanation of Luther's Small Catechism* (St. Louis: Concordia Publishing House, 1943), Question 296, p. 193.

9. Paul Zeller Strodach, *A Manual of Worship* (Philadelphia: Muhlenberg Press, 1946), p. 221.

10. Edward W. A. Koehler, *A Summary of Christian Doctrine* (Detroit and Oakland, 1939), p. 200.

11. **Ibid.**, pp. 201-202.

12. Cf. the lengthy discussion in Martin Reu, *Lutheran Dogmatics*, Third Edition (Wartburg, Iowa, Wartburg Seminary, 1951), pp. 296-298; Martin Chemnitz, *The Lord's Supper* translated by J.A.O.

Preus (St. Louis: Concordia Publishing House, 1979), pp. 91-139.

13. **Ibid.**, p. 294.

14. Tappert, *The Lutheran Confessions*, **op. cit.**, p. 483.

15. **Ibid.**, p. 489

16. C. M. Zom, *Die Zwei Episteiln St. Paul and die Korinther* (Zwickaus: Verlag des Schriftvereins, no date), pp. 95-96. Paul E. Kretzmann, *Popular Commentary of the New Testament* (St. Louis: Concordia Publishing House, 1924), II, pp. 141-142.

17. Reu, **op. cit.**, p. 293.

18. **Ibid.**, p. 294.

19. *Popular Symbolics*, **op. cit.**, p. 93.

20. *Popular Symbolics*, **op. cit.**, p. 94. *Formula of Concord*, VII, Epitome, 24; *Augsburg Confession* XXII, *Apology of Augsburg Confession*, XXII, Smalcald Articles, Part III, VI, p. 3.

21. Weidenschilling, **op. cit.**, p. 52.

22. *Popular Symbolics*, **op. cit.**, p. 94.

23. E. Hove, *Christian Doctrine* (Minneapolis: Augsburg Publishing House, 1930), p. 352.

24. *Formula of Concord*, Th.D., VII, 83f, *Popular Symbolics*, **op. cit.**, p. 94; C. H. Little, *Lutheran Confessional Theology* (St. Louis: Concordia Publishing House, 1943), p. 160.

25. *Augsburg Confession X, The Apology X, Smalcald Articles*, Part IV, VI; *Large Catechism*, V. 8f; *Formula of Concord* II, *Solid Declaration* VIII, 2f, 92f; Epitome XII, p. 24.

26. John Theodore Mueller, *Christian Dogmatics* (St. Louis: Concordia Publishing House, 1955), p. 530.

27. **Ibid.**, pp. 530-531.

28. Weidenschilling, **op. cit.**, p. 55.

29. C. P. Krauth, *The Conservative Reformation and Its Theology* (Minneapolis: Augsburg Publication House, reprint in 1889 Edition), p. 609.

30. "The Heidelberg Catechism," in Philip Schaff, *The Creeds of Christendom* (New York: Harper and Sons, 1877), III, p. 335.

31. "The Westminster Confession," Schaff, **op. cit.**. III, p. 666.

32. E.G. Schwiebert, *Luther and His Times* (St. Louis: Concordia Publishing House, 1950), pp. 700.

33. F. R. Zucker, "The Lord's Supper," in Theo Laetsch, Editor, *The Abiding Word* (St. Louis: Concordia Publishing House, 1947), II, p. 429. **Ibid.**, p. 429, Cf. also Francis

Pieper, *Christian Dogmatics* (St. Louis: Concordia Publishing House, 1953), III, pp. 337-349.

34. **Ibid.**, Zucker, **op. cit.**, p. 429.

35. Joseph Stump, *The Christian Faith* (New York: The Macmillan Company, 1932), pp. 353-354.

36. Hove, **op. cit.**, pp. 354, 356.

37. Stump, **op. cit.**, p. 350.

38. L. Berkhof, *Systematic Theology* (Grand Rapids: Wm. B. Eerdmans Publishing Company, 1950, p. 654.

39. *Catechism of the Catholic Church* (Rome: Urbi et Orbi Communications, 1994), p. 654.

40. "The Lord's Supper," in *Popular Symbolics*, **op. cit.**, p. 416.

41. *Popular Symbolics*, **op. cit.**, p. 354.

42. Hove, **op. cit.**, p. 354.

43. **Ibid.**, pp. 353-354.

44. Werner Elert, *The Lord's Supper Today* (St. Louis: Concordia Publishing House, 1973), p. 44.

45. Heinrich Schmidt, *The Doctrinal Theology of the Evangelical Lutheran Church*. Third Revised Edition by Charles A. Hay and Henry E. Jacobs (Minneapolis: Augsburg Publishing House, 1961) pp. 552-582.

46. Mueller, *Christian Dogmatics*, **op. cit.**, p. 538.

47. Letter to the Synod, February 22, 1993.

48. **Ibid.**

49. A Report of the *CTCR, Theology and Practice of the Lord's Supper*, May 1983, pp. 20-24.

50. Mueller, *Christian Dogmatics*, **op. cit.**, p. 540.

51. *The Apology of The Augsburg Confession*, Article XXIV, 18, *Concordia Triglotta* (St. Louis: Concordia Publishing House, 1921), p. 389.

52. Koehler, **op. cit.**, p. 198.

53. **Ibid.**, p. 198.

54. *Augsburg Confession*, XXIV 30, **Ibid.**, p. 394.

55. *Popular Symbolics*, **op. cit.**, p. 99.

56. F. E. Mayer, *The Religious Bodies of America* (St. Louis: Concordia Publishing House, 1956), p. 17.

57. **Ibid.**, p. 17.

58. *Orthodox Conf., Questio CVII, Conf. Dositheus, Decretum XVII*, Longer C. Wus 315-50, in Frank Gavin, *Some Aspects of Contemporary Greek Orthodox Thought* (The Hale Lectures) New York: Morehouse Publishing Co., 1923.

Questions

1. Do the Lutheran Confessions have much to say about the Lord's Supper? ____

2. Some different names of the Lord's Supper are ____.

3. Why do Lutherans today generally avoid the use of the term Mass? ____

4. Is the term sacrament a Biblical term? ____

5. What Roman Catholic rites do not meet with the Lutheran criteria for "sacrament?" ____

6. Jesus referred to "New Testament" to point out ____.
7. Is the Lord's Supper as first observed in the Christian Church based on John 6? ____
8. Proponents of "High Lutheranism" claim that John 6:26,52 refers to ____.
9. Do the Lutheran Confessions reject this interpretation? ____
10. Is the body of Christ eaten in a Capernaitic manner? ____
11. The paschal lamb was a type of ____.
12. Why should Christians observe the Jewish Seder? ____
13. Should grape juice be used for the Eucharist? ____
14. What is the nature of the Bread to be distributed? ____
15. Must the bread be broken? ____
16. Vatican II restored the cup also to ____.
17. All attending the Lord's Table, whether contrite sinners or unbelieving people receive ____.
18. What is the sacramental union? ____
19. Zwingli held that the word "is" means ____.
20. Christ Himself calls His Holy Supper ____.
21. Has the Lutheran Church ever recognized consubstantiation? ____
22. With the last distribution at the Communion rail the ___ ceases.
23. Who requires the reservation of the host? ____
24. Are the Bread and Wine changed into the Lord's Body and Blood? ____
25. The sacrifice of the Mass is ____.
26. What contradicts the doctrine of justification by faith alone? ____
27. When is Christ's Body really and essentially present in the Eucharist? ____
28. The Lord's Supper is intended only for ____.
29. The Sacrament must be withheld from ____.
30. Who practices closed communion? ____
31. Not the privation, but ____ of the Sacrament condemns.
32. The Sacrament of the Altar is not a ____.
33. Does the validity of the Sacrament depend on the person who administers it? ____
34. What gives power to the Sacrament? ____
35. Do the Sacraments profit without faith? ____
36. How is the Eucharist viewed in Eastern Orthodoxy? ____
37. Why does Eastern Orthodoxy practice infant communion? ____

An Evaluation of Millennialism and Dispensationalism of Proponents Using the Gulf War to Interpret the End Times Millennialism and Israel Today

Christian News, **March 18, 1991**

Because of the Gulf War millennialism and dispensationalism are being promoted with a vengeance and great attention is being accorded to the state of Israel, and there is now being promoted considerable interest in what is termed "Biblical prophecy."[1] While all dispensationalists believe in a millennium, not all millennialists are dispensationalists. Historicity speaking, each of these two movements had different origins and different promoters.[2] In the center of this new interest given to the Gulf War is the attention focused on the State of Israel and the events which allegedly will characterize the end time, in which the second coming of Christ to this earth for the establishment of his earthly kingdom is paramount.

The Scofield Reference Bible, originally published in 1909 and 1917, has been the purveyor of dispensationalism; it was revised in 1966 as *The New Scofield Reference Bible*. One of the seven revisers was John E. Walvoord, now Provost of Dallas Theological Seminary, Dallas, Texas.[3] Time magazine, February 11, 1991 has called attention to his latest book, *Armageddon, Oil and the Middle East* (a revision of his 1974 work), which up to February has sold in a million copies.[4] Another member of the Dallas Seminary faculty is Charles Dyer Who has authored *The Rise of Babylon, The Sign of the End Times*, in which Saddam Hussein is said to be rebuilding Babylon and proclaiming himself as Nebuchadnezzar and in his book Dyer claims that Biblical prophecy about Babylon is being fulfilled.[5] Cal Thomas wrote a column using the books of Walvoord and Dyer predicting that Armageddon may be near.[6]

Dallas Theological Seminary (originally Evangelical Theological (College) for over sixty years has been a vigorous proponent for dispensationalism through its theological quarterly, Bibliotheca Sacra[7] and through the many books written by such professors as Walvoord, M. Unger, the two (Chafers, R.T. and the Lewis Sperry), Ryrie,[8] Pentecost,[9] Lincoln and many others not connected with the seminary. Many Bible Colleges (formerly called Biblical Institutes) have also helped to disseminate the brand of dispensationalism sponsored by Scofield. Chafer's Systematic Theology in eight volumes has been the book on dogmatics, impregnated with dispensationalism and millennialism to which thousands of students have been exposed for at least six decades.[10] One of its graduates was Hal Lindsey, the author of *The Late Great Planet Earth*, *Satan Is Alive and Well*, *There Is A New Earth Coming*, three books which sold in the millions.[11]

1812

Millennialism Antedates Dispensationalism

Dispensationalism, to be discussed later in this essay, has many features in common with millennialism or millenarianism or chiliasm. Millennialism goes back to the Jewish rabbis and to even Christ's disciples who up to the day of the Ascension were looking for the restoration of an earthly Davidic kingdom (Acts 1:6). Christian writers like Ireneus, Tertullian, Methodius were chiliasts. One of the authors in *Popular Symbolics* proclaimed that "chiliasm had considerable vogue in the early church, but was fought by and eliminated from Christian theology by Clement of Alexandria and by Origen, and in the Western church by Augustine."[12]

Millennialism in America in the 19th Century

In America chiliasm was sponsored by many fundamentalists. *Popular Symbolics* contended that "American Chiliasts have introduced the term dispensationalism as properly descriptive of their modification of older millennialistic teachings."[13]

Early Millennial Proponents

One of the earliest millenarians was Anna Lee, who came to America from England in 1774 and became the founder of the Shakers. William Miller, a converted deist, lectured extensively in New York State and in 1831 fixed the date of Christ's second coming as occurring in 1843, which never happened and he acknowledged his mistake. Out of those who had accepted Miller's eschatological views eventuated the Adventist movement which has always been premillennialistic. Another church group that turned out to be millennialistic were the Latter Day Saints or Mormons. "Pastor" Russell organized the "Millennial Dawn" movement known as the Jehovah Witnesses.[14]

Revival of Millennialism in 1914-1917

At war times there appears to be much more of an interest in Christ's second coming and the events that will be a prelude to the end of world history. This happened in connection with the first World War. After 1917 there were many so called prophetic congresses.[15] A factor which must be noted in connection with the burgeoning of interest in Christ's second coming and the adoption of millennialism and eventually of dispensationalism was the liberalism which invaded the Protestant Churches during the latter half of the 19th century and the early decades of the 20th with its substitution of sociology, economics and psychology for the Christian message together with its questioning of all supernatural truths. This led to a reaction in fundamentalism, which would not brook a system of interpretation that would only accept the literal interpretation and not permit a figurative interpretation for many of the Biblical prophetic passages found in Isaiah, Jeremiah, Ezekiel, Daniel, Amos, and Zechariah in the Old Testament and especially Revelation in the New Testament. Many clergymen in the Presbyterian, Baptists, Methodist and other churches became ardent devotees of millennialism. Wrote Mayer: "All Fundamentalist Associations, as well as holiness and Pentecostal groups have written premillennialism into their creed."[16] The establishment of the State of Israel in 1948 led further on an interest in millennialism and the imminent return of Christ.

Different Form of Millennialism

Millennialism, also called millenarianism, or chiliasm has been historically active in two forms.[17] One school holds that Christ's second coming will occur after (post) the millennium, hence called postmillennialism. The other type holds that Christ's second coming will precede the thousand year rule of Christ in Palestine. Mayer claimed that postmillennialism ignores the fact that the human race "will increasingly be afflicted by wars, disorders, catastrophies."[18] Postmillennialism has practically died out, while premillennialism has a large following today. Those who reject the premillennial and dispensationalist views are called a millennialists.[19]

John Nelson Darby and Dispensationalism

Bowman in his article on "dispensationalism" began it this way: "Dispensationalism is a term descriptive of a fantastic type of interpretation of the Scriptures which originated toward the beginning of the last century among certain groups of people in England who later became organically related and since have styled The Plymouth Brethren."[20] One of their earliest leaders was John Nelson Darby, a graduate of Trinity College, Dublin (1819), who is credited with suggesting that world history and Biblical history be divided into seven dispensations. In 1908 Blackstone published his book, *Jesus Is Coming*, in which he assumed seven dispensations, each comprising a thousand years.[21] Blackstone called a dispensation an **aion**. According to the former these are: 1. the Eden, the aion of innocence, ending in expulsion; 2. the Antediluvian, the aion of freedom, during which conscience was the only restraint, and it terminated in the Flood and the reduction of the human race to eight people, consisting of Noah and his family; 3. the Postdiluvian, the aion of government, man placed under civil authority, ending in the destruction of Sodom and Gomorrah; 4. the Patriarchal, the pilgrim aion, terminating in the overthrow of Pharaoh and his armies in the Red Sea; 5. the Mosaic, the Israelite aion, ending in the crucifixion and the destruction of Jerusalem; 6. the Christian aion, the aion of mystery ending in the great tribulation, the coming of Christ, the judgment of the nations, and another great reduction of the world's population. During this aion the Jewish people are scattered among the nations; 7. the Millennial aion, the time of manifestation, Rom. 8:19, ending the Satan's last deception and the judgment of the great white throne. Blackstone was interested in the latter end of the Christian eion.[22] Basic to his discussion of this latter part of the Christian aion is the denial of a general judgment. Many of the views expressed by Blackstone will be found in dispensationalism and in millennialism.[23]

Revelation 20 in Millennialism

Premillennialism has made a number of basic assumptions which constitute the premises on which premillennialism rest and constitutes its formal character. A key Bible section, Revelation 20:1-10, is foundational to its view that Christ will establish an earthly kingdom on earth, in which Christ will rule as King in peace for a thousand years.[24] Millennialists as well as dispensationalists follow a literal system of interpretation relative to explaining the contents and teaching of the Apocalypse or Revelation.[25]

The interpretation of John's vision or apocalypse has been the battle ground for centuries.[26] There are at least four principal schools of interpretation: (1) Praeterist; (2) Historic; (3) Futuristic; (4) Spiritual. The first interprets the vision as having reference to episodes in Jewish and Christian history up till the fall of Jerusalem and Rome; the second, that we have here in vision the entire course of all the centuries of the Christian era; the third, postpones the significance of the vision to events accompanying the second coming of Christ; the fourth, holds that in the signs and symbols we have the never ending conflict between good and evil portrayed.[27]

Relative to the literal interpretation of the number 20, of a thousand years of a visible reign of Christ it must be noted that in Revelation there is a symbolical use of numbers. Four represents the four corners of the earth; seven the number of completion; while three and a half the number of imperfection and incompletion; ten stands for the world; twelve for the Old Testament congregation of believers; twenty-four the number of the Old and New Testament believers; six hundred and sixty-six a great opponent of Christ; one hundred and forty-four thousand the total number of those who will be saved; the number thousand represents the entire rule of Christ between His two comings.[28]

Premillennialists and dispensationalists take the number one thousand literally and reject a symbolic interpretation as violating the basic principle of Biblical interpretation that the literal sense is the normative rule in the interpretation of Scripture. Which raises the question: Is all of the Apocalypse to be taken literally. On the basis of what principle are some chapters and verses to be taken literally?

According to the premillennial and dispensational interpretation of Revelation 20, the saints are said to rule with Christ on earth. But 20:4 describes those that rule with Christ as being "the souls of those that were beheaded for the witness of Jesus and for the Word of God," so that the vision in Revelation DOES NOT DESCRIBE AN EARTHLY RULE, BUT A HEAVENLY RULE. Furthermore, 20:1-10 is so difficult and obscure that it cannot be used as **sedis doctrinae** (the seat of a doctrine) for the idea of a physical rule of Christ on earth for a thousand-year period.[29] The latter is true because reputable Biblical exegetes have understood this chapter in different ways. Since the last judgment in chapter 20 follows immediately after the "little season," the reference to the millennium must be the Messianic era, which began with the preaching of John the Baptist and is concluded with Christ's second and final coming for judgment. Since Revelation is replete with obscure visions and the allegorical and quais-enigmatical forms, difficult to interpret. Revelation's teaching must be understood according to the analogy of faith. The dark and difficult passages must be interpreted in the light of the clear passages.[30]

Because of the interpretation that Christ will rule as a visible monarch in Jerusalem, in Palestine, a premise of millennialism is that all Messianic passages that describe Christ as king, must be understood as still unfulfilled and still pertain to the future. Such passages are Psalm 2, 110, Isaiah 11, Daniel 7:13-14 and especially 2 Samuel 2:12-18, prophecies many Christians believe have already been fulfilled with Christ's first coming and in connection with his spiritual rule during the Messianic era.[31] Still to happen are supposedly that prediction that Jesus, the Jewish Messiah needs to bring to earth an era of good will, peace and harmony.

Is There a Difference Between the Kingdom of God and the Kingdom of Christ?

Some premillennialists postulate a difference between the kingdom of God and the kingdom of Christ.[32] The kingdom of God or kingdom of heaven is said to be the Holy Christian Church, while the Kingdom of Christ will be a kingdom in Jerusalem. Thus it is contended that when Christ first came he intended to establish the earthly kingdom as a descendant of David. He planned to reestablish the kingdom of David, which ceased in 587 B.C. But the Jews of Christ's time opposed Jesus' efforts between A.D. 26-39. The establishment was postponed because of the opposition of the Jewish leaders and instead proclaimed the nearness of the kingdom, which constituted the church, and this initiated the "church dispensation" or the dispensation of grace. The Christian Church which began at Pentecost will be terminated at the second coming of Christ, to be followed by the dispensation of the kingdom.[33] The last two thousand years of church history have been denominated the "great parenthesis."

Three Alleged Purposes for Israel

Another millennialist premise is that assumption that God has three purposes in view for Israel,[34] namely, 1) the production of a Messiah, a descendant of David, 2) the giving of the Old Testament Bible, and 3) that Israel was to be a light to the nations (Is. 43:12; 66:14). This third purpose still has to be realized, because Israel still needs to be converted and as a nation they still need to accept Christ The conversion is said to be occasioned by Christ's power and glory in the future, "when all Israel is supposed to be saved." If the Jews will be overpowered by Christ's power and glory and in consequence will accept Christ, why could not Jesus have done the same when he offered to become their king earlier?

The General Conversion of the Jewish People?

Another premise and assumption of premillennialism is that there will be a general conversion of the Jewish people.[35] The statement of Romans 11:26 is proof for this contention. Paul wrote: "And so all Israel will be saved."[36] In Romans chapters 9-11 Paul takes up the question: "Why is Israel not being saved in view of all the god-given advantages it had enjoyed?" Thus Paul wrote: "They are the people of God. They are made God's children. They have the glory, the covenants, the Law, the worship and the promises. They have the ancestors, and from them, according to the human nature, came Christ, who is God over everything, blessed forever" (Romans 9:5). Paul teaches that while many Jews are being lost there will always be a remnant of Israel that will be saved: "there is a remnant who will be saved." The "all Israel" of Romans 11:26 refers to the spiritual Israel, the elect among Jews and Gentiles.[37] Paul argues just as not all Israelites at Elijah's time were fallen away, but there was a remnant that did not bow the knee to Baal (7,000), so not all Israelites will be lost, but there is an elect remnant, which precludes the contention of premillennialists and dispensationalists that all Jews in the future will be saved. In 11:7 the apostle asserts: "There is a remnant according to the election of grace." Paul is clear that all Jews will not be saved. In 11:7: "What then? Israel did not receive what it wanted but those who God chose did receive it."

In Romans chapters 9-11 Paul distinguishes between the spiritual Israel (Israel **kata pneuma**) and the carnal Israel (Israel **kata sarka**), the former is and will be saved and the latter lost.[38] In chapter 9:8 Paul wrote: "This means that Abraham's children who are born in a natural way are not counted as the children of God. Only the children of the promise are counted as his descendants." In support of his view that not all Israel according to the flesh will be saved, the apostle quoted Isaiah 10:22-23: "Though the people of Israel are as many as the sand by the sea, only a remnant will be saved. For the Lord will execute His sentence on the land, completely and decisively." Again Is. 1:9: "If the Lord had not left us some survivors, we would have become like Sodom and Gomorrah." Again in verse 31: "Israel, which followed after the law of righteousness, hath not attained to the law of righteousness."

When Paul toward the latter part of his discussion of the fate of Israel, as to why they were being lost, emphasized the truth that a Jewish remnant was being saved, he warns the Gentiles not to boast because they were like a wild olive branch that had been grafted on the tree of God's chosen people, that both the elect remnant among the Jews and the elect among the Gentiles constituted the real spiritual Israel of God. It is this true Israel that Paul had in mind when he declared and "so all Israel will be saved." This saving of the elect of Israel and of the elect Gentile will take place during the "time of the Gentiles." The expression the fullness of the Gentiles denotes those of the Gentiles who are the elect of God.

Mueller asserted concerning this expression the "fullness of the Gentiles:" The determination of time until (Rom. 11:27) (**archi hou**) the fullness of the Gentiles be come in, stresses the truth that, as long as Gentiles shall be converted and saved, so long shall the elect in Israel be brought in, that is unto the end of the world, Matthew 24:14. The words "and so" (Rom. 11:26: **kai houtos**) describes the manner in which "all Israel" shall be saved, namely, by the divine calling of the elect in Israel through the Gospel, by which also the fullness of the Gentiles shall come in, (Romans 10:13-18).[39]

The Apostle Paul followed this principle and proclaimed the Gospel of repentance and remission of sin which was to be proclaimed unto the end of the age (Matthew 28:18-20) and that His disciples should preach both to Jews and Gentiles (cf. Acts 13:14-52). During the New Testament period of grace the Gospel was proclaimed to "all Israel" so that the fullness of the Gentiles might come in (Romans 10:1-4). It is the duty of the Christian Church to announce the truths of the Law and the Gospel to all nations, which includes also the Jews, the physical descendants of Abraham.[40]

The State of Israel Established in 1948

Millennialists and dispensationalists are claiming that the establishment of the State of Israel in Palestine is the harbinger of events which will culminate in the second coming of Christ to establish his earthly kingdom. Even though Israel condemns and persecutes Christian today, this does not matter, because eventually this scenario will be changed when Jews living when Christ appears will by Christ's sheer power become his followers.[41] The establishment of Israel in Palestine is based on such prophecies as Isaiah 11:1-12; Micah 4:1-4; Amos 9:11-15; Ezekiel 40-48; Zechariah 8:12 and chapter 14. However, what these passages describe is the building of the New Testament Church employing Old Testament phraseology.

Are There Two Judgments Prior to the Second Coming of Christ?

Both premillennialism and dispensationalism teach that there will be a number of judgments.[42] The "first judgment" is said to take place at the beginning of the millennium and has only one standard of judgment, namely, mankind's attitude toward the Jews. The "second judgment" will occur after the millennium. Thus Ludwigson asserted: "There are two great judgments, one preceding the millennium, then 'first resurrection' (Rev. 20:4-5) and one following the millennium, the great 'white throne' judgment (Rev. 20:5,11,15)."[43] The apostolic Scripture knows only one public judgment, described in Matthew 25:31-46. The Word of God also teaches that as soon as man has died, he will be judged. "It is appointed unto man once to die, and then the judgment" (Hebrews 9:27). John 3:16 and 36 clearly teach that each person's destiny is determined at death, whether he has accepted Christ as his personal Savior and has given evidence of his faith by good works. The final judgment of the world involves all people, all nations and people, including those who have been raised from the dead.[44]

Are There Two Different Resurrections?

Millennialists and dispensationalists operate with two different resurrections, one occurring at the beginning of the thousand-year reign of Christ on earth and the other prior to the final judgment.[45] There are also two different kinds of resurrection: 1. a resurrection of the just, or better resurrection and a resurrection of the wicked, a resurrection to condemnation. The basis for the two-resurrection theory is Revelation 20:1-6. Passages that just refer to one resurrection that is final, such as John 5:28-29; Luke 14:13-14; Hebrews 11:5 are forced into a predetermined scheme of the last things. In John 5:28-29 Jesus asserted: "Do not wonder at this, because the hour is coming in which all who are in the graves shall hear his voice and shall come forth, those who have done good into a resurrection of life (and here millennialists insert a long time space) those who have done evil to a resurrection of condemnation."[46] Such a procedure to divide a verse in half, assigning one part to one time period and the second part of the verse to a much latter time does violence to the Biblical text. There is only one resurrection and one final judgment, namely the one on the last day.

The Activity of the Antichrist

Dispensationalists and millennialists make much about the activity of the Antichrist, finding him in passages where he is not mentioned. The name "anti-Christ" is only found in 1 John, and used of those who deny the humanity of Jesus and thus oppose a basic truth about the Savior. Millennialists and dispensationalists have identified the antichrist with many different personalities and forces.[47] C. I. Scofield claim he is the last ecclesiastical head, an apostate from Christianity. H. Ironside believes he is the last ecclesiastical head, an apostate Jew (the beast out of the earth). Darby, Newell, J. Seiss, Dwight Pentecost, Hal Lindsey, and W. A. Criswell claim the antichrist is the first beast of Revelation 13; the second beast is the false prophet who supports him.[48] Many other identifications will be found in the writings of theologians of the last two thousand years of church history.

Calvin, Luther and the Lutheran Confessions[49] contend that the antichrist has been described by Paul in 2 Thessalonians 2:1-10, where he is called "the man of sin," the "man of lawlessness," who sits in temple of God and claims to be Christ's regent and authority on earth and this person has been represented by the papacy, whose activity was already evident in the early centuries. The papacy has been the great opponent of Christ because of its denial of the doctrine of justification by faith apart from works and because of its many new and unscriptural teachings which it has promoted and foisted upon men.[50]

The Battle of Armageddon

Ludwigson has described Armageddon as "the final cataclysm battle at the very end of the tribulation period when the kings of the earth under antichrist will gather together to invade Israel and go to war against the King of Kings, the Lord Jesus Christ. The future struggle of Armageddon has been called the battle of God Almighty (Rev. 16:14)."[51] From the lands of the rising sun, the armies will cross the Euphrates. "They will be gathered by unclean spirits at the command of the beast, the dragon, and the false prophet." According to the alleged understanding of Revelation 17,14 they are the armies of the last kings that will rule, on earth. Antichrist has joined them and together they rule in a confederacy of power for a brief period at the end of the age just before the second coming of Christ. The enemies of Christ will turn against Babylon and burn it. Then will occur the Battle of Armageddon.[52] In the battle in which Christ will lead His armies, Christ will be victorious (Rev. 19:11-12). As a result of Christ's supposed victory the beast and the prophet will be cast into the lake of fire, Satan will be bound and the armies which were killed will be consumed by birds and vultures. How Christ will destroy Antichrist is supposedly poetically set forth in Zechariah 14:2-3; Zech. 12:6; 2 Thess. 2:8-9. It will take Christ's followers seven months to dispose of all the weapons left behind.

Does the Scripture Know Anything of the Battle of Armageddon?

Armageddon is mentioned once in the Bible, namely, in Revelation 16:14-15. The pass of Megiddo leads through the Carmel range and has been the scene of many battles. There is nothing in chapters 38-39 of Ezekiel that mentions Armageddon but the nations, led by Gog of Magog, are directed against the mountains of Israel (Ezek. 39:4).[53] Ezekiel 38-39 simply states that the true Israel of God, the spiritual Israel, during the Messianic age, will experience the activity of great enemies. If the Ezekiel chapters are to be taken literally, as millennialists dispensationalists claim, this would mean that the many nations mentioned in chapter 38 would use bow and arrows, shields and bucklers as they allegedly fight against Christ. In view the great sophisticated weapons now available, such an interpretation seems utterly unlikely. It will take seven months to bury all the bodies of the slain armies. Would that not present a stench problem and be a source for diseases to spread? Where will all the birds come from who will be devouring the dead bodies?

The view of Christ riding forth at the head of an earthly army contradicts the teachings of Christ that His kingdom is not of this world but that it is established with the sword of the spirit, namely, the Word of God. Furthermore, it should be noted that Biblical scholarship does not know where a number of the nations mentioned in Ezekiel are to be found and what nations supposedly would be involved in this mythical battle of Armageddon.

The Place of Tribulation in Premillennialism

In the Mount Olivet discourse Jesus announced that before the Parousia of the Son of Man, there will be great tribulation and that immediately the Son of Man will appear in the sky (Matt. 24:30). He also announced in the same address that before the fall of Jerusalem there would be great tribulation. Many of the sufferings before Jerusalem's fall were types of similar happening toward the close of the age.

Millennialists claim that there will be tribulation in the millennial age.[54] Millennialism claims that the millennial period will be ushered in by Christ's invisible return to remove the believers from the earth during "the great tribulation."[55] After the church has been raptured, the great tribulation of a period of seven years (Dan. 9:26-27) will come upon the Jewish nation (Dan. 12; Luke 21:25,26; Acts 15:13-17). The Mount Olivet discourse simply teaches that the end of the age will be characterized by tribulation accompanied by great astronomical phenomena in nature.

The millennial and dispensational placing of the tribulation at different places in their eschatological schemes, is artificially contrived. The whole series of events allegedly to happen to Jew and Gentile is forced into a preconceived and non-Biblical eschatological scheme of happenings.

Whose Enemy Is Satan?

Premillennialism depicts the Devil or Satan as the enemy of the Jews rather than the adversary of Christ. This concept contradicts the whole tenor of the New Testament's teaching about Satan. Christians are warned by Peter to be on their guard, for the Devil as a roaring lion goes about seeking whom he may devour (1 Peter 5:8). It was Satan who entered the heart of Judas to go to the high priest and the Sanhedrin and betray Jesus for thirty pieces of silver, it was the Devil who entered the minds of Ananias and Sapphira to lie unto Peter about the amount of money they had received for their property. Throughout the ministry of Christ the Devil made a number of attempts to cause Jesus to deviate from his mission. Paul frequently warns Christians about the Devil (1 Cor. 7:5; 2 Cor. 2:11; 2 Cor. 4:4; 2 Cor. 11:3; Eph. 2:2; 4:27; 6:11-14; Col. 1:13).

The Church During the Millennium

Premillennialism has depicted the Church as an institution of splendor during the millennium,[57] but the New Testament teaches that the Church will be covered and hidden. The Church will be covered by the Cross until the end of time. Jesus said to His disciples "fear not little flock, for it is the father's good pleasure to give you the kingdom?" The Bible portrays the end of the age as a time when iniquity will abound and the Church will experience hard times and persecution.

The Misrepresentation of Christ as an Earthly Warrior

Millennialism claims that Christ will come to Jerusalem to establish an earthly kingdom[58] which He first planned to establish when He became incarnate, while Augustus was emperor and, Jesus much later, as already shown, supposedly will lead His armies against Gog of Magog (Ezek. 38-39). Millennialism is guilty of making Christ's kingdom during the millennium an earthly, instead of a heavenly one and spiritual in nature.

This depiction of Christ as an earthly ruler and warrior contradicts the teaching of Christ, who told Pontius Pilate that He was not a rival of Caesar and that His kingdom was not of this world. If it were, my disciples would fight for me. He forbade Peter to use the sword to defend Him. Jesus was a spiritual king and never gave (instructions to build up the kingdom of God by the use of force. Paul reminded the Christians of Asia Minor that the weapons of our Warfare are not carnal but Spiritual, 2 Cor. 10:4).

The Alleged Chronology of Millennialism's Eschatology

The center of millennialist theology is not soteriology but eschatology of a preconceived and predetermined nature. There is no agreement among millennialists as to the sequence of happenings that characterize the millennium. Mayer claimed that there are five major events agreed to by most scholars who are advocates of premillennialism.[59]

1. Christ's visible return will usher in the millennial period. This will occur during the great tribulation. At the first resurrection the dead believers will be made alive and living believers will be transfigured (1 Thess. 4:10, Philippians 3:26; 1 Cor. 15:51,52). The raised dead and the living believers will be raptured into heaven, so that they may escape the imminent tribulation (Luke 21:36). The raptured believers will be presented to Christ as the pure bride after the long betrothal period (1 Cor. 11:2; John 5:25-35) and will be married to the Lamb (Rev. 19:7).

2. The great tribulation, a period of seven years (Dan. 9:26,27) will afflict the Jewish nation (Dan. 12; Luke 1:25-26, Acts 15:13-17). In the midst of the week (in the midst of the week of Dan. 9:27) Antichrist will be revealed (2 Thess. 2:3; Rev. 11:3-7) and as a result of God's pouring out His wrath abundantly on Israel (Psalm 2:1-3) Israel accepts Christ (Zech. 12:10-16; 13:6-9).

3. After Israel has accepted Christ, the revelation of Christ takes place, and He establishes His millennial kingdom (2 Thess. 1,7-8; Zech. 2:10; 14:4; Matt. 24:29-30; 2 Thess. 1:7; especially Is. 59:20). Then Christ as an earthly king will cause all nations to come together to judge the nations because of their treatment of the Jews and the great nations will be destroyed, Matt. 25:31ff. Then according to some proponents of millennial views "the first judgment" occurs at the beginning of the millennium. The standard by which nations will be judged is their treatment of the Jews (Ezek. 38 and 39.)

4. After the first judgment the real millennium will begin. Both Jews and Christians will participate with Christ who will literally fulfill all Messianic prophecies that depict Christ as King. Satan will be unleashed toward the end of the millennium (Rev. 20:7-10), and will make an attack with the rebels against Christ, only to be utterly destroyed.

5. At the end of the millennium the second resurrection will occur (John 5:20; Dan. 12:2) culminating in the judgment at the great white throne (Rev. 20:11-15). Then hell and death will be destroyed (Rev. 20:14; 1 Cor. 15:26). The millennium will be terminated as God makes a new heaven and earth (Is. 66:25).

Evaluation of Millennialism's Eschatological Scheme

One gets the impression that this complicated chronology of eschatological events was a construction into which certain Bible passages were forces. Passages are placed next to each other which are not true parallels to each other and also that many verses are taken out of context and do not teach what they are alleged to set forth. Basic rules of hermeneutics are violated to produce a scheme of happenings which confuses the average student of the Bible.

Differences Between Premillennialism and Dispensationalism

Mayer contended that even though dispensationalism has many theological interpretations in eschatology with premillennialism, they do differ sharply on certain issues.[60] Premillennialism does not subscribe to the concept of seven major dispensations. Scofield borrowed either from Darby or Malachas Taylor, a Brethren disciple, the concept of seven dispensations and eight covenants.[61]

The "Dispensations" of Scofield and Dispensationalism

Scofield's whole system of theology is based upon the idea that the history of the world should be divided into seven time periods, beginning with the creation of the universe until the great white throne judgment, and all events are to be placed into seven dispensations. Scofield has defined a dispensation "as a time period during which man is tested in respect to obedience to some specific revelation of the will of God."[62]

Alleged Proof for the Idea of Seven Dispensations

Dispensationalists claim that there are a number of suggestions in the Old Testament for seven dispensations. Seven dispensations has its counterpart in seven creation days. Since each creation day of Genesis 1 had its specific creative happening, so each dispensation has something special which must characterize it. Furthermore, Israel's religious calendar is built up on the number seven, a week of seven days, a week of seven weeks between Passover to Pentecost, a week of seven months from Passover to the Day of the Atonement, another week of seven years ending with a sabbatical year, a "week" of seven years to the fiftieth year, the jubilee year. On the basis of these facts of Israel's religion, dispensationalists justify their seven-fold division into seven distinguishing time periods.[63] The dispensations are created out of data that have no relationship to the imaginary dispensations, which must be labelled as wishful speculation and forcing Biblical teachings into a theological straight jacket.

Some dispensationalists also claim on the basis of 2 Peter 3:8 that a prophetic day is a thousand years, and so 6,000 years of world history have already transpired leaving not too much time left in seventh prophetic day, which would mean that the parousia of Christ is not too far away. The observant reader of dispensationalist literature will discover that there is no unanimity as to what actually transpires during a dispensation.[64]

Misuse of the Word "Dispensation"

The word in the Greek New Testament **oikonomia** translated "dispensation," which means "stewardship," "administration," "arrangement." "The office of a steward" are words without temporal significance. John Wick Bowman claimed that Scofield's use of the word is not correct English. "For in our own tongue not to speak of Greek or Hebrew, the word never has any temporal connotation, as reference to any of the standard dictionaries will indicate."[65] The fact is, that the Bible has no such word which divides history into seven dispensations!

The Triadic Form of Each Dispensation

Each dispensation is characterized by a three-fold movement and assumes "(a) that God's primary relationship to man is that of Judge, (b) that each dispensation is conditioned by it own distinctive manner of testing which differs from that discovered in other dispensations and that (c) that God deals with man, accordingly in different periods and under different conditions of world history today."[66]

Reformed Theologians and Dispensations

There were a number of Reformed theologians who have written of two, three or four dispensations, as Berkhof, Hodge.[67] But they disagree with Scofield and Chafer, contending that there was but one plan of salvation during all dispensations that they distinguish.

Although some Reformed theologians have spoken of time dispensations, they have never accepted the seven dispensations of Scofield and Lewis Chafer. The following are the seven dispensations of dispensationalism:[68]

1. The dispensation or era of Innocence, which began with creation and ended with the fall of Adam and Eve.

2. The dispensation from the fall to Noah entering the ark. The responsibility was to do good, to use blood sacrifice but the world became extremely wicked and the failure resulted in judgment, a universal flood.

3. The Dispensation of Human government. The Noahic covenant, given after the flood, put man under a new test. He was to scatter and repopulate the earth, but he did not scatter and because of this failure the tongues were confused as judgment.

4. The dispensation of grace or promise, beginning with Abraham (Gen. 12:1-3 to Exodus 19). This dispensation was under the Abrahamic covenant and was exclusively Israelite. According to Leon Bates, the responsibility was to dwell in Canaan (Gen. 12:1-7), the failure was to dwell in the Land of Canaan and because of this failure they were placed in the Egyptian bondage.

5. The Mosaic dispensation, beginning with the giving of the law at Mount Sinai (Ex. 19) terminates with the sacrifice on Calvary. According to Bates the responsibility of the laws was not kept by the Jews, because they did not keep the whole law, they frequently apostatized and the judgment was the scattering of the Jews among the nations all over the world (Deut. 26:63-66; Luke 21:29-21).

6. The Church dispensation or dispensation of grace. This dispensation began with Pentecost and will end with the great tribulation, the judgment of the nations and the destruction of Antichrist. According to Scofield this is the time period during which people are saved by faith in Christ Jesus. When the Jews failed to comply with this responsibility by the rejection of Christ, according to Bates, the punishment was the great tribulation.

The Covenants of the Dispensational System and Theology

Intertwined with the seven dispensations of Scofield and Chafer, is a system of eight covenants.[69] These are the Covenant in Eden and corresponds to the dispensation of innocence:

1. The Covenant with Adam after the fall and pairs of with the dispensation of conscience;

2. The Covenant with Noah corresponding to the dispensation of Human Government;

3. The "Abrahamic Covenant," which was confirmed with Abraham at the time God was establishing the dispensation of promise, but not necessarily being coterminous with the dispensation which gave Palestine unconditionally to his descendants;

4. The "Mosaic Covenant," which corresponds to the dispensation of the Law, which was given to only Israelites and not to Christians. The Church is not under the covenant with Moses, a Law dispensation, but Christians are under grace;

5. The Covenant relating to Israel's entrance and securing the land of Canaan;

6. The Covenant with David—this covenant was made with David and later to Mary at the annunciation and is unchangeable;

7. The New Covenant, to which no conditions are applied which man is required to fulfill. As a result the New Covenant is everlasting.[70]

Here the reader will find the same situation that the convents of these covenants are determined by dispensationalism's preconceived eschatological conceptions and has resulted in the denial of Scriptural truth and misinterpretation of clearly revealed Biblical doctrines. It is questionable whether God made a covenant with Adam in Eden; the Noahic covenant was meant for mankind as a whole, promising the people after the flood that never would the world be destroyed by a flood. The Abrahamic, the Davidic and the New Covenants are all concerned with the plan of salvation, which was the same for Jews and Gentiles. They are all soteriological and in different ways set forth various truths about salvation, to be effected by Christ.

Evaluation of Millennialism in General

Although premillennialism and dispensationalism have many teachings in common, the premillennialists do not accept the dispensations or covenant theory of dispensationalism. On pages 131-133 there is a serious of criticisms about millennialism by the authors of *The Popular Symbolics*.

Engelder, Arndt, Graebner and Mayer make this judgment against Premillennialism: "Millennialism obtains much of its doctrine by literalizing the figurative language of Scripture." Isaiah 2:2-4; 11:6-9; Joel 2:21f., Micah 4:1-4 and similar passages foretell the spiritual peace of the Church of the New Testament and its wondrous growth, mediated by the Gospel, Is. 9:2-6; 11:9; Matt. 10:34; Luke 2:13f; John 14:27; Acts 2:16f., 15:13; Ephes. 6:15; Heb. 12:22. Millennialism appeals chiefly to Revelation 20. But in that chapter the second coming of Christ is not so much as mentioned as establishing the millennium. The reign of the saints there mentioned is not exercised on earth — but the souls lived and reigned with Christ. The number 'thousand years,' a symbolical number designates a long period and fixed period of time, began with the spread of the Gospel of Christ throughout the world.[71] The *Augsburg Confession*, Article XVII asserts: "They condemn also others, who are now spreading certain Jewish opinions, that before the resurrection of the dead the godly shall take possession of the kingdom of this world, the ungodly being everywhere suppressed."[72]

Evaluation of the Views of Dispensationalism

Engelder, Arndt, Graebner and Mayer list 21 objections against the eschatological views of dispensationalism.[73] The majority will be produced in what follows:

1. Dispensationalism follows a system of hermeneutics that overstresses the literal principle of interpretation to the detriment of the figurative in Daniel, Joel, Jeremiah, Isaiah, Zechariah, Ezekiel and Revelation.

2. Dispensationalism ignores the Biblical truth that in both Old and New Testament time, salvation was only by faith in Christ Jesus.

3. Dispensationalism denies that from the very beginning of His ministry, Christ established his kingdom of grace, spiritual in character, which also His disciples perpetuated (Matt 12:18; Luke 11:19; 1 Cor. 4:2). Christ in Matthew 28:18-20 instructed His disciples to preach repentance and remission of sins to the end of the age.

4. Dispensationalism falsely distinguished between the kingdom of Christ and kingdom of God, for they are terms employed interchangeably in the New Testament.

5. Dispensationalism materializes the true nature of Christ's kingdom and secularizes it.

6. Dispensationalism assigns the Jews a preeminence which the New Testament does not.

7. Dispensationalism fails to distinguish properly between the use of Law and Gospel, as is done in both the Old and New Testaments.

8. Dispensationalism teaches a general conversion of the Jewish people, effected not by repentance and faith.

9. Dispensationalism makes irresistible grace as the means for the conversion of the Jewish nation.

10. Dispensationalism ignores the truth that the last times will be filled with iniquity before the second coming of Christ and there will be no age of alleged peace for a thousand years.

11. Dispensationalism ignores the way the Bible uses the term "the latter days" as designating the Messianic period, the beginning of the Gospel age, which began with Christ's first coming and will terminate with His final second coming.

12. Dispensationalism teaches two different resurrections separated by a thousand years, despite the fact that the Bible teaches that the resurrection of the ungodly and godly will take place at the same time (Matt. 24:30-35 ; 25:31-46; 2 Thess. 1:7-10).

13. The revelation of Jesus Christ is not made known in Rev. 19, but in chapter 21, and takes place after the second coming and not before it.

14. The assumption that a millennial temple will be built in which sac-

1826

rifices are offered contradicts the Epistle to the Hebrew which teaches that by one sacrifice Jesus has sanctified has perfected all saved.

15. Dispensationalism contradicts the fact that now Christ is in the state of exaltation and it would be inconsistent for Christ to bring the glorified saints down from heaven to earth.

16. Since there will be no physical rule on earth by Christ, climaxed by a great physical battle against His enemies, all prophecies in the Old Testament which describe Christ's kingship have been fulfilled during the Apostolic period and during the Messianic age.

17. Dispensationalism disparages the Gospel and detracts from the true work of Christ.[74]

18. The rapture occurs at the final appearance of Christ, not before.

Theodore Engelder has subjected millennialism to a searching analysis in his three articles, entitled "Notes on Chiliasm": *Concordia Theological Monthly*, March, 1935, pp. 161-172; April, pp. 241-253; May, pp. 321-334; June, 401-412; July, 481-495. Add to these articles his article "Dispensationalism Disparaging the Gospel," *Concordia Theological Monthly*, VIII, pp. 649ff. The Commission on Theology and Church Relations of The Lutheran Church-Missouri Synod, September 1989 published its *The End Times, A Study on Eschatology and Millennialism,* 65 pages. A very useful and instructive study for members of the Lutheran Church-Missouri Synod and for those interested in knowing a traditional Lutheran stand on millennialism and dispensationalism.[75]

Footnotes

1. Michael Hirsley, "The end is near?" *Fort Wayne News Sentinel,* February 1, 1991, pp. 1a, 6A; John Elson, "Apocalypse Now" *Time,* February 11.
2. F. E. Mayer, *Religious Bodies of America* (St. Louis: Concordia Publishing House, 1956), p. 426.
3. Raymond F. Surburg, "The New Scofield Reference Bible," (*The Springfielder,* 31:4, Winter 1968), 6-24.
4. Elson, **op. cit.**, p. 33.
5. Charles H. Dyer, *The Rise of Babylon - Sign of the End Times* (Wheaton, III.: Tyndale House Publishers, 1990).
6. Cal Thomas, "Gulf War May Mean Armageddon is Near," *St. Louis Post-Dispatch,* February 11, 1991.
7. *Bibliotheca Sacra*, since its purchase from Xenia Theological Seminary has published hundreds of articles dealing with every possible phase of Scofieldian dispensationalism.
8. Charles Caldwell Ryrie, has written two helpful books for the understanding of premillennialism and dispensationalism, namely. *The Rise of the Premillennial Faith* (New York: Loizeaux Brothers, 1953) 160 pp. and Dispensationalism Today (Chicago: Moody Press, 1965), 221 pp.
9. J. Dwight Pentecost, *Things to Come, A Study in Biblical Eschatology* (Grand Rapids: Michigan: Dunham Publishers Company 1953), 633 pp.
10. Lewis Sperry Chafer, *Systematic Theology* (Dallas: Dallas Seminary Press, 1947-1943), 3 volumes.

11. Hal Lindsey, and C.C. Carlson, *The Late Great Planet Earth* (Grand Rapids: Zondervan Publishing House, 1970). Lindsey, *Satan is Well and Alive* and Hal Lindsey, *There's a New Earth Coming* (New York: Bantam Books, 1974.

12. Th. Engelder, W. Arndt, Th. Graebner and F.A. Mayer, *Popular Symbolics* (St. Louis; Concordia Publishing House, 1934), p. 367.

13. **Ibid.**

14. **Ibid.**

15. F. A. Mayer, *The Religious Bodies of America* (St. Louis: Concordia Publishing House, 1956), p. 422.

16. **Ibid.**

17. Floyd Hamilton, *The Basis of Millennial Faith* (Grand Rapids: Wm. B. Eerdmans Publishing Company, 1942), pp. 31-43. Cf. also D. H. Kromminga, *The Millennium in the Church* (Grand Rapids: Wm. B. Eerdmans Publishing House, 1945), pp. 242-253; 270-273.

18. John Walvoord, *The Millennial Kingdom* (Grand Rapids: Dunham Publishing Company, 1959), pp. 13-30. Millard J. Erickson, *Contemporary Options in Eschatology* (Grand Rapids: Baker Book House, 1977), pp. 55-72.

19. Erickson, **op. cit.**, pp. 73-90. Cf. William E. Cox, *Amillennialism Today* (Philadelphia: Presbyterian and Reformed Publishing Company, 1975), 140 pp.

20. John Wick Bowman, II. "Dispensationalism," Interpretation, 10:170, April, 1956.

21. *Popular Symbolics*, **op. cit.**, p. 363.

22. **Ibid.**, p. 363.

23. Bowman, **op. cit.**, p. 171.

24. Ludwigson, *A Survey of Bible Prophecy* (Grand Rapids: Zondervan Publishing House, 1973), p. 170.

25. Rollin Thomas Chafer, *The Science of Biblical Hermeneutics* (Dallas: Bibliotheca Sacra 1939, O, p. 90; Merrill C. Tenney, *Interpreting Revelation* (Grand Rapids: Wm. B. Eerdmans Publishing House), 1957, p. 89.

26. A. Berkeley, Mickelsen, *Interpreting the Bible* (Grand Rapids: Wm. B. Eerdmans Publishing House, 1963), p. 304.

27. Merrill C. Tenney, *The New Testament, Historical and Analytic* (Grand Rapids: Wm. B. Eerdmans Publishing House 1953), pp. 404-407.

28. D.A. Hayes, *John and His Writings* (New York: The Methodist Book Concern, 1917), p. 296.

29. For a Lutheran interpretation of Rev. 20, cf. C. H. Little, *Explanation of the Book of Revelation* (St. Louis: Concordia Publishing House, 1950) pp. 202-212; Siegbert W. Becker, *Revelation - The Distant Triumph Song* (Milwaukee: Northwestern Publishing House 1935), pp. 296-318. Luther Poellot, *Revelation - The Last Book in the Bible* (Milwaukee: Northwestern Publishing House, 1976), pp. 255-271. F. C. G. Schumm, *Does Revelation 20 Teach A Millennium?* (St. Louis: Concordia Publishing House, 1962 (Sixth Printing), 33 pp.

30. John Theodore Mueller, *Christian Dogmatics* (St. Louis Concordia Publishing House, 1955), p. 624.

31. Mayer, **op. cit.**, p. 423.

32. Lewis Sperry Chafer, *Systematic Theology*, **op. cit.** VII, p. 224.

33. *Unger's Bible Dictionary*, cf. Covenants, p. 269.

34. Mayer, **op. cit.**, p. 423.

32. Lewis Sperry Chafer, *Systematic Theology*, **op. cit.**, VII, p. 224

33. *Unger's Bible Dictionary*, cf. Covenants, p. 269.

34. Mayer, **op. cit.**, p. 423.

35. For a discussion of Romans 11:26, cf. Victor Bartling, "All Israel Shall Be Saved," *Concordia Theological Monthly*, 12:641-52, Sept., 1941. cf. also William Hendricksen, "And So All Israel Will Be Saved" (Grand Rapids: Baker Book House, 1945), 36 pp.

36. C.M. Zorn, Der Brief an die Roemer Zwickau, Germany (Verlag Druck Johannes Herman, no date), pp. 151-153.

37. Francis Pieper, *Christian Dogmatics* (St. Louis Concordia Publishing House, 1953), III, p. 528.

38. John Theodore Mueller, *Christian Dogmatics* (St. Louis; Concordia Publishing House, 1955), p. 624.

39. **Ibid.**, p. 625.

40. **Ibid.**, p. 625.

41. Mayer, **op. cit.**, p. 425.

42. C. I. Scofield, *Rightly Dividing the Word of Truth*, 2 Timothy 2:15. (Westwood, N.J.: Fleming H. Reveall based on 1896 edition, pp. 28-33.

43. Ludwigson, **op. cit.**, p. 65.

44. Joseph Stump, *The Christian Faith* (New York: The Macmillan Company, 1932), pp. 405-412.

45. Ludwigson, **op. cit.**, p. 167. Scofield, **op. cit.**, pp 26-27.

46. Translation of Helen Barrett Montgomery, *The New Testament in Modern English. The Centenary Translation* (Philadelphia: The Judson Press, 1924), p. 255.

47. Cf. the listing in Ludwigson, **op. cit.**, pp. 25-26.

48. **Ibid.**

49. Theodore H. Tappert, *The Lutheran Confessions* (Philadelphia: The Fortress Press, 1959), pp. 217, 259, 263, 314, 297, 263.

50. Theodore Hoyer, "The Papacy," in Theodore Laetsch, *The Abiding Word* (St. Louis: Concordia Publishing House, 1947), pp. 709-766.

51. Ludwigson, **op. cit.**, p. 27.

52. Cf. *Unger's Bible Dictionary* (Chicago: Moody Press, 1957), p. 39a.

53. Cf. Daniel C. Moeller, *The Evaluation of the Divergent Interpretations of Ezekiel 38 and 39* (Fort Wayne: Concordia Seminary, M. Div. dissertation, 75 pp.

54. Chafer, *Systematic Theology*, **op. cit.**, VII, p. 307.

55. Ludwigson, **op. cit.**, p. 136.

56. Mayer, **op. cit.**, p. 425.

57. **Ibid.**, p. 425.

58. Bowman, **op. cit.**, p. 174.

59. Mayer, **op. cit.**, pp. 424-425.

60. Mayer, **op. cit.**, p. 426.

61. Bowman, **op. cit.**, pp. 171, 173.

62. Scofield, **op. cit.**, pp. 12-15; Chafer, *Systematic Theology*, VII, pp. 121-123.

63. Meyer, **op. cit.**, p. 426.

64. **Ibid.**, p. 427.

65. Bowman, **op. cit.**, p. 175.

66. **Ibid.**, p. 176.

67. Allen Killen, "Dispensation," *Wycliffe Bible Encyclopedia* (Chicago: Moody Press, 1975), I, p. 465.

63. Leon Bates, *Colored Chart of the Seven Dispensations*, called "God's Plan for the Ages, Texas, 1969; Theodore H. Epp, *Rightly Dividing The Word, A Study of Dispensations* (Lincoln, Nebraska: Back to the Bible Publishers, 1954; Bowman, **op.**

cit., pp. 173-174; 1. Edwin Hartill, *Biblical Hermeneutics* (Grand Rapids; Zondervan Publishing House, 1947), pp. 13-15 lists eight dispensations instead of seven.

69. Bowman, **op. cit.**, p. 178.
70. Lewis Sperry Chafer, *Dispensationalism*, Reprinted from the Bibliotheca Sacra, Number 372, volume 93, Oct.-Dec., pp. 429-243, Pentecost, **op. cit.**, pp. 65-128.
71. *Popular Symbolics*, op, cit., p. 131.
72. F. Bente, *Concordia Triglotta* (St. Louis: Concordia Publishing House, 1922), p. 51.
73. *Popular Symbolics*, **op. cit.**, pp. 373-375.
74. Theodore Engelder. "Dispensationalism Disparaging the Gospel," *Concordia Theological Monthly*, 3:649-666, September, 1937.
75. The "End Times" *A Study on Eschatology and Millennialism - A Report of the Commission on Theology and Church Relations of The Lutheran Church-Missouri Synod*, September, 1939, 56 pages.

Questions

1. The Scofield Reference Bible originally published in ____ has been a purveyor of ____.
2. Cal Thomas predicted that ____.
3. Dallas Theological Seminary is a vigorous proponent of ____.
4. Hal Lindsey is the author of ____.
5. Millennialism goes back to ____.
6. Christian writers like Irenaeus, Tertullian, Methodius were ____.
7. The Adventist movement has always been ____.
8. What did "Pastor" Russell do? ____
9. Who became ardent devotees of millennialism? ____
10. Postmillennialism ignores the fact that ____.
11. The establishment of the State of Israel in 1948 led to ____.
12. A millennialists rejects ____.
13. John Nelson Darby was credited with ____.
14. In Revelation there is a ____ use of numbers.
15. The vision in Revelation does not refer to an ___ rule by a ____ rule.
16. The "all Israel" of Romans 11;26 refers to ____.
17. Will all Jews be saved? ____
18. Scripture teaches only ____ judgment.
19. Each person's destiny is determined at ____.
20. The ___ has been the great opponent of Christ because of its denials of ____.
21. The future struggle of Armageddon has been called ____.
22. Premillennialism depicts Satan as the enemy of ___ rather than the adversary of ____.
23. Millennialism is guilty of ____.
24. Millennialism claims that Christ will come to Jerusalem to ____.
25. What does Article XVII of *The Augsburg Confession* say about millennialism? ____
26. Hebrews teaches that by one sacrifice Jesus ____.
27. Dispensationalism disparages the ____.

The Teachings About The Holy Spirit in The Book of Acts

Christian News, May 8, 1989

Pentecost, May 14

In the liturgical churches of Christendom its members are mentally, emotionally and spiritually prepared for the celebration of Christmas and Easter. During the Advent season there are in some churches Advent services designed to prepare for the birth of Christ. Although, as a result of the commercial celebration of Christmas beginning with Thanksgiving, the Christmas festival is remembered in churches during the Advent season, as is evidenced by candlelight Christmas carol services a few weeks prior to the official liturgical beginning of the festival of the Incarnation on December 24, at 6 p.m. In the church in which the writer worships there are Christmas trees, fully decorated, standing on the first Sunday in Advent. There is no doubt about it, church worshippers are prepared for the celebration of the birth of Christ, born of the Virgin Mary.

For the celebration of Christ's resurrection likewise the followers of Christ in liturgically-oriented churches are prepared by Lenten service and by the services of Holy Week, with its sacred Maundy Thursday and Good Friday. Both at Christmas and Easter church choirs have put in hours of preparation for the singing of joyous anthems commemorating the birth and resurrection of Christ. Thus the first two persons of the Trinity are accorded considerable attention; the Father in sending His Son into the world and also in raising Him from the dead.

On the fortieth day after Easter Christ ascended into heaven, a truth which has been questioned by even Lutheran liberal scholars. The Ascension of Christ was the climactic event of His earthly life. However, this important historical event docs not receive much attention in Christendom. In Lutheran churches there may be special Ascension services, but if they are held they are sparsely attended. Since this festival always falls on a Thursday, it is practically ignored. The Sunday after the Ascension is not called the Sunday after the Ascension, as it should be, but the seventh Sunday in Easter.[1] No anthems of jubilations are rendered by church choirs in commemoration of this great event in Christ's life. The event which constituted a climax in Christ's life thus actually becomes anticlimactic!

One of the blessings Christ promised as a result of His physical ascent into heaven was the sending of the Holy Spirit.

Like Ascension the Festival of the Holy Spirit does not receive the attention given to Christmas and Easter. People do not look forward with anticipation, as they do for Christmas and Easter, for the coming of Holy Spirit, the Paraclete. This year Pentecost falls on Mother's Day, May 14th. It does not take too much imagination to realize what will happen to the celebration of the Holy Spirit when churches, to please mothers, will put mother on a par with the Holy Spirit. When Pentecost comes late as it does in some years around the middle of June, the summer home occupants will have left for their summer cottages and Pentecost will not have the large attendance normally the case at Christmas and Easter services. Thus there has developed a neglect of emphasizing the person and work of the Holy Spirit, although Pentecost is the Sunday after the last Sunday in Easter and so in a way is observed, but not in a manner it should be.

Twenty-five years ago Professor Lorenz Wunderlich wrote a book, entitled *The Half-Known God - The Person and Work of the Holy Spirit*.[2] At the time this book appeared there emerged a movement in the mainline churches of Christendom which adopted the teachings of Pentecostalism relative to the Holy Spirit. The charismatic movement began go emerge with its overemphasis on the work of the Holy Spirit and its depreciating the Biblical doctrine of the Means of Grace.[3] The gifts of the Spirit, such as speaking with tongues, divine healings,[4] emphasis on "baptism with the Holy Spirit," new revelations and prophecy became the center of the theology and practice of various groups of Protestants, including Lutherans. The Roman Catholic Church was also greatly influenced by this unhealthy spiritual movement. The result has been that from an underemphasis on the person and work of Holy Spirit there had now developed an overemphasis, and a slighting of the person and work of God the Father and of God the Son. What the Christian Church needs is a correct Scriptural balance relative to the Person and Work of the Holy Spirit as given in the Scriptures of the Old and New Testaments.

Both testaments contains teachings about the Spirit of God. Only those who believe in the Holy Trinity are in a position to appreciate the teachings of God's Word given before and as well after Christ's coming. The Old Testament teaches that there was a Holy Spirit, separate from the Father and the Son. The Holy Spirit was active in Israel in Old Testament times.[5] The New Testament has references in the Gospels, in Acts, the Pauline and Central Epistles.[6]

With the great outpouring of the Holy Spirit in Jerusalem in the year 30, a new era in world history began, because now the Spirit was even more in evidence than before.[7] Various New Testament writings have teachings about the person and work of the Third Person of the Trinity. A book of Scripture which is especially instructive relative to the Holy Spirit is the Book of Acts, which has been chosen in this essay for a brief analysis and description of its pregnant teaching on the Holy Spirit. Many years ago (1918) Professor Hayes wrote: "No writer in the New Testament emphasizes the personality of the Holy Spirit as Luke does."[8] Matthew says: "If ye then being evil, know how to give good gifts to your children, how much more shall your heavenly father give good gifts to them that ask him (Matthew 7:11)." Luke prefers to summarize all other good gifts in the greatest, namely, the Holy Spirit. Luke's second volume is a prolongation and justification of this standpoint. It is to Luke that we owe the baptism with the Spirit as marking the beginning of the dispensation that was inaugurated with Pentecost and has not yet ended.[9]

Any number of scholars have noted the importance of the Holy Spirit as reflected in the twenty-eight chapters of the Book of Acts. Thus Ross wrote: "According to some, the book might be more correctly called 'The Acts of the Holy Spirit.'"[10] Again the same writer remarked: "The Ministry of the Spirit is the theme of the book and in keeping with the theme the book divided itself into two unequal parts: I. The Ministry of the Spirit to the Jews, and II. The Ministry of the Spirit to the Gentiles."[10a] Another writer Scroggie averred: "The ACTS is essentially a record of the activities of the Holy Spirit, and here He is seen related to every aspect of the believer's life and the Church's life and work." It is as Scroggie has said: "The ACTS is the record of a Spirit-begotten, Spirit-filled, and Spirit-guided Church."[11]

The Purpose of the Book of Acts:

According to Ross the purpose of Acts is the following:

"The purpose of the book is apparent throughout, to set forth clearly the account of the fulfillment of the Promise of the Father to Christ, and through Christ to the Church, by the descent of the Holy Spirit. There are no less than fifty-seven passages in the book which directly refer to the Holy Spirit. It is the special book of Scripture that is devoted to this theme, and we are therefore not surprised to find that the verses in which the Holy Spirit is mentioned by name are nearly as many as in all the four gospels. We are told more about the Holy Spirit in this book than anywhere else in the whole Bible."[12]

The Importance of Acts for the Doctrine of the Holy Spirit

The Book of Acts has many values. It is the only divine inspired book that deals with church history. Luke's reliability as an historian has been established by a number of scholars. Those interested in biography will find many important and unimportant individuals discussed in its twenty eight chapters.

Jews and Gentiles, Christians and Pagans, rulers and subjects, philosophers and artisans are here. At least 75 different people are discussed and alluded to. Further, Acts is the authorized missionary manual of the church. What an inspiration Paul's journeys and other activities by Peter and John have motivated many through the Christian centuries to go on missionary journeys to every continent of the world and to many islands in the great seas and oceans of the world. Acts also has dispensational value, not in the sense of what is commonly known as Scofeldian dispensationalism, but in the sense that the Old Dispensation which terminated with the death of Christ, when the veil in the temple was rent, indicating that a new dispensation had broken upon the world. Acts shows us how the great changeover was made from Judaism to Christianity. Even the apostles had to learn the important truth that God is not a respecter of persons, but that in all nations, whoever fears God and accepts His Son as Savior, Redeemer and Lord can be saved. The Person intertwining all these values is the Holy Spirit. Correctly Scroggie has asserted: "The ACTS is essentially a record of the activities of the Holy

Spirit, and here is seen related to every aspect of the believer's life and work."[13]

The activities of the Holy Spirit have been summarized by Scroggie as follows:

"He is the Spirit of Power (chapter 2), of Healing (chapter 3), of Boldness (chapter 4), of Judgment (chapter 5), of Administration (chapter 6), of Steadfastness (chapter 7), of Evangelism (chapter 8), of Comfort (chapter 9), of Guidance (chapter 10), of Prophecy (chapter 11), of Deliverance (chapter 12), of Missions (chapter 13), of Protection (chapter 14) of Councils (chapter 15), of Restraint and Constraint (chapter 16), of Opportunity (chapter 17), of Revelation (chapter 18), of Purpose (chapter 19), indeed the Spirit dominates the whole story."[14]

The Pre-Pentecost Prediction of the Holy Spirit's Coming

Luke began his second treatise to Theophilus in this manner: "In my first book, Theophilus I wrote to you about everything that Jesus did and taught till the day He was taken up to heaven after giving orders by the Holy Spirit to the apostles He had chosen." (1:1).[15] On the Mount of Olives, ten days before His ascension, Jesus said to His disciples: "John baptized with water, but in a few days you will be baptized with the Holy Spirit." In the first of speeches or addresses by Peter, the apostle declared to the assembled 120 in the Temple: "Brothers, long ago the Holy Spirit spoke through David about Judas, who led the men that arrested Jesus. And what he wrote came true."[16] Here Peter taught that the Holy Spirit was active in Old Testament times and that he spoke through the lips of David. This is in agreement what Peter later in the sixties wrote to the congregations of Asia Minor: "Holy men of God speaks they were moved (carried along as a ship by its sails, which the winds propels) by the Holy Spirit." (2 Peter 1:21)

On the day of the Ascension Jesus also promised the disciples the Holy Spirit who would give them power and the ability to proclaim the Good News to both Jews and Gentiles.

The Unique Outpouring of the Holy Spirit in the Year A.D. 30

In chapter 2 of Acts the promise Christ gave the disciples on the Mount of Olives was kept. Thus the reader has a clear case of prophecy and fulfillment. The day of Pentecost in A.D. 30 or 33 (as some hold) witnessed a phenomenon never again happened in world history. This is the way Gerstner described what is recorded in verses 1-13 of Acts 2:

A rushing wind was heard, tongues descended, and one rested on each of them and all began to speak. On the day of Pentecost, people from the entire Dispersion scattered all around the Mediterranean area were present. To these different language-speaking groups the Christians began to speak. In one group, standing near Thomas perhaps, several different native dialects were spoken, none of which Thomas knew. But as he spoke some of the people realized that he was speaking in their language even though he had never learned it.

Those who knew Thomas were amazed to hear him speaking in their own language; others in the group might have thought he was speaking some kind of gibberish. Meanwhile, Philip was speaking in another area, and the same thing was happening. Some understood him speaking in their own language; others thought he was mad or drunk (2:4-13).[17]

In this chapter of Acts we have an illustration of the hermeneutical principle: "Scripture interprets Scripture," for Peter stated to his Jerusalem audience that the remarkable events that were transpiring before their eyes were a fulfillment of the prophecy of Joel. The Holy Spirit informs every New Testament reader that when Joel uttered the words found in the Hebrew Bible in chapter 3:1-4 (In the English Bible, 2:28-32) that Joel, whether he knew it or not, was predicting the great outpouring of the Spirit that occurred on Pentecost of the year 30 or 33 B.C. and that this was the inauguration of a new dispensation. P. E. Kretzmann wrote as follows concerning chapter 2:12-17 of Acts:

God Himself promised through the prophet that in the latter days of the world He would pour out His spirit upon all flesh, that as a result of this miracle both the sons and daughters of the people would prophecy, would be able to unfold the future, that young men would receive revelations in dreams. And still more was included in this miraculous occurrence. And even bonded servants, the slaves, both male and female, would receive the same gift of the Holy Spirit, so that they too, would be enabled to prophesy. Persons of all nationalities and of every station and rank in life world thus become partakers of the Spirit and His wonderful gifts. And this phenomenon would not be confined to a single occasion, but would continue until the day when God would show and give signs of His majesty on the earth beneath, blood and fire and smoke and vapor. The sun would be changed entirely, losing his brightness and turning into darkness and the moon likewise would be changed into a bloody mass. Bloodshed and devastation of war would precede the last great day of the Lord, whose purpose will be clearly visible as it dawns over the demoralized world. Cp. I Thess. 5,2; I Cor. 1,8; II Corr. 1,14; 2 Thess. 2,8.16).[18]

In Acts 2 Peter showed clearly the relationship of the Old Testament Messianic prophecies to Christ. Any person denying predictive Messianic prophecies is forced to do violence to Peter's Pentecost sermon, where the apostle stated unequivocally that the death and resurrection of Christ as promised Messiah was foretold in psalm passages.

Peter concluded his Pentecost sermon with the following appeal: "Repent and be baptized, every one of you, in the name of Jesus Christ so that your sins will be forgiven, and you will be given the Holy Spirit. What is promised belongs to you, to your children, and to all who are far away, all whom the Lord our God will call (2:38-39)."[19]

Absence of the Mention of the Holy Spirit in Chapter 3

While the Holy Spirit is not specifically mentioned by name in Chapter 3 the Biblical student will see in both chapters 3 and 4 of Acts the power of the Holy Spirit at work, enabling Peter and John to proclaim fearlessly a message they knew the leaders of the Jews rejected and whose proclamation would get them arrested and punished. Here the promise of Christ given the disciples, on the day of Pentecost, namely; "But when the Holy Spirit comes on you. . . you will receive power and will testify of me in Jerusalem, in all Judea, and Samaria, and to the uttermost parts of the world." (1:8), was fulfilled.

Holy Spirit in Acts 4

Chapter 4 comes from the Jerusalem period of the history of the apostolic Church, established with a membership of 3,000 on Pentecost. In it Peter and John are portrayed as proclaiming before the Sadducees the truth that the dead rise, arguing for this obviously on the basis of Christ's resurrection from the dead. The Sadducees denied the doctrine of man's resurrection. Both apostles were cast into prison, however the next day they were brought before Annas the high priest, Caiaphas, John, Alexander and asked by what power they had healed the cripple in Chapter 3. Luke reported in his fourth chapter of his second treatise to Theophilus: "And Peter was filled with the Holy Spirit," and then proceeded to preach Christ and Him crucified and also accused the Jewish leaders with killing Christ, the promised Messiah of the Old Testament Scriptures. The outcome of the trial before the Jewish ecclesiastical leadership was that Peter and John were told to cease preaching their message about Christ's death and resurrection. Chapter 4 ends with a quotation from Psalm 2, a Messianic Psalm. After Peter and John related what had happened, the multitude that receive them, so Luke states, raised their voices together and said: "You said by the Holy Spirit through our ancestor David; 'Why do the nations rage, And the people imagine a vain thing, The kings of the earth stand ready. And their rulers get together. Against the Lord and His Anointed."[20] Herod and Pontius Pilate were the two great enemies of whom Psalm 2 predicted as opposing Christ, God's only begotten Son.

Chapter 4 concludes with this statement about the Holy Spirit: "When they had prayed, the place where they were meeting was shaken, and they are all filled with the Holy Spirit and boldly spoke God's Word."[21]

The Holy Spirit in Chapter 5

Chapter 5 brings the interesting experiment in connection with a free-willing form of holding their property and goods in common.[22] This was an expression of faith and of Christian love. Ananias and Sapphira also voluntarily decided to participate in this experiment. They sold their property but decided to keep part back but tell Peter that they were giving it all. This was deception and lying so when they presented their gift, Peter said to Annanias. "Ananias, why did Satan fill your heart so that you should lie to the Holy Spirit and keep back some of the money you got for the lands. While you had the land, wasn't it your own? And after it was sold, couldn't you have done as you pleased with the money? How could you think of doing such a thing? You didn't lie to men, but to God"

(vv. 3-5).[23]

Unfortunately, Sapphira continued to lie and her fate for lying to the Holy Spirit, was that she dropped dead. The Holy Spirit was directly involved in the building and growth of the first Christian congregation, which grew to 5,000 members. Further, Luke reported in Acts 5, that the apostles performed many miracles. For this activity the apostles were seized and put in public prison by the Sadducees, who denied the doctrine of the resurrection, held by the Pharisees, but proclamation or Christ's resurrection was doubly offensive to them. However, the angel from the Lord freed the apostles so that the next day Peter and John were found preaching the doctrine they had been forbidden to proclaim. When summoned by the leaders of the Jews, they willingly appeared before them. When the apostles were told that they had been forbidden to proclaim that the Jewish leaders had killed Jesus and filled all Jerusalem with the message of Christ Crucified and Risen, the apostles responded: "We must obey God rather than men. You hanged Jesus on a cross and murdered him. But the God of our fathers raised Him and took Him up to His right side as Leader and Savior in order to have the people of Israel repent and forgive their sins. We are witnesses of these things — we and the Holy Spirit, who God has given those who obey Him."[24]

The Holy Spirit in Chapter 5 is clearly defined as God and that it was necessary to believe in the fact of Christ's death and resurrection

The Holy Spirit in Chapters 6 and 7

In chapter 6 Luke, physician and historian, has given an account of how the early apostolic church was given appointment of church officers, who were to supervise the distribution of alms. The stipulation for selection for this office, as specified by the apostles, was that the seven men were to be men of good report, full of the Spirit and of wisdom. This suggestion of the apostles met with favor and they selected seven men, one of whom was Stephen, a man full of the Holy Spirit. (6:6) Because of his being filled with the Holy Spirit, he performed miracles among the people, and also proclaimed with great power the Good News. He engaged Jews who had rejected Christ in dialogue and the latter were angered and claimed that Stephen, a deacon, had blasphemed God and thus was worthy of death. Being brought before the Sanhedrin, Stephen's enemies made false charges against him. He was accused of having blasphemed the Temple and Law. Chapter 7 gives the reader an account of what might be termed Stephen's *Apologia Vita Sua*. In this defense Stephen showed how all Old Testament history has pointed to Christ by means of specific prophecies and how the Hebrew people had killed their own promised Messiah. Stephen charged: "O stiff-necked men, uncircumcised in heart and ears you are continually at strife with the Holy Spirit (7:51)" As they seized him to drag him out and stone him, Stephen was "full of the Holy Spirit and looking up to heaven saw the glory of God, and Jesus standing at God's right hand" (7:55).[25]

From Stephen's Defense for His Life we infer that the Holy Spirit was active in the Old Testament, just as He was during the ministry of Jesus and now after Pentecost, the contemporaries of Stephen in Jerusalem were opposing the Holy Spirit.

The Holy Spirit Active in Samaria in Chapter 8

As a result of the persecution that broke out in Judea, believers were scattered abroad and Philip, one of the seven deacons, preached in Samaria.

Many believed among the Samaritans, including Simon Magus (8:13). When the Jerusalem apostles heard of this remarkable happening, they sent Peter and John to sit with the new converts, who after they arrived, so Luke informs his readers, "prayed for them that they might receive the Holy Spirit," (8:16) for he had not as yet fallen on any of them. Then the apostles laid their hands upon them, and they received the Holy Spirit (8:17).

The latter portion of chapter 8 records how Philip met the Ethiopian eunuch, who had come from Queen Candace in Africa.[26] It was the Holy Spirit who told Philip the evangelist to meet the eunuch. "Go and join the chariot" was the Spirit's command. After Philip showed the African how Chapter 53 spoke specifically of Christ and of nobody else, the high official of Queen Candace was baptized and the chapter concluded with this interesting information: "Then the Spirit of the Lord caught Philip away, and the eunuch did not see him again" (8:38).

The Holy Spirit in St. Paul (Chapter 9 of Acts)

Chapter 9 of Acts records one of the greatest historical events of human history, the conversion of Paul of Tarsus, bitter opponent and hater of Jesus of Nazareth on the Damasus road. Jesus intervened and changed the whole course of Paul's life, after the miracle of the Damascus road Paul became the most ardent devotee of Jesus Christ and suffered the loss of all things, yes, even life itself.[27] Ananias, sent by the Lord, to go to Paul who had been led to Damascus by his associates, said to the apostle of the Gentiles: "Saul Brother, The Lord — even Jesus who appeared to you on a journey — has sent me, that you might recover your sight and be filled with the Holy Ghost."[28]

Paul was filled with the Holy Spirit and it was under His inspiration that Paul penned at least thirteen epistles, some even hold that Paul may have written Hebrews. In his letters Paul has considerable to say about the work of the Holy Spirit in the lives of Christians.[29]

The Holy Spirit and the Romans (Chapter 10 of Acts)

Chapter 10 is a key chapter in the book of Acts, as was chapter 8.[30] It took some time before the early Christian Church learned the important lesson that the old Judaism was a matter of past history, that now membership in the true and spiritual Israel was there for all "who called upon the name of the Lord" and accepted Christ as Redeemer and were justified by faith in the shed blood of Christ. Peter, a Jew, brings the Gospel to a people considered unclean by Old Testament standards. Peter was prepared for this revolutionary experience by a unique happening in the city of Joppa along the Mediterranean coast. On the rooftop of the house of Simon the tanner Peter saw a sheet coming down from heaven, on which were different unclean animals, prohibited for eating according to the ceremonial law. A voice from heaven said to the apostle: "Kill and eat!" Three times this command came. Peter shrank back in horror. The sheet with all manner of unclean quadrupeds was removed. He was told by the heavenly voice: "What God has cleansed, you must not regard unclean." As he thought about this unusual experience, a delegation appeared from Cornelius of Caesarea asking Peter to come. The Spirit of God told Peter to accompany the men and do what Cornelius was asking him to do.

In the home the Roman centurion Peter preached his Gentile Pentecost sermon and described among other things how the Gospel of peace characterized the earthly ministry of Jesus and how Jesus of Nazareth was anointed by the Holy Spirit and with power (10:38).[31] As the Roman audience was listening to Peter's message, the Holy Spirit was poured out upon them of the Jewish people, who had accompanied Peter to Caesarea, Luke records, that they "were astonished that on the Gentiles also the gift was poured out. For they heard them speaking in other languages and extolling the majesty of God."[32] The result was that Peter asked: "Can anyone forbid the use of water for the baptism of these people-men men who had received the Holy Spirit just as we did (10:49)?"[33]

Later at the Jerusalem council, held probably in A.D. 48[34] Peter addressed the assembly and related his experience at Caesarea, stating that God had chosen him to bring the Gospel to non-Jews, so that they might believe. "And God, who knows our hearts, showed them He approved by giving them the Holy Spirit as He gave Him to us. And by cleansing their hearts by faith He has declared we are not different from them" (15:8-9).[34a]

The Holy Spirit in Chapter 11

When Peter returned from Caesarea to Jerusalem the party of the circumcision challenged Peter that he had consorted and eaten with non-Jews. They rebuked Peter, but the latter defended himself by relating his experience on the house of Simon the tanner and how God had told him not to consider people unclean whom God did not. Peter said that what he did was done under the Holy Spirit's guidance. "The Spirit told me to go with them and not to treat them as different people.

These six fellow disciples went with me and we came into the man's house." (11:12)[35] In verse 15 Peter told his accusers: "No sooner had I begun to speak then the Holy Spirit fell upon them, just as he fell on us at the first. Then I remembered the Lord's words, how he said: 'John will baptize you with water, but you shall be baptized in the Holy Spirit. If God gave them the same gift as He gave us when we believed in the Lord Jesus Christ, why who am I to be able to thwart God?'"[36]

Holy Spirit in Antioch (Acts 11)

As a result of the persecution that broke out after Stephen's death, Christians spread throughout Palestine. Men came from Cyrene and Cyprus and preached the Good News among the heathen of Antioch. "The Lord's hand was with them, and a large number believed and turned to the Lord" (11:21)[37] When the Jerusalem Church heard about these conversions in Antioch, they sent Barnabas to Antioch to investigate the matter. Barnabas was thrilled by what he found in Antioch and encouraged the new converts in their faith. Luke described Barnabas as "a good man, full of the Holy Spirit and faith" (11:24).

Chapter 11 concludes with the coming of the prophet Agabus to Antioch, who by the Spirit predicted that there would be a big famine all over the world, of which Luke said that it occurred during the reign of Claudius.

The Holy Spirit and Paul's First Missionary Journey (Acts 13)

The Holy Spirit is not mentioned in chapter 12 of Acts. Luke tells his readers that there were a number of prophets living in Antioch, who were also teachers of the church, namely, Barnabas, Symeon, called Black, Lucius from Cyrene, and Manaen. While the Christians prayed the Holy Spirit said; "Set Barnabas and Paul apart for Me to the work I called them for (13:2)."

So Barnabas and Paul set out for the island of Cyprus. At Paphos they met up with a Jewish magician and false prophet, Bar Jesus by name. When the Proconsul Sergius sent for the two Antiochene missionaries to hear the word of God, Elymas, the sorcerer, tried to prevent the Proconsul from accepting the Christian faith. Then Saul, later called Paul, was filled with the Holy Spirit and fixed his eyes on Elymas, called him a son of perdition, a son of the devil and a foe of all that was right. The Lord's hand is upon you and you will be blind for a season and unable to see the day light."[38] Instantly Elymas was afflicted with blindness and the result was that Sergius Paulus believed. From Cyprus Barnabas, Mark and Saul proceeded to Asia Minor.

At Antioch in Pisidia Paul preached in the synagogue to the Jews showing them from various Scriptures in the Old Testament that in Christ the Messianic prophecies were fulfilled.[39] The next Sabbath the whole city came together to hear the word of the Lord (13:24). This caused the Jews great anger, when they saw the crowd and they opposed Paul and abused him. The response of Barnabas and Paul was that "we were bound to proclaim the word of God first to you. But since you spurn it and judge yourselves unworthy of eternal life — well, we turn to the Gentiles."[40] Again they cited Isaiah 49:6 to the effect that God gave Jesus as a light to the Gentiles (13:47). The Jews then stirred up persecution against Paul and Barnabbas and drove them out of the district. The apostles shook the dust of their feet as a protest against them and came to Iconium, and as far as the disciples were concerned, Luke, a reliable historian, reported; "they were more and more filled with the Holy Spirit (13:52)."[41] The Holy Spirit was a mighty force in causing the Gospel to be proclaimed fearlessly and also with great success.

The Holy Spirit and the Apostolic Council (Acts 15)

In Acts 15 Luke has given New Testament readers a report on the first great church convention, a gathering of Christian people that discussed an issue vital to the nature of Christianity itself. The great issue debated at the convention, at which Peter, Paul and James spoke was this: was it necessary for Gentiles to become circumcised and observe the ceremonial laws of the Old Testament in addition to accepting Christ as their Savior and being justified by faith. The Judaizers claimed it was necessary, but Peter, Paul and James asserted that it was not. The Judaizers taught and contended for the position that circumcision and observance of the ceremonial law was a sine qua non for membership in the Israel of God. Peter related his experience in the house of Simon the tanner, and as a part of his argumentation against the Judaizing position declared." And God who knows all hearts, gave His testimony in their favor of bestowing the Holy Spirit on them just as He did on us (15:8) and He made no difference between us and them, in that He cleansed their heads by their faith (15:9)."[42]

The outcome of this important apostolic gathering was that the Gospel of God's free grace in Christ prevailed. It was decided to send a letter to the congregations, written by the apostles and elders and the whole church, in which it was asserted among other things: "For it seemed good to the Holy Spirit and to us to lay upon you no burden heavier than these necessary requirements. You must abstain from things sacrificed to idols, from flesh of strangled animals and from fornication. Keep yourselves clear of these things, and it will be well with you. Farewell (15:24)."

The Holy Spirit and Paul's
Second Missionary Journey (Acts 16)

On his second missionary journey Paul had a different missionary partner, namely, Silas or Silvanus.[43] Barnabas and Paul separated because of a difference of opinion about taking Mark along as helper, who had abruptly left them on their short first journey. Paul and his new associate began their journey by passing through Syria and Cilicia, strengthening the churches found on the first missionary journey. In Asia Minor, at Lystra they found a disciple named Timothy — the son of a Greek father and a Christian Jewish mother. After having Timothy circumcised, Paul took him along as a third member of the missionary party. These three men travelled from town to town, handing to the brethren the letter adopted at the apostolic council (16:4). As a result of this pastoral activity the church was strengthened and also grew numerically. Luke further reports in chapter 16: "Then Paul and his companion passed through Phyrgia and Galatia, having been forbidden by the Holy Spirit to proclaim the word of God in the province of Asia. When they reached the frontier of Mysia, they were about to enter Bithynia, but the Spirit of Jesus would not permit this."[44]

The Holy Spirit and the Disciples of John the Baptist
(Acts 19)

Paul spent a long time in Ephesus in the beginning of his third missionary journey.[45] When Paul first came to Ephesus he met disciples of John the Baptist, whom he said: "Did you receive the Holy Spirit when you believed?" They replied: "No we have not even heard whether there was a Holy Spirit (19:2-3)." Here Paul met people who had been baptized by John the baptizer. Paul's response to them was: "John baptized those who were sorry for their sins and told the people to believe in the One coming, that is, Jesus." When these disciples of John heard this, they were baptized into the name of the Lord Jesus. Luke further reports that Paul laid his hands on them and the Holy Spirit came upon them and they started to speak in other languages and to speak God's Word (5-6).

The Holy Spirit and the End of Paul's Third Journey

Next reference to the Holy Spirit is found in chapter 20, where Luke records that Paul was homeward bound, heading for Jerusalem. At Miletus Paul delivered a touching farewell address.[46] In the course of this pastoral address Paul declared: "And now you see that the Spirit compels me to go to Jerusalem. I didn't know what will happen to me there, except the Holy Spirit keeps warning me from town to town that chains and troubles are waiting for me. I don't count my life worth anything. I just want to finish running my race and doing the work the Lord Jesus entrusted to me, declaring the good news of God's love" (vv. 22-24).[47]

Paul also told the leaders of the churches from Ephesus: "Take care of yourselves and the whole flock in which the Holy Spirit has made you overseers to be shepherds of God's church that he bought with His own blood."[48]

On his way back to Jerusalem Paul came to Caesarea, where he stayed with Philip the Evangelist. While there, there came a prophet named Agabus, who took Paul's girdle and bound his own feet and arms with it, and said: "The Holy Spirit says 'This is how the Jews in Jerusalem will tie the man to whom this belt belongs to and hand him over to non-Jews'" (21:11).[49]

The Last Reference to the Holy Spirit in the Book of Acts

Although there are a total of 57 different references in Acts, only one reference to the Holy Spirit is found after chapter 21:11, and that is found in chapter 28, in connection with Paul's first Roman imprisonment. Paul met with a delegation of Jews from Rome and proclaimed to them that Christ was the promised Messiah on the basis of the Law and the Prophets and that he had come to establish the kingdom of God. Paul spoke with the Jewish contingent from morning to evening. Some people believed while some did not. As the Jews were leaving Paul added a statement: The Holy Spirit spoke the truth to your fathers through the prophet Isaiah and then cited the passage from Isaiah 6:9-10, which announced the hardening of hearts of the Jewish people, a passage also cited by Christ in the Gospels.

McDonald's Summarization of the Teachings on the Holy Spirit in Acts

H.D. McDonald in his Living Doctrines of the New Testament discussed the teachings on the Holy Spirit as a part of his presentation of the teachings of the Book of Acts. He treated the doctrine of the Holy

Spirit homiletically and then doctrinally.[50]

The former professor of the University of London listed no less than sixteen points about the Holy Spirit's activity as given in Acts.[51] The foundation of the Christian Church is intimately bound up with the outpouring of the Spirit. It was only after the outpouring of the Spirit that the Christian Church was founded and organized. 2. Service to the Church was dependent on the presence of the Holy Spirit. 3. The fellowship of the newly founded Church was dependent on the presence of the Spirit of God. 4. The Advance and progress of the Church was dependent on the Spirit. It was the Spirit who inspired Peter, John, Stephen, Philip and directed Paul. 5. The Sins of the Church are sins against the Holy Spirit. 6. The Spirit's Coming was the fulfillment of Christ's promise to send another Paraclete. 7. The Spirit's speaking occurred in the Old Testament, so the Early Church believed. The Spirit spoke through Jesus and He still speaks through the Word of God recorded in Acts. 8. The Holy Spirit separated Paul for the apostalate. 9. The Holy Spirit was the efficient cause for sending Barnabas and Saul on their first missionary journey. 10. The Holy Ghost vindicated the true cause of God by punishing Ananias and Sapphira for lying to Peter. 11. The Holy Spirit was also the Indicator in motivating to decisive action by showing dangers of a path (Acts 11:26;21:4) and the rightness of decision (Acts 15:28). 12. The Holy Spirit comforted the Church in that he caused its members to walk in the fear of the Lord and in comforting (Acts 9:31). 13. The Holy Spirit was the Empowerer throughout Acts is the assurance that power would come upon the apostles. 14. The Holy Spirit as Giver of Guidance as may be seen from 11:12, where Peter was told by the Spirit to go to Caesarea. 15. The Holy Spirit as Witnesser, The Holy Spirit, stated Peter, was given to those who obey God. The Holy Spirit is found among men as a witness to the realities of the Gospel (cf. Acts 16:1-2). 16. The Holy Ghost as Filler. The Spirit of God filled men and women with power, abundance and adequacy. It was because of this activity that the Christian Church was able to carry out the Great commission of Christ, to bring the Gospel to Jerusalem, Judea, Samaria, Antioch, Asia Minor, Greece, Italy and even Spain.

Doctrinal Teachings According to McDonald

1. The Personality of the Holy Spirit is clearly taught in Acts. The Spirit is not merely an influence. The Spirit, as a person, speaks to people and there are ascribed the actions of person, The Spirit is the great divine "I." Barnabas and Paul were set apart for the Spirit.[52]

2. The Spirit is sent from God. On Jesus the Son of Man the father poured the Holy Spirit so that Jesus could serve with power and success. After His ascension the glorified Christ then sent His Spirit upon the Church for a life of power and service. The Holy Spirit at the same time was also the promised gift of the Father.[53]

3. In a special sense Pentecost marked the beginning of a new age. Since Pentecost of the year 30 or 33 A.D. one can properly speak of the age of the Spirit. The miracle of Pentecost took place on the feast of the

first fruits, when passages from Exodus 19, Psalm 29, Psalm 69 and Ezekiel 1 were read, passages which are full of the display of the power and might of God. In a unique way God's power was manifested and the Old Dispensation was being fulfilled in the New Dispensation the prophetic was merging into the historic.[54]

4. The coming of the Spirit was by a sovereign act of God. It was not the praying of the disciples which caused the Spirit being sent upon the disciples, but the work of God.[55]

5. The baptism of the Spirit seems to refer to the oneness of the church. It is for that reason that we have two Pentecosts, one in chapter 2 and the other in chapter 10. It was into the Spirit and by the Spirit that Jews and Gentiles were baptized. [56]

Footnotes

1. *Lutheran Worship*, Prepared by The Committee on Worship of the Lutheran Church-Missouri Synod (St. Louis, Concordia Publishing House, 1932), p. 56.

2. Lorenz Wunderlich, *The Half-Known God - The Person and Work of the Holy Spirit* (St. Louis: Concordia Publishing House, 1963), chapter 1, pp. 15-23.

3. Harry W. Love, *Speaking in Tongues - A Brief History of the Phenomenon Known As Glossolia or Speaking in Tongues* (Omaha: Pacific Press, Publication Association, 1965), cf. last part of book; Frederick Dale Brunner, *A Theology of the Holy Spirit* (Grand Rapids: William B. Eerdmans Publishing Company, 1970), pp. 19-34.

4. Don Hillis, *Tongues, Healing and You* (Grand Rapids: Baker Book House, 1969), 63 pp.

5. Leon Wood, *The Holy Spirit in the Old Testament* (Grand Rapids: Zondervan Publishing House, 1976), 160 pp. W. H. Griffith Thomas, *The Holy Spirit of God* (Grand Rapids: Wm. B. Eerdmans Publishing Company, 1955), pp. 9-17; Michael Gree, *I Believe in the Holy Spirit* (Grand Rapids: Wm. B. Eerdmans Publishing Company, 1975), pp. 13-31. Ernst F. Scott, *The Spirit in the New Testament* (London; Hodder & Stoughton, 1923), Chapter 1 treats the doctrine of Holy Spirit in the Old Testament, pp. 11-44.

6. Henry Barclay Swete, *The Holy Spirit in the New Testament* (Grand Rapids: Zondervan Publishing House, 1976), a reprint of the edition of 1910, 417 pp.

7. J.J. Ross, *Thinking Through the New Testament* (New York: Fleming H. Revell Company, 1921), *p*. 78.

8. D.A. Hayes, *The Synoptic Gospels and the Book of Acts* (New York: Methodist Book Concern, 1919), p. 306.

9. **Ibid.**

10. Ross, **op. cit.**, p. 77.

10a. **Ibid.**

11. Graham Scroggie, *Know Your Bible*. Vol. II. *Analytical, The New Testament* (London; Pickering & Inglis, no date), p. 76.

12. Ross, **op. cit.**, p. 78.

13. Scroggie, **op. cit.** p. 76.

14. **Ibid.**, p. 76.

15. William Beck, *The Holy Bible An American Translation* (New Haven: Leader Publishing Company, 1976), N.Y., p. 149.

16. **Ibid.**

17. John H. Gerstner, "Acts," in Carl F. Henry, editor, *The Biblical Expositor* (Philadelphia: A.J. Holman Company, 1960), III, p. 138.

13. P. E Kretzmann, *Popular Commentary of the Bible - New Testament* (St. Louis: Concordia Publishing House, 1923), 1, p. 540.

19. Beck, **op. cit.**, p. 149.

20. **Ibid.**, p, 153.

21. **Ibid.**, pp, 153-154.

22. F.F. Bruce, *The Acts of the Apostles - The Greek Text With Introduction and Commentary* (Grand Rapids: Wm. B. Eerdmans Publishing Company, 1952), p, 133,

23. Beck, **op. cit.**, p. 154.

24. F.F, Bruce, *New Testament History* (Garden City: Doubleday, 1971), pp. 220-226.

25. Beck, **op. cit.**, p, 158,

26. Cf. Alford, *The New Testament for English Readers* (Chicago: Moody Press, no date), p. 706.

27. David Smith, *The Life and Letters of Paul* (New York: George H. Doran, date), pp. 45-64.

28. Helen Barrett Montgomery, *The New Testament In Modern English* (Philadelphia: The Judson Press, 1924), p. 335.

29. Cf. Swete, **op. cit.**, pp. 410-411 where are listed all the passages from Paul's Letters that refer and deal with the Holy Spirit.

30. Cf. Swete, **op. cit.**, p. 98.

31. Gerstner, **op. cit.**, p. 204.

32. Beck, **op. cit.**,

33. Beck, **op. cit.**, p, 164,

34. H. W. Wayne House, *Chronological and Background Charts of the New Testament* (Grand Rapids: Zondervan Publishing House, 1977), p. 118,

34a. Beck, **op. cit.**, p. 164.

35. **Ibid.**, p. 164.

36. Richard Weymouth, *The New Testament in Modern English* (Boston: Pilgrim Press, 1934), p. 301.

37. Beck, **op. cit.**, p, 164.

38. Montgomery, **op. cit.**, p. 3;1.

39. Olaf Moe, *The Apostle Paul - His Life and Work* (Minneapolis: Augsburg Publishing House, 1950), pp. 195-199.

40. **Ibid.**, pp. 220-221.

41. Montgomery, **op. cit.**, pp. 353.

42. **Ibid.**, pp, 354-355.

43. Smith, **op. cit.**, pp. 116-124.

44. Translation of the Greek text.

45. Gerstner, **op. cit.**, pp. 217-218.

46. Smith, **op. cit.**, p, 462.

47. Beck, **op. cit.**, p. 175.

48. Beck, **op. cit.**, p. 178.

49. **Ibid.**, p. 179.

50. H. D. McDonald, *Living Doctrines of the New Testament* (Grand Rapids: Zondervan Publishing House, 1972), pp, 135-142,

51. **Ibid.**, pp. 135-137,

52. **Ibid.**, p, 137.
53. **Ibid.**, p. 138.
54. **Ibid.**
55. **Ibid.**, p. 139.
56. **Ibid.**, p. 140.

Questions

1. The Ascension of Christ was the climatic event of ____.
2. Ascension Day services are practically ____.
3. What book did Lorenz Wunderlich write? ____
4. The charismatic movement depreciated the ____.
5. What correct balance does the Christian church need? ____
6. Scroggie said that Acts is the record of ____.
7. Acts shows us how the great changeover was made from ____ to ____.
8. Any person denying the predictive Messianic prophecies is forced to ____.
9. The Sadducees denied ____.
10. "You didn't lie to men, but to ____" Peter told Ananias.
11. Stephen showed that all Old Testament history points to ____.
12. The conversion of Paul of Tarsus is ____.
13. Luke described Barnabas as ____.
14. What was the great issue debated at the first great church convention? ____
15. Why did Paul and Barnabas separate? ____
16. Who was Timothy? ____
17. It was only after the outpouring of the Holy Spirit that ____.
18. Jews and Gentiles were baptized into the ____.

Biblical Teachings Rejected and Contradicted by the Practitioners of Human Abortion

Christian News, May 27, 1991

Today two diametrically opposed philosophies of life are vying for the hearts and minds of the people of the Americas and of Western civilization, namely, the Judeo-Christian and the atheistic, agnostic and pragmatic humanism taught in many grammar; high schools, colleges and universities the world over.[1] The Judeo-Christian **Weltanschauung** which has dominated Western civilization for at least sixteen hundred years was also the view of life espoused by the founding fathers of the United States of America.

Generally speaking, the founding fathers were Christians or deists, who even though they differed on a number of theological issues, were proponents and defenders of the sacredness of human life. Their understanding of law in general was based on the Bible and the idea that one could kill his offspring deliberately after its conception as legal, legitimate and human was certainly not ever entertained by them.

How the situation has radically changed today, after the influence of evolution, higher criticism, which with the help of Pierce and Dewey and their ilk, has influenced the field of ethics and its pragmatic values have taken over in American education. The humanistic media (said to be about 86 percent liberal), together with the movie industry, television and radio have propagated a **Weltanschauung** that promotes the view that anything which gives people pleasure, short of murder, violent behavior toward others, stealing and slander, is permissible. An unwanted pregnancy, it is claimed hurts no other individual, but may even enhance the physical and psychological well-being of the person becoming pregnant by removing the unwanted irritant new life.

These views about the sanctity of human life are completely opposed to the ethical concepts as contained in the Constitution and the Bill of Rights. Many of the moral values and practices people are now witnessing and practicing are against the religious and philosophical beliefs of the writers of the U.S. Constitution and its Bill of Rights.

Immorality, nudity, the practice of homosexuality and lesbianism, free love, abortion and euthanasia are being heralded as guaranteed rights of the American Constitution. As already stated, the authors of the American Constitution and the Bill of Rights were Christians or deists, who would never have dreamt or imagined that the documents that they gave the thirteen colonies would be interpreted as supporting viewpoints completely opposed to the Bible and that murder and euthanasia would be defended in these legal documents they authored toward the closing years of the eighteenth century. When the founding fathers wrote the

Constitution and Bill of Rights, they were doing this out of a context of the moral and Biblical principles that had dominated Western civilization for centuries in Europe and parts of Asia and Africa and it was these principles they brought to the American shores from England, Ireland, Scotland, France, Switzerland, Holland, Austria and Germany.

Views about abortion, divorce, euthanasia, aberrant sex practices, aids through intravenous injection, caused by illicit sex committed by adulterers and fornicators are defended as perfectly moral as long as its practitioners act out of love. The humanists claim that man is not accountable to God but only to society and to himself or herself. People do not need to exercise stewardship as they use their lives for they are captains of their own ships. They contend that there is no day of judgment, when their creator and sustainer, will call them to account on the great judgment day.

Christians Often Influenced by the World

Paganism is more in evidence in our time, than it has been the case for a long time.[2] When everybody is doing something wrong, Christians are frequently persuaded to join the crowd and follow suit. Abortion can be a convenient way of hiding adultery or immorality, when an infant is allowed to develop and thus publicly advertise the fact of one's sinful act. Having an abortion might interfere with the practice of a career that is profitable and makes many comforts available which might be lost if a beginning life is given the opportunity to develop fully and eventually emerge as a small baby boy or little baby girl. For more individuals aborting solves what they believe is belief from a whole host of complex of problems.

Unbelievers, in most cases, will take the easy way out, and decide to eliminate the new person within a woman's womb. Those who believe in no hereafter and that the grave writes the end to a human life, do not have a problem with murdering another life. But how about individuals who believe in an afterlife, who are convinced that a woman's sexual organs were not just given for pure gratification and that a woman's sexual organs were given a woman for the purposes of pro-creation?

A Christian woman or for that matter, a man who insists that his pregnant wife submit to abortion, should be aware that there are a whole series of Biblical teachings which the abortionists violate and contradict. In the following essay the writer will point out and discuss those Biblical doctrines which prohibit abortion and show that those who destroy a beginning human person are negating and rejecting God's directives and teachings. Abortion, basically rejects, the doctrines of creation and providence, the doctrine of predestination, the lost eternal destiny of the unbaptized child and above all it is a flagrant violation of God's commandment: "Thou shalt not kill."

Every Person Created by God

The idea that a woman can control her body and therefore, can if she so wishes, dispose of her offspring conceived in her, is totally against God's Word. In Job 10, the patriarch Job confessed: "Thy hands have fashioned me..."[3] "Remember that thou hast made me of clay and wilt thou turn me to dust again? Thou didst clothe me with skin and flesh, and I am knit together with bone and sinews; Thou hast granted me life and steadfast love, and thy care has preserved my spirit."[4] In verse 18 of chapter 10 Job asserted: "Why didst thou bring me forth from the womb?"[5] Job had a very clear understanding about his human origin. His friend, Elihu confessed: "The Spirit of God hath made me, and the breath of the Almighty hath given me breath."[6] The same Elihu also confessed: "But none saith, Where is God my maker?"[7]

The existence of each human person is a mediate creation of the Triune God,[8] using the body of the woman, which the Triune God had made and equipped so that woman can conceive, become pregnant and eventually give birth to offspring. The author of Psalm 100 stated clearly: "Know ye that the Lord he is God, and it is he that hath made us and not we ourselves, we are his people and the sheep of his pasture."[9] Ezra, who may be the author of Psalm 119, averred: "Thy hands have made me and fashioned me."[10] The writer of Psalm 138 declared: "The Lord will perfect that which concerneth me; thy mercy, O Lord, endureth forever, forsake not the work of thy hands."[11] Psalm 139 clearly and unequivocally teaches the truth of man's creation by God. When the psalmist thinks of his marvelous body, he exclaimed: "I will praise thee: for I am fearfully and wonderfully made; marvelous are thy works and that my soul know it very well."[12] Solomon wrote: "Lo, this only have I found, that God hath made man upright."[13] The prophet Isaiah predicted that the Syrians would look to a time when "a man shall look to his maker and his eyes shall have respect to the Holy One of Israel."[14] Isaiah surely did not believe that any humans could argue that they were not created by God, for he asserted:

"Thus saith the God, the Lord, he that created the heavens, and stretched them out; he that spread forth the earth, and that which cometh out of it; he that giveth breath unto the people upon it; he that giveth spirit to them that walk therein."[15] The same prophet a few chapters later in his prophetical book taught: "I have made the earth, and created man upon it; I, even my hands, have stretched out the heavens, and all are the work of my hands."[16] Toward the conclusion of his book, Isaiah instructs his readers: "But now, O Lord, thou art our father, and thou our potter and we all are the work of thy hands."[17] The prophet Malachi asks the question: "Have we not all one father, hath not one God created us?"[18]

No woman accepting Holy Writ as God's Word can say that any offspring conceived in her can deny that God did not make conception possible and that she has no stewardship obligations to God how she conducts herself and how she takes care of her body during the time period a life different from hers is being formed by processes with which God has endowed her to begin with.

God Has Something To Do With Conception
The Bible teaches that women who could not become pregnant were given pregnancy by God. Sarah, who was too old to have children by herself, was given the ability to conceive and bare a son. Rebekah, too many years was unable to have a child by her husband Isaac, did become preg-

nant by the action of Yahweh. In Judges 13:3-24 the reader will find the interesting account how Manoah's wife was given conception by Yahweh and she eventually bore Samson, one of the judges, who delivered the children of Israel from the Philistines. The mother of Samuel was infertile, a condition which made her very sorrowful, and she prayed to Yahweh to open her womb. According to 1 Samuel 1:19-20, Hannah's prayer was answered and she was able to conceive and bear one of the greatest prophets of the Old Testament Samuel. Elizabeth, the wife of Zecharias, also was unable to have an offspring. As With Sarah, Rebekah, Manoah's Wife and Hannah, God also caused Elizabeth to become fertile and conceive and bear the great waypreparer for the Son of God, namely, John the Baptizer.

The most remarkable birth of all time was the conception of Mary, a maiden of the house and lineage of David, who without having sexual relations with any man, least of all with Joseph, became pregnant as a result of the work of the Holy Spirit upon her.

God, certainly, is involved with every woman, who conceives and is with child. God can withhold from couples children. Inasmuch as he has made the way woman is sexually constituted, ultimately God is the author of all human life. To abort is to question this fundamental fact of woman's creation. She cannot impregnate herself but her ovum needs the sperm of the male of the human species, no woman can claim that a new life in her is her right only to determine whether to abort or not to.

Human Personality Begins From the Time of Conception

According to the Supreme Court's Roe-Wade decision, after conception the new life in the womb is not a person for at least nineteen weeks. That was certainly an arbitrary decision, designed to make it possible for women to murder potential human beings. This decision goes against common sense and reason and is one that certainly has no warrant in Holy Writ. David in speaking about himself as a sinner confessed: "Behold, I was brought forth in iniquity and in sin did my mother conceive me."[19] As far as David was concerned his existence began with conception and from that very moment on he was a sinner in God's sight. God told Jeremiah: "Before I formed you in the Womb, I knew you. Before you were born I sanctified you. And I ordained you a prophet to the nations."[20]

Clearly, both David's and Jeremiah's existence began with conception. They were persons from the very moment their mothers conceived them or were impregnated by their fathers Jesse and Hilkiah respectively. Both David and Jeremiah acknowledged that from the very beginning of their existence; as tiny as it was at first, they were personalities. In Psalm 139, the reader will find clear teaching about the part played by God in the forming of a life in a human womb. Thus David, so magnificently wrote: "For thou didst form my inward parts, thou didst knit me together in my mother's womb, I praise thee, for thou art fearful and wonderful, wonderful are thy works. Thou knowest me right well; my frame was not hidden from thee. When I was being formed in secret, intricately wrought in the depths of tile earth, Thy eyes beheld my unformed substance; in thy book they were written, every one of them. The days as yet there was none of them, the days that were formed for me, when as yet there was none of them."[21] Job declared: "Thy hands fashioned men, and now thou dost turn to destroy me."[22] Is not that precisely what those are doing who abort and make it impossible for those to live for whom God has plans and as the possible elect of God are destroyed without ever having the opportunity to see their election result in their glorification?

Human Reason and Medical Science Teach
That Human Personality Begins With Conception

On August 9, 1989 *The Fort Wayne Journal Gazette* published the following letter written by a Fort Wayne physician. We reproduce it here. The caption of the letter given to it was: "A LIFE IS A CONTINUOUS PROCESS THAT BEGINS AT CONCEPTION." Here is the letter:

When does life begin? Is it at birth? Every mother can tell us the baby was alive and kicking long before that. Is it when the baby can survive outside its mother? The point of viability gets earlier and earlier all the time because of medical progress. Should we just pick some round number such as 20 weeks, (halfway through the pregnancy)? The trouble with that is that a fetus at 21 weeks isn't any more "alive" than a fetus at 19 weeks, just bigger and better developed.

What about the point at which the heart starts beating, 25 days (not 25 weeks) after conception? Surely a beating heart is a good criterion of life. But every day in Fort Wayne, people's hearts are deliberately stopped for heart surgery and they're still alive. How about the point at which a pregnancy test becomes positive? Could we say that if the embryo is too small to detect by a pregnancy test, it isn't alive? No, because the whole science of embryology shows that it is alive.

But is the early embryo really "alive" or only "potentially alive?" What is human life anyway? Are the sperm and ovum "alive?"

We have to draw the line somewhere, and it seems to me that the most logical and scientific place to draw the line is at conception, because the ovum and the sperm each only have half the number of chromosomes to make a person, the fertilized has the full number. Generally the fertilized ovum has all the characteristics that the individual will ever have, such as blood type, gender etc. The embryo growing inside the mother is not just her own tissue, but a new and separate individual with a unique combination of characteristics different from its mother. Biologically, a person's life is a continuous process from conception till death, nominally in old age. Birth is an important event in that process, but the process itself started nine months earlier, at conception.

Ian M. Cook, M.D.

Abortion Interferes With the Decree of Predestination

According to the Scriptures of the New Testament especially, God's plan of salvation begins in eternity.[23] Those Christians who will be saved and enjoy eternal life are called the elect of God. Before the world began the Triune God in love in Christ chose those who will be saved. The elect of God are brought to faith by the call through the Gospel, which may be either

1851

baptism or the preaching of the Word. Those who are called are justified by grace. They are kept in the faith through sanctification which eventually by God's grace and mercy eventuates in the glorification of the elect.[24]

We have already seen that Jeremiah was chosen before he was conceived and born by Hilkiah's wife and was before the conception and eventually birth of Jeremiah he had been chosen to be a prophet to Judah and other nations of the Near-East. When a woman deliberately aborts her own flesh how does she know that she is not countermanding God's plan for her child? What creature of God has the right to kill a human being that God formed in a woman's womb and concerning which God has great plans possibly in this life and assuredly for eternity?

What Happens to the Souls

According to the Bible each human person has a body and a soul.[25] Differences of opinion have existed in the Christian Church whether or not man has just a body and soul or whether human beings have a body, soul and spirit. At this juncture the writer will not take up the views of the dichotomists and that of the trichotomists.[26] However, this may be safely asserted, namely, that both groups believe that man is more than body. Both groups would admit that man has both a body and a soul. Luther and the older Lutheran dogmaticians were dichotomists. Luther in the first article asserted that "God has given me my body and soul."[27] According to the Lutheran Dogmatician Stump: "The soul or spirit is the immaterial part of man which inhabits and moves the body, and which constitutes man's real self. It is an entity created by God. It is not a part of God's spirit, not God's spirit dwelling in man, not God coming to consciousness in man. Nor on the other hand, is it the result of the functioning of the matter of the brain, not heap of sensations, nor simply a stream of consciousness. It is a finite spiritual being made in God's image, and like Him possessed of self-consciousness and self-determination."[28]

Every Human Fetus Possesses a Soul the Origin of Souls

When was the soul created? Three different answers have been given to this important question, namely by the theories of pre-existence, creationism and traducianism. Plato, Philo, Origen, Kant, Fichte, Schelling, Schleiermacher, Julius Mueller, William Coleridge, Wordsworth and others have been individuals who maintained that all souls came into existence by God in the beginning and entered the body propagated by human parentage.[29] Stump in describing this stance wrote: "It involves the necessity of a fall of human souls in a previous state and then would stand in conflict With the account of the fall of man in Genesis 3, and with Romans 5:12-18."[30]

The second view is called creationism and would involve that only the body is propagated by the parents, and that a new soul is created by God for each child which is born. Stump evaluated this view as follows: "But according to this theory it would follow, either there is no original sin, or that it inheres in the body or that God is the creator of sinful souls and thus the author of sin."[31] Since sin inheres in the personality and not in

1852

the body, and since God cannot be Scripturally conceived of as the author of sin, the theory of Creationism is not tenable. Further, Creationism apart from the body, militates against the unity of the race and its descendant from the first human pair, Adam and Eve.[32]

The third view is that of Traducianism which holds that both body and soul of a child are propagated by the parents. This view agrees with the implications of numerous Scripture passages that teach that body and soul are derived from the parents. Thus teach Genesis 1:21; 5:3; Ps. 51:5; Job 14:4; Acts 17: 21-26.[33] Traducianism as an explanation of the origin of souls is in agreement with the doctrine of the unity of the human race and the universality of original sin. Stump has pointed out: "It is corroborated by the experiences of the race, which shows that not only physical, but mental characteristics are inherited by children from their parents. There is, of course, a sense in which God creates the child body and soul, but it is a mediate creation through secondary sources."[34]

A human fetus is an individual going through stages of development, ultimately resulting in a full body and soul. The soul is the animating force of the developing human being in its mother's womb.[34a]

In God's creative plan and method, plant and animal life all begin in a small manner. This also is the case with human beings. What happens to the soul of a fetus which now according to the law established by five jurists on the Supreme Court can now be destroyed during the first twenty weeks? What happens to the soul? Since the new life forming in its mother's womb is sinful and not a child of God, what, pray happens to it? Christian denominations like the Roman Catholic, Eastern Orthodox, high Episcopalian and traditional Lutheran believe that each new life needs to be born again spiritually and this is accomplished through baptism. Jesus taught: "He that believeth and is baptized shall be saved."[35] St. Peter wrote: "So baptism now saves us."[36] Jesus gave the command to make disciples of all nations by baptizing them in the name of the Father, and of the Son and of the Holy Ghost."[37] How can fetuses, distinct human beings, be baptized when they are destroyed? Is not a mother consigning her offspring to eternal condemnation? Baptism creates faith in a child to believe in Christ. Christian mothers who plan on abortion should seriously ask themselves this question: 'What am I doing to my unborn fetus?'"

Mankind Created in the Image of God

In Genesis I the reader is told that the Triune God made male and female in His image.[38] The fact that human beings are created in the image of God distinguishes male and female babies from male and female animals. Since God does not have a body but is pure spirit (John 4:24), the likeness referred to is not bodily but spiritual. The original image involved in Adam's creation and also that of Eve meant that the first man was created in righteousness and holiness and simultaneously possesses self-consciousness and the ability to make choices.[39]

J. T. Mueller wrote about the image and likeness in which God created Adam, as follows: "In his original state man bore a resemblance to God, because He Himself was the pattern, or the archetype, after which man was made. According to Scripture, Adam was created after the likeness of the Triune God, Gen. 1:26, and not after that of Christ alone."[40] There are Bible passages which speak of the fact that the image of God in man was lost, and which must be restored (Col. 3:10 and Ephes. 4:24). On the other hand, there are also verses in Scripture which describe man as still possessing God's image (Genesis 9:6 and James 3:9).

After the Flood God said to Noah: "Whosoever sheds man's blood, by man shall his blood be shed, for in the image of God He made man."[41] James warns his readers against the misuse of the tongue, for "with it we bless God and the Father and with it we curse men; who are made in the image of God."[42]

When a fetus is destroyed, the person doing this act, is guilty of destroying a person made in the image of God.[43] Plants and animals, all forms of life, are never described in the Bible as made in the image of God. When abortionists destroy potential human beings[44] with the approval of the United States Supreme Court, they are desecrating Gods image in those aborted fetuses and are guilty of negating and rejecting another teaching of God's Word.[45]

The Correct View and Attitude
Relative to Newborn Offspring

The marriage ceremony used by this writer for many years had this statement from Psalm 126: "Thy wife shall be as a fruitful vine by the sides of thy house, thy children like olive plants around thy table. Behold, that thus shall be the man be blessed that feareth the Lord."[46]

Footnotes

1. Francis A. Schaeffer, *How Should We Then Live? The Rise and Decline of Western Thought and Culture* (Old Tappan, New Jersey: Fleming H. Revell, 1970); pp. 144-245.
2. **Ibid.**, pp. 205-245.
3. *The Holy Bible. The Old Testament*, Volume II, Esther-Malachi (New York: Thomas Nelson & Sons, 1952), p. 1002.
4. **Ibid.**, p. 1002 (Job 10:10-11).
5. **Ibid.**
6. Job 33:4 in *The Revised Standard Version*, **op. cit.**, p. 1080.
7. Job 35:10 in *The Revised Standard Version*, **op. cit.**, p. 1040.
8. Conrad Emil Lindberg, *Christian Dogmatics and Notes on the History of Dogma*, translated by Rev. C. Hoffsten (Rock Island, IL: Augustana Book Concern, 1928), p. 146, footnote*.
9. Psalm 103:73 in *The Revised Standard Version*, **op. cit.**, p. 1201.
10. Psalm 119:73 in *The Revised Standard Version*, **op. cit.**, p. 1237.
11. Psalm 138:10 in *The King James Version* (New York: American Bible Society, no date).
12. Psalm 139:14 in *New American Standard Bible* (Philadelphia: The Holman Company, 1973), p. 456.
13. Ecclesiastes 7:29 in *The* Revised Standard Version, **op. cit.**, p. 1348.
14. Isaiah 17:7 in *King James Version*, **op. cit.**, p. 636.
15. Isaiah 42:5 in *King James Version*, **op. cit.**, p. 655 .
16. Isaiah 45:12 in *King James Version*, **op. cit.**, p. 658.
17. Isaiah 64:1, in *King James Version*, **op. cit.**, p. 672.
18. Malachi 2:10 in *King James Version*, **op. cit.**, p. 847.

19. Psalm 51:5 in *King James Version,* **op. cit.,** p. 545.
20. Jeremiah 1:5, *The New King James Version* (New York: Thomas Nelson & Sons, 1979), p. 728.
21. Psalm 139:1016, in *The Revised Standard Version,* **op. cit.,** p. 1260.
22. Job 10:5, **Ibid.,** p. 1260.
23. Cf. Ephesians 1:4; 2 Thessalonians 2:13; Also cf. A.L. Graebner, *Outlines of Doctrinal Theology* (St. Louis: Concordia Publishing House, 1910), p. 44.
24. Cf. 2 Thessalonians 2:13-14; Erwin L. Lueker, *Lutheran Cyclopedia* (St. Louis: Concordia Publishing House, 1954), article on "Predestination," pp. 839-840.
25. Genesis 2:7; also cf. Graebner, **op. cit.,** p. 56; Joseph Stump, *The Christian Faith* (New York: Macmillan Company, 1032), p. 98.
26. Revere Franklin Weidner, *The Doctrine of Man* (Chicago: Wartburg Press, 1912), p. 13.
27. Theodore Tappert, *The Book of Concord* (Philadelphia: Fortress Press, 1959), p. 345.
28. Joseph Stump, **op. cit.,** p. 99.
29. **Ibid.,** p. 101, footnote 5.
30. **Ibid.,** p. 101.
31. **Ibid.,** p. 101.
32. **Ibid.**
33. **Ibid.,** p. 102.
34. **Ibid.,** p. 102, footnote 7.
34a. Martin Reu, *Lutheran Dogmatics,* 2nd Revised Edition (Decorah, Iowa: Wartburg Press, 1952), p. 83.
36. I Peter 3:21; cf. also Francis Pieper, *Christian Dogmatics* (St. Louis: Concordia Publishing House, 1953), III, pp. 263ff.
37. Matthew 28:18 according to the Greek text.
38. Genesis 1:26.
39. Stump, **op. cit.,** p. 103.
40. J.T. Mueller, *Christian Dogmatics* (St. Louis: Concordia Publishing House 1955), p. 205.
41. Genesis 9: 5; cf. also the statement of Christ: "Put up thy sword into his place, for all they that take the sword shall perish with the sword" Matthews 26:52.
42. James 3:9.
43. Exodus 2:3; Deuteronomy 5:17; many Bible Translations have: "You shall not murder."
44. Proverbs 6:16-17 in *The Revised Standard Version,* **op. cit.,** p. 1284.
45. Amos 1:13 in *The Revised Standard Version,* **op. cit.,** p. 1870.
46. *The Pastor's Companion* (St. Louis: Concordia Publishing House; no date) p. 44 which cites Psalm 27:3-4.

Questions

1. Generally speaking the founding fathers were ____.
2. The humanistic media is said to be about ____.
3. What is against the U.S. Constitution and Bill of Rights? ____
4. Abortion can be a convenient way of ____.
5. The most remarkable birth of all times was ____.
6. Who is ultimately the author of all life? ____
7. According to the Supreme court's Roe-Wade decision ____.
8. When does life begin? ____
9. Human Reason and medical Science teach that ____.
10. What is a dichotomist? ____
11. Traducionism holds that____.

Dr. Raymond F. Surburg (1909-2001)

Dr. Raymond F. Surburg (1909-2001) Teacher and Friend Ascended Home to Heaven

A Tribute
By Dr. Phillip B. Giessler
Christian News, May 28, 2001

"Back to Revelation and God's Word! If anyone does not speak according to this Word, there is no light dawning for him." (Isaiah 8:20-AAT)

As we feebly celebrate Ascension Day during this week of 2001, a scholars' scholar is now celebrating it firsthand with his ascended Lord Jesus.

With the Christian passing of Dr. Ray Surburg (May 19), former pastor and professor, a vanishing "stand-for-the-truth" breed dwindles by one more. Like the Ludwig E. Fuerbringers, the Walter A. Maiers, the P. E. Kretzmanns, the Theodore Laetsches, and the Alfred Rehwinkels of conservative Lutheranism, Raymond Surburg was one who theologically knew "truth from error." And he had the courage—when asked as a leading teacher in the church—to express such with a "yes" or "no" without fear of differing with colleagues! His was a focus on his Lord and his Lord's Scriptures (as the Isaiah 8 passage above so aptly sums up Surburg's didactic approach). What a breath of fresh air in a day of anemic preaching, wild exegetical speculation, and less than "thus-says-the-Lord" teaching!

To know Surburg was to know research to its depths; exegetical warfare to seldom-witnessed heights of conviction; and scholarship mixed with humility at its best.

As a pastor in New Jersey and New York, Surburg mixed very personal, pastoral care with difficult academics at such schools as Columbia University, American Theological Seminary, and Fordham University, learning many languages such as Arabic, Aramaic, Syriac, and Akkadian as well as Biblical hermeneutics, ancient church history, and comparative religions. Even in his last days at an assisted-living nursing home in Bloomington, IN, he was studying Japanese and Chinese. (Of course, we who knew him best give much credit to Lillian, his wife-to-be, who bought him one new book each week out of her secretarial salary.)

As to his love for wife Lillian and his books, one cannot forget the story of his arrival at Concordia Teachers College – Seward, NE. There was Dr. Surburg sitting outside in a chair, reading, as Lillian directed students carrying his books to an upstairs office—and then directing them down again as the administration decided on an office downstairs when they feared the upper floor would not hold the weight. Some of us students who loved his book collection were in awe of his two rooms of books in his office at Concordia Theological Seminary—Springfield, IL and the three floors of books at his home on Walnut one can only imagine the task when the seminary moved to Ft. Wayne, IN!

But lest it be forgotten, we also marveled at the saintly, and also now sainted Lillian, who mowed the lawn as Ray again sat reading in his yard. And Dr. Surburg had two other great loves – his son Paul and sports. He followed Paul's athletic endeavors all the way to Paul's teaching career at Indiana University, becoming an avid fan of Bobby Knight's Hoosiers—and also sitting at the TV and hoping against hope that the Chicago Cubs could just win one World Series. (At the "sem" we used Ray, then in his 60s, as a pitcher on our softball team.)

We his students stood in amazement of his other love: His Students.

He gave his very best!

There he was in the middle of a lecture, grabbing book after book to back up his arguments with quote upon quote! Then he reached again, but the next book wasn't there! Out of the room he raced; back to his office; and then back into the room with about 10 more books that he had forgotten.

It was in one of those classes that a student complained that Dr. Surburg expected them to know too much in addition to all that was in the basic class textbook. So what does Surburg do? He redesigns the whole course for the next semester, now basing his lectures on the class textbook.

And you may have guessed it! In the middle of the course, a student complained that Surburg was insulting their intelligence since they could read the textbook on their own; he should be using other sources more! Thus the ongoing fulfillment of Jesus' words: "everyone will hate you because of My Name" (Mk. 13:13—NET).

But what a teaching talent—and versatile, both in topic and literary endeavor!

Is or was there a more prolific teacher and writer in the conservative Lutheran Church of our day? I doubt it!

Surburg holds the all-time record at the seminary for the most courses taught that differ in subject matter – and maybe the most credit hours taught in a quarter. Besides all the Old Testament books he taught from Genesis to Isaiah, Jeremiah, Ezekiel, etc., he taught Messianic prophecies, Old Testament theology, Hebrew, Biblical archaeology, the Intertestamental Period, Biblical hermeneutics, and on and on and on.

In the area of publishing, what topic did he not cover? There were the class manuals, accompanied by books like *How Dependable is the Bible?* (Lippincott/Holman, 1972); *Introduction to the Intertestamental Period* (Concordia, 1975); etc., added to with periodicals and articles on varying topics, such as "The Bible in the Balance"; "Why Should a Christian Study the Old Testament?"; "Jesus and the Canon"; "Defending the Book of Daniel"; "The Removal of Satan or the Devil from the Old Testament by Modern Lutheran Theologians"; "The Forgotten Sesquicentennial of Charles Darwin's Beagle Voyage"; "The 450th Anniversary of the Apology"; "The 'Identity Crisis' in American Lutheranism and The Lutheran Church-Missouri Synod"; "The Text, Music and Employment of the Bible in Handel's Greatest Oratorio: 'The Messiah'"; "In What Language Did Christ and the Apostles Speak?"; "An Evaluation of the Divergent Interpretations of the Lord's Mount Olivet Discourse"; "The Teachings About the Holy Spirit in the Book of Acts"; "The Misuse of the Bible to Falsely Support Homosexuality and Lesbianism"; "In Defense of Luther"; "Millennialism and Israel Today"; "Did Zoroastrianism Influence the Religion of the Old and New Testament?"; and so forth.

(Only when you note Christian News' listing of Surburg's many articles (coming June 4, 2001) will you really appreciate Surburg's versatility and willingness to sacrifice for the education of Christ's people!)

There was yet another all-encompassing love that dominated Dr. Surburg's life – his two grandsons (how he cared about them!) And his fellowship with his fellow professors like Klug, Huth, R. Preus, Stahlke, Tepker, etc., and especially in his last days with those colleagues who really befriended him after the death of his very beloved Lillian – namely, Dr. Walter A. Maier, Jr. (and Leah) and Richard Muller (and Kay).

One cannot give valid tribute to the importance of Surburg's contributions to the defense of the Christian faith in our age without noting his approach to Scripture. First of all, as Isaiah 8:20 above says, for Dr. Surburg it was Scripture first and alone that revealed Christ. As such, all of

Surburg's teachings were Christ-centered! And second, in support of this type of an approach our "now heaven present" Dr. used two more principles – to their utmost – for the interpretation of Scripture, namely, "Scripture interprets Scripture" and "the unity of the Scriptures." In other words, Surburg was a solid, steady exegete of Scripture. He said what Scripture said, careful not to add or subtract or be fanciful (Rev. 22:18,19); and for him all of Scripture spoke with one unified voice, not contradicting itself. These three hermeneutical approaches make Dr. Raymond Surburg one of the greatest teachers of Messianic interpretation ever.

We should also mention Surburg's courage in being a frequent contributor to Christian News. Thus, he was also there with Becker, Hoerber, Honsey, Hummel, and Kiehl when asked to help revise The Holy Bible: An American Translation (AAT) into what became known as the New Evangelical Translation (NET New Testament).

There are so many more things to say about this special servant of Christ. We could mention his appreciation for Christian music and other things beyond, but it was his personal faith in Christ Alone that made his love for everything else so remarkable!

As one of Dr. Surburg's students who was encouraged to attend grad school under the famous Edward J. Young at Westminster Theological Seminary—Philadelphia said, I would like to make this tribute: It was Dr. Siegbert Becker, who initially formulated my advance theology and ability to teach; Dr. Wm. F. Beck, who opened my world to Bible translation and communication; Dr. Robert Preus, who led me into the deeper depths of dogmatics; Professor David Kuske, who opened the vistas of Greek insight; but it was Surburg who became my favorite teacher, opening up the Old Testament with its Hebrew and Christ-centered truth and creating a love for its total interaction with the New Testament. He taught me research and bibliography and sparked an interest in Ugaritic. And it was he and his wife who put their faith into practical action by treating me as a "son" in their home and lives to the end.

May we the Church of our Messiah and Savior Jesus continue to benefit from Dr. Surburg's servanthood, scholarship, and Scriptural approaches! Thank you, Doctor! *Soli Deo Gloria!!!*

Questions
1. Raymond Surburg theologically knew ____ from ____.
2. To know Surburg was to ____.
3. Surburg mixed very personal pastoral care with ____.
4. What was Surburg doing during his last days? ____
5. Was there a more prolific writer and teacher in The Lutheran Church-Missouri Synod? ____
6. All of Surburg's teachings were ____.
7. Surburg was one of the greatest teachers ever of ____.

Dr. Raymond F. Surburg At Rest In Heaven
by Dr. Phil Giessler
Christian News, June 4, 2001

One attendee at Dr. Raymond F. Surburg's funeral service at Concordia Theological Seminary, Ft. Wayne, IN, commented: "That was the most beautiful service I've ever attended."

How true!

From the liturgy and Scripture selections to the organ music and choir presentations to the sermon delivery and content— yes, it was superb, moving, and beautiful.

And how apropos!

Dr. Surburg's life was a beautiful one from his dedication to Christ's word to his life of faithful living (sanctification).

We praise the Lord of the Church for it all!

His Last Years

After the death of his beloved Lillian, wife of 65 years, the last three years were very difficult and lonely for Dr. Surburg, even though surrounded by family and friends.

After a short stay in a nursing home in Ft. Wayne, Surburg spent the last year at Meadowood Health Care in Bloomington, IN, to be closer to where his son Paul lives and teaches at Indiana University.

Last year the 90-year-old Surburg still used the teaching talents that distinguished him for over 30 years as a professor at Concordia Theological Seminary, Ft. Wayne. With son Paul, Ray jointly taught a congregational Bible class. And as Paul says, when the tough questions were asked—like "How long did it take Joshua's army to march around the city of Jericho?"—He called upon his father, who immediately informed the class that by the size of the walls uncovered by archaeologists it would have taken about 40 minutes (on each of the first six days) or 4 hours and 40 minutes on the seventh day (seven times around).

Called Home

Finally at age 91 Dr. Surburg was called to heaven on Saturday, May 19, 2001. A funeral service was conducted in Bloomington on Tuesday the 22nd and the next day a second service was held at Kramer Chapel on the Ft. Wayne Seminary campus.

The Concordia Service

The choir rendition of Psalm 30 with congregational antiphon ("You turned my wailing into dancing; I will give you thanks forever") moved every worshipper to reaffirm that our greatest focus is to be on eternity's heaven and our Lord and Savior JESUS! (What a Christian talent at composing and arranging is Kantor Richard Resch, Dean of the Chapel!)

And what a job the Seminary Kantorei did! To this reporter's ears, it may have been the very best he has ever heard. Dr. Surburg, a great lover of Christian music, would have cherished the moment to thank both choir and organist for their excellent accomplishments.

The preacher for the occasion was Dr. Walter A. Maier III, Associate

Seminary Professor of Exegetical Theology. He used a text from Isaiah since Surburg's specialty was the Old Testament.

Maier—in the tradition of his famous Lutheran grandfather and father—delivered an electrifying, down-to-earth, convicting, comforting, and uncompromisingly direct sermon. Surburg the sinner and forgiven sinner, Surburg the chosen and believing child of God, as well as Surburg the warrior who stood against the false and destructive method of historical criticism— were expounded.

The Attendees

It was most edifying to see so many former colleagues of Dr. Surburg at the funeral. The family was most appreciative. (Pictures are interspersed with this article.)

The Committal

Dr. Ray Surburg's body was laid to rest at St. Peter's Lutheran Cemetery, Ft. Wayne. President Dean O. Wenthe of Concordia Theological Seminary conducted the graveside service.

Reception

Afterwards, family and friends assembled for a meal in Luther Hall on the seminary campus.

Dr. Surburg's son Paul added extremely interesting comments about his father and the whole family at the reception. President Wenthe's gracious touch provided a very fine closing to all the events. (With the news just in as we write this article, we wish President Wenthe the richest blessings upon him, his family, and the whole Concordia community after a recent tornado did serious damage all over the campus. For example, a quarter of the roof was taken off the Wenthe home.)

Dr. Surburg's Family

Paul Surburg, only child of Ray and Lillian Surburg, was present with his wife Ellen (nee Stahlke).

Dr. Surburg's two grandsons— Mark and Matthew— were also on hand. Mark is a seminary graduate and is presently working on his doctorate at Southern Methodist University (SMU) where he is concentrating his thesis in the area of Pauline theology, doctor, now being ready for residency. Both grandsons have wives named "Amy," who are trained specialists with higher degrees in their chosen field. Mark's Amy is a nurse practitioner, while Matthew's Amy is a chemical engineer. In addition, each couple blessed Surburg with a grandchild. Thus, Dr. Surburg boasted a grandson Timothy and a granddaughter Naomi.

In Closing

For our teacher and friend who will be greatly missed, it was a full life with all the spiritual blessings and many earthly gifts. REST IN PEACE, DEAR DOCTOR!

The Rev. Dr. Raymond F. Surburg
Called to the Church Triumphant

Christian News, June 4, 2001

(Fort Wayne, IN) – The Rev. Dr. Raymond F. Surburg, long-time professor of Exegetical Theology at Concordia Theological Seminary (CTS), Fort Wayne, died on Saturday, May 19, 2001, in Bloomington, Ind. Dr. Surburg served the seminary from 1960 to the time of his retirement in 1979, and he continued to teach classes at the seminary until he fully retired in 1993. He was 91 years old at his death.

Raymond Frederick Surburg was born in Chicago, IL, on July 3, 1909, to Frederick and Hulda (nee Messerschmidt) Surburg. He was married to his wife, Lillian (nee Werbeck) on July 3, 1933, and they were blessed with one child, Paul Raymond Surburg, who was born on September 8, 1937.

The funeral service for Dr. Surburg will be held Wednesday, May 23, 2001, at 10:00 a.m. in Kramer Chapel on the CTS campus. The Reverend Doctor Walter A. Maier III, Associate Professor of Exegetical Theology at CTS, will deliver the sermon.

Dr. Surburg pursued his academic studies in a vigorous manner. After graduating from Concordia High School in Milwaukee, receiving his diploma in 1929 with special emphasis on religion and languages, he immediately entered Concordia Seminary, Saint Louis, from which he graduated in 1933. From 1933 to 1935 he attended Columbia University, New York, and completed the A.M. degree in Aramaic and Syrian. From 1939 to 1942 he studied at American Theological Seminary, Wilmington, Delaware, which awarded him the Th. D. with a major in ancient church history and comparative religions, and a minor in biblical interpretation. In 1946 he received the Master of Religious Education (M.R.E.) from the Biblical Seminary of New York City in 1950. His thesis was titled, "An Evaluation of the Educational Philosophy of Hermann Harrell Horne."

In addition to his academic work, Dr. Surburg served the church faithfully. He was ordained into the Office of the Holy Ministry on February 23, 1936, after having received a call to Trinity Lutheran Church, Clifton, New Jersey. He served this congregation from 1936 to 1941. He later served Bethlehem Lutheran Church, Brooklyn, New York, as pastor from 1941 to 1954. From 1950 to 1953 he directed the Brooklyn Bible Institute. In 1954 Concordia Teachers College, Seward, Nebraska, called him as assistant professor of religion, and in 1956 raised his rank to associate professor. From 1956 to 1960 he served as assistant professor of biblical interpretation at Concordia Theological Seminary, Springfield, Illinois. He advanced to the rank of associate professor in 1962 and professor in 1966. Dr. Surburg chaired the department of exegetical theology at the seminary from 1968-1978.

Dr. Surburg was Book Review Editor of the *Springfielder* (1965-1976) and the *Concordia Theological Quarterly* (1977-1979). He is the author of a number of books, including *Readings in the Lutheran Philosophy of Ed-*

ucation and Darwin, Creation and Evolution. He also wrote numerous articles whose topics ranged from Lutheran education to biblical interpretation.

Dr. Surburg's dynamic and inquisitive mind will be missed at the seminary. He remained active in the life of the community as long as he possibly could. With his death, the seminary loses a long-time friend and the church loses a faithful servant. Quoting the conclusion of an article by Dr. Surburg that appeared in *Ohio Concerns* (no. 12, November 1976 and no. 13, December 1976): "There is an old Lutheran saying that we would quote in conclusion. In German it says: "Gottes Wort und Luthers Lehr Vergehet nun und nimmer mehr." God's Word and Luther's teaching will not depart now or forevermore. Luther's teaching was based foursquare on the Bible, of which our father's said: 'Verbum Dei manet in aeternum.' The Work of God remains into eternity. Let us hold and defend God's Word as taught by Martin Luther!"

Dr. Surburg is survived by his son, two grandchildren, and two great-grandchildren.

Dr. Raymond Surburg " Brave Warrior"
Called by Name, Belonging to God
Is. 43:1c

By Dr. Walter Maier III
Christian News, June 18, 2001

At the funeral of Raymond Surburg, Ph.D., Th.D.,
Concordia Theological
Seminary Chapel, Ft.
Wayne, Indiana, May 28, 2001.

We are gathered here in honor of the Rev. Dr. Raymond Surburg hereafter called "Raymond." Even as a member of this seminary's faculty I
could only call him "Dr. Surburg." However, a number of his colleagues
referred to him as "Ray." "Raymond," then, seems to be a good compro-
mise.

Is. 43:1c was chosen as the text for the funeral message at the request
of Raymond's son, Paul. Paul explained that for many years a banner
hung in his father's office, which both Raymond and Paul appreciated,
and which had been made by a student. The banner read, "Raymond, I
have called you by your name; you are mine." It seems most appropriate
that a text from the Old Testament be chosen for the homily at Raymond's funeral.

Although God spoke the words of our text, through Isaiah, initially to
the nation Israel, these words are true for they apply to any believer. Yet,
CALLED BY NAME, BELONGING TO GOD – what does this mean?

I.

This means, first, salvation. These words emphasize that salvation is
an individual, personal matter. Salvation is one on one - involving God
and a person. God loved the whole world, yes, and He loves each one of
us. Christ redeemed all humanity, yes, and He paid for the sins of each
one of us.

When did God call Raymond by name? Actually, He did this in eternity, before the foundation of the earth. Before creation God saw Raymond, and us, God knew us as individuals, and He elected, or
predestined, us for salvation.

After creation, God later called Raymond, and us, to faith, making us
members of the one, holy, Christian Church. Each person in the Church
has been called individually by God, called through the Gospel. For Raymond, and most of us here, that call came in our baptism, through which
we received the blessings of salvation.

Raymond would have been the first to confess, "I could never save my-
self, because I am a sinner." That confession is our confession. By nature
we were lost, enemies of God, in the kingdom of Satan, and headed for

hell. The fact that we are going to die is undeniable testimony that we are sinners.

But Raymond took great comfort in the Gospel, as we do. He rejoiced in the grace of God. He exulted in the good news of Christ's substitutionary life, atoning death on the cross, and triumphant resurrection. He was assured by his baptism, through which he was made a believer in the Triune God, a follower of Jesus Christ, and through which God took possession of him. He boasted in Christ, as a member of Christ's kingdom. Raymond knew that, through faith in Christ, the Deliverer promised in the Old Testament, he had forgiveness, he was clothed with Christ's righteousness, he had everlasting life, and was an heir of heaven.

As one called by name, called by God to faith, Raymond belonged, and belongs, to God. God owned and owns Raymond, and He owns you and me, brothers and sisters in the faith. That means He will hold on to us, as He did Raymond.

This is why Raymond delighted in making use of the means of grace. He read, marked, learned, and inwardly digested God's Word, because through this Word God strengthened and preserved his faith. He delighted in going to the Lord's Supper, through which he received the same blessings. Christ, giving His body and blood to Raymond, again and again bestowed on him, in a very individual, personal way, the forgiveness of sins.

So God preserved Raymond in faith, until He called Raymond home to heaven. This is the result of a person being called by name and belonging to God — being taken to celestial splendor and joy. But that is not the final result. Raymond is looking forward to, as we are, the resurrection and the new creation.

Therefore, in this time of grief, let us nevertheless celebrate Raymond's victory in Christ, a foreshadowing of our victory. We give thanks that God called him, and us, by name, and that Raymond, and we, belong to God. Thus we look forward to the heavenly reunion and life together, forever, in the world to come.

II.

Besides salvation, the words of our text, applied to believer, also mean service. Elsewhere in the Old Testament, when God said that he had called a person by name, God was marking that person as one chosen to carry out special work for the Lord. God has called each of us to faith, and to show forth the fruits of faith in our lives. We are reminded of what Paul writes in Eph. 2 where, after speaking in verses 8 and 9 of our salvation by God's Grace through faith, he goes on to state in verse 10: "For we are His workmanship created in Christ Jesus for good works, which God prepared beforehand that we should walk in them."

God certainly had a lot of work for Raymond to do, much service to render, to God's glory, and for the good of other people. In essence God said to him, "You belong to Me, Raymond. You are My servant."

Combine that thought with the biblical concept of "name"— that which designates the character of the named one, as well as the work he was to carry out or the role he was to fill. In calling Raymond for service, what names did God use?

God used the names "Husband" and "Patriarch." Raymond was a loving, devoted, caring husband to Lillian, who preceded him in death by about two and one-half years. God allowed their union, such a beautiful, powerful witness to what God intended in marriage, to last for over 65 years. Further, Raymond was a loving father, grandfather, and recently, great-grandfather.

God also used the name "Zealous One." Not just that Raymond was a zealous walker and zealous Cubs fan. Much more than that he was zealous for Christ, devoting his life to the Savior, and to ministering to his fellow human being. He zealously studied God's Word for his own benefit and the benefit of others. He preached and taught Christ during his 18 years in the parish ministry, six years at Concordia, Seward, and 33 years at the seminary.

Thus, Raymond was a blessed influence in the lives of many, many people. I speak from personal experience, for I, as a seminarian, had Dr. Surburg for five courses. I can still picture him lecturing, sometimes with his eyes closed, as he presented his tremendous research and learning to the students. As a seminary professor, he taught a wide range of courses, from Hebrew and Syriac to Old Testament Theology to Archaeology. His first love always remained the Old Testament, especially the Messianic prophecies. His classes were characterized by scholarly rigor and sound doctrine.

His zeal was seen in his earning two doctorates, the better to equip himself as a servant of the Lord. His Ph.D he earned while serving full time as a pastor in Brooklyn, New York, and no one in the congregation, except for the president, knew that he was engaged in such graduate work. Raymond did much of his studying as he traveled on the subway from Brooklyn to the Bronx, and back home again.

Raymond's zeal for the Lord was seen even in his walking. He did this for exercise, to be sure, as a good steward of the body God had given him. However, he started such walking in Brooklyn also to save money. His congregation gave him a transportation allowance, but instead of driving, he would walk and use the subway, so that he could use his transportation allowance to buy books.

In addition, God used the name "Brave Warrior" for Raymond God raised him up to be a courageous fighter against the Historical-Critical Method, which had infiltrated our synod, and caused unrest in the '60s and '70s. Raymond stood firm on the inspiration and inerrancy of Scripture. He upheld the hermeneutical principles of the Reformation of the Lutheran Confessions.

Finally, God used the name "Prolific One" in calling Raymond to His service. Raymond was a true, and most productive, scholar. His prolific reading has already been alluded to, and this aided him in his writing. What a prolific writer he was: Books, and hundreds of articles, spanning a broad range of subjects! Through his writings his influence continues today. By God's grace, he maintained his scholarly productivity well into his later years. All of his writings had either a direct or indirect connection with the Word of God, and so ultimately to Jesus Christ.

In fact, the theme running throughout Raymond's life, in his various roles, was Jesus — who has the name which is above every other name. Raymond lived, taught, preached, wrote about Christ, the promised Messiah of the Old Testament, the seed of Adam and Eve, the Son of God, the Savior of the world, who lives and reigns to all eternity.

In this way, Raymond's life is a witness to us, and an encouragement. Here was a humble, yet mighty servant of God. We see how a person called by God belonging to God, and motivated and empowered by God through His Word and Sacrament, can be a fruitful tree for the Lord, in whatever position God has placed him or her. Raymond's life is testimony to the veracity of Ps. 1, which likens the godly person, who meditates on God's Word, to a tree: "He shall be like a tree planted by the rivers of water that brings forth its fruit in its season, whose leaf also shall not wither." We are reminded, too, of Ps. 92, which says of believers, "They shall still bear fruit in old age; they shall be fresh and flourishing, to declare that the Lord is upright."

Therefore, at this funeral service of Raymond Surburg we say, "Hallelujah." Raymond would have liked that. "Hallelujah" is a good Hebrew, Old Testament term meaning "Praise Yahweh" - "Yahweh" being the covenant name of the God of Israel, the one true God, the God of salvation.

Hallelujah! - that God called Raymond, and us, by name. Hallelujah! - that God says to Raymond, and to us, "You are mine." Hallelujah! – that God saves us, and enables us to serve Him. Hallelujah! Amen.

Questions

1. Salvation is an ____ matter.
2. Surburg would have been the first to confess ____.
3. Surburg took great comfort in ____.
4. Surburg was zealous for ____.
5. Surburg earned his PH.D. while serving as ____.
6. His transportation allowance was used for ____.
7. He was a courageous fighter against ____ Method.
8. God used the name ____ in calling Surburg to His service.
9. Surburg's influence today continues through his ____.
10. The theme running through Surburg's life was ____.
11. Hallelujah means ____.

Index

Names

Abraham – 592
Adam – 1235
Adams, James Edward – 1256,1288
Albright, W. F. – 445
Allan, Robert S. – 369
Allegro, John – 771,1438,1445
Alleman, Herbert C. – 219
Allen, Robert S. – 477
Allis, Dr. Oswald – 469,1235
Allison, Dr. B. Gray – 491
Althaus, Paul – 928,1745
Anderson, Bernhard W. – 404,841
Anderson, David – 1365,1369,1377
Anderson, Ray Sherman – 511
Ankerberg, John – 325
Aquinas, Thomas – 1515,1545
Archer, Gleason – 469,477,506
Armstrong, Herbert W. – 1605
Arndt, William – 266,313,386,542,557,
 563,686, 930,1236,1369,1463,1468,
 1477
Augustin, Cardinal Bea – 1540
Augustine – 1254
Aulen, Gustav – 597,927
Bach, Johann Sebastian –
 1167,1195,1365
Barry, George Duncan – 1254
Barth, Karl – 238,370,386,1368,1632
Bartling, Walter – 315,1291,1292
Bavinck, Herman – 507
Beasley-Murray, G. R. – 498
Beck, John Tobias – 57
Beck, William – 128,310,322,452,580,
 1859
Becker, Dr. Siegbert – 1859
Beecher, William – 83
Beethoven, Ludwig von – 1365
Belshazzar – 443
Berkhof, L. – 1003,1779
Berkhouwer, G. C. – 384
Bertermann, Dr. Eugene – 1293
Bertram, Robert – 1291
Bishop Pike – 371
Blecker, L. – 213
Boer, Harry – 485
Bohlmann, Ralph – 33,59,515,686,1293
Boice, James Montgomery – 477,506
Bonhoeffer, Dietrich – 890,1632

Borg, Marcus – 1612
Bornkamm, Guenther – 594
Boss, Edgar W. – 1301
Boswell, John – 1489
Bouman, Herbert J.A. – 59
Bousset, Wilhelm – 1537
Braaten, Carl – 403,596,929, 1756
Bratcher, Robert – 497
Brekke, Milo, L. – 10
Brennan, Justice – 1414
Bretscher, Paul G. – 365,473
Briggs, Charles Augustus – 26,372
Bring, Ragner – 51
Bromiley, Geofrey – 506
Broomall, Wick – 1015
Brown, Raymond – 1540,1546
Brown, Robert McAfee – 373
Bruce, F. F. – 384,434,1476
Brueckner, Robert M. – 432,452,458
Brunner, Emil – 62,497,503,922,1369
Buddha – 593,1371,1612
Bultmann, Rudolf – 221,238,240,242,
 354,593,840,863,890,929,1252,1455,
 1637
Burrows, Millar – 34,1000
Burtschaell, James – 381
Buszin, Walter – 1208
Caapari, C. P. – 1435
Caemmerer, Richard – 686
Cain, Marvin F. – 437,451
Calixt, Georg – 1276
Calvin, John – 1622
Carnell, E. J. – 384
Carroll, B. H. – 497
Carter, Nicholas – 1452,1473
Caspari, W. – 213
Cassian, John – 1042
Cassuto, U. – 469
Charles V – 78
Chemnitz, Martin – 32
Christ – 955,1475,1656
Chrysostom – 794
Clark, Gordon Haddon – 503
Coffin, William Sloan – 373
Colson, Howard P. – 369
Confucius – 1371
Conzelmann, Hans – 841
Criswell, Dr. W. A. – 491
Cullmann, Oscar – 240

Cwirla, William – 1298
Cyrus (King) – 270
Daane, James – 401,485,510
Danby, H. – 258
Daniel – 437,449,1509
Danker, Fred – 315,686
Darby, John Nelson – 1814
Darius of Mede – 444
Darwin, Charles – 362,1339
David – 290,316,318
Davidman, Helen Joy – 1298
Davies, A. Powell – 1438
Davis, Richard – 534
Dayton, Donald W. – 395,480
De Koster, Dr. Lester – 484
Delitzsch, Franz – 741,1433,1434,1500
Dentam, R. – 315
Dewey, John – 786
Dittes, James, E. – 10
Dobshansky, Theodosius – 1421
Dodd, C. H. – 497
Driver, S. R. – 446
Duncan, D. – 325
Dunn, Henry – 781
Dupont-Sommer – 1438,1445
Durr, L. – 213
Dwyer, Robert J. – 1249
Dyer, Charles – 1812
Ebeling, Gerhard – 239
Ebrard – 1275
Eckhardt, Ernst – 310
Edersheim, Alfred – 258
Edwards, David L. – 892
Ehlen, Arlis – 315,366
Eichhorn, Albert – 1537
Eichrodt, W. – 213,315
Elder, Dr. John – 1607
Elert, Werner – 928,1745
Elford, George – 10
Elijah – 1186
Elliott, J. Keith – 891
Engelder, Theodore – vii,306,322,1756, 1827
Engnell, I. – 212
Erasmus – 25,79
Essenes – 1438,1440
Eve – 1235
Faberberg, Holstem – 29
Fahling, Adam – 1242,1477
Farrar, Dean – 26
Feinberg – 273
Ferre, Nels – 243,857,895
Filson, Floyd – 1560

Fink, Ronald – 452
Fitzmyer, Joseph – 1546
Fleming, Ambrose – 599
Forde, Dr. Gerhard O. – 893,892
Fosdick, Harry Emerson – 372
Frame, John M. – 376
Francisco, Clyde – 498
Franzmann, Martin – 1291,686
Fretheim, Terrence E. – 461
Frey, John D. – 386,557
Friberg, H. Daniel – 1291
Fritz, J. H. C. – 686,1710
Fuchs, Ernst – 139
Fuerbringer, Alfred – 686
Fuerbringer, Ludwig – vii,263,306,309, 563,686,1509
Fuller, Charles E. – 375,501
Fuller, Daniel – 370,502,510
Fuller, Reginald – 517
Gabler, John Philip – 1503
Gadamer – 239
Gaebelein – 273
Gaenssle, Dr. – 463
Gast, William – 1293
Gaussen, L. – 1250
Geissler, Dr. Norman – 325,506
Gerhard, Johann – 32,1003
Gerstner, John – 376,477,506
Giessler, Phillip B. – 1856,1860
Glock, C. Y. – 9
Gloege, Dr. Gerhard – 594,1368
Glueck, Nelson – 1470
God - 1638,1759
Goppelt, Leonard – 319
Gordon, Dr. Cyrus – 459
Graebner, Augustus Lawrence – 306, 322,563
Graebner, O. – 306
Graebner, Theodore – 686,1287
Graesser – 315
Grant, Frederick C. – 62.381,1253
Grasser – 686
Gray, James – 785
Greene, Dr. L. – 1293
Greenleaf, Simon – 598
Gresham Machen, J. – 356,371
Gressman, Hugo – 212,1537
Grotius, Hugo – 1277
Grounds, Vernon – 1560
Gruber, L. Franklin – 89
Gunkel, Hermann – 212,244,461,1537
Habel, Norman – 315,1731
Hadden, J. K. – 9

Haley – 1477
Hall, Robert Jr. – 1355
Halley, Henry – 325
Hals, 1731
Hamman, Henry – 472,1298
Handel, Friedrich – 1130,1167,1217
Hanke, Howard A. - 325
Hanson – 1731
Harnack, Theodosius – 58,1387
Harris, R. Laird R. – 1251
Harrison, Everett F. – 369
Harrison, M. – 890,891
Harrison, R. K. – 441,46
Harrisville, Dr. Roy – 895
Hase, Gerhard – 1001
Hay, Charles A. – 603
Haydn, Joseph – 1216
Hebert – 315
Heck, Joel D. – 1298
Hefner, Philip J. – 1746
Hegel, Friedrich – 1280
Hegel, Wilhelm – 1506
Heidegger – 843
Heitmueller, Wilhelm – 1537
Heldebrand – 718
Hendricks, William L. – 489
Hengstenberg, Ernst Wilhelm – 57, 1499
Hengstenberg, William – 1434
Henry, Carl F.H. – 369,379,402,478, 481
Herod – 1474
Herring, Ralph A. – 488
Hitler, Adolph – 1633
Hobbs, Herschel H. – 488
Hodge, Charles – vii
Hoeneckes, Adolf – 124
Hoffmann, Dr. Oswald – 643
Hoffstein, C. E. – 603
Hofmann, J.C.K. – 315
Hollyfield, Noel W. – 499
Holmer, Paul – 1312
Homrighausen, Dr. Elmer – 360
Horne, H. H. – 785
Horton, Walter Marshall – 243
Hovey, Alvah – 362
Hoyer, Theodore – 686
Hubbard, Dr. David – 370,374,474,502
Hubble, Edwin P. – 1421
Hughes, John Jay – 1248,1289
Hull, William E. – 477,497
Hummel, Horace – 319-321,323,469
Huxley, Thomas H. – 1423

Isaiah – 989,942
Jacobs, Charles M. – 147
Jacobs, Henry E. – 603
Janzow, Walter, T. – 9
Jefferson, Thomas - 1387
Jeremiah - 265
Jeremias, Alfred – 1026
Jeremias, J. – 258
Jerome – 680
Jeske, Dr. Richard – 892,896
Jess, John D. – 1274
Jesus – 432,1080,1371,1759
Jewett, Dr. Paul King – 370,486,503
John the Baptist – 771,942
Johnson, Arthur L. – 10,212
Johnstone, Maury – 1490
Jonah – 393,1237
Jones, Peter R. – 315,376,686
Josephus – 433,1457,1474
Judas Maccabaeus – 1173
Jungkuntz, Richard – 33,1292
Kadai, Heino – 1291
Kaiser, Walter C. – 325
Kalin, Everet - 315
Kallas, James – 1730,1731
Kant, Immanuel – 54
Kantzer, Kenneth – 477,506,1252
Karsten, Ernst – 387
Kauffeld, Eugene P. – 325
Keil, K. F. – 1431
Keller, Walter E. – 365,797
Kelly, Page H. – 498
Kersten, Lawrence, L. – 9
Keyser, Leander S. – 1020
Kiehl, Dr. Erich – 1293
Kierkegaard, Soren – 497
Kilby, Clyde – 1305
King, Martin Luther – 1377
Kitchen, K. A. – 447
Klann, Richard – 686,1293
Klassen, Ben – 1473
Klausner, J. – 543
Kleinhans – 797
Klingermann – 943
Kloha, Jeffrey – 891
Koch, Henry – vi,83
Kraft, Charles – 511
Kramer, Fred – 32
Kretzmann, Dr. Martin – 1287,1288
Kretzmann, Paul E. – vii,306,310,322, 543,563, 586,686,1025,1034,1685
Kretzschmann, T.W. – 219
Kuemmel, Werner George – 929

Kung, Hans – 1367
Kuske, David – 1859
Ladd, George – 384,502
Laetsch, Theodore – vii,306,308,322, 686
Lake, Kirsop – 1568
Lampe, G.W.H. – 315
Lamsa, G. M. – 1269,1507
Lapide, Pinchas – 1370
Larson, Martin A. – 1437
Latourette – 1536
Le Roy, E. E. – 1543
Lefebvre, Marcel – 1540,1559
Leo XIII – 1541
Leupold, H. C. – 442
Lewis, C. S. – 1298,1299
Lewis, Edwin – 208
Lewis, Jack P. – 442
Lewis, John M. – 495
Lindsell, Dr. Harold – 355,369,1252
Lindsey, Hal – 1812
Lockyer, Hebert – 325
Loisy, A. – 1543
Lönning – 886
Lucian – 1475
Luck, C. – 273
Ludwig, Emil – 543
Lueker, Erwin – 686
Luoma, J. K. – 19
Luthardt, E. – 58
Luther, Martin – vii,74,147,170,180, 225,581, 676,1094
Macgregor, G. H. C. – 922
Machen, J. Greshen – 1537
Mack, Edward – 208
Magdalene, Mary – 602
Maier, Dr. Walter III – 437,895,1860, 1865
Maier, Walter A., Sr. – vii,35,306, 309,322, 469, 583,587,686
Manly, Basil – 493,497
Manske – 1528
Marquart, Kurt – v, vii,890,1292
Martin, Ralph P. – 511
Marty, Dr. Martin – 355,391,1632
Marx, Karl – 74
Mary – 587
Matthew – 1245
Mayer, F. E. – 1706
Mayer, Herbert – 1286
McCall, Duke – 390,490
McDowell, Josh – 1345,1365
McNeil, Father John – 1490

McQuilken, Dr. J. Robertson – 511
Melanchthon – 40
Mendelssohn, Felix – 1181
Mendenhall, George – 746
Menking – 1525
Mennicke, Victor – 32,311,689
Messiah – 1172
Metzger, Bruce – 384
Meyer, Dr. Dale – 643
Micah – 939,948
Miller, H. S. – 408
Mitchell, Timothy A. – 1558
Moellering, H. Armin – 1291
Mohammad – 1371,1476,1576
Mohr, George – 1293
Montgomery, Dr. John Warwick - 355, 376,1290,1456,1485
Moody, Dr. Dale – 498
Moon, Sun Myung – 1605
Moore, Mrs. Jamie – 1298
Morgan, C. – 273
Morgan, G. Campbell – 783
Morphew, Clark – 114,1612,1769
Morris, Henry – 1354,1419,1424
Morrison, Frank – 599
Morton, R. F. – 784
Moses – 337
Mounce, Robert – 371
Mowinckel, Sigmund – 221
Mueller, John Theodore – 69,295,306, 307,322, 686,1698
Mueller, Prof. Max – 121,1353,1361
Murphy, Roland – 1546
Myers, Edith – 354
Nafzger, Samuel H. – 1806
Neiswender, Donald R. – 1291
Nelson, Byron C. – 220
Neuhaus, Richard – 387
Newman, Barclay – 496
Nichols, David R. – 474
Nida, Eugene – 712
Niebuhr, Reinhold – 1633
Niemoeller, Martin – 1633
Nobile, Phillip – 1315
Noth, Martin – 315
Ockenga, Dr. Harold J. – 355,369,391
Ogden, S. H. – 243
Ohlendorf, Ray R. – v
Opik, Ernst J. – 1421
Orr, James – 355
Otten, Herman – v,vii,124,890,1291, 1692
Packer, J. I. – 376,506

Packer, James I. – 477
Pagels, Dr. Elaine – 1315
Palmer, Earl – 474
Palmer, Edwin H. – 484
Pannenberg – 595
Pannenberg, Wolfgang – 1550
Pardiek – 306,322
Pasteur, Louis – 1421
Payne, J. Barton – 325,449,1003
Peerman, Dean – 1632
Pelikan, Jaroslav – 79,1375
Petigru, James – 494
Petreus, Johann – 85
Pfeiffer, Charles – 771
Pfeiffer, Robert – 1439
Philippi, F. A. – 1435
Phillips, Marshal Alan – 1489
Pieper, Francis August Otto – vii,63,
    306,307,322,538,585,686,1650,1745
Pieper, Reinhold – 312
Pieper, Walter C. – 1698
Piepkorn, Dr. Arthur C. – 1268
Pinnock, Clark – 356,376,402,481
Piper, Otto A. – 210
Pius XII – 1543,1545,1553
Plagens, G. – 1407
Plass, Ewald – 159,337
Polack, wg – 686
Pope Leo XIII – 1255
Pope Paul VI – 1266
Pope Pius IX – 141
Pope Pius XIII – 1540
Pope, W. B. – 1502
Potter, Charles – 1438
Prenter, Regin – 596,1746
Preus, Christian – 23
Preus, David – 386
Preus, Dr. J.A.O. – 33,368,387,452,
    1256,1289
Preus, Dr. Robert – 45,312,323,324,
    366,472,506,686,753,1859,1291,
    1293,1859
Preus, Ed – 123
Provan, Charles – 1468
Quebedeaux, Dr. Richard – 513
Rambachan – 115
Ramm, Bernard – 474,481,1698
Ratzinger, Josef – 1554
Rehnquist, Justice – 1414
Reimnitz, Elmer – 1293
Repp, Arthur – 315,686
Reu, Martin – 148,422,603
Reumann, John – 927

Reynolds, Diane – 1642
Richardson, Alan – 33,1252
Robertson, A.T. – 390,497,1061
Robinson, Dr. Edward – 1241
Robinson, James M. – 921
Robinson, John A. T. – 630,1257
Roehrs, Walter – 315,316,323,686,
    1291
Roensch, Dr. Manfred – 1293
Rogers, Jack – 474,506
Rosenberg, Alfred – 403
Rosenthal, Franz – 447
Rowley, H. H. – 1000
Rowley, J. H. – 772
Runia, Dr. K. – 244
Rutherford, Samuel – 507
Saffen, Wayne – 452
Saint James – 831
Saint Philip – 831
Sampey, John R. – 390,494
Samson – 1172
Sasse, Hermann – 123,1291,1293
Saul – 1171
Scalia, Justice Antonia – 1414
Schaeffer, Francis A. – 477,478,506,
    1293
Schaff, Phillip – 1274
Scharlemann – 686
Scharlemann, Dr. Robert – 894,896
Scharlemann, Martin – 515
Scherer, James, A. – 19
Schleiermacher, Friedrich Daniel –
    56,1387,1507
Schmid, Heinrich – 603
Schuetz, Heinrich – 1215
Schuller, Robert – 546
Schweitzer, Albert – 540,1387
Schweitzer, W. – 33
Schwiebert, Ernest - 173
Scofield, C. I. – 541
Scott, E. F. – 211
Seeberg, Reinhold – 62
Segal, J. B. – 258,469,470
Sellin, E. – 213
Shanks, Hershel – 1448
Shehan, Lawrence Cardinal – 1540
Sheppard, Gerald T. – 478,512
Shinn, Roger – 1640
Smith, Wilbur M. – 208,369,384,592
Sohn – 1287
Sohns, Wilbert – 1293
Sommer, Du Pont – 771
Somner, Martin – 1287

Sproul, R. C. – 376,477,506
Spurgeon, Charles Haddon – 203,356
St. Jerome – 197
St. Jude – 898
St. Luke – 897
St. Mark – 830
St. Matthias – 805,1095
St. Paul – 800,1092,1183
St. Peter – 798
St. Simon – 898
St. Timothy – 801,1090
St. Titus – 803
Stagg, Frank – 496
Stalsett, Gunnar – 1293
Stark, R. – 9
Starr, William S. – 486
Stauderman, Albert – 385
Staus, D. F. – 1280
Steinmueller, John E. – 895,1249,1551
Stewart, Don – 1345
Stoeckhardt, Dr. George –
    vii,306,322,563,1433, 1698
Strommen, Merton, P. – 10
Strossmayer, Josef – 144
Stump, Joseph – 603,932
Suetonius – 1475
Sullivan, Dr. John – 701
Surburg, Dr. Raymond F. – v,353,405,
    437,449,472,679,839,988,1229,1291,
    1298,1374,1437,1467,1530,1649,1856,
    1862
Tacitus – 1475
Tate, Marvin E. – 498
Taylor, Vincent – 629
Terry, Milton – 25
Tessman, Alfred – 1293
Thielicke, Helmut – 923
Thompson, Frank C. – 325
Thompson, Fred P. – 483
Tietjen, Dr. John – viii,365,373,1230,
    1248
Titus – 1092
Toland, John – 1278
Townsend, Cameron – 712
Tyrrell, G. – 1543
Underwager, Ralph – 10
Unger, Merrill – 273,469
Van Bruggen – 719
Van Til, Dr. Cornelius – 485,1637
Vasady, Bela – 505
Vilmar, August – 1435
Vine – 273
Vischer – 337

Voegtle - 925
Von Harnack, Adolf – 403,840
Von Hoffmann, J.C.K. – 58,317
Von Rad, Gerhard – 315,841,999
Von Rohr Sauer, Alfred – 229,314,315,
    686
Von Schenk, Berthold – 890
Vriezen – 999
Wagner, Alvin E. – 1293
Walther, C. F. W. – vii,32,55,305,394,
    562,585, 686,1285
Walvoord, John F. - 394
Warfield, Benjamin –
    vii,136,325,356,1252
Warth, Prof. – 1293
Weber, Edwin C. – 1293
Weiss, Dr. Bernhard – 522
Weiss, Johannes – 1537
Weldon, John – 325
Wenger, Frederick – 312
Wengert – 315
Wenthe, Dean O. - 1861
Werning, Waldo J. – 1293
Westermann, Claus – 220
Weyehauser, C. David – 370
Widengren, G. – 212
Wiederaenders, Dr. Roland – 1289
Wilhelm, Georg – 1280
Williams, Donald – 498
Williamson, Bishop Richard – 1540,
    1558
Wilson, Clifford – 467
Wilson, Edmund – 771,1438
Wilson, Ian – 1369
Wilson, Robert Dick – 469,1468
Winrod, Gordon – 195,667
Wolff, Hans W. – 315,404
Wollenburg, George – 1293
Woods, Bryant T. – 1470
Woolcombe, K. J. – 315
Wright, C. F. W. – 1699
Wright, J. S. – 435
Wunderlich, Lorenz – 686,1832
Yamauchi, Edwin – 449,1447
Ylvisaker, Johs – 1242,1477
Young, Dr. Edward – 230,361,398,
    439,449,1508, 1674,1679
Zechariah – 260, 265,270
Zimmerli, Walther – 315,404
Zimmerman, Paul – 1293,1420
Zwingli, Ulrich – 69

Subjects

1 Peter 3:18 – 1752

A Christian Handbook on Vital Issues – 1291

A Mighty Fortress – 202

A Project of Biblical Hermeneutics – 1292

A Study of Generations – 10,19,371, 1710

A. J. Holman Company – 1407

Abiding Word – 1287

Abiding Word, The – 32,563,688

Abortion – 1847

Abrahamic Messianic Covenant – 289

Acts – 152,183,1831

Advent – 910,939,955

Advent and Christmas Hymns – 1071

AELC – 129

Age of the Universe – 1421

All Saints Day – 900

Allegorical – 28

Allegorization – 567

Allegory – 658

Almah – 225,229,316,321

Amos – 105

An American Translation – 128,311, 580,1859

Analogy of Faith – 715

Anatomy of an Explosion – 1292

Angel of the Lord – 295

Angelology – 526

Angels – 601, 1733

Animals – 1343

Annunciation – 814

Anti-Christ – 669, 1819

Anti-Semitic – 667

Apocrypha – 1323

Apologetics – 1272, 1284

Apology of the Augsburg Confession – 39

Apostles' Creed – 1120

Aramaic – 447, 1409

Archaeology – 740

Armageddon – 1819

Arminianism – 23,1706

Ascension – 832, 920,1106

Ascension Day – 988,1048

Asceticism – 1520

Ash Wednesday – 810, 1026

Assumption – 143

Assumption of Moses – 435

Athanasian Creed – 890, 1121

Atonement – 1684

Augsburg – 10

Augsburg Confession – 1622

Augsburg Confession, The – 364

Augsburg Publishing House – 473

Baal or God – vii,1298,1692

Babi – 1525

Bach Revival – 1191

Baha'u'llah – 1526

Bahaism – 1525

Banner, The – 484

Baptism – 797,1115,1116

Baptist Hymnal – 489

Barmen Declaration – 1633

Battle for the Bible, The – 355,374,476

Beagle Voyage – 1339

Beatitudes – 534,544

Beck's Bible – 1329

Beck's translation – 393,607

Benedictus – 1074

Bethula – 229,230

Bible – 23

Bible in the Balance – 472

Bible Translations – 712

Biblical miracles – 12

Bigotry – 1468

Bondage of the Will, The – 337

Book of Enoch – 1439

Book of Joshua – 1547

Bow-wow theory – 1350

Brief Statement, The – 363

Broadman Press – 495

Buchmanism – 1605

Buddhism – 119, 1612

Calvinism – 23,1706

Canate – 829

Canon – 432

Canonical Books – 189

Catholic Biblical Association of America – 1544

Celibacy – 1520

Celibate – 1401

Cemetery – 164

Centenary Translation of the New Testament – 1778

Chalcedon – 1122

Charismatic Movement – 16

Chochmah – 420

Christ Myth – 1454

Christ Seminary in Exile – 133

Christ's Resurrection - 1366

Christian Century – 477

Christian Dogmatics – 928

Christian News – 1272, 1291, 1547

Christian Reformed Church – 483

Christian Science – 23; 1605

Christianity – 911; 1468, 1530

Christianity Today – 355
Christianity's Unknown Gospel – 473
Christmas – 910, 955, 1535
Christmas Prophecies – 939
Christmas Texts – 976
Christology – 337, 1501
Christos – 1187
Church – 1521
Church and Ministry – 324
Church Music – 1212
Church of the Reformation – 1029
Church Year – 793
Circumcision – 1079
Civil Year – 795
Closed Communion – 1806
Colossians – 186
Columbia University – vi
Commission on Theology and Church
    Relations – vii,32,33,1291
Communication Theory – 713
Conception – 1849
Concordia Cyclopedia – 40, 1434,1499
Concordia Self-Study Commentary –
    586
Concordia Seminary, St. Louis – viii,
    686,1229
Concordia Theological Monthly – 463,
    686
Concordia Theological Seminary, Ft.
    Wayne - 1860
Confessional Lutheran, The – 1290
Confucianism – 119
Confusion of Language – 1360
Confutation – 39
Conservative Reformation and its The-
    ology – 1627
Contradictions – 1463,1477
Coptic Brotherhood International –
    1335
Coptic Church – 1333
Coptic Gnostic Texts – 1315
Coptic Language – 1334
Cost of Discipleship – 1635
Council of Presidents – 1289
Counterfeit Gospel – 1452
Creator's Tapestry, The – 323
Creeds – 1120
Cresset, The – 365
Crisis in Lutheran Theology – 1291
Cross – 1377
CTCR – 303,322
Currents in Theology and Mission –
    892
Daniel – 104

Dead Sea Scrolls – 770,1437,1478
Death – 159
Demthologization – 850
Der Heiland – 308
Der Lutheraner – 1287
Descent into Hell – 1756
Deuteronomy – 96,746
Devil – 14,1728
Dia – 1779
Dialog – 129,892-894,896
Dibelius – 535
Didaskalia – 416
Ding-dong theory – 1350
Direct Prophecy – 235
Dispensation – 1823
Dispensationalism – 1812
Divino Afflunte Spiritu – 683,1250,
    1541,1543, 1544
Divorce – 1521
Doctrine – 1662
Documentary Hypothesis – 458,865,
    1232
Domino Effect – 1716
Douay Bible – 682
Dutch Catechism – 923
Dynamic Equivalence – 712,720
Easter – 825,1024,1098
Easter Controversy – 1365
Ebla – 467,745
Ecclesiastes – 98,99
Ecclesiastical Music – 1167
Ecclesiastical Year – 795
Ecclesiology – 529
Ecumenical Century – 1287
Eisegesis – 462
ELCA – 1769
Ephesians – 185
Epiphany – 793,1043,1087
Epistles of Saint John – 188
Erlangen School – 58
Essene – 1531
ESV – vii
Ethical Concerns – 1725
Eucharist – 1311,1398
Evangelical Counsels – 1519
Evangelical Lutheran Church – 170
Evangelicals – 356
Evangelism – 905
Evolution – vii,1289,1414,1453
Evolutionists – 1349
Exaudi – 833
Exegesis – 462,747
Existentialism – 842
Exodus – 96

Ezekiel – 102, 103
Family – 1520
Flood – 1229,1234
Form criticism – 25,461
Formula of Concord – 1755
Forty-four – 1287
Forum Letter – 387
From Atheism to Christianity – 1298
Fuller Theological Seminary – 369,374
Fullness of Time – 607,959
Fundamentalism – vii,388,400
Fundamentals, The – 400
Galatians – 185
Galatians 4:4 – 607
Gathering Storm in the Churches, The – 9
Genealogies – 910,959
Genesis – 424,578
Genesis 3:15 – vii,95,207,1551,1589
Genesis 4:1 – vii
Genesis Commentary – 79
Geneva Bible – 1329
Gloria in Excelsis – 1075
Gnosticism – 1273
God and Gender – 1374
God's Word: Today's Bible Translation – 1777
Good Friday – 1028
Good News Bible – 720
Gospel – 149,182,345
Gulf War – 1812
Habakkuk – 107
Haggai – 109
Half-Known God, The – 1832
Heart – 551
Hebrews – 118
Heilsgeschichte – 313,419
Hell – 1751
Hermeneutical Principles – 28
Hermeneutics – 32,67,238,562,753
Hermeneutics Committee – 1291
Higher Criticism – 650,1507,1546,1554
Higher Things – 1298
Hinduism – 119
Historical Critical Method – 132,763, 921,1289, 1728
Historical-Grammatical Method – 23,132,657
Hoax – 1473
Holy Monday – 1027
Holy Scriptures – 1679
Holy Spirit – 523,1058,1113,1786,1831
Holy Thursday – 1621
Holy Trinity – 1119

Holy Tuesday – 1028
Holy Week – 815
Homo loquens – 1350
Homosexuality – 1489,1725
Hosea – 104
Humani Generis – 1545
Humanism – 1416
Humiliation – 906
Hymnal – 78
I Corinthians – 184
I Timothy – 186
Identity Crisis – 18
II Corinthians – 185
II Epistle to Timothy – 187
II Peter – 188
Immaculate Conception – 143
Immanuel – 946
Incarnation – 578,607
Inerrancy – vii,358,401,474,502,1229, 1248
Infallibility – 138,144
Inspiration – 1289,1574
Inspiration and Canonicity of the Bible – 1251
International Center of Confessional Studies - 1649
Is – 1802
Isagogical Views – 94
Isaiah – 101
Isaiah 53 – 1153
Isaiah 7:14 – 225,228,234,944
Isaiah 9:5-6 – 321
Islam – 1525,1572,1605,1607
Isogogics – 643,646
Israel – 1816,1818
Israel in Egypt – 1170
Jainism – 119
James – 152
Jehovah Witnesses – 1605
Jeremiah – 102,118
Jerome Biblical Commentary – 925, 1540,1545, 1547,15551
Jerusalem Bible – 1547
Jesus Seminar – 1612
Jesus Through the Centuries – 1375
Jewish Book – 723
Jews – 345,723
Job – 97,425
Joel – 105
Jonah – 106
Journal of Historical Review – 1437
Jubilate – 829
Judaism – 119,1587
Jude – 152,190

Judgment of God – 1360
Judiasm – 723
Judica - 815
Justification – 14,44,85,1516,1777
Justification by Faith – 41,288
Kersten Study – 1710
Kingdom of God – 547
Knowledge – 1666
Koran – 1476
Kotholischer Kurz Kathechismus – 1389
Lambentabilis Sane Exitu – 1542
Lampra – 825
Language – 1266
Law & Gospel – 571
Law/Gospel Dichotomy – 1695
Lehre und Wehre – 33,1286
Lent – 810,1024
Lesbianism – 1489,1725
Leviticus – 96,1688
Liberal Lutherans – 114
Liberal Theology – 1761
Liberalism – 141
Liberty Bell – 1452,1467,1468
Life – 1662
Life after death – 13
Light - 1044
Ligonier Statement – 376
Limbus Patrum – 1753
Logos - 955
Lord's Supper – 1621,1796
Love – 1519
Loyal Lutheran – 1374
Luke's Gospel – 1071
Luther's Attitude Toward Scripture – 62
Lutheran Book of Worship – 449
Lutheran Brotherhood – 10
Lutheran Church in America – 219
Lutheran Church Year – 1032
Lutheran Church-Missouri Synod
    (LCMS) -18,32, 128,129,132,363,
    396,606,515,1697
Lutheran Congress – 1292
Lutheran Cyclopedia – 32
Lutheran Hour – 643
Lutheran Orthodoxy – 1195
Lutheran Perspective – 515
Lutheran Reformation – 122
Lutheran Witness – 432,1287
Lutheran Witness Reporter – 386
Lutheran World Federation – 593
Lutheran, The – 385
Lutheranism – 23
Malachi – 109
Malicious desertion – 1521

Manual of Disciple – 1442
Marburg Colloquium – 1621
Mary's Magnificat – 1073
Matthew's Genealogy – 910
Maundy Thursday – 1028
Means of Grace – 1624,1651
Messiah, The – 1217
Messianic Prophecy – 205,207,313,957
Metaphysics – 80
Method in the Study of the Bible – 781
Micah – 106
Millennial – 273
Millennial Darwinism – 23
Millennialism – 1812
Misericordias Domini – 829
Mission Board – 1288
Mission Festival - 904
Missions – 13
Missouri District – 323
Missouri Synod – 1284
Mithraism – 1534
Modernism – 1543
Monogenesis – 1356
Monotheistic religious – 998
Mormonism – 23
Mormons – 1601
Mosaic Authorship – 95,1230
Mount Olive Discourse – 625
Muratorian Canon – 1462
Music – 1130
Mythologization – 1637
Nahum – 107
National Association of Evangelicals –
    483
National Catholic Register – 1249
Naturalism – 1418
Nazism – 1633
Neo-evangelical – 474
New American Bible – 1547
New Berkeley Bible – 581
New Berkeley Version – 947
New Catholic Commentary – 1544
New Catholic Encyclopedia – 1540
New Catholic Encyclopedia, The – 19
New Hampshire Confession of Faith –
    487
New International Version – 484,581
New Testament – 151
New World Translation – 1778
News and Views – 1291
News Sentinel – 1525
Newsweek – 1540
Nicene Creed – 1120
Non-Christian Religions – 114

Numbers – 96
Nunc Dimittis – 1076
Obadiah – 106
Objective – 975
Old Catholic Church – 142
Old Missouri – vi
Old Testament – 149,286,304,337,403, 840,863, 998,1004,1638,1728
Oratorio – 1131,1212
Origin of Language – 1348
Origin of Life – 1421
Origin of Man – 1423
Origin of Paul's Religion – 1537
Origin of Speech – 1350
Origin of the Universe – 1419
Original Languages – 694
Origins of Christianity – 1452
Orthodoxism – 52
Outlook, The – 484
Paideia – 418
Paleontological Record – 1344
Palm Sunday – 1027
Papacy – 138
Parables – 637
Paraclete – 344
Pascha – 826
Passion Week – 1027
Passover – 247
Peacemakers – 551
Penance – 1399
Pentateuch – 452,1229
Pentecost – 825,834,1113,1786,1831
Persecutions – 345
Perspecuity – 566
Perspicuity of Scriptures – 71
Pesharim – 1442
Peshitta – 578,1270
Peshitta Bible – 1409
Peter – 187
Philemon – 187
Philippians – 186
Physical Death – 1403
Pietism – 52,1207
Poh-pooh theory – 1351
Polemics – 1272,1284
Polygenesis – 1356
Pope – 138
Popular Symbolics – 1698
Postal System – 613
Post-Reformation Theology of Lutheranism – 756
Prayer – 1519,1649
Prayers for the Dead – 1310
Predestination – 1851

Prefaces – 94
Premillennialist – 501
Presbyterian – 1293
Presentation – 804
Princeton Religious Research Center – 1650
Pro Ecclesia – 1558
Process Theology – 595
Prophecy – 324
Protestant Reformation – 24
Prot-evangelium – 1589
Proverbs – 98
Providentissimus Deus – 1541
Psalm 16 – 322
Psalm 22 – 290,322
Psalm 46 – 201
Psalm 8 – vii,322,468
Psalms – 97,1654,1739
Psychoanalysis – 1455
Purgatory – 159,1310,1403
Quartodecimans – 826
Quasimodogeniti – 829
Qumran – 770,1441,1572
Rationalism – 1207,1506
Reformation – 134,170,899,1001
Reformation Sunday – 1513
Reformed – 1621
Reformed Journal, The – 484
Repristination theology – 1505
Resolution 3-09 – vii
Resurrection – 290,592,1098,1550,1559, 1598,1638
Resurrection of Christ – 1769
Revelation – 154,190,522,1289,1291
Revelation 20 – 1814
Revised Standard Version – 1355,1489
Revisionist – 1468
Rheims Bible – 682
Rogate – 829
Roman Catholic – 47,353,381,587
Roman Catholic Biblical scholars – 1249
Roman Catholic Biblical Studies – 1541
Roman Catholic Church – 140
Roman Catholic Ethics – 1513
Roman Catholic Short Catechism – 1389
Roman Confutation – 30
Roman Empire – 1484
Romanism – 23
Romans – 183
Romans 3:28 – 85
Rome – 153
Rosicrucianism - 1605
Roto Magazine – 1315
Ryrie Study Bible – 633

Sacraments – 14
Salvation – 346
Sanctification – 14
Satan – 1728
Schwan Foundation – 1298
Scofield Reference Bible – 633,1741
Second Servant – 1157
Seminex – viii,33,1245
Sensus Literalis – 758
Septuagesima – 1025
Sermon on the Mount – 534
Servant Songs – 1151
Seventh-day Adventism – 1605
Shrove Tuesday – 1026
Singing – 177
Six Days of Creation – 1427
Six million Jews – 1468
Sodom – 1491
Sola fide – 15
Sola gratia – 15
Solas – 114,122
Solomon – 98
Songs of Songs – 100
Souls – 1852
Southern Baptist Convention – 390,
    488,499
Southern Baptist Seminary – 498
Southwestern Journal of Theology – 489
Speaking the Truth in Love – 1287
Spiritualism – 23
Spiritus Paraclitus – 1543
St. Andrew's Day – 897
St. Matthew Passion – 1219
St. Olaf College – 115
Stainer's Crucifixion – 1214
Stance Document, The – 33
State of the Dead – 1020
Subjective Justification – 975
Suffering Servant – 1238
Sufficiency of the Scriptures – 71
Supernaturalism – 1418
Supplication – 906
Supreme Court – 1414,1415
Swoon Theory – 1365,1567
Symbiotic Relationships – 1344
Synod of Jamnia – 1331
Synoptic Problem – 1239
Syriac – 1409,1411
Taoism – 119
Te Deum Laudamus – 1073,1126
Teacher of Righteousness – 772,1445
The Concordia Self-Study Bible – 322
Theft Theory – 1567
Theology of Fellowship – 1291

Thessalonians – 186
Third Use of the Law – 1708
TIME – 10
Titus – 187
Tradition – 174
Transfiguration – 798,1017
Trinity – 998,1001,1605
Truths – 1023
Type – 318
Typology – 324
Ultramontism – 141
Unam Sanctam – 143
Unification Church – 1605
Union Theological Seminary – 372,1633
United Church of Christ – 371
United Methodist Church – 371
United Presbyterian Church – 371
Unity School – 1605
Universal Language – 612
Universalism – 115,1385
Universality-with Particularity – 1386
Valparaiso University – 473
Vatican Council – 141
Vatican II – 1513
Veritas Splendor – 1559
Vicarious atonement – 1308
Virgin Birth – 15,943,958
Vision Theory – 1365,1567
Visitation – 833
Vulgate – 24,90,195,578,679
Wanderer, The – 354
Weltanschauung – 1847
Westminster Theological Seminary – 361
Westmont College – 370
White Sunday – 825
Whitsunday – 1786
Wisconsin Evangelical Lutheran Synod
    (WELS) -324
Word Becoming Flesh, The – 319
World Council of Churches – 33
World Lutheranism – 123
Worldwide Church – 1605
Worship – 793
Wycliffe Bible Translators – 712
Yom – 1417
Young Life Institute – 486
Zechariah – 108
Zend-Avesta – 1586
Zephaniah – 108
Zondervan Publishing House – 374
Zoroastrianism – 119,1584